Encyclopedia of
ENDANGERED
ANIMALS

Encyclopedia of
ENDANGERED
ANIMALS

AMY-JANE BEER, PAT MORRIS AND OTHERS

Grange BOOKS

Contents

This edition published in 2005 by Grange Books
Grange Books plc
The Grange
1-6 Kingsnorth Estate
Hoo
Near Rochester
Kent ME3 9ND
www.grangebooks.co.uk

© 2005 The Brown Reference Group plc

ISBN 1-84013-797-5

Editorial and design:
The Brown Reference Group plc
8 Chapel Place
Rivington Street
London
EC2A 3DQ
UK
www.brownreference.com

Contributors:
Amy-Jane Beer, Pat Morris
(Introductory Essays and Mammals)
Jonathan Elphick *(Birds)*
Robert and Val Davies *(Reptiles)*
Tim Halliday *(Amphibians)*
John Dawes *(Fish)*
Andrew Campbell *(Insects and Other Invertebrates)*

Editorial Director: Lindsey Lowe

Project Director: Graham Bateman

Editors: Virginia Carter, Penelope Mathias, Jo Newson, Shaun Barrington

Art Editor and Designer: Steve McCurdy

Cartographic Editor: Tim Williams

Picture Managers: Becky Cox, Claire Turner

Production: Alastair Gourlay, Maggie Copeland

Printed in Singapore

Title page: **Mountain gorilla**
Half title: **Macaw**

Giant panda

Dunnart

Flying fox

Monk seal

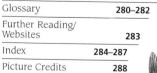

Introduction—What Is an Endangered Species?

Some animals are naturally rare, but many more are now scarce because of recent changes that have sharply reduced their numbers. Endangered species are those that are likely to continue their rapid decline and will become extinct (die out) within the foreseeable future. Even more species risk becoming endangered as we see the repeat of processes that have led to some species becoming extinct.

If a very small number of an animal species exists in one small place and its numbers are in rapid decline, it is severely endangered. However, threatened and endangered species also include some that are quite numerous; but because they are confined to the same areas, they may be critically threatened by a single factor. For example, thousands of bats may hibernate in a single cave that is about to be quarried away; lots of seabirds may nest on a single island safe from predators, but the accidental release of rats there from a shipwreck endangers them all.

Other species might be spread out over a huge area, but are now so thin on the ground that they are in danger of not being able to meet and breed. A widespread species often becomes broken up into little groups that die out one by one. The cheetah is a good example. Other animals might be threatened, despite being numerous, because they are very specialized. For example, snail kites need large water snails. A threat to this special food supply—through drainage of marshland, for example—endangers the whole kite population. Similarly, many reptiles may be in danger because they depend on temperature conditions. Climate changes—or even simply growth of vegetation shading out the sun—pose serious threats that would not bother some other species.

Many rare animals (such as albatrosses, elephants, and sharks) reproduce only slowly. They can become endangered as a result of rapid losses by hunting,

poisoning, or even natural causes, simply because they cannot breed fast enough to replace those losses. Nowadays it is possible to make estimates of the future numbers of a species by feeding information into special computer programs. They can figure out what the population is likely to be in, say, 10 or 50 years. The technique, called population modeling, allows predictions to be made and helps us understand what might happen.

So, there are many and varied reasons why animals become endangered. Some things that threaten one species are no trouble to others, but certain threats are a danger to all. Such issues are discussed more fully in this volume.

Animals in This Book

The *Encyclopedia of Endangered Animals* reviews over 122 extinct or threatened animals. Our selection does not cover all the world's threatened species because there are too many of them. Moreover, many species are so rare that they have only been seen once or twice, and virtually nothing is known about them. A few of these obscure creatures are included. Overall we have tried to feature a selection of species that illustrate different reasons for their precarious state. There are examples from all the major groups of animals. In the data panel in each entry related endangered species are also listed; an asterisk (*) indicates that the species is also featured in the book.

This book covers most parts of the world. But note that some species (such as the gray wolf) may be rare in some countries but widespread and relatively common in others. It is also true that some species become rare at the edge of their distribution, where local varieties (subspecies) may be the subject of major conservation concern—the Florida panther, for example—but elsewhere the main population of the

species is relatively secure. European readers will be familiar with stories about the conservation of red kites and pine martens, while people in Australia are more focused on the fate of dunnarts and koalas.

Often the reasons for decline are similar whether the animal is an insect, a mammal, or an amphibian. Nevertheless, all endangered animals share one thing—they are on their way out. A book on endangered animals might be gloomy; but the good news is that the problems are now much better understood. We must all hope that this will result in better protection for wildlife and reduce the numbers of species that become extinct.

Not all endangered *animals are as famous as the tiger and giant panda, but high-profile species such as these have become symbols for conservation. By preserving these so-called flagship species, conservationists are often able to help other, less well-known animals that share the same habitats.*

7

Organizations

The human race is undoubtedly nature's worst enemy, but we can also help limit the damage caused by the rapid increase in our numbers and activities. There have always been people eager to protect the world's beautiful places and to preserve its most special animals, but it is only quite recently that the conservation message has begun to have a real effect on everyday life, government policy, industry, and agriculture.

Early conservationists were concerned with preserving nature for the benefit of people. They acted with an instinctive sense of what was good for nature and people, arguing for the preservation of wilderness and animals in the same way as others argued for the conservation of historic buildings or gardens. The study of ecology and environmental science did not really take off until the mid-20th century, and it took a long time for the true scale of our effect in the natural world to become apparent. Today the conservation of wildlife is based on far greater scientific understanding, but the situation has become much more complex and urgent in the face of human development.

By the mid-20th century extinction was becoming an immediate threat. Animals such as the passenger pigeon, quagga, and thylacine had disappeared despite last-minute attempts to save them. More and more species were discovered to be at risk, and species-focused conservation groups began to appear. In the early days there was little that any of these organizations could do but campaign against direct killing. Later they became a kind of conservation emergency service—rushing to the aid of seriously threatened animals in an attempt to save the species. But as time went on, broader environmental issues began to receive the urgent attention they needed. Research showed time and time again that saving species almost always comes down to addressing the

Conservation *organizations range from government departments in charge of national parks, such as Yellowstone National Park (right), the oldest in the United States, to local initiatives set up to protect endangered birds. Here (above) a man in Peru climbs a tree to check on the nest of a harpy eagle discovered near his village.*

problem of habitat loss. The world is short of space, and ensuring that there is enough for all the species is very difficult.

Conservation is not just about animals and plants, nor even the protection of whole ecological systems. Conservation issues are so broad that they touch almost every aspect of our lives, and successful measures often depend on the expertise of biologists, ecologists, economists, diplomats, lawyers, social scientists, and businesspeople. Conservation is all about cooperation and teamwork. Often it is also about helping people benefit from taking care of their wildlife. The organizations involved vary from small groups of a few dozen enthusiasts in local communities to vast, multinational operations.

THE IUCN

With so much activity based in different countries, it is important to have a worldwide overview, some way of coordinating what goes on in different parts of the planet. That is the role of the International Union for the Conservation of Nature (IUCN), also referred to as the World Conservation Union. It began life as the International Union for the Preservation of Nature in 1948, becoming the IUCN in 1956. It is relatively new compared to the Sierra Club, Flora and Fauna International, and the Royal Society for the Protection of Birds (see panel on pages 10–11). It was remarkable in that its founder members included governments, government agencies, and nongovernmental

organizations. In the years following the appalling destruction of World War II, the IUCN was born out of a desire to draw a line under the horrors of the past and to act together to safeguard the future.

The mission of the IUCN is to influence, encourage, and assist societies throughout the world to conserve the diversity of nature and natural systems. It seeks to ensure that the use of natural resources is fair and ecologically sustainable. Based in Switzerland, the IUCN has over 1,000 permanent staff and the help of 10,000 volunteer experts from 181 countries. The work of the IUCN is split into six commissions, which deal with protected areas, policy-making, ecosystem management, education, environmental law, and species survival. The Species Survival Commission (SSC) has almost 7,000 members, all experts in the study of plants and animals. Within the SSC there are Specialist Groups concerned with the conservation of different types of animals, from cats to flamingos, deer, ducks, bats, and crocodiles. Some particularly well-studied animals, such as the African elephant and the polar bear, have their own specialist groups.

Perhaps the best-known role of the IUCN SSC is in the production of the Red Data Books, or Red Lists. First published in 1966, the books were designed to be easily updated, with details of each species on a different page that could be removed and replaced as new information came to light.

So far the Red Lists include information on over 18,000 types of animal, of which over 11,000 are threatened with extinction. Gathering this amount of information together is a

The IUCN Red Lists *of threatened species are published online and can be accessed at:*
**http://www.
iucnredlist.org**

huge task, but it provides an invaluable conservation resource. The Red Lists are continually updated and are now available in CD ROM format and on the World Wide Web. The Red Lists are the basis for the categories of threat used in this book.

CITES

CITES is the Convention on International Trade in Endangered Species of Wild Fauna and Flora (also known as the Washington Convention, since it first came into force after an international meeting in Washington D.C. in 1973). Currently 167 nations have agreed to implement the CITES regulations. Exceptions to the convention include Iraq and North Korea, which, for the time being at least, have few trading links with the rest of the world. Trading in animals and their body parts has been a major factor in the decline of some of the world's rarest species. The IUCN categories draw attention to the status of rare species, but they do not confer any legal protection. That is done through national laws.

Conventions serve as international laws. In the case of CITES, lists (called Appendices) are agreed on internationally and reviewed every few years. The Appendices list the species that are threatened by international trade. Animals are assigned to Appendix I when all trade is forbidden. Any specimens of these species, alive or dead (or skins, feathers, etc.), will be confiscated by customs at international borders, seaports, or airports. Appendix II species can be traded internationally, but only under strict controls. Wildlife trade is often valuable in the rural economy, and this raises difficult questions about the relative importance of animals and people. Nevertheless, traders who ignore CITES rules risk heavy fines or imprisonment. Some rare species—even those with the highest IUCN categories (many bats and frogs, for example)—may have no CITES protection simply because they have no commercial value. Trade is then not really a threat.

The Greenpeace ship, *seen here in Antarctica, travels to areas of conservation concern and helps draw worldwide media attention to environmental issues.*

WILDLIFE CONSERVATION ORGANIZATIONS

BirdLife International
BirdLife International is a partnership of 60 organizations, most of which are national nongovernmental conservation groups such as Nature Kenya, the Malaysian Nature Society, and the Canadian Nature Federation. Others include large bird charities such as the Royal Society for the Protection of Birds in Britain, Birds Australia, and the Wild Bird Society of Japan. By working together within BirdLife International, even small organizations can be effective globally as well as on a local scale. BirdLife International is a member of the IUCN.

Conservation International (CI)
Founded in 1987, Conservation International works closely with the IUCN and has a similar multinational, multidisciplinary approach. However, CI offers help in the world's most threatened biodiversity hot spots.

Durrell Wildlife Conservation Trust (DWCT)
Another IUCN member, the Durrell Wildlife Conservation Trust was founded by the British naturalist and author Gerald Durrell in 1963. The trust is based at Durrell's world-famous zoo on Jersey in the Channel Islands. Jersey was the world's first zoo dedicated solely to the conservation of endangered species. Breeding programs at the zoo have helped stabilize populations of some of the world's most endangered animals. The trust trains conservationists from many countries and works to secure areas of natural habitat to which animals can be returned. Jersey Zoo and the DWCT were instrumental in saving numerous species from extinction, including the pink pigeon, Mauritius kestrel, Waldrapp ibis, St. Lucia parrot, and the Telfair's skink and other reptiles.

Fauna & Flora International (FFI)
Founded in 1903, this organization has had various name changes. It began life as a society for protecting large mammals, but has broadened its scope. It was involved in saving the Arabian oryx from extinction.

National Association of Audubon Societies for the Protection of Wild Birds and Animals
John James Audubon was an American naturalist and wildlife artist who died in 1851, 35 years before the society that bears his name was founded. The first Audubon Society was established by George Bird Grinnell in protest against the appalling overkill of birds for meat, feathers, and sport. By the turn of the century there were Audubon Societies in 15 states, and in 1905 they all became part of the National Association of Audubon Societies for the

WILDLIFE CONSERVATION ORGANIZATIONS

Protection of Wild Birds and Animals. The Audubon Societies fund scientific research and education programs, publish magazines and journals, manage wildlife sanctuaries, and advise state and federal governments on conservation issues.

Pressure Groups

Friends of the Earth, founded in Britain in 1969, and Greenpeace, founded in 1971 in British Columbia, were the first environmental pressure groups to become internationally recognized. Greenpeace became known for its sometimes dangerous "direct, nonviolent actions," which drew attention to major conservation issues. (For example, campaigners steered boats between the harpoon guns of whalers and their prey.)

The organizations offer advice to governments and corporations, and help those that seek to protect the environment, while continuing to name, shame, and campaign against those who do not.

Royal Society for the Protection of Birds (RSPB)

This organization was founded in the 1890s to campaign against the slaughter of birds to supply feathers for the fashion trade. It now has a wider role and has become Britain's premier wildlife conservation organization, with over a million members. It is involved in international activities, particularly in the protection of birds that migrate to Britain.

The Sierra Club

The Sierra Club was started in 1892 by John Muir and is still going strong. Muir, a Scotsman by birth, is often thought of as the founder of the conservation movement, especially in the United States, where he campaigned for the preservation of wilderness. It was through his efforts that the first national parks, including Yosemite, Sequoia, and Mount Rainier, were established. Today the Sierra Club remains dedicated to the preservation of wild places for the benefit of wildlife and the enjoyment of people.

World Wide Fund for Nature (WWF)

The World Wide Fund for Nature, formerly the World Wildlife Fund, was born in 1961. It was a joint venture between the IUCN, several existing conservation organizations, and a number of successful businesspeople. Unlike many charities, WWF was big, well-funded, and high profile from the beginning. Its familiar giant panda emblem ranks alongside those of the Red Cross, Mercedes Benz, or Coca-Cola in terms of instant international recognition.

Categories of Threat

Two types of classification are used throughout this book. The IUCN categories that appear in the data panel for each species are based on those published by the International Union for the Conservation of Nature. They provide a useful guide to the current status of the species in the wild, and governments throughout the world use them when assessing conservation priorities and in policy-making. However, they do not provide automatic legal protection for the species.

Animals are placed in the appropriate category after scientific research. More species are being added all the time, and animals can be moved from one category to another as their circumstances change.

Extinct (EX)

A group of animals is classified as EX when there is no reasonable doubt that the last individual has died.

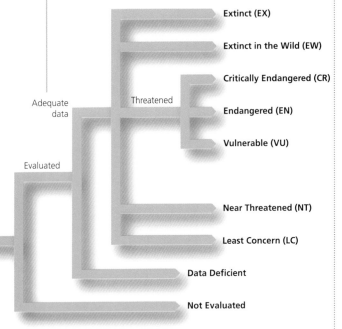

- Extinct (EX)
- Extinct in the Wild (EW)
- Critically Endangered (CR)
- Endangered (EN)
- Vulnerable (VU)
- Near Threatened (NT)
- Least Concern (LC)
- Data Deficient
- Not Evaluated

Adequate data
Threatened
Evaluated

Extinct in the Wild (EW)

Animals in this category are known to survive only in captivity or as a population established artificially by introduction somewhere well outside its former range. A species is categorized as EW when exhaustive surveys throughout the areas where it used to occur consistently fail to record a single individual. It is important that such searches be carried out over all of the available habitat and during a season or time of day when the animals should be present.

Critically Endangered (CR)

The category CR includes animals facing an extremely high risk of extinction in the wild in the immediate future. It includes any of the following:

- Any species with fewer than 50 individuals, even if the population is stable.
- Any species with fewer than 250 individuals if the population is declining, badly fragmented, or all in one vulnerable group.
- Animals from larger populations that have declined by 80 percent within 10 years (or are predicted to do so) or

The IUCN categories *of threat. The system displayed has operated for new and reviewed assessments since January 2001. See pages 14–15 for a summary of the earlier categories.*

three generations, whichever is the longer.

• Species living in a very small area—defined as under 39 square miles (100 sq. km).

Endangered (EN)

A species is EN when it is not CR but is nevertheless facing a very high risk of extinction in the wild in the near future. It includes any of the following:

• A species with fewer than 250 individuals remaining, even if the population is stable.

• Any species with fewer than 2,500 individuals if the population is declining, badly fragmented, or all in one vulnerable subpopulation.

• A species whose population is known or expected to decline by 50 percent within 10 years or three generations, whichever is the longer.

• A species whose range is under 1,900 square miles (5,000 sq. km), and whose range, numbers, or population levels are declining, fragmented, or fluctuating wildly.

• Species for which there is a more than 20 percent likelihood of extinction in the next 20 years or five generations, whichever is the longer.

Vulnerable (VU)

A species is VU when it is not CR or EN but is facing a high risk of extinction in the wild in the medium-term future. It includes any of the following:

• A species with fewer than 1,000 mature individuals remaining, even if the population is stable.

• Any species with fewer than 10,000 individuals if the population is declining, badly fragmented, or all in one vulnerable subpopulation.

• A species whose population is known, believed, or

The American bison *was almost wiped out by overhunting. With the population reduced to just 800 by about 1875 (below), intensive conservation measures saved the species from extinction. These bison (left) have radio-transmitter collars that allow scientists to track their movements.*

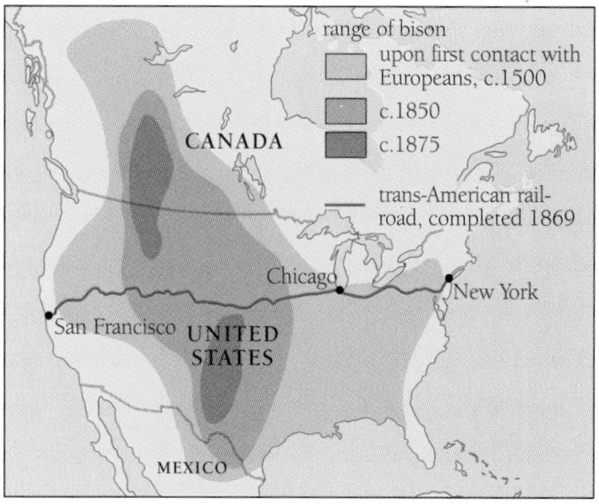

range of bison
upon first contact with Europeans, c.1500
c.1850
c.1875
trans-American rail-road, completed 1869

CANADA

Chicago
New York
San Francisco   UNITED STATES

MEXICO

expected to decline by 20 percent within 10 years or three generations, whichever is the longer.
• A species whose range is less than 772 square miles (20,000 sq. km), and whose range, numbers, or population structure are declining, fragmented, or fluctuating wildly.
• Species for which there is a more than 10 percent likelihood of extinction in the next 100 years.

Near Threatened/Least Concern (since 2001)

In January 2001 the classification of lower-risk species was changed. Near Threatened (NT) and Least Concern (LC) were introduced as separate categories. They replaced the previous Lower Risk (LR) category with its subdivisions of Conservation Dependent (LRcd), Near Threatened (LRnt), and Least Concern (LRlc). From January 2001 all new assessments and reassessments must adopt NT or LC if relevant. But the older categories still apply to many animals until they are reassessed, and will also be found in this book.
• **Near Threatened (NT)**
Animals that do not qualify for CR, EN, or VU categories now but are close to qualifying or are likely to qualify for a threatened category in the future.
• **Least Concern (LC)**
Animals that have been evaluated and do not qualify for CR, EN, VU, or NT categories.

Lower Risk (before 2001)

• **Conservation Dependent (LRcd)**
Animals whose survival depends on an existing conservation program
• **Near Threatened (LRnt)**
Animals for which there is no conservation program but that are close to qualifying for VU category.

By monitoring *populations of threatened animals like this American rosy boa, biologists help keep the IUCN Red List up to date.*

CITES regulations mean that elephant tusks can no longer be traded. The Kenyan government has destroyed its stockpiled ivory.

• **Least Concern (LRlc)**
Species that are not conservation dependent or near threatened.

Data Deficient (DD)

A species or population is DD when there is not enough information on abundance and distribution to assess the risk of extinction. In some cases, when the species is thought to live only in a small area, or a considerable period of time has passed since the species was last recorded, it may be placed in a threatened category as a precaution.

Not Evaluated (NE)

Such animals have not yet been assessed.

Note: a colored panel at the top left of each entry in this book indicates the current level of threat to the species. The two new categories (NT and LC) and two of the earlier Lower Risk categories (LRcd and LRnt) are included within the band **LR**; the old LRlc is included along with Data Deficient (DD) and Not Evaluated (NE) under "**Other**," abbreviated to "**O**."

CITES lists animals in the major groups in three Appendices, depending on the level of threat posed by international trade.

	Appendix I	Appendix II	Appendix III
Mammals	228 species 21 subspecies 13 populations	369 species 34 subspecies 14 populations	57 species 11 subspecies
Birds	146 species 19 subspecies 2 populations	1,401 species 8 subspecies 1 population	149 species
Reptiles	67 species 3 subspecies 4 populations	508 species 3 subspecies 4 populations	25 species
Amphibians	16 species	90 species	
Fish	9 species	68 species	
Invertebrates	63 species 5 subspecies	2,030 species 1 subspecies	16 species

CITES APPENDICES

Appendix I lists the most endangered of traded species, namely those that are threatened with extinction and will be harmed by continued trade. These species are usually protected in their native countries and can only be imported or exported with a special permit. Permits are required to cover the whole transaction—both exporter and importer must prove that there is a compelling scientific justification for moving the animal from one country to another. This includes transferring animals between zoos for breeding purposes. Permits are only issued when it can be proved that the animal was legally acquired and that the remaining population will not be harmed by the loss.

Appendix II includes species that are not currently threatened with extinction, but that could easily become so if trade is not carefully controlled. Some common animals are listed here if they resemble endangered species so closely that criminals could try to sell the rare species pretending they were a similar common one. Permits are required to export such animals, with requirements similar to those Appendix I species.

Appendix III species are those that are at risk or protected in at least one country. Other nations may be allowed to trade in animals or products, but they may need to prove that they come from safe populations.

CITES designations are not always the same for every country. In some cases individual countries can apply for special permission to trade in a listed species. For example, they might have a safe population of an animal that is very rare elsewhere. Some African countries periodically apply for permission to export large quantities of elephant tusks that have been in storage for years, or that are the product of a legal cull of elephants. This is controversial because it creates an opportunity for criminals to dispose of black market ivory by passing it off as coming from one of those countries where elephant products are allowed to be exported. If you look up the African elephant, you will see that it is listed as CITES I, II, and III, depending on the country location of the different populations.

Threats to Animals

Animals face a variety of dangers, including direct persecution (hunting) by people for their skins and meat or because they are considered dangerous. However, many threats are indirect and less obvious—habitat loss, environmental damage, and pollution, for example, all take a toll.

HABITAT LOSS

The problem of habitat loss is an extension of one of the oldest battles in nature—that of competition between species for space. In this contest, however, one species (our own) competes more aggressively for space than any other. The human population has exploded over the last few centuries (it now exceeds 6 billion), so it is no surprise that other species are losing out. The problem is vast and widespread, and it affects animals of all kinds.

A large proportion of the land (and the water) lost to wildlife is taken over for a range of agricultural practices. Some traditional forms of land management evolved in harmony with nature, creating seminatural habitat such as meadows, hedgerows, and managed woodlands. Often they supported many species of plants and animals, sometimes more even than truly natural habitats. Sadly, most of them are now threatened by the advance of modern agriculture. Huge fields and heavy machinery now dominate the countryside in many areas, notably on the American prairies. The scope of modern agriculture is truly vast, including cereal and root crop production, vineyards, fruit and timber plantations, livestock, and aquaculture (farming water plants, fish, and seafood). Agricultural technology is now so advanced that almost any habitat can be farmed, destroying everything else from mangrove swamps to tropical jungle; even lakes and parts of the sea can be turned into dry land or used for fish farming. All this activity automatically wipes out the natural wildlife of the area, except for a few pests and opportunist species that move in to take advantage of the new crops and products.

Pasture

Farming also involves grazing animals, often creating large areas of grassland where there was once forest. Grasslands are usually less productive than other land habitats, and grazed pasture supports relatively few animals. When forests are cleared to make pasture, hundreds of species and thousands of individuals may lose their home overnight. Once the trees are cleared, if grass does not grow quickly, the ground is no longer shielded from the sun, wind, and rain. In wet weather the soil is trampled into mud, while in the dry season the soil may turn to dust and blow away. In hot, dry countries this begins the process of desertification,

Grazing livestock *can put huge pressure on an ecosystem. Sheep and cattle—even scraggy native zebu cattle (left) that are adapted to life where water is short—compete with wild herbivores for food, causing overgrazing. At this site in Western Australia (right) overgrazing has been caused by overstocking of sheep. This in turn leads to desertification.*

where plants struggle to grow in fierce heat and with little water, while being constantly attacked by nibbling cattle, sheep, and goats. If plants do not succeed, their roots will not stabilize the soil, and little foliage will grow to protect it from the sun and wind. Then, even more soil is lost, and even fewer plants can survive. Gradually, a desert develops where almost nothing can live. This problem has devastated the wild mammals of the southern Sahara. As the desert has grown larger, fewer migrant birds manage to cross it during their annual journeys to and from Europe. While protected in Europe, many European songbirds are now rare because of what is happening in Africa.

As well as taking up large areas of habitat, grazing livestock can also cause other problems, bringing new diseases and sometimes even interbreeding with wild animals. This is a particular problem for many species of cattle such as the banteng and yak. Wild herbivores are also killed or driven away to prevent them from competing with domestic stock, and large predators may find themselves victims of hunting by ranchers wanting to protect their animals.

Industries and Settlements

Primary industries such as mining (for coal, metal ores, coral, precious metals, and jewels), quarrying of building stone, extraction of sand, gravel, oil, and groundwater, and the felling of nonplantation forest or collection of fallen timber for firewood all lead to degradation of natural habitats on a massive scale. Primary industries also need a workforce, and so they often bring people into previously uninhabited parts of the world. Thus, even if most industrial activity is concentrated in a small area, or even underground, the settlements that spring up around the site can have a considerable impact on the surrounding habitats. Manufacturing industries often locate close to the source of raw materials or fuel to cut down on transportation costs, bringing yet more people, service industries, and infrastructure such as roads and traffic, with their harmful effects on wildlife.

The areas occupied by human settlement are relatively small compared to those lost to agriculture and industry. However, they are often located in sensitive places—on the banks of rivers or lakes, by

DRAINAGE AND IRRIGATION

Natural potholes *like this one in Alberta, Canada, are vital to breeding waterbirds, but they are often drained or filled in because they are a nuisance to farmers.*

One of the most significant ways that people alter habitats is through changing the water balance. Marshes and mangroves can be drained, deserts irrigated, and rivers diverted or dammed. Major alterations like these almost always result in loss of species.

For example, when the swamps of Borneo were drained, the proboscis monkey not only lost large areas of habitat, but also became vulnerable to hunters who had previously been unable to penetrate the dense muddy undergrowth. Drainage also prevents water birds from feeding properly and removes the insects and vegetation on which may other animals depend. When water is pumped onto

the land to irrigate crops, much is lost due to evaporation, and the rivers and wetlands are left much drier. Where water runs back from irrigated land into a river or lake, it may carry pesticides and fertilizers that disrupt the natural balance among aquatic plants and animals. Again, this has damaging consequences for the mammals and birds that feed on them.

While many wetlands are threatened with having too little water as a result of drainage, others (especially along rivers) are in danger of being submerged in too much water as a result of building dams. A dam also changes flowing water into a large static lake, often endangering rare species such as the river dolphin, as well as many specialized fish, insects, and other wildlife.

The clearing of *tropical forests for agriculture (right) is disastrous for humans and wildlife alike because the soils on which the forests grow are actually very poor. All the nutrients come from the constant addition of dead plant material. Once the forest has been cleared, the soil deteriorates fast and can only support crops for a season or two, after which the land is abandoned.*

Even selective logging *can have a profound effect on a forest ecosystem. Slow-growing trees such as teak (below, at a site in Myanmar) and mahogany are usually considered most valuable, and loggers often lay waste to a swath of forest in order to fell and extract one prime tree.*

the sea, or in sheltered valleys. None of these settlements is isolated, and networks of connecting roads and railways, pipelines and power supplies carve up the relatively untouched areas of habitat in between. Ironically, in some more developed countries rail and roadside edges cover such large areas that they are now considered a valuable conservation resource. Undisturbed edges provide a home for a variety of insects, reptiles, small mammals, and predatory birds such as owls and kestrels. However, these animals are making the best of a bad situation. Roads, dams, and the like create barriers to many species, splitting habitats and populations into dangerously small fragments.

Tourism

Other kinds of development, such as tourism, are often located in especially sensitive areas: Their unspoiled beauty is exactly what attracts visitors there in the first place. Watersports and waterside activities such as boating, diving, and fishing can harm coastal wildlife directly and indirectly. Dozens of Florida manatees die each year as a result of collisions with boats, and many more bear the scars of close encounters with propellers. Careless divers and boaters have done untold damage to coral reefs in the Caribbean especially, simply by standing on the coral, running aground, or dropping anchors into it.

There are similar problems with inland tourist resorts. National park authorities have to balance the conflicting interests of wildlife and the people who come to enjoy it—even ecotourism has its cost in terms of habitat loss or modification. Hotels not only occupy natural habitat but generate pollution.

HUNTING

Humans have been killing wild animals for thousands of years. There is evidence that long before the advent of sophisticated weapons humans were capable of hunting species to extinction. The fossil record tells us

THE BATTLE FOR THE BEACHES

Tourists have much the same taste in beaches as sea turtles and monk seals. Both once used the wide sandy beaches of the Mediterranean for breeding.

Female turtles once came ashore by the thousand to bury batches of eggs well above the high-tide mark. The newly hatched babies made a mad dash for the relative safety of the sea, relying on safety in numbers to avoid ambush by predators such as foxes and gulls. But as tourist resorts sprang up, turtle numbers plummeted. The females were unnerved by the presence of people, and many eggs were crushed or exposed to predation by gulls. Those babies that did hatch were often confused by bright lights along the beachfront and ended up heading up the beach instead of down, greatly diminishing their chances of survival.

In the case of the Mediterranean monk seal even minor disturbance is enough to make mothers abandon their newborn pups, and there are now so few suitable breeding beaches that the species is on the brink of extinction.

A washed up turtle *specimen on view in Turkey.*

Tourists *are often drawn to environmentally sensitive parts of the world—as here at the saltmarshes of Calpe, Alicante, in Spain (left). The infrastructure needed to transport and accommodate thousands of visitors seriously affects wildlife in terms of habitat loss, pollution, and disturbance.*

21

that many large mammals went extinct about 10,000 years ago, about the time that modern humans began to advance. More recently hunters reduced the American bison almost to extinction.

In the past hunting animals was a matter of life and death not only for the animals but for the people who relied on their meat and skins. These days in the developed world wild-caught meat is a supplement to farm-reared foods, and hunting is as much for sport as for subsistence. However, in poorer regions such as

Central Africa, South America, and Asia hunting is still a way of life. "Bushmeat" is the term used to describe a wide variety of animals killed in the wild for food. Hunting for subsistence is one thing, but the bushmeat trade is becoming increasingly commercial. In recent years civil unrest has damaged aspects of traditional life. Soldiers deployed in the forests and people dispossessed of their land and livestock kill more wildlife than ever before, some to feed themselves, but a large proportion is to sell.

Minke whales *are the smallest of the baleen whales. Commercial hunting has been banned since 1986, but countries such as Japan and Norway continue killing them for "scientific purposes."*

The sight of monkey meat on sale in African markets is shocking, but there is nothing new about the hunting of threatened species for profit. Killing rhinos for their horns or elephants for their ivory tusks is still a serious threat to their continued survival in many areas.

The hunting and slaughter of the world's great whales during the 20th century is perhaps the most savage and shameful episode in the history of animal exploitation. Between the start of the century and the late 1960s tens of thousands of blue, fin, humpback, and sperm whales were killed every year, except for a brief respite during the two world wars. Even after that the hunting continued, but with diminished success, since by the 1970s there were so few great whales left. In addition, international opposition to the slaughter was stiffening, and eventually in 1986 a worldwide ban on hunting large whales was introduced. The fight to "save the whale" is a high-profile one, but the ban is not total. Some nations persist in exploiting loopholes that allow a small catch for research purposes.

The world's fisheries operate on an even bigger scale. Perhaps because fish live out of sight and yet can be caught in huge numbers, humans have treated them as an inexhaustible resource, hauling them out by the millions without giving nearly enough consideration to sustainability. Fishing techniques such as drift nets and dynamiting are extraordinarily efficient and take advantage of the fact that many commercially important species seek safety in numbers by living in large shoals. Because so little attention has been paid to monitoring fish stocks, often the first sign that something is wrong comes when catches drop. All too often the first response to that is to increase the fishing effort in order to maintain a profit.

These grisly *gorilla remains (above) and severed shark fins (right) are just two examples of the continued trade in endangered species.*

The average size of fish caught decreases to include immature fish that have not yet had a chance to breed. Once this happens, the population will crash. Such is the economic importance of fishing that conservation measures are only taken seriously once a fishery is no longer financially viable. By this time the future of the species is in doubt, and recovery takes many years. In 1993 Canada was forced to take the drastic step of closing Atlantic cod fisheries. Years later stocks are beginning to show signs of recovery, but it will still be some time before they can withstand renewed commercial fishing.

23

Luxury Products

There is more to a dead animal than meat. Some species owe their demise to other characteristics, such as warm fur, skins that make good leather, or horns that can be carved into tools. Others are unlucky enough to have body parts that we covet for less practical purposes—musk for perfume, ivory for decorative carvings, fine wool and feathers for fashionable outfits, and shells and pearls for trinkets and jewelry. Body parts are used in medicines or magical rituals. The more difficult a certain resource is to come by, the greater its value. So as a species becomes more rare, the

Tourists are prime targets for unscrupulous traders. A fur like this bought in a Chinese market may land its purchaser in serious trouble with customs authorities.

The Raggiana bird of paradise *is one of the most dramatic examples of plumage and display among birds.*

One of the problems with big-game hunting was that it tended to focus attention on certain large species, often large predators that were relatively rare anyway. Only the most superior specimens were shot, thereby removing the finest individuals and reducing the numbers of young that they could produce. Some hunters took particularly large numbers of key species. The Maharajah of Cooch Behar in northeastern India, for example, shot 365 tigers in his lifetime.

Victorian trophy hunters *often achieved celebrity status by killing large numbers of wild animals—the bigger and more dangerous the better.*

rewards for hunting it increase. There is nearly always someone prepared to break the law in order to make a profit on the black market.

War

War and civil unrest are usually measured in terms of human tragedy; but when large areas are devastated by fighting, animals suffer too. Some die in crossfire or by setting off landmines; others are killed to feed military personnel in the field. Large movements of human refugees have a carryover effect on the environment. Wars also disrupt conservation projects.

Superstition

Some animals, even certain very rare ones, are perceived as pests, and many have been driven to the edge of extinction by systematic persecution. All kinds of animals can find themselves targeted: herbivores with a tendency to raid crops; rodents, birds, and insects that feed on stored produce; along with large carnivores that are seen as a threat to livestock and people. Some species are killed because of local superstitions or simply because people do not like or understand them. The bad reputation of animals like snakes, bats, and wolves, for example, has more to do with human misunderstanding and prejudice than with any real threat, but it results in large numbers of animals being killed just the same.

For centuries humans have made sport out of pitting their wits against wild animals in order to hunt them down and kill them, using crossbows, spears, shotguns, rifles, fishing lines, trained dogs, or falcons.

In some cases the aim is little more than target practice, in others it is the challenge of defeating a large, potentially dangerous animal. People still pay large sums of money for the opportunity to capture or kill elephants and sharks.

EXPLOITATION OF LIVE ANIMALS

A major problem with the trade in living animals is that for every one that arrives safely at its final destination, be it a family home, a zoo, or a research laboratory, many others will have died or been injured in the process.

Young primates are usually captured at the cost of the mother's life; and having been thus orphaned, there is little chance for the youngster to learn many important life skills. Even if the animal is subsequently rescued, it will not survive in the wild without intensive and expensive rehabilitation.

The trade in live animals is huge. In 1996 alone the United States imported over 1.7 million reptiles, including nearly 694,000 iguanas. Between 1991 and 1995 over 50,000 Senegal chameleons were imported into the United States. In 1990 India exported 5,546 Alexandrine parakeets legally, plus who knows how many illegally. In nine months (1994) 187,361 African birds were exported through Dar es Salaam airport in Tanzania, despite attempts to control the situation by having much lower quotas. Many bird species have suffered from overcollection for the pet trade, especially parrots. The impressive hyacinth macaw is particularly popular with zoos and collectors, and there are now probably fewer than 3,000 of these handsome birds left in the wild in South America.

The aquarium trade is responsible for the loss from the wild of millions of fish and aquatic invertebrates

Baby orang-utans *are highly appealing, but they do not make good pets. Orang-utans taken from the wild usually end up neglected or abandoned; only a very few are lucky enough to be rehabilitated.*

Fish collectors *use paralyzing chemicals to catch live fish for the aquarium trade. For every fish that survives the procedure, dozens die.*

every year. Reef species are especially popular, and fish are captured in large numbers, not in nets that might damage them, but by using a chemical (sodium cyanide). It causes temporary paralysis in the fish, which can then be collected by hand. The fish recover, but for other reef-dwelling animals the outcome is

27

death. Fish are also often selected for their appearance rather than their suitability for captivity.

POLLUTION

With some forms of pollution the damage is obvious and extreme. When the supertanker *Exxon Valdez* ran aground in Alaska's Prince William Sound in 1989, the death toll included almost 1,000 sea otters, several whales, a third of a million seabirds, and millions of fish and invertebrates. Disasters on this scale are shocking, but not all pollution is so obvious or newsworthy. Accidents such as large oil spills or mass poisonings represent a relatively small proportion of the damage done by man-made pollutants.

The careless disposal of everyday domestic refuse leads to gradual accumulation in the environment. The main problem is that plastics and much other modern litter do not rot away as does natural waste. Plastic shopping bags and other plastic packaging, bottles, and tape kill about 100,000 whales, seals, sea otters, and turtles every year and up to 2 million birds. Often these animals become entangled in the waste and

BIOACCUMULATION

Many substances that find their way into the environment—such as heavy metals, pesticides, and industrial compounds—are impossible to metabolize. Once picked up by an animal, they cannot be broken down or excreted. Instead, they build up in its tissues. Short-lived species, or those near the bottom of the food chain, may never consume enough of a particular chemical to do any real harm, but in a long-lived carnivore such as an otter or bird of prey the accumulated dose can be fatal.

European otters *were almost entirely wiped out by the accumulation of the pesticide DDT in their bodies during the late 20th century.*

Water polluted *with acid, heavy metals, and cyanide—all by-products of the mining industry—has poisoned this entire valley in Arizona.*

drown. Other animals try to eat rubbish—plastic bags are often mistaken for jellyfish by turtles—and choke to death.

Atmospheric Pollution

Industry and transportation are the main contributors to atmospheric pollution. The burning of fossil fuels such as coal, gas, oil, and derivatives like gasoline releases large quantities of fine, sooty particles and noxious compounds such as carbon monoxide and nitrous oxides—as well as excess carbon dioxide—that contribute to global warming.

Huge swaths *of Scandinavian pine forest have been destroyed by acid rain generated elsewhere in Europe and carried north by the prevailing winds.*

Acid Rain

Acid rain is another side effect of the burning of fossil fuels. Although the acid is not strong enough to kill most animals outright, over a period of months and years it can destroy vast areas of habitat, killing trees and other vegetation, and poisoning the soil.

Pesticides

One of the most effective ways of controlling pest or nuisance species, be they insects, fungi, weeds, or rodents, is by poisoning them using pesticides. There are a number of problems associated with the use of pesticides. First, it is very difficult to be sure that only the pest species will be affected. Poisons intended to kill coyotes all but wiped out the swift fox in North America, and the rare and beautiful Shaus swallowtail

butterfly of the Florida Keys has suffered as a result of insecticide sprays to control mosquitoes.

Second, once the pesticide is in the environment, its properties can change. The breakdown products can be as damaging to some wildlife as the original compound. However, one of the greatest problems with many pesticides is that they do not break down at all. Some remain in the environment long enough to cause problems years and years after they were originally used.

DDT is one of the most effective insecticides ever invented. It has saved thousands of human lives through its use on mosquito-infested lakes and rivers in malaria-stricken parts of the world. It was also widely used on crops to control insect pests. While deadly to insects, the concentrations at which DDT is applied are in themselves nowhere near enough to harm a large animal or bird. However, through the process of bioaccumulation top predators can ingest most of the DDT ever eaten by all their prey and their prey's prey. Their intake can end up being thousands of times the original concentration. For some animals the dose is fatal; in others the effects are more subtle. During the 1950s and 1960s the North American

29

declines occurred in other predators, including ospreys and the European otter. The use of DDT is now widely banned, and some affected predator populations are beginning to recover.

Other kinds of bioaccumulating chemicals, including heavy metals (such as lead, copper, zinc, and mercury) and polychlorinated biphenyls (PCBs), are giving cause for concern. They have a variety of damaging effects on wildlife, including causing paralysis, reproductive failure, immune deficiency, and death through poisoning.

Modern farming methods often rely on fertilizers containing phosphates and nitrates in order to make otherwise poor soils productive. These chemicals are often applied so liberally that every time it rains, large quantities are washed out of the soil and into rivers and streams. There they enrich the water and cause sudden explosive growth of water plants. Algae are the first plants to benefit, and they can grow so fast that in a matter of days they block off the light to other plants and choke the river. Some algae produce toxins that will harm animals and people using the river for drinking. Once all the nutrients are used up, the algae die and begin to rot. The decomposition process uses a lot of oxygen, which is bad news for the entire ecosystem. In the aftermath of an algal bloom a river can be almost devoid of life.

Heat, Noise, and Light

The effluent from factories and power stations is often warmer than the river into which it is emptied. In some industrialized regions this can significantly increase the overall temperature of the river. The heat can damage aquatic wildlife because warm water carries less oxygen than cold. This can be a particular problem in the tropics, where water is already warm and oxygen deficient. It is also a problem in cooler areas where fish and other aquatic animals are not accustomed to warm water.

Human beings are noisy creatures, far more so than our feeble ears would have us believe. It is easy

Even low levels of pollution *can lead to serious problems, as happened in this Spanish wetland. A serious drought increased the concentration of chemicals in the water to lethal levels, killing thousands of carp.*

population of peregrine falcons crashed. The decline was mysterious because the birds appeared healthy and did not seem to have been poisoned. It turned out that DDT in the bird's food was interfering with their metabolism in such a way that female peregrines could not produce healthy eggs. Their shells were so thin that the eggs were crushed by the weight of the incubating mother. By the time the problem was realized, the peregrine falcon was on the verge of extinction in the United States. Similar DDT-induced to forget that the world is full of sounds we cannot hear either because they are too far away or because they are too high-pitched. Sound travels much farther under water, and man-made noises such as the buzz of engines and the sonar used by submarines are damaging to marine animals. Whales are especially sensitive to sound because they use it to locate objects by measuring the time taken for an echo to return from them (echolocation) and to communicate over vast distances.

There is evidence that light pollution is also damaging to wildlife, especially migrating birds, many of which have been shown to use stars in the night sky to help them navigate. Birds disoriented by bright lights may never reach their destination, maybe missing out on the chance to breed or, worse still, perishing in an unsuitable environment.

CLIMATE CHANGE

The earth's climate is warming up. In the next 100 years we can expect the earth's temperature to rise by around six degrees Celsius. Glaciers and polar ice caps will shrink, sea levels will rise, and some low-lying areas of land will be permanently flooded. The climate will also become much more unsettled. Floods and droughts will become commonplace in many previously stable parts of the world.

The chief culprit is the greenhouse effect, caused by increased levels of gases such as carbon dioxide in the atmosphere. Carbon dioxide in itself is not harmful —we produce it in our own bodies, and plants use it as the raw material for producing essential sugars. Large quantities of carbon dioxide are also absorbed by the sea. But carbon dioxide is also a by-product of combustion. The burning of fossil fuels is producing carbon dioxide so fast that the world's oceans and depleted forests cannot use it all. The gas accumulates in the atmosphere, where it acts like the glass in a greenhouse, letting the sun's energy in but stopping heat reflected from the earth's surface from leaving.

The hazel dormouse *needs cold winters to hibernate safely. Species like this will be strongly affected by the consequences of global warming.*

The prospect of warmer winters in temperate zones may seem quite attractive to us, but for some threatened animals it could be disastrous. Hibernators such as bats and dormice will be among the first to suffer. These animals sleep all winter in order to conserve energy when there is no food around. They depend on cold weather to chill their bodies to a point where they are barely alive. They use the minimum possible amount of energy to keep from freezing, and with luck in a normal cold winter they will have just enough stored fat to survive until spring. However, if the outside temperature rises above the hibernating animal's body temperature, its heart rate will increase, and its core temperature will rise. This increased metabolism will be burning too much precious fat, and the chances of surviving until spring are poor.

There is another layer in the atmosphere made of a gas called ozone. It acts as a filter and prevents some of the sun's more harmful radiation from reaching the earth. This layer is under attack from man-made chemicals called chlorofluorocarbons

31

(CFCs). As the ozone layer gets thinner and in some places disappears, the earth is bombarded with harmful solar radiation. In humans this increases the risk of sunburn and skin cancer. The effects on animals are not known.

INTRODUCTIONS

The separateness of places is an essential factor in allowing different regions to develop their own unique kinds of animals. These days people travel around the world just to see animals different from those they encounter at home. In the past, however, homesickness and ignorance made colonists more inclined to bring familiar animals with them than to make the most of those in the new territories.

Early European settlers arrived in Australia in the 18th century, by which time at least one nonnative carnivore had already gained a firm footing. The dingo, a descendant of the Asian wolf, arrived with early settlers about 4,000 years ago. Dingos were probably responsible for the decline of the thylacine, which simply could not compete. Once white men began to colonize in earnest, they brought with them a host of useful domestic pets and livestock.

Thanks to these imports there are populations of cattle, goats, pigs, sheep, camels, donkeys, and horses as well as cats and dogs living wild all over Australia. Settlers also shipped in European wildlife to hunt and to give their new nation a flavor of the "old country." Rabbits, hares, and foxes were released into the bush, where they caused absolute havoc. Rabbits became a major pest, stripping grass from vast swaths of land and destabilizing the ground with their burrows.

Native Australian herbivores suffered in competition with the rabbit, and other harmless creatures were persecuted by association; for example, wombats were shot because their extensive burrows allowed rabbits to get underneath rabbitproof fences.

Deliberate introductions to New Zealand were even more damaging. New Zealand has no native

The introduction of species such as the cane toad (right) to Australia and the American mink (below) to Europe has led to the sudden decline of many native animals.

mammals except bats, and many of its birds have highly specialized lifestyles. When settlers introduced 150 or so nonnative birds and mammals in the space of a century, there was no time for the existing species to adapt. Not all the aliens survived, but those that found a niche did so at the expense of many native species. At least seven endemic birds have already gone extinct, and 17 more, including the blue duck and the kakapo, are now threatened. Stoats, rats, and other aliens are a danger to ground-nesting kiwis and the takahe—birds found nowhere else in the world— but they also endanger many species of unique crickets and snails.

Sailors often marooned goats, pigs, and rabbits on remote islands so that there would be a source of fresh meat for future voyages. All three species have voracious appetites, none more so than the goats, which under the right conditions can also breed very fast. The goat population of Pinta Island in the Galápagos increased from three to thousands in just 12 years and stripped the place bare. Pigs can be equally destructive—a herd left on Bermuda in the early 17th century all but wiped out the endemic

Bermuda petrel. These birds once numbered in the hundreds of thousands, and despite almost 400 years of official protection, they are still classified by the IUCN as Endangered.

American mink were first brought to Europe as fur coats. The great demand for mink fur meant that before long live animals were being shipped over to stock fur farms. Mink are exceptionally fierce predators, and those that escaped had little trouble surviving in the wild. Several thousand mink have also been deliberately set free by animal rights activists. A large proportion of the released mink are trapped or shot, while others are killed on roads. A small proportion got clean away, which presumably was what the activists wanted; but these escapees can only make a living at the expense of native wildlife. Populations of native European mink, already much depleted by hunting, cannot compete with the American mink and are now in serious decline.

Not all inappropriate introductions have been deliberate, and various animals have managed to colonize new places by hitching a ride with cargoes being transported by ship or even by plane. The Asian black rat is an expert stowaway and has found its way to almost everywhere with a port. It is known the world over as a serious pest, bringer of disease, and killer of small reptiles, amphibians, and birds.

Introduced animals do not need to be large or active to cause serious damage. Large cargo ships carry seawater in the ballast tanks to help keep them stable. The amount of ballast needed varies depending on the ship's cargo, and water is often pumped in or out close to ports. In this way the eggs and larvae of various marine animals can be transported thousands of miles from their normal range.

DISEASE

Disease is a fact of life, but in a well-balanced ecosystem virulent epidemics are rare. Disease can even be beneficial to a population, weeding out old or

Ships *that discharge waste into the sea cause a serious pollution problem. In addition, the release of ballast water may threaten the local marine ecosystem if it contains species that have been transported from other parts of the world.*

weak animals. Problems occur when a population of animals is exposed to a new disease to which it has not had a chance to build up natural immunity.

Introduced diseases can rip through unprotected populations with devastating speed. The classic example is that of the myxomatosis virus. In the 1950s a British farmer decided to use the virus (which originally came from South America) to control the rabbits on his farm. No one could have dreamed it would be so effective. The disease spread so fast that it killed 99 percent of all British rabbits within a year. But farmers barely had the chance to heave a sigh of relief before conservationists realized something was badly wrong. In the 2,000 years since rabbits were introduced to Britain, they had helped create and maintain some of the island's most treasured habitats. They had also become a vital component of the food chain, supporting predators such as foxes and various

33

birds of prey. When rabbit numbers crashed, so did national populations of red kites, buzzards, and many other predators. Fortunately for them, rabbit populations have now recovered, and a large proportion have at least some degree of resistance to the myxomatosis virus.

A balance between disease and host can only be reached in situations where the disease infects just one kind of host. Once most of the host population is dead, the infection rate becomes very low because there are few hosts left to spread the disease. This gives the host species a chance to evolve resistance. However, if the disease is carried by two kinds of animal, the more resistant species (whose numbers remain relatively high) will carry on infecting and re-infecting the other species. This is what happens when a species carrying an infectious disease is introduced someplace new. The effect on native wildlife can be very serious. For example, domestic dogs in Africa spread canine distemper to wild hunting dogs and lions, causing many to die. Horses pass on diseases to tapirs in Central America. A disease that normally affects turkeys seriously depleted the now extinct American heath hen. In cases like these the domestic animals usually suffer only mildly and often receive the benefit of veterinary medicine, while their wild counterparts can be devastated.

Animals reared in captivity have been known to spread diseases to the very populations they were intended to boost, which is one reason why reintroduction programs are really a last resort in conservation terms.

GENETICS

All animals inherit genes from their parents. The process through which a gene inherited from your mother or father gives you blue eyes or gives you a better chance of being a ballerina or a linebacker, or helps a lion become the leader of the pride, is complex. Scientists still do not have all the answers;

This lion *is being treated for the canine distemper virus. (Lines drawn on the head help in the neurological examination.) The disease was brought to Africa by domestic dogs, and the lions have no natural immunity.*

But for some species problems with genetic inheritance can threaten extinction.

Inbreeding and Interbreeding

Inbreeding is when animals mate with partners that are closely related. One effect of inbreeding is that it reduces variety in a population. Since natural variation is the key to evolution, inbreeding limits the extent to which a population can adapt to change. If all the members of a population are very similar, they effectively have all their genetic eggs in one basket.

When inbreeding becomes very extreme (for example, parents breeding with their own offspring or animals breeding with their siblings), there is an increased risk that the offspring will inherit abnormalities or genetic disorders. There are many inherited conditions that only occur when an individual inherits a copy of the faulty gene from both parents. The chances of this are much higher if both parents are closely related and therefore have a similar genome. Affected animals usually die either before

Cheetahs *appear to be very inbred. There is very little genetic variation in the population, which means that they are susceptible to birth defects and other disorders.*

North American ruddy ducks *introduced to Europe are interbreeding so successfully with the closely related white-headed duck that the latter is in danger of being wiped out.*

they are born or soon after. This problem is easy to overlook because we do not tend to see many deformed or abnormal animals in the wild. Usually the first sign that something is wrong is when a population declines. Inbreeding may be the main cause of low birth rates and high infant mortality in dozens of the world's rarest animals. Inbreeding is a problem in trying to build up captive populations and is often used as a criticism of zoo breeding programs.

Interbreeding between two species can also "dilute" the genetic pool. If wildcats breed with domestic cats, for example, eventually the things that make a wildcat a distinct species will disappear.

NATURAL DISASTERS

Not all wildlife losses are our fault, although we often make things worse. Floods, avalanches, hurricanes, fires, and landslides often happen. For animals already threatened with extinction such natural disasters can be the last straw.

Some places are more prone to natural disasters than others. Places like Japan, the Philippines, New Zealand, and the West Coast of America all have more than their fair share of active volcanoes, earthquakes, and landslides. The tropical coasts of the Caribbean, Indochina, and India are especially prone to serious storms. The pink pigeons and echo parakeets of Mauritius have been nearly wiped out by cyclones.

The destructive power of fire can be a mixed blessing. In some habitats the fire passes so quickly that while dry material such as grasses and leaves go up in smoke, large plants such as trees and shrubs escape. Ironically, by combating forest fires we can cause far more devastating losses when the fire actually takes hold because of a buildup of material over time. Some of the most devastating fires of recent times burned throughout Southeast Asia in the 1990s. Unusual weather patterns had created large areas of dry vegetation; once the fires took hold, even healthy jungle went up in smoke, and life across much of the region ground to a halt. We will never know how many rare animals were lost.

Asiatic Lion

Panthera leo persica

The African lion may be familiar and still relatively numerous, but the Asian subspecies is becoming scarce and is now confined to a single reserve in northwestern India.

Lions are widespread over much of Africa south of the Sahara, but one subspecies—the Barbary lion—used to occur only in the north. The Barbary was the animal seen in Roman arenas fighting gladiators to the death. At one time the Barbary lions and their close relatives were found from northern Africa throughout the Middle East to India. All are now extinct; but a similar subspecies, the Asiatic lion, survives in the Gir Forest in northwestern India.

A Shrinking Range

Because of the threat that lions pose to humans and livestock, they have been systematically eradicated from most of their former range. The last European lions were killed about 1,000 years ago; and once guns became widely available, they disappeared rapidly from the Middle East along with other large animals. In India British soldiers and Indian nobles hunted the Asian subspecies for sport. By 1900 only a few dozen were left; they lived in the Gir Forest, where a local prince protected them.

At that time the dry savanna and deciduous forest covered about 1,000 square miles (2,600 sq. km), but it has since shrunk to half that size. Much of what remains is now protected as a national park. The area is small, however, and is surrounded by cultivated land, so the lions are effectively marooned on a patch of suitable habitat of little more than 20 to 40 square miles (50 to 100 sq. km). Moreover, they do not have the forest to themselves; there are several temples in the park, and five main roads and a railway track cross it. Large numbers of people are present at all times, and some have been killed by the lions; there were 81 attacks on humans, resulting in 16

DATA PANEL

Asiatic lion

Panthera leo persica

Family: Felidae

World population: About 250–300

Distribution: Gir Forest, Gujarat State, northwestern India

Habitat: Dry forest and acacia savanna

Size: Length head/body: up to about 6.5 ft (2 m); tail: about 3 ft (1 m). Weight: male 350–420 lb (160–190 kg); female 240–260 lb (110–120 kg)

Form: Similar to African lion, but with thicker coat and longer tail tassel; more pronounced tuft of hair on elbows; males do not develop large mane

Diet: Mainly deer and medium-sized mammals

Breeding: Average of 2 or 3 cubs per litter born after 4-month gestation. Young take 4–8 years to reach maturity. Life span up to about 20 years

Related endangered species: Tiger (*Panthera tigris*)* EN; snow leopard (*Uncia uncia*) EN

Status: IUCN CR; CITES I

CHINA
PAKISTAN
NEPAL
BHUTAN
INDIA
BANGLADESH
Gir Forest
SRI LANKA

Female Asiatic lions *rear their young together and suckle cubs other than their own for up to six months. The cubs start eating meat at three months.*

deaths between 1988 and 1990. To ease the problem, the sanctuary is being extended.

However, space is limited. Over 100,000 people live with their livestock within 6 miles (10 km) of the park. Domestic animals compete for food with the wild deer that the lions need as prey. When the lions go hungry, they turn to killing cattle. The government compensates local farmers for losses, but even so, lions are killed in revenge from time to time.

The cramped conditions create another danger. With the last Asiatic lions confined to one small area,

there is a risk that the entire population could be wiped out by disease. In 1994 an outbreak of distemper left scores of African lions dead in Serengeti National Park in Tanzania, eastern Africa; a similar disaster in the Gir Forest could make the Asiatic lion extinct. One solution would be to establish another population elsewhere, but in a crowded country such as India attempts to set up a lion sanctuary are often met with local resistance. One attempt to start a new population has already failed, probably as a result of illegal poisoning and shooting of the animals.

Tiger

Panthera tigris

Tigers used to occur across Asia as far west as Turkey, and isolated populations developed into eight different subspecies.

The tiger *is the largest member of the cat family. There are thought to be about 4,500 in India, the species' main stronghold.*

Within their huge range tigers have adapted to conditions ranging from bleak mountain forests to mangrove swamps and jungle. Since the beginning of the 20th century numbers have sharply declined, usually through conflict with humans. Tigers are large and fierce animals. They need to kill to eat and will often kill domestic animals and even people. Their own habitat has been reduced by farming and logging to the point where natural prey is difficult to obtain in sufficient quantity. Humans hunt the same prey, leaving few animals for the tigers.

By the 1950s three of the tiger subspecies (Bali, Caspian, and Javan) had become extinct. The remaining populations occur in widely separate places: India, Vietnam, Sumatra, China, and Siberia. The largest subspecies, the Amur (or Siberian) tiger, once ranged throughout the forested areas of China and Korea, north to the forested edges of Siberia. However, in the late 19th century tigers were a major threat to railway construction and increased settlement, so they were persecuted. By the 1940s tigers survived only in about five separated areas. Since then they have benefited from protection, and they have now increased in numbers and distribution again. There were about 450 Amur tigers in 1996. However, climate change now poses new threats.

On Bali and Java the extinction of the tiger was a result of habitat fragmentation, loss of natural prey, and finally, in the 1960s, conflict with groups of heavily armed men hiding in the jungle as a result of civil war. In India tigers used to be a favorite target for big-game hunters, and many thousands were shot.

Throughout Asia the tiger is believed to have magical powers, and many of its body parts are highly prized in traditional Oriental medicine. Killing a single tiger, therefore, can bring huge rewards to a poacher willing to risk the penalties for breaking the law.

Captive Breeding

Tigers breed well in captivity, so they are unlikely to become extinct. However, the captive population has become seriously inbred in the past, and there has been genetic mixing between the different subspecies. In addition, tigers cost a lot to feed, so most zoos give the animals contraceptives as a way of controlling the numbers of young born. It would be relatively easy to breed captive tigers for reintroduction to the wild, but there is not enough suitable habitat left for release of captive-bred stock.

The future lies in careful management of the remaining tiger habitats and reserves. Conservation measures will include linking small, isolated groups of animals and preventing poaching and further habitat loss. It is also vital to have plenty of prey animals; huge areas of land need to be set aside to maintain the prey populations required to support just a few tigers. The dangers of inbreeding may be reduced by using captive-bred animals as a fresh gene source.

Tiger

Panthera tigris

Family: Felidae

World population: 5,000–7,500 (1998 estimate)

Distribution: From India east to China and Vietnam and south to Indonesia (Sumatra)

Habitat: Dense cover: forests, scrub, and tall grass thickets; also mangroves

Size: Length head/body: 4.5–9 ft (1.4–2.7 m); tail: 24–43 in (60–110 cm); height at shoulder: 31–43 in (80–110 cm). Weight: up to 790 lb (360 kg) in the largest Siberian tigers

Form: Unmistakable, large orange cat with black stripes and long tail

Diet: Mostly deer and wild pigs weighing 110–440 lb (50–200 kg). Occasionally smaller animals such as monkeys, fish, and even birds. Needs about 33–40 lb (15–18 kg) per day

Breeding: Two or 3 cubs per litter, born after 14-week gestation; about 2 years between litters. Life span 15 years in wild, at least 26 in captivity

Related endangered species: Snow leopard *(Uncia uncia)* EN; lion *(Panthera leo)* VU; clouded leopard *(Neofelis nebulosa)** VU; also several smaller species of cat, including Iberian lynx *(Lynx pardinus)** CR

Status: IUCN EN; CITES I

Cheetah

Acinonyx jubatus

The cheetah is well known for its lean body, great speed, and spotted coat. Years of persecution have made it one of the world's most vulnerable big cats.

The world's fastest land animal over short distances, the cheetah is also the most ancient of all the big cats. Cheetahs probably evolved on the plains of the Middle East four million years ago. Fossil evidence shows that 10,000 years ago cheetahs roamed in places as far apart as North America, Europe, Asia, and Africa. The cheetah's heyday lasted until the last ice age; since then human populations have exploded, and the cheetah's range and numbers have shrunk. In their ancestral homeland of the Middle East the Asian subspecies of cheetah is critically endangered, with very few, if any, animals left in remote parts of Iran and Afghanistan. The situation is only slightly better in Africa.

Cheetahs differ from other big cats in their adaptations for hunting. The shape of a cheetah— a narrow, elongated body and long, muscular legs— is ideal for sprinting. Unlike its cousins, the cheetah cannot completely retract its claws; it needs them to provide extra grip when running at high speeds. Cheetahs take advantage of the fact that other large predators rest during the hottest part of the day and do their hunting in the late morning and early afternoon. A cheetah first stalks its prey, then runs it down at speeds of up to 60 miles per hour (95 km/h). The flexibility of the cat's long spine allows it to take huge strides. Most chases are over in about 20 seconds—any prey that can evade capture for more than a minute will probably escape since the cheetah cannot maintain its speed for long.

Cheetahs kill by clamping their jaws around the victim's throat. This has the effect of closing off the windpipe, so the prey stops breathing. The cheetah does not have particularly big teeth, but exceptionally large nostrils ensure that, even when out of breath from the chase, it can inhale deeply through its nose while maintaining a suffocating grip with its jaws.

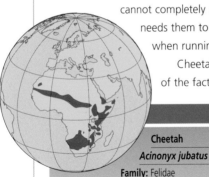

DATA PANEL

Cheetah

Acinonyx jubatus

Family: Felidae

World population: 2,000–15,000

Distribution: Sub-Saharan Africa, excluding Congo Basin; most of South Africa

Habitat: Grasslands

Size: Length head/body: 44–60 in (112–152 cm); tail: 20–33 in (51–84 cm); height at shoulder: 25–37 in (64–94 cm); males slightly larger than females. Weight: 86–143 lb (39–65 kg)

Form: Slender big cat with long, muscular legs, small head, and long, curved tail. Coat golden yellow with black spots; small, rounded ears; black stripes either side of nose

Diet: Mainly gazelles; also impala, warthogs, small antelopes, gamebirds, and hares

Breeding: Between 1 and 8 young (average 3–5) born at any time of year (peak births March–June). Life span 12–14 years in the wild; up to 17 years in captivity

Related endangered species: No close relatives

Status: IUCN VU; CITES I

Cheetah means "spotted one" in Hindi, and every cheetah has markings as unique as a fingerprint. In some Zimbabwean cheetahs the spots along the back and tail join up to form a blotchy pattern. Animals with this distinctive pattern are called king cheetahs and they were once thought to be a separate subspecies. However, it has been shown that they are simply part of the natural variation within the local population. The black "tear stripes" on the cheetah's face are thought to help protect their eyes from sunlight reflecting off their cheeks. Human athletes imitate this idea when they daub paint across their cheeks and noses.

Cheetahs breed at any time of year. A female is in heat and ready to mate every 12 days unless she already has cubs. She will give birth to three to five cubs per litter; but infant mortality is high, and fewer

A cheetah can achieve speeds of 0 to 45 miles per hour (0 to 72 km/h) in 2.5 seconds—acceleration to rival some sports cars.

than one-third of all cubs survive to adulthood. Small, widely scattered cheetah populations mean that much inbreeding occurs, and many cubs are born with genetic defects. A solution might be to release some animals from captivity, bringing in fresh genetic stock.

Tourist Attraction

Cheetahs face problems even in protected national parks. Tourists want to see the cheetahs wherever possible, and this tends to scare off prey and distracts the animals from hunting. Disturbance of cheetah kills also allows scavengers such as jackals to nip in and steal the food. Cheetahs are not good at defending themselves from this sort of interference.

Leopard

Panthera pardus

The adaptable leopard is a very widespread species and is still quite common in some parts of Africa. However, elsewhere hunting for fur, persecution by farmers, and loss of habitat have brought several subspecies to the brink of extinction.

Leopards are the most adaptable of the big cats. They can live in a wide variety of climates and habitat types, so long as they have a plentiful supply of food and secure cover in which to hide their food, rear their young, and rest during the day. Prey can be anything from large antelopes and pigs to rats, rabbits, and birds, and if times are really hard, insects.

The leopard can live in forests or open spaces and at altitudes ranging from sea level to well over 16,000 feet (5,000 m). Leopards from different places often differ in appearance, none so much as the black panther, an all black or "melanistic" leopard that inhabits dark, humid forests in Southeast Asia. Regional differences are not always this obvious; but because leopards from one population are usually isolated from those elsewhere, they are recognized as distinct subspecies.

As one would expect for such a generalist predator able to cope with extremes of climate, the leopard's distribution is large. In fact, it has the widest range of any cat. Leopards once thrived in areas ranging from the baking savannas of South Africa to the lofty Himalayas, from the Javan rain forests to windswept Siberian plateaus. They are still present in these places, but in all but their African stronghold the species is in serious trouble.

Panthera pardus panthera

DATA PANEL

Leopard	**Form:** Large, pale-buff to deep-chestnut cat marked with rosettes of dark on body and tail; head marked with smaller spots, belly and legs with large blotches; very dark or black individuals are known as black panthers
Panthera pardus	
Family: Felidae	
World population: Probably considerably fewer than the 700,000 estimated in 1988	
Distribution: Largest populations in sub-Saharan Africa, with scattered and shrinking populations in northern Africa, the Middle East, Pakistan, India, Bangladesh, Sri Lanka, China, Siberia, Korea, Indochina, and Indonesia	**Diet:** Mostly hoofed animals such as gazelles, wildebeest, deer, goats, and pigs, including livestock; also takes monkeys, rodents, rabbits, birds, and invertebrates
Habitat: Very diverse; includes forests, grasslands, and deserts, lowlands and mountains; anywhere where there is sufficient food and cover, such as trees, scrub, or rocks	**Breeding:** Between 1 and 6 (usually 2 or 3) cubs born after gestation of 13–15 weeks at any time of year in Africa, more seasonal elsewhere; weaned at 3 months; mature at 3 years; may live over 20 years
Size: Length head/body: 35–75 in (90–190 cm); tail 22–42 in (58–110 cm); height to shoulder: 17.5–31 in (45–78 cm); males up to 50% bigger than females. Weight: 61–200 lb (28–90 kg)	**Related endangered species:** Asiatic lion (*Panthera leo persica*)* CR; tiger (*P. tigris*)* EN; snow leopard (*Uncia uncia*) EN; lion (*P. leo*) VU; jaguar (*P. onca*)* NT
	Status: Varies with subspecies: LC to CR. Isolated North African leopard (*Panthera pardus panthera*), for example, is CR. All leopards CITES I

Changing Circumstances

The problems for leopards in different parts of the species' range vary so widely that the IUCN places different regional subspecies in different categories of threat. In sub-Saharan Africa leopards are still relatively numerous, especially inside national parks such as the Serengeti. Here the protection the leopards receive and the abundant prey available to them mean that they are doing very well.

The leopard is legally protected in almost every country in its range, although several nations permit limited hunting and licenses for hunting and export of skins, and mounted trophies are granted on a regular basis. The licenses are restricted by country and usually account for between 1,000 and 2,000 leopards a year. This level of hunting is probably sustainable and an improvement on the situation in the 1960s and 1970s, when over 50,000 leopards were killed a year.

Legal hunting may not be the threat it once was, but outside protected habitats (which account for only about 13 percent of the species' range) leopards are suffering from habitat loss, persecution, and poaching. Five subspecies, from northwestern Africa, the Middle East, Siberia, and Korea are listed as Critically Endangered, with populations of fewer than 250 animals and in one case as few as 17. Four other subspecies, from the Middle East, Southeast Asia, and Indonesia are listed as Endangered.

Unlike other big cats, leopards do not seem to mind living alongside people. When areas of natural habitat are settled and turned over to agriculture, the adaptable leopard does not automatically move on. Many will stick around and adjust their behavior to make the best living they can under the circumstances. Some leopards attack livestock, and others even become man-eaters, so most governments permit the shooting of problem leopards. Man-eating leopards seem to be a particular problem in India, where dozens of people are killed by leopards every year.

The leopard's *coat serves to break up its outline, especially in dappled sunlight. This camouflage is useful for hunting and allows the big cat to rest undetected in the branches of a tree during the day.*

Clouded Leopard

Neofelis nebulosa

The clouded leopard gets its name from the cloudlike markings on its coat. The hunting of this big cat for its magnificent pelt is one of several threats to its survival.

The clouded leopard is not actually a leopard at all. In fact, the species is sufficiently distinct to be classified all by itself. The skull and teeth of the clouded leopard are similar to those of big cats such as lions and tigers. However, it is unable to roar loudly like its large cousins, and its appearance is more like that of smaller cats, including lynx and ocelots.

The Malaysian name for the clouded leopard is *rinaudahan*, meaning tree tiger, and it is indeed one of the most accomplished feline climbers. Its broad, flexible paws grasp branches, and its long tail serves as an effective counterbalance. The clouded leopard also has remarkably flexible ankle joints—captive individuals have been observed dangling upside down from branches by just one back leg! Its arboreal skill is put to good use when hunting; the leopard will sometimes ambush unsuspecting prey by pouncing on them from above. It captures and kills monkeys and birds by knocking them off the branches of trees, just as a domestic cat swipes at smaller prey. Nevertheless, this adaptable cat also does much of its hunting on the ground, stalking wild pigs, deer, and cattle until it is close enough to launch a sudden fatal attack.

Starting Life

Little is known about the clouded leopard's social behavior and courtship in the wild, except that the animals appear to be solitary until the breeding season begins. Studies of individuals in zoos around the world have provided basic information about how the clouded leopard breeds. The young are born after a gestation of approximately three months. Each cub weighs 5 to 10 ounces (150 to 280 g) at birth, and its eyes remain closed for the first 10 to 12 days. The young begin to take solid food

DATA PANEL

Clouded leopard

Neofelis nebulosa

Family: Felidae

World population: Unknown, but no more than a few thousand

Distribution: Asia, including Nepal, southern China, Burma, Indochina, parts of India and possibly Bangladesh, mainland Malaysia, Sumatra, Borneo and Java, Thailand, Vietnam; probably now extinct in Taiwan

Habitat: Dense mountain forests

Size: Length head/body: 28–43 in (75–110 cm); tail: 35–59 in (90–150 cm). Weight: 25–66 lb (16–30 kg)

Form: Large, robust-looking cat with short legs and a long tail. The yellowish coat is distinctively marked with large dark patches, each with a pale, cloudlike center. The underside, legs, and head are spotted and streaked. The eyes are yellow, and the ears are rounded

Diet: Deer, cattle, goats, wild pigs, monkeys, reptiles, and birds; stalked or ambushed by day and night

Breeding: Only observed in captivity; 1–5 (usually 2–4) young born March–August. Lives up to 17 years in captivity

Related endangered species: No close relatives. Taiwanese subspecies may already be extinct

Status: IUCN VU; CITES I

after 10 to 11 weeks, but the mother will continue to suckle them until they are about five months old. They are born with plenty of yellowish-gray fur marked with dark spots. The adult coat is developed at six months, and the youngsters reach independence about three months later.

A Fragile Future

There are four geographically distinct subspecies of clouded leopard, found in Taiwan, Borneo and Malaysia, Nepal and Burma, and also China. However, there have been no recent sightings of the Taiwanese subspecies, known as the Formosan clouded leopard, and there are fears that it may already have become extinct in the wild. Elsewhere the clouded leopard survives in the most remote and undisturbed areas of mountain forests. The main problems facing the

Clouded leopards prefer to live in dense tropical forest, where they are found at altitudes of up to 7,000 feet (2,100 m). However, they will also occupy more marginal habitats such as swampy areas and sparsely forested terrain.

animal throughout its range are all too familiar. It is hunted for its magnificent pelt, and its teeth and bones are considered prized ingredients in traditional Eastern medicines. Erosion of the clouded leopard's habitat—as a result of deforestation by the timber industry and forest clearance for human settlement—is even more of a problem. Even when they are not being persecuted, the leopards are running out of places to live. Clouded leopards are being bred in captivity around the world, so reintroduction programs may be possible in the future, but that can only happen if areas of suitable habitat can be preserved.

45

Jaguar

Panthera onca

The jaguar is the most accomplished climber of all the big cats and is almost equally at home prowling the forest floor or swimming in rivers and pools. However, its adaptability is no protection against the erosion of its forest habitat or other human activities that threaten its existence.

The jaguar is the largest cat in the Americas and the only member of the big cat genus *Panthera* to be found in this region. It bears a resemblance to the leopard and is often thought of as the South American equivalent. Its coat pattern consists of black markings on a golden-tan background. Entirely black jaguars, known as black panthers, are relatively common, the all-black or melanistic condition being caused by a single gene that overrides those for normal patterning. A cub needs to inherit only a single copy of the melanistic gene from either of its parents to be born with a jet black coat. Albino jaguars have also been recorded, but they are extremely rare.

The jaguar is more heavily built than its African cousin, the leopard. Its head and jaws are substantially larger and more powerful, an arrangement that hints at its preferred method of finishing off its prey—with a crushing bite to the skull. The jaguar is the most accomplished climber among the big cats and will often ambush prey from trees. Prey includes almost anything it can catch; over 85 different species have been recorded in its diet. Nevertheless, the jaguar prefers larger mammals such as peccaries (a kind of wild pig), tapirs, and deer, though in dense rainforest where these are hard to come by, it often turns instead to fish and reptiles. It is an excellent swimmer, and with its powerful jaw and stout canine teeth it can crack open the tough shells of turtles. Indeed, it has been suggested that this ability to attack reptilian prey is one reason the jaguar survived in the New World during the Pleistocene period, when a significant proportion of large herbivore prey became extinct. In places where human settlements spread into their territory, jaguars often take livestock. In Brazil domestic cows are the main diet of many jaguars living near cattle ranches.

The jaguar would certainly be capable of killing a human; but when people have reported being "stalked" through the forest, it is likely that the jaguar was merely making sure the trespassers were leaving its territory. If it really had intended to eat the people, they would surely not have lived to tell the tale!

Jaguars can probably breed all year round, but most births take place when prey is most abundant. The two sexes only tolerate each other when courting or mating; the male has nothing to do with the raising of offspring. Only when mating does the jaguar make much noise—a deep, throaty cry is the closest it ever gets to a roar.

Cubs are born in litters of one to four, with twins being most common. The young are blind at birth and will not leave the den until they are two weeks old. The mother moves her cubs much like other cats, grasping them by the scruff of the neck. The cubs spend a lot of time playing together, and the mother is remarkably tolerant of their boisterous games, which more often than not involve clambering all over her, biting her tail, and pulling her ears! The cubs remain with the mother until she is ready to breed again, which can be as long as two years.

Threats to Survival

Jaguars were once widely hunted for their skins, which made valuable fur coats, but the trade was banned in the 1970s. Nowadays the main threat comes from cattle ranchers, who shoot jaguars that kill their livestock and may also hunt them for sport. Even more of a threat is the destruction of forests to make way for other animals. Continuous grazing by cattle and sheep prevents new trees from growing, and the vast prairies that are formed are unsuitable for the forest-dwelling jaguar.

A jaguar cub. *The animal's relatively short limbs are an adaptation for climbing; jaguars are the most arboreal of the big cats.*

DATA PANEL

Jaguar

Panthera onca

Family: Felidae

World population: Unknown, but probably in low thousands

Distribution: From Mexico to Patagonia, including Belize, Panama, Costa Rica, Guatemala, Honduras, Nicaragua, Surinam, Colombia, Ecuador, Guyana, Venezuela, French Guiana, Peru, Brazil, Bolivia, Uruguay, Paraguay, Argentina. Formerly southwestern U.S.

Habitat: Tropical forests, swamps, rivers, pools, and open country

Size: Length head/body: 44–72 in (112–185 cm); tail: 18–30 in (46–76 cm); females smaller than males. Weight: 100–250 lb (45–123 kg)

Form: Robust-looking big cat. Golden coat with black rings, rosettes, and dots; pale underside

Diet: Wild pigs, capybaras, tapirs, domestic cattle, horses, fish, frogs, turtles, tortoises, and young alligators

Breeding: Cubs born in litters of 1–4 at any time of year. Life span up to 12 years in the wild; up to 22 years recorded in captivity

Related endangered species: Other big cats, including the Asiatic lion *(Panthera leo persica)** CR and tiger *(P. tigris)** EN

Status: IUCN NT; CITES I

Iberian Lynx

Lynx pardinus

The Iberian lynx, once widespread in Spain and Portugal, may now be the world's most endangered cat. Although legally protected since the 1970s, it is still endangered as a result of habitat loss, persecution, and threats to its prey.

The Iberian lynx is smaller than the European lynx, but otherwise similar. Although previously widespread in Spain and Portugal, it is now a rare species. By the 1980s there were probably fewer than 1,200 lynxes alive. By 1999 the population had halved, and the distribution of the lynx had contracted by more than 80 percent in fewer than 30 years. Today there are probably fewer than 600 lynxes left. The main population of about 400 animals lives in the mountains of central southern Spain. The rest are widely scattered, and all these subpopulations have a total of fewer than 100 animals.

The Iberian lynxes live in open woodland with scattered pines and evergreen oaks. They also favor thick scrub, patches of open grassland, and dense thickets of dry scrub on the mountains. Rabbits comprise 80 percent of their diet, a degree of specialization that is dangerous in a changing world. To rely too much on one source of food makes any animal vulnerable if something goes wrong with the supply. In the 1950s the viral disease myxomatosis swept through the rabbit populations of Europe, killing over 90 percent of them in some places. As the years went by, the rabbit population became more resistant to this fatal disease, and numbers began to recover. However, in the late 1980s a new disaster struck in the form of rabbit hemorrhagic disease, which also killed large numbers of rabbits, again leaving few to support the lynx population.

Habitat Loss

The rapid economic development of Spain and Portugal over recent decades has been a significant threat to the lynx. Remote parts of the countryside have been opened up by the construction of new roads. Hotels and vacation homes have been built to accommodate the booming tourist industry and provide facilities for retirement communities. Overstocking of cattle and game ranches and the erection of deer fencing have also had a detrimental

FRANCE
SPAIN
PORTUGAL
ALGERIA

DATA PANEL

Iberian lynx (pardel lynx)

Lynx pardinus

Family: Felidae

World population: 500–600

Distribution: Parts of Spain and Portugal

Habitat: Open pine woodland and among dense, dry thickets of scrub on the mountains

Size: Length head/body: 31.5 in–38 in (80–96 cm); tail: 3.5–4.5 in (9–11 cm); height at shoulder: 24–27 in (60–68 cm). Weight: 22–33 lb (10–15 kg)

Form: A large, long-legged cat, with a short black-tipped tail and tufted ears. Coat pale brown with white spots

Diet: Mainly rabbits, but also young deer, rodents, and ground-dwelling birds

Breeding: Breeding season January–March, births in May. Litters of 2–3 kittens born; 1 litter per year. Life span unknown, but other lynx species live up to 15 years

Related endangered species: Cheetah (*Acinonyx jubatus*)* VU; tiger (*Panthera tigris*)* EN; snow leopard (*Uncia uncia*) EN; several other big and small cats

Status: IUCN CR; CITES I

The Iberian lynx *has an attractive gray-brown mottled coat, a broad, short head, and distinctive tufted ears. It is now one of the world's rarest mammals.*

effect on the habitat for many forms of wildlife, including the lynx. The natural mosaic of habitats that suits lynxes and their prey has been broken up, and the lynx population has been reduced and critically fragmented into nine separate subpopulations, with a total of at least 48 separate breeding groups. Increased use of roads has meant more deaths, particularly in the Coto Doñana area, and some populations of lynx already have fewer than 10 females, so even a few road kills per year could be disastrous.

Persecution

Although lynxes have been legally protected in Spain since 1973 and Portugal since 1974, many are still shot. Most live on private estates and cattle ranches, where hunting and shooting are common. Only 40 to 50 lynxes live in the protected area of the Coto Doñana National Park; very few enjoy the protection of nature reserves. Lynxes have now been infected with tuberculosis (TB) from wild pigs and deer.

Action Plan

An action plan for the lynx now exists: The European Habitats Directive has given the species more protection, and there should be money available from the European Union to manage the countryside in a manner more suited to wildlife conservation. However, it may all have come too late to save the Iberian lynx.

Florida Panther

Puma concolor coryi

The last few individuals of the once-widespread Florida panther cling precariously to their remaining habitat in the southern United States. This handsome cat now faces possible extinction.

Like the ocelot, the panther (or puma) has a very wide distribution throughout North and South America. There are various local subspecies, one of which is the Florida panther. The panther has been extinct in Arkansas, Louisiana, Tennessee, and West Virginia since the 1950s. Another subspecies, the eastern panther, has probably also died out, leaving only the Florida panther in the eastern United States.

Almost everything that has happened to its environment in the last 100 years has hit the panther hard. It is a familiar story: As the human population has expanded and increased its activities, so panthers have been eliminated. They are large predators, presenting a threat to both people and their livestock. Farm animals have been attacked, and on average one person a year is killed by panthers in North America. These few attacks may not seem significant, but they give the animals a bad public image, cause widespread fear, and result in a desire to eliminate them. Consequently, in many states hunters have been employed to kill panthers.

However, the main cause of the panther losses in Florida is change to its habitat. The creation of new farmland areas from the dense bush and palmetto (small palm) thickets has deprived the panthers of living space. New highways slice through the remaining habitat, creating areas too small to support a viable population. Young panthers normally disperse between 18 and 50 miles (30 to 80 km) from where they were born, but then the fast-moving traffic on the roads poses a danger. Roads and other barriers prevent animals from mixing and meeting, and there is then more inbreeding and consequently a loss of genetic diversity. The species then faces the threat of breeding failure, including a higher proportion of birth defects and miscarriages.

Much of Florida lies on limestone overlaid by swamps. In recent times 40 percent of the swamplands have been lost as a result of expansion of farmland. Water is pumped from underground to

Alabama Georgia
UNITED STATES

Florida

DATA PANEL

Florida panther
Puma concolor coryi

Family: Felidae

World population: Between 30 and 50

Distribution: South central Florida

Habitat: Swamp forest and dense thickets

Size: Length head/body: 42–54 in (100–130 cm); tail: 30–36 in (72–80 cm); height at shoulder: 26–31 in (62–75 cm). Weight: 66–125 lb (30–57 kg)

Form: Large, tawny or dark-brown cat with white flecks around the shoulders; long black-tipped tail, sharply kinked toward the end. Black on sides of face and backs of ears

Diet: Deer; also hares, rodents, armadillos; occasionally domestic animals

Breeding: One to 6 (usually 3) cubs born at almost any time of year after gestation period of about 3 months; mature at 2–3 years. Life span about 20 years

Related endangered species: Eastern panther (*Puma concolor cougar*) CR

Status: IUCN CR; CITES I

The Florida panther

population stands at fewer than 50 today, but the natural food supply available in Florida would once have supported about 1,300 panthers.

supply towns and irrigate crops. Swamps therefore dry up, and whole areas of forest and scrub become more susceptible to fire. Fire is devastating, not only because it kills wildlife, but also because it removes vital cover from large areas. The deer that form the main prey of the panthers are deprived of their food by the fires and also by the replacement of native vegetation by introduced plants (such as Brazilian pepper) that they do not eat, and the losses of deer affect the panther population.

In addition, panthers are at the end of a long food chain and therefore susceptible to the toxic materials that accumulate in their prey. Burning of domestic and industrial refuse in Florida gives out pollutants, which collect at every level of the food chain.

Chances of Survival

Legally protected since 1973, the Florida panther now survives only in and around the Everglades National Park and Big Cypress National Preserve. In 1995 eight females of the Texas subspecies were imported to provide fresh genes, and in 1980 a sperm bank was started to enable continued breeding of the animals. Major roads have now been fenced to reduce accidents with traffic, and habitat "corridors" are being created to allow safer movement. Nevertheless, the panther's future in Florida still looks bleak.

Wildcat

Felis silvestris

Like many predators, the wildcat has suffered extensive persecution. Today the major threat to its survival is genetic dilution of the species as it increasingly interbreeds with domestic cats.

The wildcat is a solitary and secretive animal found mainly in forested areas across continental Europe and in Scotland. Its range also extends east to the Caspian Sea, an inland salt lake that lies between Europe and Asia. Its major prey is small mammals and birds: mostly mice, voles, rabbits, and other wild species. However, wildcats have been unpopular with humans, who suspect them of being a threat to domestic stock such as lambs and chickens and a danger to children. Although these fears are greatly exaggerated, the wildcat has been trapped, shot, and poisoned widely. Moreover, in the past its skin was prized for its warmth, and its fur became a luxury fashion item for trimming clothing.

Habitat Loss

The wildcat is not seriously endangered. However, the expansion of cities and intensification of farming have resulted in habitat loss. Although some wildcats manage to live close to farms and on the edges of European towns, where they may even visit garbage dumps to feed, they have become more scarce. There are now large areas of Europe where they are extinct, and the remaining populations are widely separated.

The wildcat *looks like a domestic tabby, but is larger and has more distinct body stripes and a blunt end to the tail.*

Interbreeding Problems

The biggest threat by far to wildcats is "genetic pollution" through interbreeding with domestic cats. The wildcats of Europe are so similar to the African wildcat (from which the domestic form is thought to originate) that some zoologists think the two species are actually the same. They are certainly closely related, which is why they interbreed so easily. As a result, the natural wildcat population has begun to include crossbred animals (hybrids). This genetic dilution undermines the purity of the species. Ironically, as the wildcat's habitat has shrunk, the animal has been forced into new areas where it encounters domestic cats more often. This has led to more interbreeding and further genetic dilution. Thus the greater the wildcat's breeding success, the more uncertain its future. At the very least, hybridization will result in a confused picture, with some areas having true wildcats, and others having hybrids. In addition, interbreeding makes the species difficult to monitor.

The Berne Convention, the European Union Habitats Directive, and the national legislation of many countries recognize the wildcat's rarity and have given the animal legal protection. Yet these laws are unable to prevent the main threat of interbreeding. Moreover, since hybrids are not legally protected, the legislation is weakened because anyone killing a wildcat can claim that they thought the animal was a hybrid. Such an assertion cannot be easily disproved. If wildcats and domestic cats really are the same species then it seems impractical to give the animal legal protection, since there are millions of house cats all over the world!

Gray Wolf

Canis lupus spp.

Although still common in Alaska and some other areas, the gray wolf is now extinct or critically endangered in many parts of its former range.

The gray wolf is the largest member of the dog family. At one time it had the widest distribution of almost any land mammal, being found nearly everywhere in the Northern Hemisphere. Throughout this range wolves have inspired considerable fear over the centuries, and this has been reinforced by spine-chilling stories; they are the subject of much folklore. As people and their domestic animals have spread and increased in number, conflict with wolves has escalated, resulting in extermination of wolves in many parts of their range.

Today about 2,000 gray wolves still survive in Spain, and a few hundred more in Italy and Greece.

There are about 50 left in Sweden, and there are occasional reports of strays turning up in Norway (where unfortunately they stand a good chance of being shot by farmers). Between 1991 and 1992 wolves spread from Italy as far as the French Alps, but at least six were shot soon afterward.

Today wolves are still unwelcome residents across much of their European range. In Romania about 700 (from a population of fewer than 3,000) are shot each year. In Greece wolves face a shortage of suitable large mammal prey, and people are actively encouraged to kill them. In Italy, however, where farmers are paid compensation for sheep killed by wolves, local wolf populations seem to have stabilized or even increased a little, to about 200.

Fortunately, the wolf remains fairly abundant in northern territories particularly Alaska, Canada, and the former Soviet Union. There have also been attempts to reintroduce the animals to areas in which they had previously been eradicated. In 1995 wolves were released back into Yellowstone National Park in the United States, a move that was highly controversial. The fear of wolves runs deep, and there are concerns for the safety of

DATA PANEL

Gray wolf (timber wolf)

Canis lupus spp.

Family: Canidae

World population: Many thousands, (50,000 plus in former Soviet Union and adjacent countries, for example); rare or extinct in many parts of former range

Distribution: Canada and Alaska; also northern Asia and into Eastern Europe. Remnant populations in Spain, Portugal, Sweden, and Arabia

Habitat: Open woodland (especially coniferous forest), mountains, tundra, and bogs

Size: Length head/body: 39–51 in (100–130 cm); tail: 14–20 in (35–52 cm); height at shoulder: 26–28 in (65–70 cm). Weight: male 66–175 lb (30–80 kg); female 50–120 lb (23–55 kg)

Form: Large dog, almost white in northern latitudes; dark gray to nearly black farther south. Tail held high when running

Diet: Birds and small- to medium-sized animals; packs cooperate to kill larger species such as deer

Breeding: Between 3 and 7 cubs born per year in single litter after 9-week gestation; mature at 2 years (but often longer before they actually breed). Life span up to 20 years in captivity; probably 10–15 in wild

Related endangered species: Red wolf *(Canis rufus)* CR; Ethiopian wolf *(C. simensis)* EN; African wild dog *(Lycaon pictus)* EN; maned wolf *(Chrysocyon brachyurus)* NT

Status: IUCN VU; CITES II (some races Appendix 1)

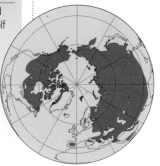

cattle and sheep in the vicinity. Such projects can only succeed with public support; otherwise the animals are exterminated before a new population has time to establish itself.

A Shortage of Suitable Prey

A serious problem for wolves in Europe and in the more densely inhabited parts of North America is that the expansion of farming has reduced the numbers of deer and other suitable prey. Without sufficient food to support them, wolf populations have fragmented. Wolves have then been forced to attack sheep and to scavenge around garbage dumps, bringing them into more frequent contact with people and increasing the risk of crossbreeding with domestic dogs.

In Spain a recent increase in the deer population was followed by a reduction in the number of sheep killed by wolves. Since the wolves were preying on the deer, they did not need to kill the sheep. This small victory is a reminder that conservation initiatives need to look at the health of the environment as a whole as well as the fate of individual species.

Perhaps there is also encouragement to be gained from Canada, where wolf-watching trips are becoming popular activities in national parks. Growing familiarity may help reduce some of the fear that people have for the wild ancestor of the domestic dog, helping make the gray wolf's long-term future a little more secure.

Gray wolves *do not attack humans, despite the legends. People are at greater risk of dying from domestic dog attacks than from wolf attacks. Wolves do attack coyotes, however, and may help keep coyote numbers in check.*

Swift Fox

Vulpes velox

The small swift fox has suffered heavy losses as a result of trapping and poisoning campaigns intended to eradicate other more abundant carnivores that were thought to be a threat to livestock.

The swift fox is sometimes regarded as a North American subspecies of the common kit fox. However, the two have a different distribution, and the distinctive DNA and skeletal structures of the swift fox justify treating it as a separate species.

Swift foxes live in small family groups, occupying underground dens with an extensive system of burrows and chambers. The tunnels provide cool shelter during the heat of the day and hiding places in open habitats. For these reasons the burrows are also attractive to rodents and other small animals such as lizards and beetles, which also occupy the dens, providing the foxes with some extra food.

Threats to Survival

Swift foxes are found in open prairie and desert habitats. They used to occur from Canada in the north to the Mexican border in the south. However, in the more northerly states much of their habitat has been taken over as farmland. Swift foxes are relatively tame, and this has contributed to their decline. They are easily trapped, and many were caught for their fur; others have been shot or killed by road traffic. Swift foxes also fall prey to the coyote, a larger relative that is the main predator of the swift foxes' cubs.

Swift foxes are nocturnal hunters. They feed mainly on rabbits and small mammals, and in so doing probably help farmers by destroying pests such as rats and mice. In addition, they do not harm chickens or other livestock. Despite this, the severe decline of swift fox numbers has been caused by their becoming unwitting victims of poisoning campaigns. Poisons directed at coyotes and other predators that are more abundant and perceived as a threat to farm livestock

have been picked up by the foxes. In many areas state and local governments have actively encouraged large-scale poisoning campaigns aimed at reducing the numbers of coyotes. As a result, swift foxes became extinct in Canada and are now also very rare in the northern United States.

Reintroduction into Canada

Attempts to reintroduce the swift fox into Canada began in the early 1980s. From 1983 to 1997 a total of 91 wild foxes were caught and taken to Canada for release. They were joined by 841 more that had been raised in captivity. Seventeen sites were selected for the release of foxes in Alberta and south-central Saskatchewan. Initially the foxes were studied carefully after release and were provided with shelters, but after 1987 they were simply turned loose. The captive-bred animals seemed to cope well with freedom, even though most had never been outside a cage.

In 1988 over 30 pups were reared in the wild, but it is still not clear whether the species will become fully established again in Canada. Despite hundreds being released, in 1997 the total Canadian population was still fewer than 200. The project has been criticized, since none of the animals were of Canadian stock, all coming from farther south. Moreover, swift foxes seem to have been slowly spreading northward on their own, suggesting that there was no need for human intervention and that recolonization of suitable areas will eventually take place naturally.

The swift fox *is similar in appearance to the common red fox, but is much smaller. Along with the kit fox, it is the smallest member of the dog family in North America.*

DATA PANEL

Swift fox

Vulpes velox

Family: Canidae

World population: Low thousands

Distribution: Confined to western U.S.; was extinct in Canada but has been reintroduced

Habitat: Open plains and deserts

Size: Length head/body: 15–20 in (36–48 cm); tail: 9–12 in (22–30 cm). Weight: 4–6 lb (1.8–2.7 kg)

Form: Small, large-eared, buff-yellow fox with black markings on either side of muzzle and bushy tail with black tip

Diet: Small mammals; occasionally large insects

Breeding: Between 4 and 7 pups born February–April. Life span up to 7 years in the wild, 20 years in captivity

Related endangered species: Falkland Island wolf *(Dusicyon australis)* EX; red wolf *(Canis rufus)* CR; Ethiopian wolf *(C. simensis)* EN; African wild dog *(Lycaon pictus)* EN; bushdog *(Speothos venaticus)* VU; dhole *(Cuon alpinus)* EN

Status: IUCN LC; not listed by CITES

Thylacine

Thylacinus cynocephalus

The thylacine—a marsupial—was once prevalent across Australia and Tasmania. Today it seems that domestic dogs and other introduced animals have outcompeted the species. It was also persecuted by farmers and is now probably extinct, although there are continued reports of sightings.

The thylacine appears to have been an unsuccessful evolutionary experiment. The largest marsupial carnivore of recent times, it was a surprisingly clumsy and rather slow-moving creature, ill equipped to be a predator. It is said to have stalked its prey at night or run after wallabies until they got tired and could be killed. Its jaws were longer than a dog's, and it had more teeth, but they were probably unable to deliver a strong bite.

The thylacine has no close relatives. Once placental mammals such as dingoes and, later, foxes and domestic dogs and cats reached Australia, the thylacine was forced to compete with these more efficient hunters and killers. It swiftly disappeared from its former wide range, although there were many reports of sightings on the mainland of Australia, even into the early 20th century.

Forced into Island Isolation

By about 1910 all remaining thylacines were confined to Tasmania, an island that initially lacked competing carnivores. The arrival of Europeans brought about a period of large-scale change to the habitat and to the species profile of the island. Once sheep farming began there, the thylacine was considered to be a serious pest, having a reputation as a livestock killer, particularly of sheep and hens. From about 1840 farmers killed them in large numbers; by about 1860 they had disappeared from the lowlands, surviving only in the more inaccessible mountain forests.

Government-Sponsored Extinction

From 1888 the killing was further encouraged by the Australian government, which offered payments for dead thylacines. Records show that rewards were paid for over 2,000 thylacines during a 20-year period, and many more must have died unrecorded. Most were shot or snared, but many were also poisoned. The species rapidly vanished from Tasmania, perhaps hastened into extinction by a disease that swept through other species of carnivorous marsupials, sharply reducing their numbers. The thylacine was given legal protection in 1936, but by then was probably already extinct in the wild.

DATA PANEL

Thylacine (Tasmanian wolf, Tasmanian tiger, marsupial wolf)

Thylacinus cynocephalus

Family: Thylacinidae (but often considered a member of the Dasyuridae)

World population: 0 (Extinct)

Distribution: Formerly mainland Australia and Tasmania

Habitat: Open woodland

Size: Length head/body: 35–50 in (90–130 cm); tail: 20–25 in (50–65 cm); height to shoulder: 14–24 in (35–60 cm); males larger than females. Weight: up to about 40 lb (18 kg)

Form: Resembles a heavy, sandy-colored dog, with bold black stripes across its haunches. Long, stiff tail

Diet: Small wallabies and kangaroos; probably also smaller mammals, birds, and reptiles

Breeding: Two to 3 young born mainly December–March. Rear-facing pouch housing 4 nipples. Life span in wild unknown; 13 years in captivity

Related endangered species: No close relatives

Status: IUCN EX; CITES 1

Victoria
AUSTRALIA

Tasmania   last known range

The last wild thylacine was captured in 1933 and lived alone in Hobart Zoo, Tasmania, where it died in 1936. There have been many reports of sightings since then, even on the Australian mainland. However, many searches—including a major venture in 1980—have failed to produce any concrete evidence that the thylacine is still alive. Photographs (that may be of another species, or even complete fakes) appear in newspapers from time to time.

A mummified thylacine body was found in a cave in 1949, but there is still disagreement over whether it had died recently or many centuries previously. In 1985 some color photographs and casts of footprints were obtained in Western Australia, but their authenticity has been questioned. Nevertheless, such reports offer the tantalizing possibility that one day a living thylacine might materialize.

In Tasmania a large area of the animal's former habitat has been set aside as a protected reserve just in case any have survived.

It has also been suggested that it might be possible to recreate a thylacine by cloning genetic material (DNA) obtained from a museum specimen. The idea is often proposed for various types of extinct animals, including dinosaurs. However, much depends on how well preserved the DNA is, and whether it is still intact. If more than a few years old, DNA is unlikely to be suitable. The chances of success are greater if it has been preserved by refrigeration or in an appropriate chemical.

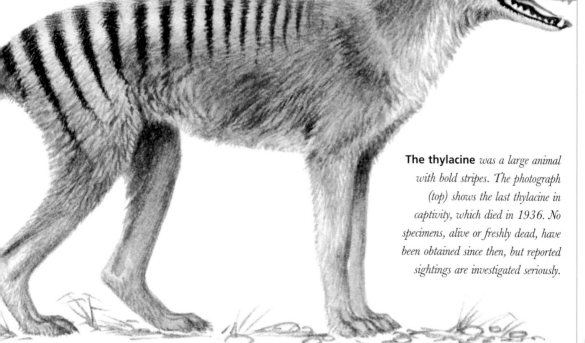

The thylacine *was a large animal with bold stripes. The photograph (top) shows the last thylacine in captivity, which died in 1936. No specimens, alive or freshly dead, have been obtained since then, but reported sightings are investigated seriously.*

Polar Bear

Ursus maritimus

The polar bear is instantly recognizable by its white coat and huge bulk. Today the population is relatively stable.

This magnificent creature is the world's largest land-dwelling carnivore and evolved from the same common ancestor as the brown bear. The most striking feature of a polar bear is undoubtedly its thick coat. The hairs are virtually colorless; they lack any pigment, but tiny bubbles within the hairs create the impression of whiteness. There are two layers to the fur; a fleecy undercoat and an outer layer of longer guard hairs. The long hairs are hollow; they trap air inside their shafts, which provides insulation and helps keep the bear afloat when it is swimming.

Giant Hunters

White is the perfect color for an Arctic predator. There is little or no cover to conceal the animal from its prey, and it would be impossible for a polar bear to surprise an alert, intelligent creature like a seal were it not for its excellent camouflage. The bear's black nose can give it away however, and there are stories of polar bears stalking seals while trying to cover their noses with a paw! Polar bears have excellent eyesight and a superb sense of smell. They can detect young ringed seals hidden in dens in the ice and use their massive, muscular forelegs to dig them out for an easy meal.

The polar bear lives at the edge of the ice, where floes break away leaving cracks and channels of water. They are just as at home in the water as on land. Their big flat feet make efficient paddles: They swim well and are accomplished divers, able to stay underwater for up to two minutes at depths of 15 feet (4.5 m). They can leap from the water on to an ice floe over 6.5 feet (2 m) tall.

True nomads, polar bears often hitch a ride on a drifting ice floe, traveling many miles at a time. They will occasionally dig a den in the snow to rest or wait out severe weather. Most of the time they are solitary creatures, but their vast ranges overlap, so from time to time they encounter other bears. They do not fight over territory, but scraps over food are common, and females with young are very aggressive.

Most polar bears remain active throughout the year, even in the prolonged twilight of the Arctic winter. Pregnant females hibernate in dens dug into the snow. During this time a female's body temperature is reduced by as much as 13°F (7°C), and her heart rate can fall as low as eight beats a minute, just enough to stay alive.

The young polar bears are born in midwinter, while the mother is in hibernation. Weighing only 24 to 28 ounces (600 to 700 g) at birth, they spend the next three months suckling rich, fatty milk from the still-sleeping mother—by March they can weigh as much as 33 pounds (15 kg). This puts a huge strain on the mother's body, and by the spring she will have lost up to 40 percent of her body weight.

Young bears stay with their mother for up to two and a half years, during which time she will teach

DATA PANEL

Polar bear

Ursus maritimus

Family: Ursidae

World population: 20,000–30,000

Distribution: Polar regions of Russia, Norway (Svalbard and Jan Mayen), Greenland, Canada, and the U.S. (Alaska)

Habitat: Arctic ice floes

Size: Length: 8.2–11.5 ft (2.5–3.5 m); height at shoulder when on all fours: 42 in (107 cm); males larger than females. Weight: females 660 lb (300 kg); males 1,100–1,320 lb (500–600 kg)

Form: A huge, stocky bear with proportionately small head, furry ears, short tail, and big, furry feet. The fur is thick and creamy-white to dirty yellow

Diet: Mainly ringed and bearded seals and the occasional young walrus; will also eat carrion, eggs, rodents, berries, and just about anything it can find

Breeding: Between 1 and 4 cubs (usually 2) born December–January

Related endangered species: Asiatic black bear (*Ursus thibetanus*) VU; Spectacled bear (*Tremarctcos ornatus*)* VU; sloth bear (*Melursus ursinus*) VU

Status: IUCN LRcd; CITES II

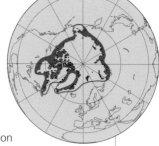

them to swim, to hunt, and build snow dens. She will not breed while she is nursing; and when the time comes for her to mate, she will drive her cubs away. The adolescent cubs may stick together for a while, but soon go their separate ways.

Polar bears were always scarce, and they suffered from severe, uncontrolled hunting during the 20th century. "International" animals, they wander widely across the Arctic wastes, where they face no real barriers, traveling from one nation's part of the Arctic to another. Until the 1960s, when the five polar bear nations (Russia, Canada, Norway, Greenland, and the

The polar bear *is the largest carnivore on land. It may cover a range of over 100,000 square miles (260,000 sq. km) in its lifetime.*

United States) signed a conservation treaty, it was difficult to protect them or to research population size. Since then numbers have increased, and today's population seems stable, with most of the bears living in northern Canada. Controlled hunting is allowed in certain places, and the bears are also an important tourist attraction.

Spectacled Bear

Tremarctos ornatus

The tree-dwelling spectacled bear is one of the larger residents of the mysterious Andean cloud forests. Its habitat is shrinking at an alarming rate.

It is easy to understand how the spectacled bear got its name: The whitish rings round its eyes are very distinctive. It is the largest member of the Carnivora in South America and is a direct descendant of the bulldog bear, which 10,000 years ago was the largest predator in the Americas. The spectacled bear is a powerful animal, and there are records of individuals killing and eating cattle. However, they feed mainly on fruit and other vegetable materials. Meat rarely amounts to more than 5 percent of the diet and is mostly in the form of insects and carrion.

Spectacled bears live in the cloud forest of the Andean mountains. Dense vegetation thrives in the damp atmosphere. Much of the interior remains unexplored, and relatively little is known about the lives of the spectacled bears. The bears appear to spend most of their time in the trees, where they clamber around up to 50 feet (15 m) above the ground, looking for fruit. They are especially partial to bromeliads, young palm fronds and figs but will seek out any sweet, energy-rich food.

Spectacled bears do not hibernate because they do not have to contend with seasonal changes in food availability. Their diet may change as different plants come into season, but at no time is there any shortage, so the bears remain active all year.

Spectacled bears mate between April and June, and pregnancies last between five and eight months. It is likely that the variation occurs because, once mated, female spectacled bears can put their pregnancy on hold: a strategy known as delayed implantation. Only when conditions seem right for the pregnancy to proceed successfully will the embryo be implanted and continue to develop. (This is speculation, but a similar process happens in polar and grizzly bears, so it is likely to occur in spectacled bears too.)

DATA PANEL

Spectacled bear

Tremarctos ornatus

Family: Ursidae

World population: Up to 2,000

Distribution: Andean mountains in northern Bolivia, Colombia, Ecuador, Peru, and Venezuela

Habitat: Cloud forests on lower Andean slopes

Size: Length: 4.2–6.2 ft (1.3–1.9 m); height at shoulder on all fours: 30 in (76 cm); females smaller than males. Weight: 175–385 lb (80–175 kg)

Form: A short-legged, brownish-black, largely arboreal bear with variable pale markings on the face and chest

Diet: Mostly plant material, including fruit, sugarcane, and corn; some small mammals, birds, and carrion

Breeding: One or 2 young (occasionally 3 in captivity) born November–February. Life span may exceed 25 years

Related endangered species: Sloth bear *(Melursus ursinus)* VU; polar bear *(Ursus maritimus)** LRcd; Asiatic black bear *(U. thibetanus)* VU

Status: IUCN VU; CITES I

Cubs are born between November and February, about six weeks before the peak fruiting period of local plants. There is plenty of food available just when the new family needs it most. The newborn cubs are blind and very small, weighing no more than 18 ounces (500 g) each. After a month they are ready to begin exploring with their mother. She spends six to eight months teaching them to fend for themselves, after which they will be on their own.

Shrinking Populations

The spectacled bear faces many problems. Its habitat is shrinking at a rapid rate as the forests are cleared for timber production and agriculture. This brings the bears into contact with human activities, reducing survival. Although the bear is legally protected, there is a thriving trade in body parts, especially skins, meat, and fat. The paws are valued too, being thought to have medicinal properties. Hunting and international trade in spectacled bears is banned, but legislation is difficult to enforce. In Peru the wild bear population is so small that inbreeding is becoming a problem: Scientists have already noted a decrease in the size of bears and the size of their litters.

Spectacled bears *are the largest carnivores in South America, though meat only accounts for 5 percent of their diet. Despite their bulk, they can climb trees with ease.*

Giant Panda

Ailuropoda melanoleuca

Adopted as the emblem of the Worldwide Fund for Nature and popular the world over, the giant panda has come to symbolize endangered animals and efforts to save them.

The giant panda is probably one of the most distinctive and instantly recognizable animals in the world, yet probably fewer than 100 have ever been seen alive outside China. Traditionally, pandas were associated with magical properties. As a result, they have been killed for their skins and body parts. Many have also been caught accidentally in snares set for the valuable musk deer.

Pandas breed very slowly: Females are fertile for only two to three days in the year. The young take over a year to reach independence and do not breed until they are at least five years old.

The giant panda is found in cool, damp, mountain bamboo forests. An individual may spend most of its time within a single square mile of a valley or mountain ridge in which it must find all the food it needs. The animals are specialized feeders. Although they will eat roots and even mice, their main diet is bamboo. Since bamboo is not very nutritious, the panda needs a great deal of it and must spend 10 hours a day feeding. It has a bony extension of the wrist—a kind of thumb—that helps it grip bamboo shoots firmly.

By the time winter arrives, supplies of bamboo in the panda's territory are running out. As temperatures drop, the animals need even more food to maintain their body heat, so they move to lower altitudes in search of more abundant growth. Such a migration is possible only so long as the main areas of panda habitat are intact. However, at lower altitudes mountain forests are being increasingly carved up for farmland; logging is also destroying the panda's forest

The giant panda, *with its stubby tail and distinctive black-and-white markings, has always been popular in zoos. Captive-breeding attempts have attracted media attention, and the species probably owes its survival to its high profile.*

habitat. Sichuan Province, the panda's main home, has lost a third of its forest in 30 years, leaving the animals isolated in small, inaccessible patches. Another problem for the giant panda is the increase in human population and settlement in lowland areas: The animals are left stranded at higher elevations.

Threats and Solutions

The contraction of bamboo habitat presents a serious threat to the giant panda. The situation is made worse by the bamboo's peculiar habit of flowering every so often and then dying, a phenomenon that appears to be on the increase as a result of long-term climate change. It takes several years for a new crop to grow. Periodically, the panda's main food supply simply dies out over large areas. In the 1970s, when three species of bamboo flowered at once and then died, over 100 pandas (more than a tenth of the entire population) are known to have starved to death.

Nowadays the population is fairly stable, although perilously small and fragmented. Attempts at captive breeding have not been very successful; a few young have been born, but their survival rate is low. Protection of the species and its habitat appears to be the most effective way to save the giant panda from extinction. Special sanctuaries have now been created, and the animal is well protected under Chinese law.

DATA PANEL

Giant panda

Ailuropoda melanoleuca

Family: Ursidae (sometimes considered one of the Procyonidae, or assigned its own family, the Ailuridae)

World population: About 1,000

Distribution: Central provinces of China

Habitat: Mountain bamboo forests up to 12,800 ft (3,900 m) above sea level

Size: Length head/body: 4–5 ft (1.2–1.5 m); tail: about 5 in (12–13 cm); height at shoulder: about 24 in (60 cm). Weight: 165–350 lb (75–160 kg)

Form: Stocky, bearlike animal with creamy-white fur; black legs, shoulders, ears, eye patches, and nose

Diet: Mainly bamboo; also bulbs and other plant materials; occasionally fish and small animals

Breeding: Up to 3 young born at a time, but normally only 1 is reared successfully. Pandas take more than 5 years to reach maturity and may not breed every year. Life span in captivity up to 34 years, probably much less in the wild

Related endangered species: Lesser panda *(Ailurus fulgens)* EN

Status: IUCN EN; CITES II

European Mink

Mustela lutreola

Once widespread in Europe, native mink populations are now in rapid decline. The animal's future is under threat both from humans and from the introduced American mink.

Like its American cousin, the European mink inhabits waterside habitats and is found along river banks and at the edges of lakes. It is mainly nocturnal, operating out of a burrow or natural den among tree roots. Some take over burrows made by water voles, but a mink can dig its own home if necessary. Mink are territorial and normally live alone: They tend to be well spaced out, with an average of only one mink per mile of river bank. They swim and dive well, aided by their partly webbed feet, and capture most of their food in the water. They also hunt on land, using their sense of smell to track down small rodents, frogs, and other prey.

Only a century ago the European mink was found across northern Europe and in parts of northern Asia. It has been extinct in most of western Europe for decades and is now also extinct in eastern European countries such as Lithuania, probably also in Finland and Poland. It remains widespread in Russia, where over 95 percent of the surviving populations live, but their distribution and exact status are uncertain.

Reasons for their decline include eager hunting and trapping for their valuable fur. Mink are easy to catch, so the temptation to overharvest them has not been resisted, and their slow breeding rate has been unable to compensate for heavy losses. Females produce up to seven young but only once a year and the survival rate is often low. Kittens are raised without help from the male and are independent at about 10 weeks. Some disperse 30 miles (50 km) or more, especially in winter, when it may be necessary to travel such distances to find unfrozen water.

Man-Made Hazards

Mink face other problems, including water pollution. They have also been affected by habitat loss, since many rivers have been dammed to provide electricity or modified to prevent floods and allow cultivation of land along their edges. Even in relatively undisturbed areas such as Belarus recent surveys show the mink has been declining. In

DATA PANEL

European mink

Mustela lutreola

Family: Mustelidae

World population: 30,000–40,000

Distribution: Belarus, Estonia, France, Georgia, Latvia, Spain, and widely in Russia

Habitat: River banks near temperate grassland

Size: Length head/body: 12–18 in (30–45 cm); tail: 4.5–7.5 in (12–19 cm). Weight: 1.3–1.75 lb (550–800 g)

Form: Small mammal resembling a small, short-legged cat; dark, glossy, brown fur with white around muzzle

Diet: Rodents, including water voles and muskrats, small birds, and aquatic invertebrates such as crayfish and mollusks

Breeding: Breeding season February–March; 4–7 young born April–June; 1 litter a year. Life span 7–10 years

Related endangered species: Wolverine *(Gulo gulo)* VU; Colombian weasel *(Mustela felipei)* EN; pine marten *(Martes martes)** O; giant otter *(Pteronura brasiliensis)** EN

Status: IUCN EN; not listed by CITES

addition to this, in 1926 American mink were imported into Europe to be reared on fur farms. Many of them escaped and now compete directly with their smaller European cousin for food, dens, and living space. It is also said that male American mink can mate successfully with female European mink. However, although the babies begin to develop, they never survive. Since mink have only one litter a year, crossbreeding means that female European mink waste a whole year's reproductive effort.

It appears that the American species is a more successful survivor, and in under 75 years it has spread throughout Scandinavia, much of Britain, and the Netherlands. Other populations are also spreading rapidly in France, Spain, Italy, and Germany. In places where both species of mink occur together, the European mink seems to die out within five to 10 years.

In 1992 a special breeding program for the European mink was established with the aim of maintaining a viable population in captivity. In 1997 there were 64 individuals in 10 zoos. In the wild the decline continues at an alarming rate, and the native wild mink seems destined to become extinct in western Europe. Efforts are being made to establish populations on offshore islands, safe from the dangers on the mainland.

The European mink *is smaller than its American cousin. Only 2 to 3 percent of the remaining population live in Europe. This one has matted fur, having just left the water.*

Pine Marten

Martes martes

In the 19th century culling by gamekeepers eliminated the pine marten from many parts of its range. Today the animal is more widely tolerated, and numbers are rising.

The pine marten is a cat-sized member of the weasel family. Its shape and size vary considerably across its range. The largest specimens are found in Denmark and western Europe; smaller ones occur farther east.

Pine martens are mainly active at night and like to use hollow trees or cavities among rocks as dens in which to sleep, shelter, and raise their young. They are forest-dwelling animals that are well adapted to climbing and leaping among the trees, and are commonly found in conifer forests up to the treeline. However, they also like to feed in open grassy areas, where they hunt for voles and ground-nesting birds. In parts of Ireland and in Switzerland pine martens also feed extensively on ripe fruit in the fall.

There is a popular belief that pine martens prey on squirrels. Although they do occasionally take juveniles, they are not as agile in the branches as adult squirrels and therefore usually leave them alone. From time to time pine martens raid the nests of wild bees for honey or eat rabbits and lemmings—particularly if they are in plentiful supply.

Easily Trapped

The pine marten is a very flexible, adaptable, and successful animal, yet it has become extinct in many areas, particularly southern Britain. Pine martens were widespread there even as late as the 19th century. However, the increasing popularity of shooting gamebirds on estates led to large numbers of gamekeepers being employed. It was their job to exterminate all predators that might kill the gamebirds, and the pine marten was especially victimized, being easily trapped or attracted to poisoned baits. The pine martens were progressively eliminated from most English counties and from Wales, although a few scattered individuals may have survived, even into the late 20th century.

With legal protection and fewer gamekeepers, the pine marten has recolonized parts of Scotland and may also establish itself in northern England once again. Recovery has been assisted by large-scale planting of conifer forests for commercial timber production. The forests not only provide the preferred habitat for pine martens but also, in their early stages of growth, support huge numbers of voles, the pine martens' favorite food.

DATA PANEL

Pine marten

Martes martes

Family: Mustelidae

World population: Probably over 200,000

Distribution: Most of Europe, from Spain to western Siberia, but scarce in many places

Habitat: Temperate pine forests up to the treeline; dens made in hollow trees and cavities in rocks

Size: Length head/body: 14–22 in (36–56 cm); tail: 7–11 in (17–28 cm); height at shoulder: 6 in (15 cm); female at least 10–12% smaller than male. Weight: 1.1–4.5 lb (0.5–2.2 kg)

Form: A long, thin cat-sized animal, with chocolate-brown fur, a bushy tail, and creamy-orange throat patch

Diet: Small mammals, particularly voles, but also birds, insects, and even seashore animals; sometimes ripe fruit

Breeding: One litter a year; usually 3 (but up to 6) young in each; mature at 14 months. Life span about 10–15 years; maximum 18 in captivity

Related endangered species: European mink (*Mustela lutreola*)* EN; various otters and other mustelids

Status: Not listed by IUCN; not listed by CITES

Changing Attitudes

Gamekeepers today are better informed about the habits of pine martens and therefore more tolerant of them. On the European continent gamekeepers were less vigorous in their extermination of the animals, so the species has remained more numerous there. Major threats now facing pine martens include busy roads and predation by eagle owls; some farmers also poison or trap the animals to protect their chickens.

In the early part of the 20th century pine marten numbers were severely depleted by the fur industry. The animal's coat was highly prized, and many thousands of pine martens were killed every year to satisfy demand. In some places commercial harvesting continues, although in Russia there has been an 80 percent drop in numbers caught since the 1920s, when pine martens were more abundant, and their fur was considered to be the height of fashion.

The pine marten

is a tree-dwelling member of the weasel family. Pine martens have been hunted heavily for their fur. They were also killed as a result of gamekeepers' efforts to eliminate predators.

Black-Footed Ferret

Mustela nigripes

Not long ago black-footed ferrets did not exist in the wild. The wiping out of prairie dog burrows in which the animals lodged started their decline. Today captive-bred stock are being reintroduced into the wild, but the population will probably never reach its original size.

The black-footed ferret was probably never abundant. Nonetheless, it used to be found across a broad swathe of the American short grass prairies, from Texas to beyond the Canadian border. It commonly made its home in prairie dog colonies (called towns), taking over part of the tunnel system for its own use as predator in residence. The prairie dogs (burrowing rodents of the squirrel family) made up over 90 percent of the ferret's diet. A single ferret could survive on what it could catch in even quite a small town, but mothers raising families normally took up residence in larger colonies. Mice and other small prey caught outside the burrow at night added to the ferret's prairie dog diet.

Black-footed ferrets do not gather in groups. Instead, they spread themselves out, often living about 3.5 miles (6 km) apart; the low density of animals presumably prevented them from overexploiting their food resources. The ferrets were so dependent on prairie dogs for both food and lodging that when—in the 20th century—prairie dog towns were wiped out wholesale to make way for farmland, the ferrets suffered along with their prey. In Kansas, a former prairie dog stronghold, over 98 percent of the prairie dog population was eliminated in less than 100 years. By the middle of the 20th century the ferrets were feared extinct, although there were reported sightings of individuals from time to time. A small population was even discovered in South Dakota, but the group had apparently died out by 1974.

Back from the Brink

In 1981 a black-footed ferret was killed by dogs on a ranch in Wyoming. Subsequent investigations revealed that a substantial wild population, numbering at least 129 animals, had survived there. The group became the subject of intensive study, but the white-tailed

DATA PANEL

Black-footed ferret

Mustela nigripes

Family: Mustelidae

World population: Probably fewer than 500, mostly in captivity

Distribution: Formerly grasslands of the American Midwest from Texas to the Canadian border; reintroduced into Montana, South Dakota, Arizona, and Wyoming

Habitat: Short-grass prairies; in prairie dog burrows

Size: Length head/body: 15–24 in (49–60 cm); tail: 5–6 in (10–14 cm). Weight: 32–39 oz (915–1,125 g)

Form: Sinuous, short-legged animal, about the size of a small cat; pale yellow in color; black legs, mask, and tail tip

Diet: Mostly small rodents, especially prairie dogs, caught inside the prairie dog burrow. Mice and other small prey caught outside at night

Breeding: One litter per year in March–April; usually 3–4 (but up to 6) young born; young stay with their mothers until early fall. Male offspring may disperse; females often stay near birth site. Life span at least 12 years

Related endangered species: Colombian weasel (*Mustela felipei*) EN; European mink (*M. lutreola*)* EN; Indonesian mountain weasel (*M. lutreolina*) EN; black-striped weasel (*M. strigidorsa*) VU

Status: IUCN EW; CITES I

prairie dogs on which the ferrets were feeding had suffered a population crash as a result of disease, and the ferrets themselves had been struck down by an outbreak of canine distemper. The last 18 ferrets were taken into captivity as an insurance against total extinction. By 1987 there were no black-footed ferrets left in the wild.

An Uncertain Outlook

In captivity the ferrets' numbers built up slowly, to 70 in 1989 and over 300 by the end of 1991—enough for some to be reintroduced to the wild. Over a period of three years 188 ferrets were released, most of which probably died soon afterward. However, the survivors produced at least six litters of young.

The captive population continued to increase, and by 1996 there were at least 400 animals in various zoos and conservation centers. The United States Fish and Wildlife Service has since carried out new reintroductions, releasing ferrets in Montana, South Dakota, and Arizona.

However, even in protected areas where prairie dogs are no longer trapped, shot, or poisoned, the future for the black-footed ferret looks uncertain. The main problem confronting the species is genetic. The entire surviving population of black-footed ferrets derives from a small handful of animals—the descendants of those taken into captivity in 1987—and as a result is dangerously inbred. Normally such inbreeding leads to poor reproductive success and a reduced chance of survival. It remains to be seen whether the newly restored populations, themselves bred from only a few dozen animals, will overcome their problems and increase to form a viable population. Even if they do, it is unlikely that they will ever again be widespread or numerous, simply because their prairie dog prey has disappeared from most of its former range.

The black-footed ferret *lives in prairie dog burrows. Its underground life and nocturnal habits explain why it is so little known. Yet despite its elusiveness, the ferret leaves tracks that are easily seen in snow, and the animal itself can sometimes be spotted at night by flashlight.*

Giant Otter

Pteronura brasiliensis

Formerly conspicuous and widespread, the giant otter is now extinct in parts of its range. Its decline is mainly a direct result of excessive and uncontrolled hunting.

The giant otter is more sociable than many otter species. It lives in family groups of up to 20 individuals, although most groups are made up of between six to eight animals. There is usually a mated pair, along with their most recently born young, and some offspring from the previous year. Unlike the more familiar river otters of North America and Europe, the group stays close together, and the adult male and female often share the same den.

Giant otters eat what they can get and cooperate with each other when hunting prey by driving shoals of fish into shallow water where they can be caught easily. They use their sensitive whiskers (vibrissae) to detect water turbulence caused by fish and other potential prey and pursue their victim underwater, catching it in their jaws. Otters often take slow-moving species, such as catfish, and will eat fish over 2 feet (60 cm) long. They wait for their partners to finish eating before moving on.

When ashore, giant otters mark out their riverbank territory with scent. One consequence of this is that it sends out a warning to other individuals or families in the area. Giant otters are also vocal, calling to each other with a wide range of squeals, barks, and whistles. Although useful for communication, such announcements make it easy for human hunters to locate and kill family groups.

Unlike many other mustelids, which are active under cover of darkness, giant otters are mainly active during the day. Coming out in daylight hours exposes the animals to many dangers, particularly from hunters with spears or guns. Another potentially fatal behavioral trait is the otter's curiosity. The animals swim around with their heads held high out of the water and will often move toward intruders, or possibly dangerous situations, to investigate them more closely. Again, such behavior makes them easy prey, and hunters are usually able to kill others of the group who linger to see what has happened.

Hunted for Fur

As in other species of otter, the fur of the giant otter is extremely dense and helps protect the animal from getting chilled when in the water. The giant otter's fur is particularly distinctive, being short, glossy, and velvety. Such qualities make it especially attractive as a fashion fur. Often a hunter will be able to sell a skin for the equivalent of two to three month's honest wages. After processing, the skin is worth five times as much to the fur trade. Official figures from Peru show that every year in the 1950s, over 1,000 giant otter skins were exported; numbers fell sharply as the giant otter population collapsed, and the trade in their pelts

and other parts was finally banned in 1970. However, it is thought likely that poaching continues, with skins being sent for export through neighboring countries such as Colombia.

The opening up of huge areas of South American forest for logging has made previously remote otter retreats more accessible to developers and others. Although the species was formerly widespread throughout tropical South America, giant otters are now extinct or nearly so in Argentina, Uruguay, and much of southern Brazil, and they have gone from many other parts of their former range. Recovery of the population is no easy task since the animal's main food—the fish in the river—is in demand to feed people as well, and there are increasing problems of pollution. A particular problem is chemical pollution from gold extraction along rivers. Settlements along river banks also make it difficult for the otters to find undisturbed places for dens.

The giant otter *is the largest of the freshwater otter species, with a distinctive flattened tail. It is still fairly numerous in the Pantanal and in parts of Peru.*

DATA PANEL

Giant otter

Pteronura brasiliensis

Family: Mustelidae

World population: Unknown, possibly 1,000–2,000

Distribution: Formerly found over much of tropical South America, south to Argentina. Probably extinct in Argentina and most of Paraguay

Habitat: Slow-moving rivers, creeks, and swamps within forested areas

Size: Length head/body: 36–58 in (86–140 cm); tail: 14–42 in (33–100 cm). Weight: males 57–75 lb (26–34 kg); females 48–57 lb (22–26 kg)

Form: Large otter with short, glossy-brown fur that appears black when wet. Often white or creamy nose and throat. Feet webbed; tail tapering and flattened with a flange along each edge

Diet: Mainly fish; also freshwater crabs and occasionally mammals

Breeding: Up to 5 young in a single litter per year, born after gestation of 65–70 days. Life span over 14 years in captivity

Related endangered species: Marine otter *(Lutra felina)* EN; southern river otter *(L. provocax)* EN; hairy-nosed otter *(L. sumatrana)* DD; European otter *(L. lutra)* NT; smooth-coated otter *(Lutrogale perspicillata)* VU

Status: IUCN EN; CITES I

Sea Otter

Enhydra lutris

Excessive hunting lead to the extermination of the sea otter from most of its range along north Pacific coasts. It recovered to about half its previous population levels through international protection, but is declining again.

The sea otter is one of the few mammals that uses tools: It employs a stone to smash open crabs, sea urchins, and mollusks caught on its shallow dives to the seabed. Intelligent animals, sea otters have learned to rip open sunken, discarded drink cans in which a small octopus may hide. Sea otters are important ecologically since they control the numbers of sea urchins, which eat a lot of growing kelp. Exposed coasts are protected against heavy wave action by the kelp beds. Where sea otter numbers have declined, urchins have increased and prevented proper growth of the floating kelp beds.

Sea otters are generally solitary animals, although they sometimes gather in groups. They are exclusively marine and usually fairly sedentary, but some occasionally go on long journeys, of about 100 miles (160 km) along the coast.

The sea otter lives in the cold waters of the north Pacific and spends a lot of time floating at the surface, grooming, or sleeping among the kelp beds. It is one of the smallest sea mammals and needs very effective insulation to reduce loss of body heat. Its fur is the densest known, with more than 600,000 hairs per square inch (93,000 per sq. cm)—twice the density of a fur seal's coat.

For centuries the thick pelt was highly valued, and the sea otter was ruthlessly hunted off the coasts of Kamchatka in Russia and in the eastern Pacific. Explorations by 18th-century navigators expanded the trade in skins, and colonization of Alaska by the Russians intensified the pressures on the species across the north Pacific. The skins became the world's most valuable fur, each pelt worth the equivalent of a seaman's wages for an

DATA PANEL

Sea otter

Enhydra lutris

Family: Mustelidae

World population: About 15,000 (1999)

Distribution: Coasts of California, eastern Russia (Kamchatka and Commander Islands). Successfully reintroduced to coasts of Alaska, Oregon, and Washington

Habitat: Rocky coasts and kelp beds

Size: Length head/body: 30–36 in (75–90 cm); tail: 11–13 in (28–32 cm); height at shoulder: 8–10 in (20–25 cm). Weight: 30–85 lb (14–40 kg)

Form: Dark-brown coat with a cream, blunt-looking head. The feet are completely webbed, the hind ones forming flippers

Diet: Crabs, shellfish, sea-urchins, fish, and other marine animals; about 13 lb (6 kg) daily

Breeding: Breeds all year round, but most births occur in early summer. Only 1 pup is born each year. Life span can exceed 20 years

Related endangered species: Giant otter (*Pteronura brasiliensis*)* EN; European mink (*Mustela lutreola*)* EN

Status: IUCN EN; CITES II

entire year. Records show that over 750,000 sea otters were killed between 1750 and 1850, and that a single shipment of 17,000 skins was made in 1803.

Sea otters were easily hunted from kayaks; hunters chased the animals until they were too breathless to dive, then speared them. Each body would be skinned in the kayak and the next otter sought out. Living along the coast, and with no safety at sea, the otters could be hunted until every last one had been caught.

Success Story

Sea otters do not breed rapidly, so they became extinct over wide areas. In 1911 the Russians, Americans, and British (on behalf of Canada) agreed on total protection for the sea otter throughout the north Pacific. Gradually numbers have increased, and they are appearing again in many of their former

A sea otter floats on its back. In such a position the animal can open a mollusk shell, crab, or sea-urchin by smashing it against a stone balanced on its chest.

habitats. It was thought that sea otters were extinct on the California coast, but in 1938 a few were found. Numbers have grown to more than 2,000. In fact, fishermen now complain that there are too many. Animals have been transported to Washington state, Oregon, and Alaska, successfully repopulating those coasts; reintroductions to the Pribilof Islands off Alaska appear to have been less successful.

The sea otter, having been reduced to fewer than 1,000 animals in the whole North Pacific, seems to have made a comeback. However, the otters still face a variety of threats—some of them natural, such as the risk of predation by killer whales. Others are man-made and include oil spills and other pollution.

Steller's Sea Lion

Eumetopias jubatus

Steller's sea lion was once considered a pest because of the quantities of fish it "stole" from humans. Now the situation has been reversed; Steller's sea lions are in decline because we eat too much of their food.

Although it is a widespread species, the number of Steller's sea lions has been declining since the 1980s, when there were about 290,000; today there are fewer than 89,000. The western population, which extends across the Aleutian Islands to Japan, appears to be shrinking relatively slowly. The main losses seem to have occurred in the eastern population along the coasts of California, Oregon, British Columbia, and southern Alaska. Although the population there may still number about 39,000, it has declined by 83 percent in 30 years. If an animal population decreases that fast, action must be taken before it is too late.

Steller's sea lion used to be hunted for its meat, hide, and blubber, but commercial hunting stopped in the 1970s. About 400 are still killed each year for traditional uses by the indigenous peoples of Alaska (the skins make good canoe covers). Marine mammals in American waters have full legal protection, so large-scale killing of Steller's sea lions or disturbance of their breeding places should be prevented now and is unlikely to be the main cause of their decline. However, the animals are sometimes caught up in fishing nets. Around Vancouver Island licenses were issued to kill a few sea lions that were causing problems in fish-farming areas, and some illegal killing still goes on.

Oil spills and contamination of food by chemicals pose another threat to Steller's sea lion, as they do to many other species. Around Japan high levels of tributyl tin (TBT) have been reported in the bodies of sea lions. This is a poisonous substance found in the paint used to prevent barnacles from attaching to the hulls of boats.

Despite such hazards, the basic problem for Steller's sea lion seems to be a reduction in its food supply. The animals feed on fish,

DATA PANEL

Steller's sea lion (northern sea lion)

Eumetopias jubatus

Family: Otariidae

World population: Fewer than 89,000

Distribution: Edges of North Pacific and Bering Sea

Habitat: Coastal waters, offshore rocks and islands; also sea caves

Size: Length: male 9.2–10.5 ft (2.8–3.2 m); female 7.5–9.5 ft (2.3–2.9 m). Weight: male 1,240–2,470 lb (566–1,120 kg); female 580–770 lb (263–350 kg)

Form: Seal with coat of short, coarse hair; small ears; longer flippers than true seals. Males have manes

Diet: Fish, particularly pollock, salmon, herring, mackerel; sometimes squid and octopus

Breeding: Single pup born per year after 12-month gestation. Mature at about 4 years. Life span over 30 years in females, lower in males

Related endangered species: Guadeloupe fur seal (*Arctocephalus townsendii*) VU; Galápagos fur seal (*A. galapagoensis*) VU; Juan Fernandez fur seal (*A. philippii*) VU; northern fur seal (*Callorhinus ursinus*) VU; Hooker's sea lion (*Phocarctos hookeri*) VU

Status: IUCN EN; not listed by CITES

which they catch on or near the seabed, sometimes diving down to more than 1,200 feet (400 m) to get them. Trawlers harvest the same fish by dragging huge nets across the seabed. This competition for fish is a problem for the sea lions, especially around sea lion breeding colonies, where mother sea lions feed for up to three days at a time before returning to suckle their pups on the beaches.

Action against Fishing

Intensive commercial fishing has left fish stocks—especially walleye pollock—severely depleted. Trawlers were banned from fishing near sea lion breeding places throughout the 1990s. Exclusion zones were then extended to keep trawlers at least 22 miles (35 km) away from the colonies, and fishing restrictions were imposed all year round, not just in the breeding season. Fishermen were also made to spread their activities to reduce the pressure on fish stocks in certain areas. Around the Aleutian Islands, for instance, restrictions were placed

Steller's sea lion *is in decline as a result of overfishing, but other factors may be at work too, including changes in sea currents.*

on fishing for mackerel (another important food for the sea lions), and trawling for pollock was forbidden.

Such measures have come about partly as a result of lobbying by environmental campaigners. They must be taken seriously in order for us to prevent unpredictable and possibly irreversible damage to the North Pacific ecosystem and the extinction of Steller's sea lion.

Mediterranean Monk Seal

Monachus monachus

Although the monk seals of the Mediterranean are no longer hunted, they are extremely sensitive to disturbance of any kind. As many tourists know, undisturbed beaches in the Mediterranean are now few and far between.

The Greek philosopher and scientist Aristotle made the first scientific record of a seal in the 3rd century B.C. Since the Mediterranean monk is the only seal to inhabit the waters off southern Europe, there is little doubt that it was the species to which he referred. Ancient place names derived from the Greek word *phoca,* meaning seal, occur throughout Greece and Turkey, suggesting that the seals were once widespread in the region.

A few Mediterranean monk seals also live outside the Mediterranean. In fact, one of the largest remaining populations occurs in the tropical waters of Cap Blanc on the coast of Mauritania in northwestern Africa. One of the most remote and vulnerable populations lives around the Desertas Islands, a small group of rocky islets off Madeira. In 1989 that population contained just 10 individuals.

Environmental Disturbance

In more recent times the main hazard facing Mediterranean monk seal populations has come from environmental disturbance; the region's fishing and tourism industries are mostly to blame. Early records suggest that the seals used to pup on wide, sandy beaches, like those favored by their relative the Hawaiian monk seal. Yet today the same beaches are lined with hotels and visited by sunbathers and yachts. Consequently, the sensitive seals now rarely breed away from secluded coves surrounded by high cliffs, which are inaccessible to people. Most seals choose the even greater security of sea caves that can only be reached through underwater entrance tunnels.

Pregnant females are especially sensitive to disturbance, and even fairly minor incidents can cause them to miscarry. Although they are physiologically capable of having one young every year, in reality they rarely do so, and the overall reproduction rate is relatively low.

Another serious problem for the remaining scattered populations is competition with fishermen. The Mediterranean is one of the most intensively fished areas of water in the world. Humans and seals have similar tastes in seafood, including fish, octopus, and squid. Fishermen are none too willing to share their catch, and the seals make themselves very unpopular when they tear holes in the

DATA PANEL

Mediterranean monk seal

Monachus monachus

Family: Phocidae

World population: About 500

Distribution: Scattered populations around the Mediterranean and on the Atlantic coast of Mauritania in northwestern Africa

Habitat: Sheltered subtropical coast; small beaches and sea caves

Size: Length: 7.5–9.2 ft (2.3–2.8 m). Weight: 550–660 lb (250–300 kg)

Form: Large seal with short, dark, variably patterned coat; pale patch on belly

Diet: Fish, octopus, and squid

Breeding: Single pup born May–November after gestation of 9–10 months; weaned at 6 weeks but stays with mother for 3 years; mature at 4 years. May live up to 23 years

Related endangered species: Hawaiian monk seal *(Monachus shauinslandi)* EN; Caribbean monk seal *(M. tropicalis)* EX

Status: IUCN CR; CITES I

nets and make off with the contents. They regularly become entangled in the nets and, unable to return to the surface to breathe, drown in minutes.

It is largely as a result of centuries of hunting and habitat disturbance that the Mediterranean monk seal is now one of the world's rarest mammals. The sealing industry in the Mediterranean reached its peak in the 15th century; but even after hunting went into decline, the seal population continued to fall.

Still At Risk

The remaining Mediterranean monk seals are spread over a wide geographical area, and efforts to save them require determined international cooperation. The Greek population is now relatively secure; its breeding sites are protected within the Northern Sporades Marine Park. An intensive program of education, along with compensation for fishermen whose nets are damaged by seals, should mean that persecution is a thing of the past. However, even with

Mediterranean monk seals *basking on the rocks have been linked to the ancient Greek myth of the Sirens. The story goes that these deadly sea nymphs lured seamen onto the rocks with their beautiful singing.*

protection, populations are now so small that they are increasingly vulnerable to natural hazards. In 1978 a sea cave at Cap Blanc collapsed on a breeding colony, killing up to 50 seals. Such natural disasters could harm almost any population of large mammals, but for a population of fewer than 300 it was devastating. Until the Mediterranean monk seal population is large enough to survive such incidents, it will remain one of the world's most critically endangered species.

Amazon River Dolphin

Inia geoffrensis

The world's largest river and its tributaries are home to the boto, or Amazon river dolphin. Pollution, dam-building, and overfishing are all threatening the future of this animal.

The Amazon river dolphin's range is naturally broken up into three main stretches of water, separated by extensive or perilous rapids. For this reason some scientists think that there are three distinct subspecies living in the Orinoco River in Venezuela, the Madeira River in Bolivia, and the Brazilian Amazon. However, other biologists maintain that these populations are not as separate as they seem. Every year the rivers flood, allowing large fish—and maybe also some river dolphins—to swim over and around the rapids. When the waters subside again, the dolphins become trapped, at least until the rains the following year.

This phenomenon repeats itself on a smaller scale throughout the dolphin's range, with animals moving through submerged areas of forest during the flood period and sometimes getting stranded in small lakes for the duration of the dry season.

The Risks of Isolation

The cyclic ebb and flow of flood waters is fairly commonplace in the region, and the dolphins usually manage to survive a season or two in quite small lakes, as long as there are plenty of fish trapped along with them. Problems can arise, however, when the lakes are drained to irrigate crops, or if humans compete for the same fish prey as the dolphins. Once the fish in a lake are gone, no more can arrive to replace them until the forest becomes flooded again the following year.

While local activities such as fishing and irrigation threaten isolated groups of dolphins, the building of dams for hydroelectric power and flood control can damage whole populations. Dams create permanent barriers to the dolphins' passage, cutting off whole populations. These isolated groups can become inbred and vulnerable to disease and local disasters from which there is no escape either up- or downstream.

River dolphins are not normally hunted, largely because local legend has it that they harbor the souls of drowned people. The dolphins themselves are frequent victims of

DATA PANEL

Amazon river dolphin (boto, pink dolphin)

Inia geoffrensis

Family: Iniidae

World population: Unknown

Distribution: Orinoco and Amazon river systems, South America

Habitat: Rivers and flooded forest

Size: Length 5.6–10 ft (1.7–3 m). Weight: up to 350 lb (160 kg); males can be almost twice as heavy as females

Form: Large, bluish-gray to pink dolphin with long dorsal (back) ridge and large fins and tail flukes; small eyes, long snout with peglike teeth, and bulging cheeks and forehead

Diet: Mostly fish; some crustaceans and turtles

Breeding: Single calf born May–September after gestation of 10–11 months; weaned at 1 year or more; maturity depends on size rather than age. Life span 30 years or more

Related endangered species: Yangtze river dolphin (*Lipotes vexillifer*) CR; Ganges river dolphin (*Platanista gangetica*) EN; Indus river dolphin (*P. minor*) EN

Status: IUCN VU; CITES II

accidental drowning after becoming caught up in the huge nets set by local fishermen to take river fish. When this happens, the fishermen are happy enough to make use of the unplanned extra catch by using oil extracted from the dolphins' bodies as a lubricant and lamp fuel.

Amazon river dolphins *have pink skin that contains a little dark pigment. After prolonged activity the pink color becomes more pronounced as blood rushes to the surface to help the animal cool down.*

Contamination by Mercury

Like other top Amazon predators, including giant otters, river dolphins often suffer from the effects of mercury poisoning. Mercury is used to refine the gold that is mined in the region, and as many as 340 tons (300 tonnes) are released into the river every year. There is also a certain amount of natural mercury present in the soil, and deforestation is increasing the rate at which it is washed into the river by rainfall. Mercury combines with other chemicals to produce a compound called methyl mercury, significant quantities of which then build up in the bodies of river fish. Any animal that eats a lot of contaminated fish ends up ingesting enough methyl mercury to cause serious damage, including birth deformities, muscle-wasting, nerve damage, and failure of the immune system. In humans the condition is known as Minimata disease, after the port in Japan where it was first diagnosed when a factory polluted the local water with mercury. The problem is even more severe for river dolphins, since everything they eat comes from the river.

81

Sperm Whale

Physeter macrocephalus

The extraordinary-looking sperm whale is something of a mystery. It has been hunted on and off for 300 years for its oil, but is now protected. The true extent of the damage done to the world's sperm whale population by hunting may never be known.

The sperm whale is a record breaker in more ways than one. Not only is it the world's largest living carnivorous animal, it also has the largest brain of any creature and is the deepest diving mammal. Thanks largely to the American author Herman Melville's novel *Moby Dick* (1851), it is also one of the best-known whales.

Sperm whales were first hunted in the early 18th century. What is striking about the original hunt is that, despite the huge danger and expense of hunting whales, so much of the animal was wasted. The meat, skin, and most of the bones were considered virtually worthless.

Valuable Products

One of the most valuable sperm whale products was ambergris, a gray, waxy substance that lines the whale's intestines. Its function may be to protect the animal from the bites of squid and other prey. Ambergris was widely used by the perfume industry as a fixative that helped perfumes retain their scent. Ironically, it is not necessary to kill the whales to get the ambergris, since lumps of it can be found floating in the sea or washed ashore, having been coughed up or excreted by the whales. Today many perfume makers use artificial fixatives, so this strange substance is worth much less.

Carved or decorated sperm whale teeth called scrimshaw can fetch a high price, but their value is more related to the quality of craftsmanship than the ivory itself. The true value of a dead sperm whale was always its oil. Gallons of oil could be extracted by melting down the sperm whale's blubber. In large individuals the blubber sometimes forms a layer under

DATA PANEL

Sperm whale (spermaceti whale, cachalot)

Physeter macrocephalus

Family: Physeteridae

World population: Estimates vary from 200,000 to 1.5 million

Distribution: Global; in all the world's oceans and many adjoining seas

Habitat: Mostly deep ocean

Size: Length: 36–60 ft (11–19 m). Weight: 17–55 tons (15–50 tonnes); males larger and up to 3 times heavier than females

Form: Large whale with vast, boxlike head up to one third of total length. Single S-shaped blowhole on left-hand-side of snout; skin dark bluish-gray, fading with age; often wrinkled and covered in scars; white markings around mouth. Body tapers from head to tail. Teeth only in lower jaw

Diet: Mostly squid; some octopus and fish, including sharks

Breeding: Single young born in fall after gestation of 14–16 months; weaned at 2 years; female first breeds at 8–13 years, male at 25–27 years due to social hierarchy. Life span up to 77 years

Related endangered species: No close relatives, but various dolphins and other toothed whales are threatened, including vaquita porpoise *(Phocoena sinus)* CR

Status: IUCN VU; CITES I

The sperm whale *gets its name from the oil-filled organ in its head—the spermaceti. No one is sure what the spermaceti does, but it may be used in the control of buoyancy or the production of sound.*

the skin up to 12 inches (30 cm) thick. The oil was used as a lubricant and in ointments and cosmetics. An additional 500 gallons (1,900 liters) of oil could be harvested from the spermaceti organ in a single whale's huge head. This was especially valuable since it was fine enough to be used to lubricate delicate machinery. It could also be turned into wax for making high-quality candles that burned cleanly with little soot. Spermaceti candles were popular in the late 18th and early 19th centuries, but were eventually replaced by kerosene lamps.

A Change in Hunting Practice

The sperm-whaling industry eventually declined. For almost a century the whales were not disturbed, and the world population stabilized. If hunting had not resumed in about 1930, it is estimated that there could be more than 3 million sperm whales in the world today.

The modern method of hunting is far more intensive. It peaked in the 1960s and 1970s, when 20,000 to 30,000 whales were slaughtered each year, five times as many as in the early 19th century. Although hunting is now banned, scientists still argue about the damage it actually did. Estimates of the current sperm whale population vary enormously, from just 200,000 to over one and a half million. One effect of hunting has been a shift in the sex ratio. Being much bigger, male sperm whales have always been targeted more than females. By the 1980s, when whaling ceased, there were more than twice as many females as males. It is feared that the imbalance may have led to increased inbreeding, which will damage the gene pool.

Blue Whale

Balaenoptera musculus

It took fewer than 50 years of intensive whaling to bring the largest animal the world has ever known to the brink of extinction. Whether the remaining blue whale population is large enough to make a recovery remains to be seen.

Humans have hunted whales for well over a thousand years, but it was not until the 1860s that new technology allowed whalers to hunt the largest species of all. Whaling in the late 19th century was difficult and dangerous; but by targeting the largest of the great whales, the whalers could reap enormous profits. Hunting for blue whales began in the North Atlantic; but as the populations there declined, attention turned to other oceans. In the early 1900s 90 percent of the world's quarter of a million blue whales lived in the Southern Hemisphere. When these rich hunting grounds were discovered, whaling stations were established on small islands in the Southern Ocean. At first whalers had to operate close to coastal factories and could not fully exploit the whales that remained far from land. However, with the arrival of the first factory ships in the mid-1920s, they could process their kills on the open ocean, and consequently the death toll soared.

By 1960 it became obvious that the blue whale was heading for extinction, but it was still several years before an international ban on commercial whaling was agreed. The intervening years cost the species several thousand more lives, bringing the total death toll to 350,000 in fewer than 70 years.

After the killing stopped there were high hopes that the blue whales would recover. By the mid-1980s there was evidence of a slight increase in numbers, and surveys showed that pregnancy rates had doubled, from about 25 percent in 1930 to over

DATA PANEL

Blue whale (great northern rorqual, sulphur-bottom)

Balaenoptera musculus

Family: Balaenidae

World population: About 3,500

Distribution: Three separate populations: in the North Atlantic, North Pacific, and Southern Ocean respectively; the whales migrate annually between polar and tropical waters

Habitat: Deep oceans

Size: Length: 79–89 ft (24–27 m); occasionally up to 110 ft (33 m); females larger than males. Weight: 110–132 tons (100–120 tonnes); occasionally up to 209 tons (190 tonnes)

Form: Vast, streamlined body; bluish-gray skin with pale markings and white to yellow underside. Rounded snout; deep throat furrows; 2 blowholes with large splashguard; small dorsal fin set well back on body

Diet: Krill (planktonic shrimps) and other crustaceans

Breeding: Single young born after gestation of 10–12 months; weaned at 7–8 months; mature at 10 years. May live up to 110 years

Related endangered species: Fin whale *(Balaenoptera physalus)* EN; sei whale *(B. borealis)* EN; minke whale *(B. acutorostrata)* LRnt

Status: IUCN EN, though some populations listed as VU or LRcd; CITES I

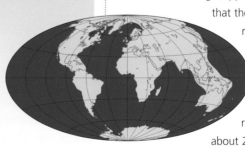

Blue whales *dive for about 10 to 20 minutes at a time before surfacing to take a dozen or so breaths, sending a spout of spray as high as 30 feet (9 m) into the air with each exhalation.*

50 percent. The total world population was estimated at the time at about 12,000 individuals.

However, the early optimism proved premature. Estimates vary as to how many blue whales there now are, but recent statistics put the world population as low as 3,500. It is doubtful whether so few whales represent a viable population.

Impoverished Oceans

The main reason why the whales' numbers have not recovered is simply because their habitat has altered for the worse. The annual catch of krill (planktonic shrimps) taken by the world's fisheries rose from practically nothing in the early 20th century to over 500,000 tons (455,000 tonnes) in 1986. An average blue whale needs about 7,700 pounds (3,500 kg) of krill a day to sustain its great bulk. Now that krill is fished on such a huge scale, there may simply not be enough food to meet the whales' requirements.

The seas are also more polluted now, and not just with chemicals. Toxins and biologically active substances that have been shown to damage other marine wildlife almost certainly affect large whales. In addition, whales are affected by noise pollution and alterations in local currents brought about by coastal developments. Large inland projects can also result in thousands of tons of silt being dumped at sea, making the water unsuitable for both whales and their food.

Humpback Whale

Megaptera novaeangliae

Having faced extinction in the 1960s, the humpback whale has responded well to protection. As long as the ban on whaling stays in place, it is set to become one of the world's best conservation success stories.

Over the past two or three decades the humpback whale has become something of a wildlife celebrity. It is one of the most widely recognized large whales, and its acrobatic displays, inquisitive personality, and intricate and varied songs have earned it a place in the affections of humans.

But the story has not always been a positive one. Prior to the worldwide ban on whaling in the mid-1980s the humpback had been one of the most widely hunted species and came within a whisker of extinction. A relatively slow-swimming animal, the humpback made an easy target, especially when large herds gathered in shallow coastal waters to breed. They were easy to approach, often coming close to whaling boats out of curiosity and discovering the danger too late. Commercial hunting of humpbacks dates back over 300 years, and before that many aboriginal peoples killed humpbacks for subsistence using simple hand-made weapons. These traditional hunts are still permitted, but the quotas are very low and are reviewed from year to year.

A Booming Industry

Now the killing has all but ceased, but there is still money to be made from humpbacks. Many former whaling communities have developed into ecotourism resorts specializing in whalewatching. There is little doubt that the profits from this rapidly expanding industry have reduced the pressure to resume hunting and played a significant part in the species' recovery. Nevertheless, it is important that the whales are not disturbed by excessive pressure from boatloads of excited tourists, especially during the breeding season.

Humpback Behavior

Humpbacks are among the most vocal of whales and their long, complex songs, hauntingly beautiful to the human ear, feature in popular music, classical compositions, and relaxation therapies. The songs, which last anything up to half an hour, vary slightly from place to place—a bit like human dialects—and they change gradually over time as whales pick up variations from each other. Like birdsong, these sounds are generally used by solitary males and are thought to attract females and let other whales know who is around.

Other fascinating aspects of humpback behavior include their feeding techniques. They generally filter feed in a similar manner to other baleen whales, but have also developed some rather special techniques of their own. One of the most impressive is bubble-netting, whereby one or more whales swims in an upward spiral around a shoal of fish, releasing a steady stream of bubbles that form a dense curtain through which the fish will not swim. The fish bunch closer together and move upward to escape the circling whales; but once they reach the surface, they are trapped, and the whales move in, swallowing huge mouthfuls of fish and water. The furrows in the whale's throat allow it to expand so that it can gulp in hundreds of densely shoaling fish at a time.

The nets used by fishing crews are curtains of death for whales as well as fish. Once entangled in the mesh, a humpback is usually doomed. Along with disturbance from boats, these nets are one of the major threats to humpback whales today.

The humpback whale *is one of the most popular species for whale-watchers; it is large, curious about boats, and often apparently full of high spirits. For an ever-increasing number of people an encounter with whales is the highlight of a vacation if not the experience a lifetime.*

DATA PANEL

Humpback whale (humpwhale, hunchbacked whale)

Megaptera novaeangliae

Family: Balaenopteridae

World population: 30,000

Distribution: Global

Habitat: Mostly deep ocean but ventures into shallower waters to breed

Size: Length head/body: 36–46 ft (11–14 m); occasionally up to 50 ft (15 m); female slightly larger than male. Weight: 33 tons (30 tonnes)

Form: Large dark-gray to black baleen whale with tapering, knobby head; pectoral fins very long (one-third body length) and patterned with irregular and unique white markings; tail flukes (lobes) also large and often marked with white

Diet: Small shoaling fish and crustaceans

Breeding: Single young born in tropics during temperate winter after 11-month gestation, usually every other year; weaned at 11 months; mature at 4–6 years. May live up to 77 years

Related endangered species: Blue whale *(Balaenoptera musculus)** EN; fin whale *(B. physalus)* EN; sei whale *(B. borealis)* EN; minke whale *(B. acutorostrata)* LRnt

Status: IUCN VU; CITES I

Steller's Sea Cow

Hydrodamalis gigas

The sea cow was a close relative of today's manatees and dugongs, and it lived in the North Pacific. It was discovered in 1741 and was extinct less than 30 years later.

In 1741 an expedition led by the Danish explorer Vitus Bering was shipwrecked on the Commander Islands off Siberia in the Bering Sea. Bering and his crew were stranded on a bleak and inhospitable coast for the whole of the following winter until they were able to rebuild their boat and escape.

The expedition's doctor and scientist was a young German naturalist called Georg Steller. He was the only naturalist ever to see sea cows alive. He had plenty of time to observe them, since the expedition depended on killing sea cows to provide food for its survival. Assuming that there were sea cows all around the islands, there may have been as many as 2,000 of them at this time. However, this represented the dying remnants of what had once been a much more widespread species. The sea cows had been eliminated from most areas, including Japanese waters, and by Steller's time it seems that they were already restricted to the Commander Islands.

The sea cow is the only type of sirenian (marine mammals that are not seals or whales, including today's manatees and dugongs) that lived in cold water. They were large, cumbersome creatures that could not come ashore like seals. Instead, they drifted slowly around in the sheltered bays along the rocky coast, moving through the offshore kelp beds, munching almost continuously on the long strands of seaweed. Steller's sea cows had no teeth, just big, horny plates with large ridges and troughs in each jaw that were used to crush the seaweeds on which they fed. In winter they became emaciated as the kelp beds died back.

Seaweed is not very nutritious, so the animals had to take in vast quantities each day to get the nutrients they needed. They spent almost all their time feeding with their head underwater, surfacing only occasionally to breathe with a loud snort. The animal's back, up to 10 feet (3 m) long, arched out of the water like a huge floating log.

It was possible for the sailors to row a boat among the herds without risk of being attacked. The sea cows were slow moving and completely harmless and had no fear of people. They allowed the sailors to

RUSSIA

Kamchatka Peninsula

Commander Islands
last known range

Aleutian Islands (U.S.)

DATA PANEL

Steller's sea cow

Hydrodamalis gigas

Family: Dugongidae

World population: 0 (Extinct)

Distribution: Formerly along the coast of the Commander (Komandorskiye) and Aleutian Islands in the Bering Sea, North Pacific Ocean. Fossil evidence from California

Habitat: Rocky coasts with extensive seaweed beds

Size: Total length of a female, probably the only one ever measured: 24.6 ft (7.5 m); circumference of body: 20.3 ft (6. 2 m); Probably grew larger sometimes. Weight: probably up to 11 tons (10 tonnes)

Form: A large, whalelike animal with small, blunt head and forked tail flipper. Forelimbs formed paddles; no hind limbs. Skin thick and brown, sometimes blotchy. Sparse, bristly hairs

Diet: Various seaweeds

Breeding: Probably only 1 young at long intervals. Life span unknown, but likely to have been at least 20 years

Related endangered species: Dugong *(Dugong dugon)* VU; Amazon manatee *(Trichechus inunguis)* VU; American manatees *(T. manatus*—includes Florida manatee *T. manatus latirostris)** VU; African manatee *(T. senegalensis)* VU

Status: IUCN EX; not listed by CITES

Steller's sea cows *were the largest of the sirenians. They moved slowly through the shallow, cold water, and browsed seaweeds, a peculiar form of feeding that is not shared by any other large animals.*

approach close enough to snare them one at a time with an iron hook on a long rope. The stricken sea cow was then speared.

Steller tells us that the animals lived in small family groups, with adult males and females accompanied by young. He thought that they had only one baby at a time and probably took at least a year to raise it. Such slow reproduction was probably adequate, bearing in mind that there would have been few natural predators in these waters that could tackle such a large, thick-skinned animal. However, such a low rate of reproduction and slow growth would have been insufficient to compensate for losses of the animals when the humans began more intensive hunting.

There for the Taking

The crew of the Bering expedition had also seen fur seals in the northern waters. When they reached the mainland, news of the fur seals spread, and expeditions set out to catch these valuable creatures. They too found sea cows an easy target and a good source of food. The animals' thick skins, almost like tree bark, made useful shoe leather and boat covers. Sea cows had to surface to breathe air, so hunters in boats could reach and spear them easily. The sea cows were said to help each other when one was distressed, so it was easy to kill several at a time. The remaining population had been wiped out by 1768.

Lost Creatures

The treacherous and inhospitable shores of the North Pacific are rarely explored, even today. The weather is poor all year round, with almost constant drizzle and fog. It is possible that sea cows survived longer in some remote bays, and sailors reported sightings even into the 20th century. However, it is virtually certain that the sea cow no longer exists.

89

Florida Manatee

Trichechus manatus latirostris

Coastal development and the impact of fast speedboats threaten the Florida manatee. However, provided that its simple needs can be accommodated, there is no reason why these charming animals should not remain reasonably numerous.

There are two subspecies of the Caribbean or West Indian manatee. One, the Florida manatee, occurs in rivers and along nearby coasts. The other—the Antillean manatee—lives farther south in similar habitats.

Manatees usually occur in small family groups. They are slow-moving, sluggish animals that normally live on the edge of the sea and in sheltered lagoons. They will not tolerate water cooler than about 68°F (20°C) and often gather in warm places such as the areas where power stations discharge warm water into the sea—Cape Canaveral, Fort Myers, and Apollo Beach in Tampa Bay, for example. In summer they disperse widely along coasts and rivers.

Dangerous Waters

Manatees cannot come ashore since they have no hind limbs. When they breathe out, they become less buoyant and sink below the surface, where they paddle gently around seeking food. They can stay underwater for up to 30 minutes before they need to come up for air. For much of the time, however, they float around at the water surface looking like large logs, with only the tops of their backs visible. When floating, they are not easy to see, nor can they see far themselves.

In the coastal areas of Florida, where there are large numbers of water skiers, fast launches, and other boats, the waters have become unsafe for manatees. Many people have houses at the water's edge and use their boats for recreation, fishing, and transport. Collisions are frequent and often fatal for the manatees.

The number of boats and the disturbance caused by the huge increase in their use along the Florida coasts and lagoons have led to a steep decline in manatee numbers. It has been calculated that a reduction in manatee deaths of only 10 percent every year should be sufficient to allow the population to increase again. However, one obstacle to recovery is that manatees are very slow breeders, and even a small increase in adult mortality leads to a rapid decline in the population.

Apart from people (and some large sharks farther south than Florida), manatees have no natural predators. Nonetheless, for centuries people have killed them for their meat. Manatees are easy prey since they cannot swim fast or defend themselves effectively. Hunting is probably the main threat to manatees outside American waters; they also get tangled up and drown in commercial fishing nets.

Florida manatees are legally protected, and in certain places where the water is clear and they can be easily seen drifting around, they have become an important tourist attraction. Visitors and local people are paying more attention to this fascinating creature.

Setting Limits

People using boats are asked to avoid shallow water near the edges of rivers and lagoons (where there is plenty of aquatic vegetation) favored by the manatees. By imposing speed limits on small craft and providing separate channels for boats, conservationists are working toward a more secure future for the Florida manatee. With such measures in place there is no reason why the manatee should not survive in reasonable numbers.

The United States Fish and Wildlife Service has recently created a special manatee sanctuary at Three Sisters Springs in the Crystal River. More than 250 manatees spend the winter there because it is pleasantly warm. Disturbances from launches and boats had been forcing the animals out into colder waters, but this area is now off limits to visitors and boats between November and March.

The Florida manatee population *suffered in 1996, when over 155 were found dead. Agricultural chemicals may have been the cause, although natural toxins from algae in the water could have been responsible.*

DATA PANEL

Florida manatee

Trichechus manatus latirostris

Family: Trichechidae

World population: Florida subspecies 2,000–3,000; rest of the species probably 5,000–10,000

Distribution: Coast of the Gulf of Mexico north to Carolinas. Antillean subspecies extends around the Caribbean to southern Brazil

Habitat: Shallow, warm coastal waters; rivers and brackish water

Size: Length: 7–13 ft (2–4 m). Weight: up to 1,300 lb (590 kg); exceptionally up to 1.5 tons (1,500 kg)

Form: Large, sluggish animal; broad head and thick upper lip with spiky bristles; flippers at front but not at rear; tail flat, horizontal, and rounded

Diet: Wide assortment of floating and submerged water weeds, including water hyacinth and sea grass

Breeding: Single calf born May–September at intervals of 2–3 years after gestation of 11–13 months. Mature at 3–4 years. Life span up to 60 years

Related endangered species: Steller's sea cow (*Hydrodamalis gigas*)* EX; African manatee (*Trichechus senegalensis*) VU; Amazon manatee (*T. inunguis*) VU; dugong (*Dugong dugon*) VU; Antillean manatee (*T. m. manatus*) VU

Status: IUCN VU; CITES I

Proboscis Monkey

Nasalis larvatus

The proboscis monkey was once fortunate enough to live in one of the world's most inaccessible and undisturbed areas. Today, despite government protection, the species is endangered because of destruction of its mangrove forest habitat.

Until quite recently the extraordinary-looking proboscis monkey was relatively common on its native island of Borneo. Even while other native primates—such as the orang-utan—were suffering dramatic population declines, the proboscis monkey appeared to be holding its own. The main reason for its success was its inaccessible habitat; the species lives in some of the most impenetrable places on the island, namely, the dense mangrove forests that once lined many of the region's rivers. Mangroves form a dense mass of branches and stems, standing in water and soft mud. It is virtually impossible to walk around in mangrove thickets, which may extend unbroken for many miles. Animals living there are fairly safe and have adapted to climb and scramble around with ease. While the stable rain forest of Borneo's interior was being felled for timber and wood pulp, or cleared for agriculture, the mangroves remained inaccessible to machinery, and the space they occupied was unsuitable for agriculture. The waterlogged forest had little commercial value and was left to the proboscis monkeys and other specialized mangrove wildlife.

A Life Near Water

Proboscis monkeys are the most aquatic of all the primates. Their partially webbed feet make them excellent swimmers, and they sometimes use the water as a convenient emergency escape route. Alarmed monkeys will readily plunge 50 feet (15 m) from a treetop to the relative safety of the water. Such a jump onto dry land would result in serious injury, even for an agile primate.

The monkeys tend not to feed in the water, surviving instead on a diet of leaves plucked from the trees. The leaves are generally tough and not nutritious, so they have to be eaten in large quantities. It has been estimated that the contents of an adult proboscis monkey's stomach accounts for about a quarter of its body weight. The huge meals pass slowly through the monkey's digestive system and are broken down by special gut-dwelling bacteria. The bacteria also break down some of the toxic chemicals produced by mangroves and many other forest plants,

---

DATA PANEL

Proboscis monkey

Nasalis larvatus

Family: Cercopithecidae

World population: About 260,000 (1986 estimate); now likely to be considerably fewer

Distribution: Borneo

Habitat: Freshwater mangrove and lowland rain forest

Size: Length head/body: 21–30 in (53–76 cm); tail: 22–30 in (56–76 cm); males twice as big as females. Weight: 17–30 lb (7–22 kg)

Form: Large, long-tailed monkey with variable red-brown fur that fades to white on underside. Feet partially webbed. Nose is small and snub in juveniles and females; large and pendulous in males

Diet: Mostly leaves of pedada trees; some fruit seeds; also flowers

Breeding: Single young born at any time of year after 24-week gestation. Life span unknown; probably at least 10 years

Related endangered species: No close relatives, but at least 35 other species of Old World monkey family Cercopithecidae are classified as Vulnerable or Endangered

Status: IUCN EN; CITES I

enabling the proboscis monkey to take advantage of food that other animals have to avoid.

A Nose for Success

The large nose of the mature male proboscis monkey is what gives the species its name, but its precise purpose is unknown. Being much larger than females, males are more prone to overheating: One theory is that the nose acts as a cooling device, radiating excess body heat. It may also be that the large nose is a badge of success, since it continues to grow throughout a male's life; the males with the largest noses are the oldest and presumably, therefore, the fittest and most successful breeders. In choosing a suitable male to father her offspring, a female may use the size of a male's nose as an indicator of his genetic desirability.

Reduced Circumstances

It would be a tragedy if proboscis monkey numbers were reduced by so much that the species became more famous for being rare than for its other unique characteristics. However, its future is uncertain. The mangroves that provide its home are now harvested for wood, and modern drainage technology has meant that the watery world of the proboscis monkey is being invaded by developers. The rivers that once flooded the forests—creating natural refuges for wildlife—have been tamed, and in just a few decades well over half of Borneo's mangrove forest has disappeared. Previously extensive mangrove swamps have been reduced to narrow fringes along rivers and no longer supply adequate habitat for the monkeys.

There are a few proboscis monkeys in captivity. However, the species is considered difficult to keep in zoos, perhaps because it is not easy to re-create its natural mangrove habitat in artificial conditions. With the entire wild population confined to one island, the priority must be the preservation of its habitat.

The male proboscis monkey's *extraordinary nose makes it one of the most easily recognized of all primates. Females and youngsters have small, upturned noses.*

Chimpanzee

Pan troglodytes

Despite its protected status, a shrinking habitat and continued poaching are major problems facing Africa's "common" chimpanzee, and populations are rapidly dying out.

Throughout central Africa human populations are expanding, and there is a growing pressure on the land from people trying to make a living. In many areas everyday human practices are putting chimpanzees at risk. Despite the fact that this animal is a close relative—we share 98 percent of our genes with chimps—it receives little sympathy when it becomes a competitor for space.

Although wild chimpanzees are protected by law in several African countries, regulations are difficult to enforce, especially in areas of central Africa torn apart by political instability and civil war. Moreover, legal protection does not include protection of their habitat.

The tropical forests, already reduced to a fraction of their original size, continue to be logged and cleared for agriculture. The remaining areas are often so disturbed by people hunting, collecting firewood, or herding their livestock that the chimpanzee population moves on or dies out. Today wild chimpanzees live in isolated patches of habitat, some of which are too small to support a healthy, viable population. As a result, levels of inbreeding increase, leading to genetic problems and birth defects.

Nevertheless, in some areas the chimpanzees are traditionally tolerated and respected, even to the extent that they are allowed to wander into crop fields and village markets. Local people do no more than "shoo" them away if they become a nuisance.

Chimpanzees are stocky, powerful animals that use a combination of brainpower and brawn to survive in a variety of habitats, including rain forests, deciduous forests, and swamp forests. They are even capable of making and using tools.

DATA PANEL

Chimpanzee (common chimpanzee)

Pan troglodytes

Family: Pongidae

World population: Unknown, but might exceed 150,000

Distribution: Tropical western and central Africa, from Senegal and Angola to Tanzania and Sudan

Habitat: Rain forest, deciduous forest, swamp forest, and savanna grassland with access to evergreen fruiting trees

Size: Length: 28–38 in (71–97 cm); height at shoulder: 39–66 in (95–165 cm); males slightly larger than females. Weight: 66–110 lb (30–50 kg)

Form: Large ape covered in long, brown-black hair. Palms and face are bare; adults are sometimes bald. Skin on face is wrinkled, usually pink or brown, darkening with age. Projecting jaw has large, expressive lips

Diet: Fruit, leaves; also seeds, shoots, bark, flowers, honey, and insects; some meat from smaller animals, including monkeys and wild pigs

Breeding: Single young born at any time of year after gestation of 7–8 months; weaned at 3–4 years; stays with mother until mature at 7 years. Life span may exceed 35 years

Related endangered species: Gorilla (*Gorilla gorilla*) EN; orang-utan (*Pongo pygmaeus*)* EN; pygmy chimpanzee (*Pan paniscus*) EN

Status: IUCN EN; CITES I

However, this kind of tolerance is the exception to the rule: In other parts of their range chimpanzees are treated as pests and killed to protect crops. Some are caught in snares or shot and eaten as bush meat. Their body parts have also been used in traditional medicines and rituals. Perhaps most disturbing of all, chimpanzees are captured live and sold as pets or for medical research. This trade represents a huge loss of life; for every young chimp that reaches its final destination, several more will have died in transit. The young chimps' mothers are often also killed in the poachers' efforts to kidnap the baby.

A Captive Future

There are large numbers of chimpanzees in captivity all around the world. Many are kept as illegal pets or held in unlicensed collections, but a great number are in zoos and conservation centers. Of those born and bred in captivity, some are of mixed race, with parents from different regions of Africa who would never normally have met in the wild. It is unlikely that any of these captive-raised chimpanzees will be successfully returned to the wild. Like human babies, young chimpanzees are born with few

instincts and must learn from their elders the skills they need to survive. Individuals born in captivity have often been hand-reared by keepers and are therefore ill-equipped for life in the wild. They are also likely to have difficulty in rearing their own young. In addition, captive chimpanzees may carry diseases that could destroy a wild population.

There is more hope for wild-born chimpanzees that have been rescued from illegal collections. Animals such as these can be taken to one of several rehabilitation centers in Africa where they can practice their "wild" skills in large enclosures before being set free. However, releases are still risky. The danger of disease, or of chimpanzees being attacked by established populations, means that they are usually released in areas from which the species has already disappeared.

Mountain Gorilla

Gorilla gorilla beringei

After years of intensive conservation efforts Africa's mountain gorilla population seemed to be overcoming the threat of extinction. However, civil war in the region has since undone much of the progress that had been made.

Mountain gorillas are particularly vulnerable to environmental pressures, both natural and man-made, because of their slow breeding rate, which makes it difficult for them to replenish their numbers. Usually only one baby is born at a time; but on the rare occasions when twins occur, one almost always dies.

Most female gorillas do not breed until they are at least 10. A female can bear young every four years; but because many infants die before they are two, the rate for successful reproduction is closer to one every eight years. Even a female living in exceptionally favorable conditions is unlikely to rear more than six offspring in her 40-year lifetime. It is more likely that she will raise between two and four young. The young are not fully weaned until the age of three and remain with their mothers for several more years.

Major Threats

The major problems facing the mountain gorilla in the mid-20th century were poaching, kidnapping, and habitat loss. Such problems can be prevented by setting aside areas of gorilla habitat and patrolling them to prevent hunting. Such refuges did exist, but the protection provided in the past was nowhere near adequate. Many hundreds were still illegally caught in snares, their flesh sold as bush meat, and their heads, hands, and feet made into trophies and tourist souvenirs. There was also a thriving market in live baby gorillas, a trade made all the more abhorrent by the fact that poachers usually killed the mother, or the entire family, to kidnap one baby. Mountain gorillas do not cope well with captivity—those seen in zoos are

of the lowland variety—and few kidnapped youngsters survive. Huge areas of mountain gorilla habitat were lost to cultivation in the 1950s and 1960s. The matter came to a head in 1968 when a single refuge, representing 40 percent of the gorillas' remaining habitat, was turned over to agriculture.

Changing Fortunes

By the late 1960s it was clear that if mountain gorillas were to escape extinction, both the animals and their shrinking habitat needed proper protection. For two decades this was provided, and at the end of the 1980s the mountain gorilla's prospects were looking much brighter. The Rwandan gorilla population had increased by over 20 percent; special reserves gave them a secure habitat, and an intensive education program helped local people realize the value of their great ape neighbors. The gorillas became a national treasure and the focus of a lucrative ecotourism industry, which in 1990 ranked as Rwanda's third highest source of income. Similar projects were also reaping benefits in neighboring Uganda and the Democratic Republic of Congo (formerly Zaire). Ecotourism brings in money, and the presence of visitors makes it more difficult for poachers to operate unseen, but the visitors also bring disease. Gorillas are susceptible to human infections, and there is a risk of passing on flu viruses and other germs to the animals when tourists visit the forests.

In the early 1990s civil war in Rwanda claimed the lives of half a million people and left 750,000 homeless. Not surprisingly the conservation of Rwanda's mountain gorillas slipped down the list of

national priorities. Conservationists stayed to protect the gorillas but were eventually evacuated. The refugee crisis caused by the war has put huge pressure on the land, and the protected status of the gorilla's habitat is again under threat; there simply is not enough room to accommodate both the gorillas and the thousands of people in need of land.

The mountain gorilla *is the world's largest primate, but despite its huge size and obvious strength, it is also one of the gentlest.*

Western Lowland Gorilla

Gorilla gorilla gorilla

The forest-dwelling western lowland gorilla is a gentle giant. It has suffered from generations of hunting, kidnapping, and habitat destruction, and its numbers are still in decline.

There are three subspecies of gorilla: the mountain gorilla and the eastern and western lowland gorillas. The mountain gorilla lives in eastern Africa; the western lowland form lives in the lowland tropical rain forests of West Africa from Cameroon to the Congo River, and the eastern form lives in the lowland tropical rain forests of what is now the Democratic Republic of Congo (formerly Zaire). All three populations face similar problems.

It is impossible to estimate how many western lowland gorillas are left in the wild. Their dense rain forest habitats are some of the least explored areas of the world, and the terrain makes surveying difficult.

Gorillas live in groups of adult males, females, juveniles, and infants. They are predominantly fruit-eaters and need vast tracts of forest in order to find food. The western lowland gorillas are constantly on the move, looking for trees with a ripe crop. An average troop needs a home range of between 10 and 15 square miles (25 and 40 sq. km) to ensure that they can always find food. The western lowland gorillas live in much smaller groups than their cousins in the east, where fruit is more abundant; a group of five to seven gorillas is less likely to exhaust the fruit supply of any tree than a group of 12 or 15.

Like all great apes, lowland gorillas breed very slowly. A healthy female will produce between three and six babies in her lifetime. The young are so well cared for that they stand a good chance of surviving as long as the troop has plenty of space to forage for food and is not targeted by poachers.

Despite their bulk and power, gorillas are peaceful creatures. Although people who have killed them often claim that they did so in self-defense, the animals are generally not agressive if left unprovoked. Even the intimidating chest-beating display of a dominant male is usually little more than a bluff.

Dwindling Habitat

Although the forests of central Africa are still vast, in the past few decades a dramatic increase in logging and clearing of trees for agriculture has greatly reduced and fragmented their extent, threatening the habitat needed by lowland gorillas. Humans have been farming in Africa for thousands of years, but this used to be

DATA PANEL

Western lowland gorilla

Gorilla gorilla gorilla

Family: Pongidae

World population: Unknown; estimates vary from 10,000 to 50,000

Distribution: West Africa, including parts of Cameroon, Central African Republic, Gabon, Congo, Equatorial Guinea, and the Democratic Republic of Congo

Habitat: Lowland tropical rain forests

Size: Height: up to 7 ft (2.1 m). Weight: 300–600 lb (135–275 kg)

Form: Brownish-black fur; long, powerful arms; legs less powerful; broad chest; large head (wider than that of mountain gorilla); heavy brow ridge

Diet: Fruit, shoots, leaves, bark, roots, and bulbs

Breeding: Single young born after gestation of 7–8 months; dependent on mother until fully weaned at 3–4 years; mature at 7–9 years (females) and 9–12 years (males). Life span up to 37 years

Related endangered species: Eastern lowland gorilla (*Gorilla gorilla graveri*) EN; mountain gorilla (*G. g. beringei*)* EN; chimpanzee (*Pan troglodytes*)* EN; pygmy chimpanzee (*P. paniscus*) EN; orang-utan (*Pongo pygmaeus*)* EN

Status: IUCN EN; CITES I

done on a relatively small scale. The rapid rise in human populations over the last century has meant that more land is being used for settlement and agriculture than ever before.

The devastation is worse in some countries than in others. For example, the western lowland gorilla had disappeared from Nigeria by 1984, while the relatively untouched forests of Gabon to the south still harbor around half the world's gorilla population. Gabon is a small country, about the size of Ohio, but around 70 percent of it is still forested, providing ideal gorilla habitat. The Gabonese hunt more gorillas than anyone else; but as far as they are concerned, this great ape is still a reasonably abundant animal.

Illegal Trade

Gorillas are killed for several reasons. They are widely eaten as bush meat, and gorilla body parts are traded as souvenirs. Hundreds, possibly even thousands of gorilla babies have been taken from the wild to supply zoos and the pet trade. They are usually kept and transported in atrocious conditions, and at least two-thirds of them do not survive the journey. It is now illegal to export wild-caught gorillas, and today most zoos refuse to take them. Nevertheless, there is still a healthy black market in the young animals.

Civil wars and political instability, especially in the Democratic Republic of Congo and parts of West Africa, have reduced the effectiveness of international legal protection. Such factors have also made it impossible to carry out surveys to find out how many western lowland gorillas remain in the wild. Even in "protected" areas the gorillas are not completely safe.

It is thought that the Kahuzi-Biega National Park in the Democratic Republic of Congo has recently lost half its gorillas as a result of poaching.

The western lowland gorilla, *in common with other gorillas, shares 98 percent of its genes with humans. Most people now realize that gorillas are peaceful creatures. Despite their huge size, they rarely act aggressively toward people.*

Orang-Utan

Pongo pygmaeus

Orang-utan means "man of the forest" in the Malay language. Once numbering hundreds of thousands, the orang-utan population has declined sharply in recent years because of loss of habitat and capture for the pet trade.

The orang-utan holds two animal records: It is the world's largest tree-dwelling mammal, and it is the only great ape that lives in Asia. Living in the trees of the tropical rain forests of Borneo and Sumatra, this ape rarely walks on the ground. It has very long, strong arms ideally suited to a life of swinging and climbing from branch to branch in the tree canopy.

Orang-utans tend to live alone or in very small groups. Most nights they build a fresh nest in the trees, only occasionally reusing a nest. Two-thirds of their diet is fruit—especially wild figs and durians —but they have a huge appetite and may spend a whole day sitting gorging in a tree.

Orang-utans can live for up to 40 years; they are mature aged between seven and 10. Females normally give birth to a single baby, though occasionally they have twins. The babies are completely dependent on the mother and are not weaned until three years old.

Decline and Fall

Once orang-utans were found throughout Southeast Asia and southern China, but today there are estimated to be fewer than 30,000 in the wild. Their numbers have declined by 30 to 50 percent in the last 10 years.

The greatest threat to orang-utans is the destruction of their habitat—tropical rain forest. Large areas of forest have been affected as trees are felled for their timber, and land cleared for farming. It is estimated that 80 percent of all forest in Malaysia and Indonesia has already been logged. In the 1990s a series of forest fires that burned for months at a time badly affected the orang-utan.

Another threat is the capture of live orangs for the pet trade. Despite legislation, it is estimated that between 1996 and 2000 about 1,000 orang-utans were captured to be sold as exotic pets. For every orang-utan that survives capture and shipment, five or six others will die in the process.

The highly intelligent species is protected by law in Indonesia and Malaysia; both countries have signed up

DATA PANEL

Orang-utan

Pongo pygmaeus

Family: Pongidae

World population: Fewer than 30,000

Distribution: Indonesia (Kalimantan, Sumatra) and Malaysia (Sabah, Sarawak)

Habitat: Tropical rain forests

Size: Height: male 54 in (137 cm); female 45 in (115 cm). Weight: male 130–200 lb (60–90 kg); female 88–110 lb (40–50 kg)

Form: A large long-haired ape; the coat is usually a reddish color but varies from orange to dark chocolate

Diet: Mainly fruit; also young leaves and shoots, insects, bark, and small mammals

Breeding: Usually gives birth to single young; mature at 7–10 years. Life span up to 40 years

Related endangered species: Western lowland gorilla (*Gorilla gorilla gorilla*)* EN; mountain gorilla (*G. g. beringei*)* EN; pygmy chimpanzee (*Pan paniscus*) EN; chimpanzee (*P. troglodytes*)* EN

Status: IUCN EN; CITES I

to CITES. The 1987
Asian Primate Action
Plan identified several
conservation measures
needed to protect the orang-
utan. They included the setting up
and managing of protected areas
(such as the Gunung National Park in
Sumatra), surveys to establish the population
and distribution of orang-utans, and a public
education program. About 60 percent of orang-utans
in Borneo could be protected if conservation laws
were more rigorously enforced.

There are a number of orang-utan rehabilitation
centers. They look after orang-utans rescued from
smugglers or those that have lost their homes because
of logging. The apes are relocated to protected areas.
There are about 645 orang-utans (1992 figures) held
in 142 zoos and collections worldwide—of which 492
were born in captivity.

Orang-utans *are
fascinating apes that share
96.4 percent of the genes
that make up the human
genetic code.*

Ruffed Lemur

Varecia variegata

The ruffed lemur is the largest of the true lemurs and is becoming so rare in the wild that its best hope for survival is now an intensive program of captive breeding and release.

The ruffed lemur of Madagascar stands out among other lemurs because of its large size and distinctively patterned coat. The patterns and colors vary, but fall into two main subspecies: the red ruffed lemur and the black-and-white ruffed lemur. By far the most endangered is the red ruffed lemur, which only occurs in the far north of the species' range. Trapping and shooting are widespread activities in the area, and the local forest is being destroyed at such a rate that the IUCN predicts that unless effective action is taken, the population will plummet by at least half in the next few years.

The prospects for the black-and-white ruffed lemur are slightly brighter, although it is still a highly endangered animal. Its range is much larger than that of the red ruffed lemur, but the population is sparsely distributed. The black-and-white ruffed lemur occurs in several nature reserves, including the small island of Nosy Mangabe, where the species was introduced in the 1930s. Here the population density is much higher than elsewhere—over 30 animals per square mile (19 per sq. km). Even at these densities there are probably no more than 150 animals in total, and the population is regularly raided by poachers.

Captive Breeding

The ruffed lemur has shown that it will take very easily to captivity, but its adaptability has been a mixed blessing. On the one hand, collecting for the Malagasy pet trade has played a large part in the species' decline. On the other, it means that there are large numbers living in the safety of zoos and conservation institutions around the world. Of the captive population, about 500 are black-and-white ruffed and 300 are red ruffed lemurs.

Over 95 percent of the population in zoos and other institutions are captive born, and there is now an extensive international breeding program, coordinated by San Diego Zoo. One problem with captive breeding is keeping the gene pool as large as possible. Although interbreeding between subspecies is strongly discouraged, there are a small number of hybrids in existence. Zoos cooperate by lending out animals for breeding so that the captive populations remain as genetically diverse as possible.

A few ruffed lemurs were successfully released back into the wild in 1998 and 1999, and at least one captive-

---

DATA PANEL

Ruffed lemur (variegated lemur)

Varecia variegata

Family: Lemuridae

World population: Unknown, but probably fewer than 10,000

Distribution: Eastern Madagascar

Habitat: Rain forest from sea level to 3,900 ft (1,200 m)

Size: Length head/body: 20–24 in (51–60 cm); tail: 22–25 in (56–65 cm); females larger than males. Weight: 7–10 lb (3.2–4.5 kg)

Form: Large lemur with thick, variable coat. Black-and-white and red forms both have a white ruff, or neck patch

Diet: Fruit, leaves, seeds, and nectar; occasionally earth

Breeding: Between 2 and 6 young born after gestation of 3–3.5 months; weaned at 19 weeks; mature at 20 months; breeds before 36 months

Related endangered species: Golden bamboo lemur *(Hapalemur aureus)* CR; broad-nosed gentle lemur *(H. simus)* CR; 5 other members of the Lemuridae family are classified as Vulnerable

Status: IUCN EN; CITES I

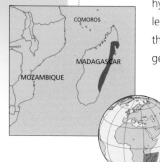

COMOROS

MADAGASCAR

MOZAMBIQUE

The ruffed lemur *has two distinct subspecies, the red ruffed (main picture) and black-and-white ruffed (inset). Even within the two subgroups the lemurs' coat patterns are extremely variable, leading some zoologists to recommend that they are further divided into seven subspecies.*

born female has raised a family since being released back into the wild. In years to come it is hoped that the captive-bred individuals will become the founders of stable new populations in specially protected areas of the species' former range.

Conservation Policies and Problems

Before the successful reintroduction of captive-bred lemurs can take place there needs to be a significant improvement in the way that Malagasy conservation law is enforced. Although conservation policies are in place, it is not easy for the government to make a real commitment to them in a country where the population is so poor, and where many other social and economic issues take priority. There have been instances, for example, where Malagasy nature reserves have been given up in favor of commercial logging. In addition, poaching has been allowed to continue virtually unchecked in areas that are supposedly protected.

The relatively recent development of ecotourism on Madagascar is now bringing money and trade to the island, showing both the government and local people that conservation can pay. A real change of attitude toward conservation of the island's wildlife by the local population would give the ruffed lemur a fighting chance of survival.

African Elephant

Loxodonta africana

The African elephant is the largest land mammal on earth. It is a remarkable creature, not only because of its size and bulk, but also because of its intelligence, memory, and behavior.

The statistics surrounding the African elephant are as impressive as the animal itself: It is the world's largest land mammal and has the longest gestation of any animal (660 days—nearly two years). An adult elephant can drink between 15 and 20 gallons (70 and 90 l) of water a day and eat about 330 pounds (150 kg) of food. Despite its size and weight, however, an African elephant can reach speeds of 25 miles per hour (40 km/h) when charging or fleeing.

The elephant's distinctive trunk has many functions. It is used for feeding, carrying, spraying water or dust to cool itself, making sounds, greeting other elephants, threatening, stroking, and even as a pacifier for baby elephants to suck on. Elephants have long tusks made of ivory that they use for fighting and digging; they flap their large ears to keep cool in the African heat.

The Romans wrote about elephants living on the Mediterranean coast of North Africa, but today African elephants can only be found on the savanna grasslands and forests south of the Sahara Desert. There they feed on the grasses and foliage, sometimes ripping trees out with their trunks and stripping them of bark and leaves. The female elephants (cows) live in herds with their calves and close female relatives. The herd is led by the oldest female elephant, called the matriarch. Male elephants (bulls) leave the herd when they reach puberty. They live alone or in small bachelor groups, only joining a herd again to mate.

Elephants live for about 70 years. They are social animals and have been known to work together—particularly in times of danger—to help sick or injured family members. They are also thought to grieve for their dead relatives.

African elephants *flap their large ears to keep themselves cool. This elephant is red from dust bathing—another way of cooling off.*

DATA PANEL

African elephant

Loxodonta africana

Family: Elephantidae

World population: Up to 543,000

Distribution: Sub-Saharan Africa

Habitat: Savanna grasslands; forests

Size: Length: up to 16.4 ft (5 m); height at shoulder: up to 10.8 ft (3.3 m); males 10% bigger than females. Weight: male up to 6.7 tons (6 tonnes); female up to 3.3 tons (2.9 tonnes)

Form: Huge gray-black body with columnlike legs, large head, large ears, long tusks, and a flexible trunk; little hair on skin

Diet: Grasses, tree leaves, and bark

Breeding: Breeds at 13 or 14 years old; gestation of nearly 2 years. Calves every 3–4 years in wet season. May live up to 70 years

Related endangered species: Asian elephant *(Elephas maximus)* EN

Status: IUCN VU; CITES I, II, and III, according to country location

African elephant populations have fallen quite dramatically. At the beginning of the 20th century there were many millions of elephants; in 1970 there were 2 million, and today there are probably fewer than half a million. They have few natural predators; their most dangerous enemies are humans.

Trade and Land

Ivory from elephant tusks is a prized material traditionally used to make carvings and jewelry. The trade in ivory began seriously in the 17th century, when Arab traders hunted elephants in West Africa. The invention of guns, and in particular the rifle, meant that hunters could kill animals more efficiently. African elephants are now protected in many countries, and there is an official ban on trade in ivory.

However, there is still a strong demand for the tusks, and illegal poaching is widespread.

Elephants are also threatened by loss of habitat. As the growing human population of Africa demands more land for expanding cities and for farmland, the elephants' habitat has shrunk, limiting their access to food. This can bring them into conflict with humans, since elephants may be driven by hunger to raid crops.

After pressure by conservation organizations the African elephant was put on Appendix I of CITES in 1989, banning international trade in the species and its products. However, several African countries want to continue trading to earn money for conservation.

Conservation groups run projects in Africa strengthening elephant conservation through anti-poaching patrols, education, and trade controls. They also work with local people to reduce conflict between elephants and humans and to promote the benefits of elephants to the local tourist industry.

Przewalski's Wild Horse

Equus przewalskii

Excessive hunting, competition with domestic stock, and interbreeding with domestic horses have effectively caused the extinction of purebred herds of Przewalski's horse in the wild.

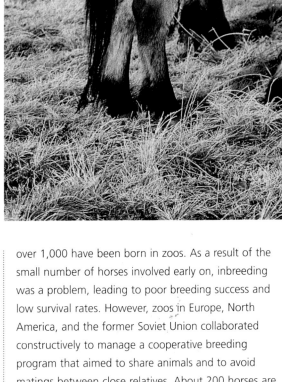

Przewalski's wild horse is named after the Russian general who discovered it while exploring Central Asia in 1879. It is, or was, the only species of true wild horse, but it is now extinct in its natural range. The horses used to live in large herds, each led by a dominant stallion, wandering the great grassy plains of Central Asia in considerable numbers. The animals would be on the move, feeding almost constantly, and always alert for danger. Although they were occasionally hunted for meat and hides, capture was not a significant threat while human populations remained low, and probably relatively few were killed. However, by the early 1900s hunting pressure had increased substantially, and the horse population began a steady decline in numbers.

The Przewalski's wild horse was given full legal protection in Mongolia in 1926. The legislation did not save the dwindling herds because the growing human population began to fence land for cultivation, excluding the horses from traditional feeding areas and vital places to drink. At the same time, the wild horses began to interbreed with domestic horses that were wandering freely in the same areas. The result was hybrid types and the steady dilution of the genetic integrity and typical features of the purebred wild horse herds. The last true Przewalski's wild horse was reported in 1968.

There now appear to be no Przewalski's horses surviving in the wild, but fortunately there are some in captivity. The horses were never domesticated but kept as a rarity in zoos. From a low point of just 13 animals numbers have been steadily increasing, and over 1,000 have been born in zoos. As a result of the small number of horses involved early on, inbreeding was a problem, leading to poor breeding success and low survival rates. However, zoos in Europe, North America, and the former Soviet Union collaborated constructively to manage a cooperative breeding program that aimed to share animals and to avoid matings between close relatives. About 200 horses are covered by this program, and purebred Przewalski's horses are now well established in captivity.

Reintroduction into the Wild

Many generations of captive breeding, artificial food, confinement in small enclosures, and living in mild climates away from Central Asia may all combine to

DATA PANEL

Przewalski's wild horse

Equus przewalskii

Family: Equidae

World population: Several hundred

Distribution: Altai Mountains of Mongolia and (formerly) adjacent parts of China

Habitat: Dry, semidesert plain; steppe grassland

Size: Length head/body: 7 ft (2–2.1 m); tail: 36 in (90 cm); height at shoulder: 4 ft (1.2 m). Weight: 450–650 lb (200–300 kg)

Form: A stockily built pony with short neck and legs. The head is relatively heavy. The fur is sandy brown, much longer in winter, with a white area around the muzzle. Stiff, blackish hairs form an erect mane on the neck

Diet: Mainly grass, but also other small plants; shrubs and bark where they are available

Breeding: One foal born in April or May after 12-month gestation. Life span may exceed 25 years in captivity

Related endangered species: African wild ass (*Equus africanus*) CR; Asiatic wild ass (*E. hemionus*) VU; Grevy's zebra (*E. grevyi*) EN; mountain zebra (*E. zebra*) EN; quagga (*E. quagga*)* EX

Status: IUCN EW; CITES I

reduce the ability of the animals to survive in the extreme conditions of their native home. In 1989 an experiment was started at the Bukhara Breeding Center in Uzbekistan to find out whether horses bred for generations in zoos could actually survive the challenge of living wild in the semidesert conditions of Central Asia. A stallion and four mares were released into a huge fenced area and studied. The horses seemed to manage well; they bred successfully and did not suffer ill-effects from mixing with wild asses also present in the area. Efforts are now being made to restore Przewalski's horse to the wild in Mongolia, where they have begun to breed successfully in a protected reserve. It is also planned to reintroduce the Przewalski's wild horse to China.

Przewalski's *is the only living species of truly wild horse. It recently became extinct in the wild but is being reintroduced to its former range (see map) using animals bred in captivity.*

RUSSIA
Lake Baikal
former range
MONGOLIA
CHINA

Quagga

Equus quagga

A form of the common zebra, the quagga used to roam the South African grasslands, but during the 19th century was hunted to extinction for its meat and hide.

The common zebra occurs as various localized and distinct varieties, and the one in southern Africa was sufficiently distinct to have been considered a separate species. It was known as the quagga, a name that was based on the loud barking-coughing sound that all zebras make.

Like the common zebra, quaggas formed large herds to exploit the vast grasslands and to achieve safety in numbers when attacked by predators. It is said that they preferred to spend the night in areas of short grass where they could not be easily ambushed. In good feeding areas the herds would stay in the same region throughout the year. However, where the grazing was poor, the quagga migrated seasonally to find better feeding places.

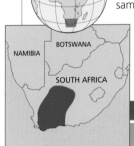

NAMIBIA

BOTSWANA

SOUTH AFRICA

In the quagga *(above) the striping that is characteristic of all zebras was confined to the head, neck, and forequarters. Breeding experiments to produce an animal resembling the extinct quagga have included a cross between a mule and a zebra, to produce a "quagga" hybrid (right). However, this animal lacks the striped head and neck of the quagga and is gray, whereas the quagga was generally brown.*

The Road to Extinction

From about 1700 settlement in South Africa by Europeans increased substantially. By the late 19th century most of the land occupied by quaggas had

---

DATA PANEL

Quagga (Bonte quagga, Burchell's zebra)

Equus quagga

Family: Equidae

World population: 0 (Extinct)

Distribution: Formerly Cape Province and parts of Orange Free State, South Africa

Habitat: Dry temperate grasslands

Size: Length head/body: about 6 ft (2 m); tail: nearly 24 in (50–60 cm); height at shoulder: 4–5 ft (1.3–1.4 m). Weight: about 450 lb (200 kg); adult males can be up to about 650 lb (300 kg)

Form: Brown zebra in which the head, neck, and forequarters had brown and cream stripes, but the hind quarters were solid brown. As in other zebras, each individual had a slightly different pattern

Diet: Coarse grasses

Breeding: Single foal born probably after a gestation of about 1 year. Independent at 6–8 months and probably capable of breeding at 2–3 years. Life span may have been up to 40 years, as in common zebras today

Related endangered species: Mountain zebra *(Equus zebra)* EN; Grevy's zebra *(E. grevyi)* EN; African wild ass *(E. africanus)* CR; Asiatic wild ass *(E. hemionus)* VU

Status: IUCN EX

been brought into use for grazing livestock and for farming. The new settlers used to shoot quaggas for sport in far greater numbers than had ever been possible by the native people. The quaggas were killed by farmers as a convenient source of meat, and their skins also provided a source of strong leather, which was used for making robust bags. They were easy animals to hunt from horseback, since the open grassland offered nowhere to hide or escape. Hunting caused disruption of the quagga herds.

Although there may have been many surviving quaggas as late as the 1860s, they were scattered into small groups, which substantially reduced their breeding success. As the older animals died, there were too few offspring to replace them, and the last wild quagga was probably killed in about 1878. A few quaggas had been kept in zoos, the last individual dying in Amsterdam on August 12, 1883.

The only photographs of a living quagga are of the female that lived at the London Zoo from 1851 to 1872. Today there is only one quagga left on the entire continent of Africa—a preserved foal in the Cape Town Museum. About 22 stuffed and mounted specimens of adult quaggas are scattered among museums elsewhere.

Re-Creating the Quagga

It has been suggested that genetic material from some of the museum specimens might be used to clone a "re-created" quagga, but that will only be possible if the DNA has remained suitably preserved (tanning the skins, for example, which is part of the preservation process, harms DNA irrevocably). Experimental cross-breeding projects and the selective breeding of zebras with different coat patterns have also produced animals that look very similar to quaggas.

Black Rhinoceros

Diceros bicornis

Formerly abundant and widespread in Africa, the black rhinoceros has been drastically reduced in numbers since the 1970s. The main culprit is the expanding international trade in rhino horn.

Although the black rhinoceros is able, if necessary, to go for five days without water, it is generally found in relatively moist areas of lush vegetation. Throughout Africa these regions are under pressure for development into farm and grazing land, effectively excluding the rhinos, which are too large and unpredictable to be tolerated close to human settlements. Yet the main threat to the animals comes not so much from habitat loss as from hunting, principally for their horns for use in oriental medicine.

For centuries rhino horn, composed of densely compressed hair, has been powdered and swallowed as a remedy for fevers and other disorders. It is made of keratin (a fibrous substance that occurs in skin, hair, nails, and hooves) and cannot be absorbed into the body, so any supposed medicinal benefits will only be imaginary. Yet the horns continue to fetch high prices, often earning more than their weight in gold.

In recent years a new factor has further complicated the situation. In Yemen in southwestern Asia there has long been a tradition of using rhino horn to make carved dagger handles. As oil money brought new prosperity to the region, the demand for these prestigious status symbols increased; in 1999 more than 100 craftsmen were employed in making and repairing such artifacts. Old and new horns were used; at the time, new horns were said to be fetching $615 per pound ($1,350 per kg), 20 percent more than they had only two years earlier.

Before hunting reduced their numbers, black rhinos could be found in the bush and savanna regions of most of Africa south of the Sahara. By the 1960s they were already becoming rare, but were still widely distributed, with substantial numbers in Kenya, Tanzania, and Zimbabwe. Although the animals enjoyed legal protection, the lucrative trade in horns could not be controlled, and the rhino died out in one area after another as hunting took its lethal toll.

Slow Breeders

The black rhino has one of the slowest reproductive rates of any large mammal, making it ill-equipped to cope with population loss. Young animals first breed at five or even 10 years, but in practice many are killed long before they reach that age. Calves are not born annually, but at intervals of up to five years. In the past this was not a disadvantage; the slow breeding rate was probably a natural adaptation to avoid producing more young than the available resources could support. Excessive hunting has, however, overwhelmed the animal's capacity to maintain its numbers, which have fallen by more than 90 percent since 1970. The total figure now seems to have stabilized, but several countries where the species was

Black rhinos *are usually tolerant of each other, but can be aggressive toward humans. Their temperamental behavior makes them difficult to manage; incidents involving rogue animals do not help the species' cause.*

once common now have fewer than 50 black rhinos, most of them confined to national parks and reserves.

Thanks to the high cash value of the horns, the killing continues; a poacher can earn more from one dead rhino than from a year's farmwork. One possible solution might be to remove the horns, which contain no nerve endings and can be painlessly cut away without disrupting the rhino's life. However, the horns grow back, so the process would have to be repeated. Even so, such a program would remove the incentive for poaching and might prove more practicable in the long run than captive breeding, which is the only other way of ensuring the rhino's long-term survival.

DATA PANEL

Black rhinoceros

Diceros bicornis

Family: Rhinocerotidae

World population: About 2,550 (1994 estimate)

Distribution: Africa south of the Sahara, in widely scattered localities

Habitat: Bush and savanna; rarely found more than a day's walk from water

Size: Length head/body: 9.5–12.3 ft (2.9–3.7 m); tail: 24–28 in (60–70 cm); height at shoulder: 4.5–5.9 ft (1.4–1.8 m). Weight: 1,500–3,000 lb (700–1,400 kg)

Form: Large, thick-skinned animal; grayish in color but often coated with dust or mud. Two horns on the snout and a pointed, mobile upper lip, used like a miniature trunk to gather food

Diet: Leaves, twigs, and branches browsed from more than 200 species of low-growing shrub

Breeding: Single calf born after 15-month gestation; suckled for up to 1 year. Life span may exceed 40 years

Related endangered species: White rhinoceros (*Ceratotherium simum*) NT; great Indian rhinoceros (*Rhinoceros unicornis*) EN; Javan rhinoceros (*R. sondaicus*) CR; Sumatran rhinoceros (*Dicerorhinus sumatrensis*) CR

Status: IUCN CR; CITES I

Père David's Deer

Elaphurus davidianus

Extinct in the wild for centuries, this species has survived only in parks and zoos. It is now being reintroduced into special reserves in its native China.

The unusual-looking Père David's deer is called "four-unlike" in Chinese, a reference to its peculiar appearance. It seems to have the antlers of a deer, broad hooves like those of a cow, a neck like that of a camel, and the long bushy tail of a donkey; yet it is also quite distinct in its appearance.

Its habitat used to be the swampy lowlands of eastern and central China. It was hunted to extinction over most of its range more than 800 years ago, though some may have survived until the 19th century on Hainan Island in the South China Sea. Meanwhile, a few were kept by the emperor in the secluded Imperial Hunting Park of Peking (Beijing), protected by armed guards and contained within a high wall over 40 miles (64 km) long. There, in 1865, the French missionary Father Armand David saw them, and he later managed to obtain two skins that he thought were from some sort of reindeer. They were studied in Europe and described in 1866 as a new species of deer. They were named after Father David.

News of the curious creatures reached the outside world, including the Duke of Bedford in England, who was particularly interested in deer. He arranged for some living specimens to be brought to his collection at Woburn Park (about 60 miles (96 km) northwest of London). The Chinese emperor also allowed some to be sent to France and Germany. The export of animals was extremely fortunate, since in 1895 massive floods destroyed part of the Imperial Hunting Park's wall. Many deer drowned; those that escaped were killed and eaten by hungry people in the surrounding countryside. About two dozen seem to have survived within the park, but they were killed and eaten by soldiers during the Boxer Rebellion in 1900.

All the deer alive today are derived from those few that had been taken to Europe. The Duke of Bedford arranged for animals to be gathered together from various zoos to add to his collection and to form a breeding group at Woburn. The herd suffered through the two world wars due to the shortage of food, but numbers steadily increased; by 1956 there were sufficient numbers to be able to send four animals to the Beijing zoo. Today the largest herd is still at Woburn, where there are about 600 to 700 animals. Another sizable herd is at Wadhurst in Sussex (in the south of England), with smaller numbers in parks and zoos around the world.

Narrow Escape

In 1985, 22 deer were sent from Woburn as a gift to the people of China. They were returned to a small 100-acre (40-ha) enclosure in part of the original Imperial Hunting Park. Another 39 animals were sent from British zoos in 1986 and released in the Da Feng Reserve 250 miles (380 km) north of Shanghai. It is a marshy coastal area, the sort of habitat originally favored by Père David's deer and within its former range. The deer bred well, and numbers have tripled within 10 years.

Fortunately, Père David's deer does not seem to be badly affected by inbreeding, despite the small gene pool from which modern populations are descended. The species has had a narrow escape from extinction; and although its total population remains small, it does seem to be secure as a semicaptive animal.

Père David's deer *are unique in that the front prongs of their antlers are branched.*

DATA PANEL

Père David's deer

Elaphurus davidianus

Family: Cervidae

World population: About 1,000–1,500

Distribution: Originally northeastern and east central China, and on Hainan Island until the 19th century. Now only in special reserves in China and zoos and parks in various countries

Habitat: Swampy lowlands

Size: Length: male 6–6.3 ft (1.8–1.9 m); tail: 24 in (60 cm); height at shoulder: male 45–48 in (114–122 cm); female slightly smaller. Weight: male 330–440 lb (150–200 kg); female about 20% lighter

Form: Resembling other deer. Coat is gray in winter, reddish brown in summer. The tail is long for a deer, with a black tip. The males have a shaggy mane. The antlers are heavy and unique in that the front prongs are branched

Diet: Grass and leaves; sometimes aquatic plants

Breeding: One young born per year; mature at 14 months. Life span up to 20 years

Related endangered species: Various other species of deer, including Kuhl's deer *(Axis kuhlii)* EN

Status: IUCN CR; not listed by CITES

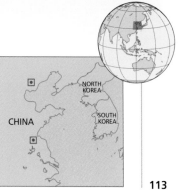

NORTH KOREA

CHINA

SOUTH KOREA

113

American Bison

Bison bison

Formerly America's most abundant large mammal and integral to the culture of native Americans, the bison was hunted to the brink of extinction during the development of North America. It is now numerous once more, and large herds live in protected areas and on ranches.

Plodding across the plains, bison look like pretty solid, sedate animals. However, they can swim, run fast—up to 30 mph (50 km/h)—and even jump over 3 feet (90 cm) into the air! They live in herds of up to several hundred animals, breaking up into smaller groups in winter. They make annual migrations to spread their feeding over a wide area. They also travel each day to drink. Today bison herds are limited in where they can roam because of towns, railways, and cattle fences. Mating takes place in July and August, when the largest numbers are gathered together. At this time the bulls make loud bellowing noises that can be heard 3 miles (5 km) away.

The bison was once abundant, with perhaps 60 million roaming across the American prairies. For many Native Americans bison were at the very center of their existence. The animals provided skins for homes and clothing; sinews were used as string or for sewing; the fur made cushions; and the meat was their main food. Paths made by the animals provided routes through dense vegetation and over rocky hills. The bison also caught the imagination of native American communities, figuring prominently in their folklore.

Slaughtered for Sport

As settlers pushed farther west, particularly during the 19th century, the plains were developed as farmland, and the bison were forced out of their ancestral range. Men like Buffalo Bill specialized in hunting the animals, particularly to feed the workers building the new railroads. The bison were also shot for sport, with hunters competing to see how many they could kill in a day. Once the railroads were running, it was also possible to export the meat and hides (bones too, for fertilizer) to distant markets. Out on the plains there was nowhere for the animals to hide, and they were ruthlessly pursued until in 1890 there were only a few hundred animals left alive.

Alaska
(U.S)

CANADA

UNITED STATES

DATA PANEL

American bison

Bison bison

Family: Bovidae

World population: About 500,000

Distribution: Midwestern U.S. and Canada

Habitat: Prairies and wooded areas

Size: Length: up to 12 ft (3.5 m); height at shoulder: up to 6.5 ft (1.9 m). Weight: 1,200–1,800 lb (500–800 kg); males up to 30% heavier than females

Form: Large, stocky animal with large hump over the shoulders; the head is held low. Dark-brown coat; forelegs, neck, and shoulders covered in long, shaggy hairs. Horns are present in both sexes

Diet: Mostly grass, also wild flowers, sedges, and shrubs such as willow, sagebrush, and birch. Active at all times, they eat over 1% of their weight per day and need water daily. In winter they scrape in the snow to get at lichens and mosses

Breeding: A single calf is born May–August after gestation of 9–10 months. It can run within 3 hours of birth and eats grass after the first week. Capable of breeding at 2–3 years. Life span up to 25 years

Related endangered species: European bison (*Bison bonasus*) EN

Status: IUCN LRcd; Canadian population CITES II

Fortunately, conservationists, led by William Hornaday, realized that one of America's national emblems was on the verge of extinction. Formed in 1905, the American Bison Society championed successful captive-breeding programs and herd management to ensure that the bison was saved from oblivion. Many have been released in areas from which they were lost long ago: Large numbers now exist in Alaska, where they were reintroduced in 1928. In many places bison now breed so successfully that they risk eating all the available food and starving during the winter. For this reason hunters are allowed to shoot small numbers each year to prevent the population getting too large. The meat is often in demand because it is less fatty than beef.

Bison are sometimes called buffalo, but they are more closely related to cattle and can breed with them. They also share similar diseases with cattle. True buffalo are quite different and are found in Africa.

Bison are the largest animals on the American plains, living in herds numbering more than 100 individuals.

Banteng

Bos javanicus

Wild banteng are shy, little-known animals, which rarely leave the seclusion of dense forests. However, it is now clear that continued interbreeding with domestic stock threatens their survival.

Domesticated banteng (often called Bali cattle) . are farmed in much of the wild banteng's range. As a result, inbreeding has taken place between the wild and domestic strains, diluting the wild genes. After generations of domestication Bali cattle have lost many of their ancestors' adaptations to life in the wild. The crossbred offspring of banteng and Bali cattle, while perfectly healthy and fertile, are poorly equipped to survive in the dense forests of Southeast Asia. For wild banteng, mixing with domestic stock holds the risk of infection from cattle diseases. Diseases spread fast through wild herds, which have limited natural immunity.

Wild banteng are naturally shy, retiring animals, and spend much of their time sheltering in dense thickets of vegetation. They venture out to graze on the vigorous plant growth at the edges of clearings, but are always ready to retreat into cover at the slightest sign of danger. They prefer to avoid all contact with people, which means that studying them is difficult. Much of what is known about their biology has been gleaned from observations of captive animals.

Diminishing Range

Banteng tend to be nocturnal in areas where they live close to human settlements; if the disturbance is too great, however, they abandon the area altogether. As a result, their range is shrinking, even in areas where suitable habitat remains.

Wild banteng herds usually consist of several females and their young with one mature male. Unattached males roam in "bachelor" groups, waiting for the opportunity to take over a herd from an old or injured male. As banteng numbers dwindle, the average

---

DATA PANEL

Banteng

Bos javanicus

Family: Bovidae

World population: May be fewer than 5,000

Distribution: Southeast Asia and Indochina, including Bali, Borneo, Cambodia, Java, Laos, Malaysia, Thailand, and Vietnam

Habitat: Dense forests and bamboo thickets

Size: Length head/body: 6.3–8.5 ft (1.9–2.3 m); height at shoulder: 5.3 ft (1.6 m). Weight: 1,320–1,760 lb (600–800 kg)

Form: Cowlike animal with short, chestnut-colored coat; darker (occasionally blue-black) in males. Lower legs white; male has upwardly curving horns; horns of female are shorter and straighter

Diet: Grasses, leaves, and shoots of trees and shrubs

Breeding: Single calf born February–March in the wild; weaned at 6–9 months; mature at 2–3 years. Life span up to 20 years

Related endangered species: Kouprey *(Bos sauveli)* CR; wild yak *(B. grunniens)** VU

Status: IUCN EN; not listed by CITES

herd size decreases. Moreover, with fewer animals on the lookout for danger, the remaining banteng face an increased risk of predation. Young calves are especially vulnerable to attack by dholes (a species of wild dog).

Declining Species

Banteng breed slowly, with females bearing only one calf a year at most. They are also hunted by humans partly for meat, but more profitably for their horns, which are carved into trinkets or simply mounted as trophies. Because the banteng currently receives no official protection, the trade in their parts continues legally. The lack of monitoring also means that there is little data from which to establish the true severity of the banteng's plight. What information there is

The banteng *is a shy wild ox that has a slight ridge on its back. It roams the lowlands and forested hills of Southeast Asia in small herds.*

indicates a serious decline. Once found throughout much of Southeast Asia, banteng are already extinct in the wild in India, Bangladesh, and probably in western Malaysia. The population in Thailand appears to have dropped by 80 percent in just 20 years. It is likely that a similar decline is underway in Cambodia, Laos, and Vietnam. In parts of northern Australia herds of banteng live wild, but these animals are outside their natural range and, having descended from domesticated stock, are not generally considered in the same light as genuinely wild banteng.

Nubian Ibex

Capra nubiana

Life is a struggle at the best of times for all desert mammals. The plight of the Nubian ibex has been made worse by trophy hunters who shoot the adult males for their horns.

Nubian ibex inhabit the rocky slopes of desert mountains in the Middle East, Arabia, and northeastern Africa. The adults are often found living alone (especially males). Females, with their young, including immature males (less than three years old), may form small groups. The ibex walks slowly among the rocks and across open slopes, searching for grasses, shoots, and leaves to eat. Like other ruminants, they will rest periodically to chew their cud before moving on in search of more food.

The Nubian is smaller than most other ibex, and the only one that is mainly adapted to life in desert conditions. Its pale, shiny coat reflects the sun's rays, helping keep the animal cool. This means that ibex can remain active even during the hottest parts of the day and wander widely in search of food.

Although there are no mammalian predators to fear in the desert, eagles and other birds of prey present a danger. Normally the ibex stay out in the open where there are plenty of escape routes and are ready to use their speed to escape attack should the need arise.

DATA PANEL

Nubian ibex

Capra nubiana

Family: Bovidae

World population: 1,200 (1986 estimate)

Distribution: Israel, Jordan, Oman, Saudi Arabia, Yemen, northeastern Sudan

Habitat: Slopes of desert mountains

Size: Length: 42–48 in (107–122 cm); height at shoulder: 24–30 in (60–75 cm). Weight: 55–150 lb (25–70 kg)

Form: A goatlike animal, sandy brown with paler hindquarters. Mature males have a dark beard and a black stripe down the back and also up the front of each foreleg. The horns sweep upward and backward in a semicircular direction, each with up to 36 prominent knobbly ridges across the outer surface of the curve. Male horns may grow to 4 ft (1.2 m); in females they are thinner and less than 14 in (35 cm) long. The young have white underparts.

Diet: Almost any type of vegetation

Breeding: Mates in late summer (or October), producing a single kid after 5-month gestation. Twins are rare. Breeds only once a year, from the age of 2–3 years onward. Life span at least 17 years

Related endangered species: Walia ibex (*Capra walie*) CR; markhor (*Capra falconeri*) EN

Status: IUCN EN; not listed by CITES

Young male Nubian ibex
like these have small horns. They remain in family groups until they are three years old.

However, in winter it can become quite cold, especially at night, when the clear skies rapidly absorb heat from the ground, and the temperature drops. At these times the ibex may seek shelter in ravines and caves. Similarly, when it rains, the animals will try to avoid getting wet.

Threats from Hunters

The ibex is prized for its meat by local people in the countries where it is found, especially since few other animals in the desert are big enough for humans to eat. In contrast to most desert animals, the Nubian ibex likes to drink daily, so it rarely lives far from water. It can be relatively easily shot or snared as it approaches water holes, especially since these are often in clefts between rock faces and only accessible via narrow tracks. In addition, wars have frequently been fought in regions where the ibex live, and the animals would have been a welcome source of food to soldiers, who were able to kill them with their powerful rifles. Moreover, the prominent curved horns of the ibex have attracted attention from trophy hunters, who seek out big males.

Like other large desert mammals, the Nubian ibex was probably always scarce, but hunting has made it even more so. There are none left in Syria, Lebanon, or (probably) Egypt, and the few animals that remain elsewhere are scattered over a very large area and live in widely separated small groups.

The Walia ibex of Ethiopia is sometimes regarded as a separate species from the Nubian. It lives on the steep slopes of the Simien Mountains, feeding among the giant heathers. It is Critically Endangered and probably now numbers only about 100 individuals.

119

Arabian Oryx

Oryx leucoryx

In the vast deserts of the Middle East the oryx was hunted to extinction in the 1970s. It has now been reintroduced to the wild from captive herds bred in zoos.

Arabian oryx live in small herds, usually with fewer than 10 animals per group, which lessens the impact of their feeding on the sparse desert vegetation. They generally feed early in the day, then rest, and feed again before finding shade for the hottest part of the afternoon. The animals move around seasonally between feeding places and may use a total area of several thousand square miles in a year. They seem able to detect rain at a distance; they travel to the area affected to feed on the new growth of plants. Oryx prefer rocky or stony plains to soft sand and steep mountains.

Big-game hunters used to pursue oryx for trophies, and for generations the animals were hunted

DATA PANEL

Arabian oryx (white oryx)

Oryx leucoryx

Family: Bovidae

World population: Over 2,000, most in captivity

Distribution: Formerly in Egypt, Iraq, Israel, Syria, United Arab Emirates, and Yemen. Reintroduced to Jordan, Oman, and Saudi Arabia

Habitat: Rocky and stony plains in desert areas

Size: Length: 5–5.5 ft (1.5–1.6 m); height at shoulder: 32–41 in (81–104 cm). Weight: 140–155 lb (65–70 kg)

Form: A white antelope with black legs, each with a white band above

the hoof. Horns (in both sexes) are straight, about 24 in (60 cm) long

Diet: Grasses and desert shrubs, from which they also get most of the water they need (although they may sometimes travel to a water hole)

Breeding: Births can occur in any month after 8-month gestation. The single calf stays with its mother for 4–5 months. Females are mature at about 3 years. Life span can be over 20 years

Related endangered species: Scimitar-horned oryx *(Oryx dammah)* EW

Status: IUCN EN; CITES I

by men riding on camels. Although some escaped, many did not, and they were steadily eliminated from countries such as Syria, Egypt, and Israel. By the 1950s the increased availability of four-wheel drive vehicles, abundant fuel, automatic rifles, and oil-based local wealth combined to make hunting in Arab countries both more widespread and more efficient. Gunmen in vehicles hunted the animals to extinction. The last wild oryx were killed in the 1970s.

Rescue Remedy

Fortunately, several Arab countries had already made efforts to keep and breed the oryx in captivity. In 1962 international cooperation between zoos made it possible to assemble a

few animals in Phoenix, Arizona (where the climate is very similar to that of the native home of the Arabian oryx), from which to breed animals specifically for release back into the wild. This was the first such international project for any endangered or extinct species, and it has been highly successful. Oryx were released in Oman in 1982, Jordan in 1983, and Saudi Arabia in 1990. There are now over 500 oryx living wild in those three areas, and many more in zoos (such as that in Los Angeles) and in large natural enclosures, including one near Eilat in Israel.

Breeding large numbers of oryx from just a few individuals has inevitably led to genetic problems. Some of the more successful breeding males fathered a disproportionate number of the captive population in the early days. As a result of inbreeding, survival

Arabian oryx *are the palest species of oryx and are superbly adapted to life in the desert. Like other species of oryx, they are characterized by their long, upright horns. They have dark patches on their faces, legs, and at the lower end of the tail.*

rates were low; this problem has been recognized, and careful management of future breeding should ensure that it is overcome with time.

Oryx are now protected and have been adopted as an important symbol of the local culture in the countries to which they have been restored. It is unlikely that the species will die out a second time through carelessness, but the herds remain small, widely scattered, and vulnerable to natural disasters such as disease and drought.

121

Wild Yak

Bos grunniens

The ultimate "survival machine," the sturdy yak is in its element even in the harshest Himalayan winter conditions. However, it is not adapted to deal with the threats of hunting, habitat disturbance, and competition from its domesticated relatives.

Yaks are the eastern equivalent of the American bison, and they are among the hardiest mammals on earth. Between 2,000 and 3,000 years ago the yak's ancestors were successfully domesticated and used for milk, beef, and wool production. Domestic yaks were also used as pack and draft animals, and their dried dung served as fuel on the Tibetan plateau, which has no trees. Today the world population of domestic yaks is probably over 12 million. By contrast, wild yaks are now extremely rare: Recent estimates have put the population at just a few hundred animals.

An immensely hardy animal, the yak survives seemingly without difficulty on the hostile, high plateaus of the Himalayas, enduring winter conditions among the harshest on earth. Temperatures in this area can fall to as low as -15°F (-26°C). The yak uses heat generated by plant material fermenting in its intestines to help keep warm; adult yaks are also covered in thick, woolly hair. However, with such adaptations to the extreme cold yaks are not so tolerant of warm temperatures. Herds that move to lower pastures to bear young in spring retreat as summer arrives, returning to altitudes of about 15,000 feet (4,550 m), where there is snow all year round.

Yaks are social animals, and most individuals will spend their lives as part of a herd. The largest herds are made up of females and young, with bachelor males forming smaller bands. There are obvious advantages to living in a group; formidable as fully grown yaks are, they still have at least one serious natural predator, namely, the Tibetan wolf.

Sure-Footed Climbers

The scarcity of good food in its habitat forces the yak to wander widely in search of grasses, lichens, and other low-growing alpine plants. Deep snow is hard to walk through, but the yaks save

DATA PANEL

Wild yak

Bos grunniens

Family: Bovidae

World population: Fewer than 1,000

Distribution: Tibetan plateau (northern Tibet); Kansu in northwestern China; eastern Kashmir in India

Habitat: Alpine tundra and steppe; spends summer above snow line

Size: Length: up to 10.6 ft (3.3 m); height at shoulder: up to 6.5 ft (2 m); females about 60% smaller than males. Weight: males 670–2,200 lb (300–1,000 kg); females lighter than males

Form: Massive ox with dense, brown-black woolly hair. High humped shoulders; low-slung head. Both sexes have curved horns

Diet: Grasses, herbs, and lichens

Breeding: Adults mate in winter; a single calf is born in the following fall. Life span up to 25 years

Related endangered species: American bison *(Bison bison)** LRcd

Status: IUCN VU; not listed by CITES

energy by walking in single file, stepping into the footprints of the animal in front. Each large cloven hoof is augmented with an enlarged dewclaw (a partly developed extra hoof), which gives a strong grip. Despite their bulk, the yaks are sure-footed climbers, able to hop from rock to rock to avoid the deepest snowdrifts. Only in the worst storms and blizzards do they come to a halt to wait out the weather, standing in small groups with their heads turned away from the driving wind and icy snow.

On the Brink of Extinction

The wild yak should surely be thriving in a habitat where no other species can match its power and suitability for the environment. It suffers from only moderate predation and has very little natural competition. However, as is so often the case, this magnificent example of natural design is being pushed to the brink of extinction by the actions of humans. Wild herds are hunted throughout much of their range; and as human settlements have expanded, yaks are finding themselves outcompeted by domestic herds or in some cases simply assimilated into them.

Wild and domestic yaks often interbreed. Consequently, the genetic purity of the wild type has been diluted, and the offspring are less able to cope with life in the wild.

The yak is a massive, powerful creature with a voice to suit its stature. Its deep, grunting call has earned it a scientific name that translates literally as "grunting ox."

Eurasian Red Squirrel

Sciurus vulgaris

Red squirrels are common across Europe, but are rapidly being replaced by American gray squirrels in Britain. Such a fate may also overtake their continental cousins.

Only 100 years ago the red squirrel was common and the only squirrel in Britain and across continental Europe. Now it is extinct in southern England, except on three islands off the coast. It is still found in Scotland and remains widespread in northern England, although its numbers there are declining fast. Apart from these areas, it survives in a few scattered localities in Wales and eastern and central England. In its place has come the American gray squirrel, introduced to Britain between 1876 and 1929. The American gray has proved a highly successful invader, becoming the squirrel commonly seen in most British woodlands, parks, and gardens.

Many people blame the grays for attacking and driving out the native red squirrel or for passing on fatal diseases. In fact, there is no evidence that it is guilty of either of these crimes, although one natural disease that kills red squirrels does not affect grays. The main problem seems to be that while the European red squirrel is satisfactorily adapted to life in coniferous woodlands, it is simply less well equipped than the gray to survive in deciduous forests.

Gray squirrels originated in the hardwood forests of North America and are at home in similar woodland areas of lowland Britain. While the reds can survive in deciduous forests on their own, they are at a disadvantage in such environments when they face competition from the grays. The result is that once the grays spread into an area, the reds disappear within about 15 years. Attempts to reintroduce them back into the areas from which they disappeared have not been successful.

A Question of Adaptation

One major problem is that red squirrels cannot digest acorns properly. Acorns are the main food available in the fall in most lowland forests. Grays thrive on them, and they also compete for hazelnuts, the reds' favorite food in deciduous woodland. Since gray squirrels normally live at double the population densities of reds, they eat at least twice as many nuts, leaving the latter with insufficient food resources. Eurasian red squirrels feed mainly in the treetops, so they cannot afford to store much fat for the winter without running the risk of becoming clumsy

---

DATA PANEL

Eurasian red squirrel (European red squirrel)

Sciurus vulgaris

Family: Sciuridae

World population: Probably at least 2 million spread over a huge area

Distribution: Europe and Asia, from Britain east to China and northern Japan

Habitat: Forest, especially coniferous forest

Size: Length head/body: 7–10 in (18–24 cm); tail: 5–8 in (14–20 cm). Weight: 9–12 oz (250–350 g)

Form: Bright chestnut red in summer, darker in winter; large bushy tail and (in winter) prominent ear tufts

Diet: Pine seeds, nuts, fruit, and fungi; occasionally insects and birds' eggs

Breeding: Usually 3 (but up to 8) young per litter; 1 or sometimes 2 litters per year after a gestation period of 5–6 weeks. Life span up to 7 years in the wild, but many die young; 10 years in captivity

Related endangered species: Some local populations and subspecies of squirrels and chipmunks in the U.S. are Critically Endangered, Endangered, or Vulnerable, but (as with the Eurasian red squirrel) whole species are not at risk

Status: IUCN NT (except in Britain where it is classified as EN); not listed by CITES

climbers. Grays, on the other hand, forage more on the ground and so can accumulate larger fat reserves because agility in the treetops is less important for them. With less fat to tide them over periods of scarcity, reds have to feed regularly, whatever the weather. Since they do most of their foraging in the trees, they are also limited in the range of food available to them. In contrast, the ground-feeding grays not only have access to a wider selection of forage but can also find enough to meet their needs in a much shorter time, a substantial advantage in spells of bad weather.

Ironically, native red squirrels have simply turned out to be less well adapted to cope with the British weather and living conditions than the invasive grays, and so they have lost out in competition with the newcomers. Sadly, the same story has been repeated in Ireland, where the gray squirrel was first released in 1913; it has now spread through the country, again at the expense of the red.

The Eurasian red squirrel *spends much of its time foraging in trees; it comes down to the ground occasionally to bury nuts.*

Still more alarmingly, grays are now spreading across northern Italy. The species was introduced there in 1948 and in 1966, near Turin. If they spread, the grays will threaten red squirrels throughout the rest of Europe. Attempts to curb the threat to Eurasian red squirrels by eliminating the grays have been stopped by animal-rights supporters, who have managed to win legal backing for their efforts to halt the killings.

The situation raises a difficult moral dilemma. If the few hundred introduced gray squirrels have a right to life, should the threatened red squirrel population not benefit from similar protection? And if so, how can their future be assured in the face of a challenge from outside, except by culling the newcomers?

St. Kilda Mouse

Apodemus sylvaticus hirtensis

The St. Kilda mouse is typical of many subspecies of small mammals that form tiny populations in remote places and are highly vulnerable, being found nowhere else in the world.

The St. Kilda mouse does not face any particular threats. However, it is found only on the tiny island of Hirta in the North Atlantic and perhaps one other of the St. Kilda archipelago. These windswept, precipitous islands lie 40 miles (65 km) from the most westerly of Scotland's Outer Hebrides. Hirta was only occupied by the British Army, which had a missile range there. It is now a nature reserve.

If there were a major natural disaster on Hirta, the mice could disappear, and they may die out anyway through inbreeding for many generations. Visitors may carry rats, dogs, or cats, to the island, a serious threat to island mammals. Fortunately, this never happened during the time that the island was occupied.

However, the St. Kilda mouse population remains small and highly vulnerable. It is typical of many island races of small mammals (and other animals) that have become stranded in remote places and undergone their own process of private evolution until they no longer resemble the mainland forms from which they are descended.

The St. Kilda mouse is derived from the common wood mouse, which is found widely on the mainland of Britain and Europe. We know that the St. Kilda mouse must have arrived quite recently and evolved rapidly (within a few centuries at most) on its remote island home because at the end of the Ice Age (10,000 years ago) the islands were still covered by solid ice. The deep sea surrounding St. Kilda means that the mice could only have got there with human help. They must have been transported accidentally among thatching materials or supplies of food carried from the mainland.

Studies of skull similarities suggest that the original wood mice reached St. Kilda over 1,000 years ago and that they arrived from Scandinavia, not the nearest parts of mainland Scotland. They were probably carried to St. Kilda by the Vikings during their famous voyages. The islands have no mammalian predators and no other small mammals

DATA PANEL

St. Kilda mouse

Apodemus sylvaticus hirtensis

Family: Muridae

World population: About 1,000

Distribution: Outer Hebridean island of Hirta, St. Kilda group, off the west coast of Scotland

Habitat: Windswept, grassy slopes; in ruined buildings

Size: Length head/body: 4.5–5 in (11–13 cm); tail: 3–4 in (8–10 cm). Weight: 1.4–1.8 oz (40–50 g)

Form: Brownish above, creamy-gray below; large eyes and long tail. Coat thicker and woollier than in mainland mice

Diet: Plants, insects, and seeds

Breeding: About 6–8 young per litter; 2 or 3 litters per year. Average life span likely to be only a few months, but in captivity can live at least 2 years

Related endangered species: Poncelet's giant rat (*Solomys ponceleti*) EN; Anthony's wood rat (*Neotoma anthonyi*) EN; western small-toothed rat of Indonesia (*Macruromys elegans*) CR; Balkans mole-rat (*Spalax graecus*) VU; Florida mouse (*Podomys floridanus*) VU

Status: Not listed by IUCN; not listed by CITES

St. Kilda Group

IRELAND   UNITED KINGDOM

FRANC

apart from some house mice, which died out soon after people left the island in 1930.

Adapt and Survive

Left to themselves and cut off from the typical wood mice of the mainland with whom they would have bred, the island mice gradually changed to suit their new home. Over many generations they became better adapted to the windswept, rainy conditions on their treeless island. Their fur is now dense and woolly, quite unlike the sleek, thin coat of mainland mice. They also grew much larger than their mainland relatives—more than twice the size. They became quite tame too, having nothing to fear from predators. St. Kilda mice now look quite different from common wood mice, having changed by natural processes.

Isolated Populations

The IUCN lists more than 125 other rat and mouse species of the family Muridae (that to which the St. Kilda mouse belongs) classified as Endangered or Critically Endangered. Often they, like the St. Kilda mouse, live in small numbers in remote places. Many have evolved to be different precisely because of the remoteness of their populations

on islands, mountaintops, or in other isolated patches of habitat. Isolation tends to cause change, and it happens fastest in the smaller species of mammals, particularly mice, because they breed very quickly. Each generation takes a small step toward the creation of a new form.

Isolated habitats tend to generate new forms of small mammals that are found nowhere else. Often they are not properly studied because their remote homes are rarely visited. Sometimes such peculiar creatures are not seen for decades and are known only from a few skins and skulls in museums, perhaps collected over a half-century ago. The extinction of such species would take away fascinating examples of evolution in action.

The St. Kilda mouse *evolved from the common wood mouse. It lives on a windswept island, sheltering among the ruined buildings left behind after people moved away.*

Garden Dormouse

Eliomys quercinus

The garden dormouse can be locally abundant, but the species as a whole is in decline in many parts of Europe. No one really knows the reasons why.

The garden dormouse is one of about 20 species in 10 genera in its family. Its bold, black "mask" (a stripe on each side of its face) gives it the look of a bandit. It is widespread in Continental Europe, where it is a familiar sight on farms and in villages. It also comes into people's houses, so it is often seen and identified.

Ground-Dwelling Lifestyle

Most dormice live in trees, but garden dormice spend much of their time on the ground, living in burrows or among rocks. They may also make nests in crevices of buildings or in abandoned birds' nests. Like other dormice, they are excellent climbers, even managing to scale relatively smooth surfaces. Despite their agility, garden dormice do not travel far and rarely venture more than 200 yards (150 m) from their nest.

Garden dormice live mainly in deciduous or coniferous woodland, but they are also found in gardens, vineyards, sand dunes, and on bare rocky screes high in the mountains. This suggests that they can survive in a variety of conditions by eating a range of different foods. The dormouse's diet ranges from acorns to bird eggs and beetles. Its narrow snout enables it to poke under stones and logs to seek out insect larvae and hidden seeds.

In winter garden dormice hibernate, a factor that aids their survival in cold countries such as Finland and at high altitudes in Bavaria, Germany, where the ground is covered with snow, and food is hard to find.

Mysterious Decline

The garden dormouse is a very flexible and adaptable species and can be locally abundant, with up to 20 animals per acre (50 per ha). However, the species has been getting scarcer throughout the 20th century. It is now extinct in Croatia and parts of Slovakia, and is rare across eastern Europe in Lithuania, Latvia, the Czech Republic, and eastern Germany. Along with other dormouse species the garden dormouse is legally protected by the Berne Convention and the laws of individual European countries.

In Corsica the garden dormouse is said to be suffering from competition with brown rats. However, rats are normally rare or

DATA PANEL

Garden dormouse

Eliomys quercinus

Family: Gliridae

World population: Unknown, but in the thousands

Distribution: Europe south to the Mediterranean and North Africa, north to Finland, and east to Russia

Habitat: Mainly woodland; also dry habitats, including vineyards and mountains up to 6,560 ft (2,000 m)

Size: Length head/body: 4–6.5 in (10–17 cm); tail: 3.5–6 in (9–15 cm). Weight: 1.6–4.2 oz (45–120 g). Weight increases before hibernation to 7.4 oz (210 g)

Form: Reddish brown or gray rodent with black stripe on each side of its face; large ears; white belly and paws; long, furry tail with white, flattened tuft at the end

Diet: Buds, nuts, fruit, insects, eggs; occasionally baby mice and birds

Breeding: One or 2 litters of 4–6 (up to 9) young born per year after 4-week gestation. Life span can exceed 5 years

Related endangered species: Black-tailed dormouse *(Eliomys melanurus)* LRnt; Japanese dormouse *(Glirulus japonicus)* EN; Chinese forest dormouse *(Dryomys sichuanensis)* EN

Status: IUCN VU; not listed by CITES

absent in the forests and rocky mountainsides where many garden dormice live, so competition with rats cannot be the only explanation for its disappearance over such a wide range of different habitats and in so many countries.

Humans pose no direct threat. Unlike the edible dormouse—the largest of the dormice (also known as the fat dormouse and considered a delicacy in Roman times, when they were specially reared for food)—the garden dormouse has never been hunted; nor is its skin of value. Animal predators such as owls do not represent a substantial threat and are certainly unable to exterminate whole populations. All dormice have an

The garden dormouse *has distinctive black markings around the eyes. A nocturnal animal, it lives in small social groups on the ground and in trees and bushes. Dormice hibernate and have a reputation as sleepy animals. The edible and common dormice stay dormant for longest: from September to April.*

interesting adaptation to evade capture. If a predator grabs at the tail, the thin skin slips off, allowing the dormouse to escape. The tail later drops off, but the dormouse survives. As yet no one knows why, despite such adaptability and resilience, the garden dormouse is in decline, or what can be done about it.

Volcano Rabbit

Romerolagus diazi

The volcano rabbit is one of the world's rarest mammals, yet it lives within a short distance of one of the world's most densely populated human settlements: Mexico City.

The high ground overlooking the Valley of Mexico is studded with volcanoes, some more active than others. The lower southern slopes of the valley are dominated by natural forests of pine and alder, with a dense understory of scrub. At higher altitudes these forests give way to tussocky "zacaton" grassland made up of bunch grasses such as *Epicampes* and *Festuca* species. The volcano rabbit, or zacatuche, lives at the treeline, where the forests meet the zacaton.

The volcano rabbit has been rare for as long as records have been kept; whether the low numbers are due to natural causes or centuries of persecution is not certain. However, the rabbit's specialized habitat requirements suggest that it has never been widespread. The zacaton habitat is unique to this part of Mexico and is itself at risk.

Volcano rabbits are smaller than their more familiar cousins, but in other respects have much in common with them. For example, volcano rabbits are great diggers and, like their relatives, will also develop a network of overground runways that crisscross through the dense grass. The most important similarity from a conservation point of view, however, is the volcano rabbit's relationship with local farmers—the animal is just as unpopular in Mexico as North American cottontails and European rabbits are with farming communities in their ranges. Under normal circumstances the rabbits feed mainly on the new shoots of wild grasses, but the temptation of cultivated oats and corn is too much to resist; given the chance, they will readily take advantage of the bountiful food supply.

A Change of Image

Local people have long regarded the volcano rabbit as a pest, and their attempts to eradicate it have very nearly succeeded. The rabbits have never been hunted for meat, but farmers have seen them as pests and shot them indiscriminately. They were also used for target practice by quail hunters.

Grazing cattle compete with the rabbits for food, and

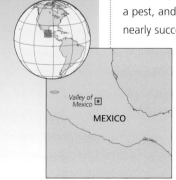

DATA PANEL

Volcano rabbit (zacatuche, teporingo)

Romerolagus diazi

Family: Leporidae

World population: About 1,000–1,200 (1964 estimate)

Distribution: Volcanic rim of the Valley of Mexico, near Mexico City

Habitat: Tussock grass on volcanic basalt at the edges of pine forests; found at altitudes of 9,200–14,000 ft (2,800–4,250 m)

Size: Length: 11–14 in (27–36 cm). Weight: 0.8–1.3 lb (390–600 g)

Form: Small and compact, with small ears and virtually no tail

Diet: Young zacaton grasses and leaves of other low-growing plants; bark from alder trees; some crops, including oats and corn

Breeding: Between 1 and 4 furry young born after gestation of 5–6 weeks at any time of year (with peak births in March–July); weaned at 3 weeks

Related endangered species: Amami rabbit *(Pentalagus furnessi)* EN; hispid hare *(Caprolagus hispidus)* EN; several other rabbit and hare species

Status: IUCN EN; CITES I

Valley of Mexico

MEXICO

their trampling feet alter the nature of the grasslands. The rabbits dig out their burrows and nests at the foot of big tussocks of grass. After heavy grazing these tussocks disappear, leaving the rabbits without shelter. The grasses are also harvested for thatch, becoming too closely cropped to offer cover from predators. Swathes of forest have been cleared, bringing settlements right up to the rabbits' habitat.

The volcano rabbits are now protected in several ways. The area where they live is designated as a national park. Hunting the rabbits is strictly illegal, although it undoubtedly still happens. The close proximity of Mexico City and the dramatic local scenery mean that the area is increasingly popular with

Volcano rabbits *look like smaller, slightly dumpier versions of their cousins, the North American cottontail and European rabbits, but their ears are noticeably smaller, and they have no powder-puff tail.*

tourists. The presence of tourists may help reduce incidences of illegal shooting. However, the increase in human traffic also brings a growing risk of forest fires. Before ecotourism projects can be set up, much remains to be done to encourage local people to respect a creature they currently view as vermin.

There are volcano rabbits in captivity. The British naturalist Gerald Durrell was one of the first to recognize the plight of the species; in the mid 1960s he established a small colony at Jersey Zoo in the Channel Islands, where the animals bred successfully for several years. Today volcano rabbit colonies are doing well in Mexico City Zoo and at other conservation centers in Mexico.

Giant Otter Shrew

Potamogale velox

The giant otter shrew occupies a large range in Central Africa. Nevertheless, it is poorly known, and its future is blighted by hunting, deforestation, pollution, and general lawlessness in areas of political instability.

The three species of otter shrew living in Africa are the only mainland members of the tenrec family, which is otherwise found exclusively on the island of Madagascar. Tenrecs were among the first mammals to colonize Madagascar from mainland Africa. For many thousands of years they had the place to themselves, and they diversified into an extraordinary range of forms and habits.

However, the mainland cousins of these early mammalian pioneers did not have it quite so easy. With other kinds of mammals already occupying niches in Africa's diverse habitats, they had to find alternative specializations in order to survive. The mainland otter shrews have evolved so much and become so different to the Malagasy branch of the family that some zoologists place them in a separate family of their own. Two small species live in tiny areas of West Africa and Uganda, but the giant otter shrew occurs widely across Central Africa.

Coveted Creatures

The giant otter shrew is one of the world's largest aquatic insectivores, almost as big as a true otter. Its common name is an apt one, since its specialization to an aquatic lifestyle makes it look much like a small otter or mink. Like both otters and mink, the giant otter shrew has fine, dense fur. The hairs trap an insulating layer of air, giving the shrew a silvery appearance under the water and helping keep it warm—even in tropical Africa mountain streams can be chilly.

Unfortunately, the animal's splendid pelt is coveted by humans, and the giant otter shrew has been hunted for its skin in many parts of its range.

DATA PANEL

Giant otter shrew (giant African water shrew)

Potamogale velox

Family: Tenrecidae

World population: Unknown

Distribution: Central Africa, including Nigeria, Gabon, Cameroon, Central African Republic, Uganda, Kenya, Democratic Republic of Congo (formerly Zaire), Rwanda, Burundi, Tanzania, Zambia, and Angola

Habitat: Fast- and slow-moving streams from sea level to 5,900 ft (1,800 m)

Size: Length head/body: 11.5–14 in (29–35 cm); tail: 9.5–35 in (24.5–90 cm). Weight: 12–14 oz (340–400 g)

Form: Otterlike animal with cylindrical body, powerful tail, and short legs; fur short and dense, brown to black above, pale below; head has broad, flat snout with stiff whiskers, small eyes, and small ears

Diet: Freshwater crustaceans (mainly crabs); also mollusks, fish, insects, and amphibians

Breeding: Two litters of 1 or 2 young born at any time of year

Related endangered species: Nimba otter shrew *(Micropotamogale lamottei)* EN; pygmy otter shrew *(M. ruwenzorii)* EN; aquatic tenrec *(Limnogale mergulus)* EN

Status: IUCN EN; not listed by CITES

While hunting is to be discouraged, the decline in giant otter shrew numbers probably has more to do with habitat destruction than with direct killing. The animals live in streams that pass through forested areas. They do not venture far from the water, and it is possible that they could survive with only a narrow strip of trees on either side of the watercourse. It would certainly cost the timber companies little to leave such areas alone when they cut down the rest of the forest. However, such narrow corridors of habitat are less useful to the majority of nonaquatic, forest-dwelling mammals, and most conservationists would prefer to see much larger areas of forest being protected so that other animals could also benefit.

Habitat Erosion

One of the side effects of deforestation is a dramatic increase in soil erosion. Soil and silt—no longer bound up by tree roots or protected and enriched by a layer of humus—are washed into streams and rivers every time it rains. In the wet season especially, a clear stream becomes a torrent of muddy water, and the effect is not limited to deforested areas. The mud is carried miles downstream, contaminating habitat that would otherwise still be suitable for otter shrews.

The giant otter shrew *has many of the characteristics of a true otter, including a powerful tail for swimming. It also has a flattened snout, with the nose, eyes, and ears near the top of the head, allowing it to see, hear and breathe with only a fraction of its head above water.*

The shrews have poor sight at the best of times and tend to rely more on scent and touch to find their prey. With the help of their other senses they are able to trap prey in cloudy water, even if visibility is reduced to zero. However, otter shrews can only hunt successfully if there is plenty of prey around. With mud and silt blocking out the sunlight, few aquatic plants can grow, so plant-eating stream creatures are scarce. The gills and filter-feeding mechanisms of fish and crustaceans become clogged, and they soon die off, leaving the otter shrews with nothing to eat.

There are no otter shrews in captivity, and nobody knows how many survive in the wild. However, the rapid destruction of their habitat by local and upstream deforestation means that they are facing a serious decline, and the situation is worsening.

133

Kitti's Hog-Nosed Bat

Craseonycteris thonglongyai

Kitti's hog-nosed bat is the smallest bat in the world. It was discovered only recently in a forest habitat in Thailand that had already been largely destroyed.

Imagine a creature with a body smaller than the top of an adult's thumb. Kitti's hog-nosed bat is the world's tiniest bat and probably the smallest of all mammals. A miracle of miniature engineering, all the organs found in the human body fit into a space the size of a large bumblebee; the bat's heart is scarcely bigger than a pinhead. Yet these minute and delicate mammals fly in the dark, pursue insects on the wing, and raise young just as other bats do.

Kitti's hog-nosed bat was only discovered in 1973. It has no close affinities with any other bat species, being classified in a family of its own. Its nearest relatives are thought to be the mouse-tailed bats of Africa and Asia that have similar piglike snouts.

However, these species have long, threadlike tails, while Kitti's hog-nosed bat has no tail at all; instead, its rear-end anatomy resembles that of the sheath-tailed bats of Africa and South America.

Hog-nosed bats come in two different shades of brown. The variation is often a distinction between young and old in bat species and may be so in Kitti's also. The bats have tiny eyes that are almost hidden in the fur of the face.

The only place where Kitti's hog-nosed bats are known to live is along the Kwai River at Sai Yok in western Thailand, a region riddled with small limestone caves. An area of about 2.5 square miles (6.5 sq. km) has been designated a national park where the bats are protected. Kitti's hog-nosed bats have been found in about two dozen caves, some outside the protected area.

Colonies in the Caves

The caves offer both protection and shelter from the daytime sun. The bats are sometimes found alone, but more often in small colonies of about 20 individuals. Even so, they tend to keep apart and do not cluster together as many bats do. They also feed alone and appear to be rather territorial.

As in other bat species, the females bear a single offspring, giving birth in the dry season from April to May. At birth the baby is about one-third the size of the mother. Although she may carry it with her on short journeys when flying from one part of the cave to another, she will leave the baby behind in the roost when going out at night in search of food.

DATA PANEL

Kitti's hog-nosed bat

Craseonycteris thonglongyai

Family: Craseonycteridae

World population: 2,000–2,500

Distribution: Western Thailand, along the Kwai River

Habitat: Deep caves in forest

Size: Length: 1.1–1.3 in (2.9–3.3 cm); wingspan: about 5.5 in (13.5 cm). Weight: about 0.07 oz (2 g)

Form: Minute bat with no tail; piglike snout with flattened end that is swollen around nostrils. Ears large and pointed

Diet: Tiny insects caught in flight

Breeding: Single young born once a year between April and May. Life span unknown, but likely to be at least 5–10 years

Related endangered species: No close relatives, but 1 mouse-tailed bat (*Rhinopoma macinnesi*) is listed as Vulnerable. Among sheath-tailed bats *Coleura seychellensis* and *Taphozous troughtoni* are Critically Endangered, *Balantiopteryx infusca* and *Emballonura semicaudata* are Endangered, and 9 other similar species are Vulnerable

Status: IUCN EN; not listed by CITES

MYANMAR
LAOS
THAILAND
VIETNAM
CAMBODIA

Kitti's hog-nosed bat *is a shy creature, seeking refuge in the darkest recesses of its limestone cave. Its wings are relatively broad, a shape that is associated in other species with fluttering flight and the ability to hover. The adaptation may have helped the bats maneuver among dense foliage.*

Kitti's hog-nosed bats seem to be most active in the first hour after dark. They then rest for a few hours, becoming active again shortly before dawn, when they return to their daytime roosts.

Like other bats, Kitti's hog-nosed use echolocation to find their way around in the dark, emitting sounds at high frequencies that are inaudible to the human ear, and then listening for the echoes to indicate potential obstacles in their path. Sound reflects well from cave walls, so echolocation is a good way of navigating in the total darkness of their underground homes. However, the sense is probably of less use to them when hunting; it seems likely that they also use their acute hearing to detect the wing beats of insects.

Habitat Changes

At one time Kitti's hog-nosed bats hunted among the dense foliage of the tropical forest, snatching insects from the air and hovering to pick spiders and insect larvae off leaves. However, much of the forest was cleared in the 1950s to make way for farmland and teak plantations, and the bats now feed among fields of cassava or kapok, taking mostly tiny flies. They seem to be active in the open, rarely flying near the vegetation or more than 15 feet (5 m) off the ground, and so have presumably been forced to alter their feeding behavior in response to the habitat changes. It is difficult to confirm this fact, however, because the bats are not just tiny but also nocturnal, and so are unusually hard to observe in their natural habitat.

Kitti's hog-nosed bat is considered to be endangered because of its restricted range in a region that has been heavily affected by human activity. Even though their caves are now mostly protected, the animals still risk occasional disturbance from visitors eager to see the world's smallest bat species.

135

Ryukyu Flying Fox

Pteropus dasymallus

The Ryukyu flying fox is typical of many fruit bats living on islands; it faces a range of threats, and already one subspecies seems to be extinct.

There are five local varieties of the Ryukyu flying fox, which vary in size and color. They each live on different islands; and because their habitats are mostly small, the animals have probably never been very numerous.

The flying foxes are not foxes at all, but large fruit-eating bats. They live in the warmer regions of Asia and on islands in the Pacific and Indian Oceans. Like other flying foxes, they form colonies, hanging like furled umbrellas, spaced out along the bare branches of trees. Sometimes the colonies are large and conspicuous. Their habit of hanging out in the open makes the bats vulnerable to the slightest disturbance and to being shot or captured.

Capture is a common problem for all the larger fruit bats, since they are meaty and good to eat. Large numbers have been routinely collected for food, often by plundering the nursery colonies where the young bats are reared. Such disturbance results in the loss or abandonment of many youngsters. Like other bats, if the young

fall to the ground before they can fly properly, they are generally unable to get airborne again. Often they are killed by dogs, land crabs, and even armies of ants. Bats also produce only one young a year, so replacement of losses is a slow process.

Ecological Eating

Fruit bats feed mainly on soft fruit borne by trees in the forest. They often just squeeze the fruit in their mouths and swallow only the juice, spitting out (or dropping) most of the pips and pulp at some distance from the tree. Any swallowed pips or seeds pass undamaged through the digestive tract and are discarded with the feces, often miles from where the fruit was collected. This is an important mechanism for dispersing the seeds of forest trees. Many fruit bats, including the Ryukyu flying fox, also feed on flowers at certain times of the year and help pollinate them, thus performing another essential ecological role. Consequently, the preservation of fruit bat populations is needed for the continued survival of a sustainable forest ecosystem.

DATA PANEL

Ryukyu flying fox

Pteropus dasymallus

Family: Pteropodidae

World population: A few hundred

Distribution: Ryukyu (Nansei) Islands, Japan

Habitat: Forest, fruit trees

Size: Length: 8 in (22 cm); wingspan: over 3 ft (1 m). Weight: 1 lb (400–450 g)

Form: Large fruit bat with typical "foxy" face and big eyes. Varies in color from pale brown to black, sometimes with pale collar or chest

Diet: Variety of fruit, especially figs; also flowers, insects, and leaves

Breeding: One young born per year. Life span unknown but could be 20 years

Related endangered species: Rodrigues flying fox *(Pteropus rodricensis)* CR. The IUCN lists 34 other species of *Pteropus* among the threatened mammals, including 5 others that are Critically Endangered

Status: IUCN EN; CITES II

A Fragile Future

The conservation of flying foxes and other fruit bats is essential, yet many species are threatened and fast disappearing. For example, numbers of the Taiwanese subspecies of the Ryukyu flying fox have declined sharply as a result of poor enforcement of protection laws. Recent surveys have failed to find any individuals, and this flying fox may already be extinct. Elsewhere, other subspecies of the Ryukyu flying fox are threatened by loss of habitat in which to roost and feed as trees are removed for the timber industry, fuel, and to create farmland.

In the past hunters have killed large numbers of flying foxes, reducing the population drastically. In some places the bats also sustain losses through flying

The Ryukyu flying fox, *like other species of flying fox, has a doglike face and large ears. Flying foxes navigate using their eyesight and sense of smell to locate the fruit and flowers on which they feed at night.*

into overhead electricity and telephone wires. Contact with the wires can result in electrocution, strangulation, or broken wings.

The Japanese government has given the Ryukyu flying fox legal protection. However, it has not created any protected areas in which the bats can live undisturbed. Although the flying fox is reported to be numerous on a couple of the islands around Japan, forest removal is still badly affecting the Ryukyu group.

Mulgara

Dasycercus cristicauda

Mulgara numbers fluctuate widely throughout much of their range. Nevertheless, there is little doubt that in the 200 years since Europeans settled in Australia, the mulgara's range has shrunk and the population declined.

The status of the ratlike mulgara of central Australia is something of a mystery. It seems that local mulgara populations are prone to dramatic peaks and troughs, probably brought on by the unpredictable rains and droughts in their desert habitat. The mulgara population is more stable in some parts of its range than in others. It is considered common in the Northern Territories of central Australia, for example, while the few mulgara populations in neighboring Queensland fluctuate wildly; they are sometimes thought to be extinct, only to reappear at a later date.

To add to the confusion, it now seems that many of the animals formerly regarded as mulgaras may, in fact, be a different species, known as the ampurta. Ampurtas live in the east of the mulgara's range, and it is virtually impossible to tell the two types—be they species or subspecies—apart except by analysis of their DNA.

Shrinking Range

Mulgaras were once common over a wide area, including what are now the Northern Territories, South Australia, and Western Australia. There were also stable populations in Queensland and New South Wales. The only place they appear to be doing well now is the Northern Territories. Isolated populations survive in parts of Western Australia and also in a few sites on the borders of the Northern Territories with Queensland and South Australia.

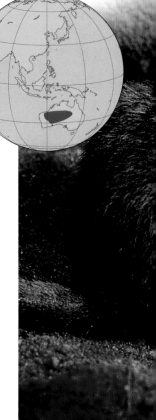

DATA PANEL

Mulgara (crest-tailed marsupial mouse)

Dasycercus cristicauda

Family: Dasyuridae

World population: Unknown; thought to fluctuate widely

Distribution: Widespread, but patchy in Western Australia, southern Northern Territories, and northern South Australia

Habitat: Sandy, semiarid grasslands

Size: Length: 5–8 in (12.5–22 cm); tail: 3–5 in (7–13 cm); males up to twice as large as females. Weight: 2–6 oz (60–170 g)

Form: Sandy-brown, ratlike marsupial; crest of black hairs blends into black fur on second half of tail; female lacks true pouch

Diet: Small mammals, reptiles, and invertebrates; seeds and root tubers

Breeding: Between 6 and 8 young born in May–June after 4-week gestation; remain attached to teat in fold of skin on belly for up to 2 months; independent at 4 months. Life span unknown

Related endangered species: Several other small species of insectivorous marsupial in Australia and New Guinea listed as VU or EN

Status: IUCN VU; not listed by CITES

The main causes of decline are predation by dingoes and introduced cats and dogs. The mulgara's habitat has also been altered and destroyed in places. The largest and best-known population is protected in the Uluru-Kata Tjita National Park in the Northern Territories, but even here not enough is known about the precise requirements of the mulgaras to ensure that the land is managed appropriately.

Picky Eaters

Mulgaras appear to be extremely fussy about their habitat. They live in burrows dug in dry, sandy soils and hunt for food among shoots of spinifex (a spiny-leaved inland grass also known as porcupine grass). However, mulgaras appear to prefer clumps that are about 10 years old, moving on when the centers of large old clumps begin to die off. They also avoid the new growth that springs up in the years after the grasses have been burned. Livestock farmers use regular controlled burning to keep down scrub and to encourage the growth of fresh new grass to feed their cattle and sheep. Cycles of natural burning and regrowth are a normal part of the mulgara's habitat; but when the farmers artificially set fire to the vegetation, the cycles are shorter. As a result, the spinifex rarely has long enough to develop and mature to the mulgaras' satisfaction.

The specific conditions favored by the mulgara are similar to those required by two other vulnerable Australian animals, the southern marsupial mole and the great desert skink (a type of lizard). Currently, conservationists are working on plans for controlling predators and maintaining suitable habitat that will benefit all three species.

__The mulgara__ is small and ratlike in appearance. It feeds mainly on insects and small animals, and has many small, sharp teeth.

Kangaroo Island Dunnart

Sminthopsis aitkeni

Seen only eight times in a quarter of a century, the Kangaroo Island dunnart is both rare and elusive. Efforts are underway to find out more about the animal so that it can be conserved.

Until the late 1960s there were thought to be no dunnarts of any species living on Kangaroo Island off the coast of South Australia. However, in 1969 a domestic dog captured and killed two specimens of what appeared to be the common dunnart. It was reported that the dog had caught the mouselike animals as they fled from yacca trees that were being felled to make way for farmland. At the time common dunnarts were considered to be relatively abundant and widespread on the mainland of Australia. However, since they had never before been found on Kangaroo Island, the corpses were considered important enough to be sent to the Museum of South Australia in Adelaide.

By the mid-1980s science had progressed sufficiently to allow closely related species to be distinguished by biochemical differences. As a result, many similar-looking animals could now be separated out and

given the full species status they deserved. The common dunnart was a worthy candidate for such treatment. When specimens from different parts of Australia were processed in 1984, it became clear that there were, in fact, four species of "common dunnart" that had been grouped together because they looked so similar. Three of them—the common dunnart (from southeastern Australia), the little long-tailed dunnart, and Gilbert's dunnart (both from Western Australia)—appeared to be relatively secure. However, the newly named Kangaroo Island dunnart was an immediate conservation worry because no populations existed anywhere else.

Lack of Information

The Kangaroo Island dunnart appears to live in a variety of natural heathland habitats on the island; but the species is incredibly elusive, and its precise requirements are not known. The lack of sightings can be partly explained by the fact that the animals are

DATA PANEL				
Kangaroo Island dunnart (sooty dunnart) *Sminthopsis aitkeni* **Family:** Dasyuridae **World population:** Unknown, but tiny **Distribution:** Kangaroo Island, South Australia **Habitat:** Mallee (scrub) heathland		**Size:** Length head/body: 3–4 in (7.6–10 cm); tail: 3.5–4 in (9–10 cm); male about 10% larger than female. Weight: 0.7–0.9 oz (20–25 g) **Form:** Mouselike marsupial with long, tapering snout and long tail; fur grayish tinged with sooty black on back **Diet:** Probably insectivorous, like the closely related common dunnart		**Breeding:** Probably similar to common dunnart, with large litters born after short gestation; young weaned at about 2 months **Related endangered species:** Boullanger Island gray-bellied dunnart (*Sminthopsis grisoventer*) CR; Julia Creek dunnart (*S. douglasi*) EN; sandhill dunnart (*S. psammophilla*) EN; Butler's dunnart (*S. butleri*) VU; Queensland common dunnart (*S. murina tatei*) LRnt **Status:** IUCN EN; not listed by CITES

probably nocturnal. Like some of their mainland relatives, they may also go into a kind of hibernation during food shortages, seeking out secure refuges in which to hide. The absence of more detailed information is not due to a lack of effort. Indeed, there have been several attempts to survey the population using standard live-trapping techniques. So far all that biologists have learned is that the dunnart is rare—and cautious. After numerous trapping attempts only six individuals have been found, bringing the total of recorded specimens to just eight. What is almost certain is that wherever dunnarts live and breed on the island, they are at risk of dying out.

In 1983 laws were passed to protect native Australian vegetation, over 60 percent of which had already been cleared from Kangaroo Island for agriculture. Without knowing more about the dunnart's habitat, it is impossible to judge what effect land clearance might have had on numbers, or to take measures to safeguard its future.

Interim Measures

The manner in which the first Kangaroo Island dunnarts were discovered—they were caught by a domestic dog—showed only too clearly that introduced predators, including pets, are a serious threat to dunnart populations. The fact that such animals did not exist on Kangaroo Island until relatively recently may be the only reason the dunnarts have survived as long as they have. Until more is known about the species, the removal of predators and a complete ban on habitat disruption are the only measures that will have any chance of helping this endangered island mammal.

An extra-long tail *and black-tinted fur are the characteristics that set the Kangaroo Island dunnart apart from its common relative on the mainland. It was only recognized as a distinct species in 1984.*

Marsupial Mole

Notoryctes typhlops

Of all Australia's mammals, the marsupial moles of the western desert are certainly among the more unusual species. Since they normally spend almost their entire lives buried in the sandy soil, they are also among the least well understood.

Before declaring an animal Endangered, the IUCN normally needs convincing scientific evidence that the species is likely to become extinct unless the causes of the declining numbers are removed. In most cases the evidence for a species' decline is not difficult to come by—we can often easily see there are fewer individuals than there once were. Occasionally, however, there are exceptions; in the case of the marsupial moles of Australia the IUCN agreed to classify the species as Endangered even though most scientists who have tried to study the species admit that they have no idea how many marsupial moles there may be.

Marsupial moles are extraordinary for many reasons. In lifestyle and appearance they are very similar to African golden moles; but other than the fact that both are mammals, they are only distantly related. The similarities are a stunning example of what biologists call convergent evolution, where two completely different types of animal evolve into very similar forms because it is the best way of dealing with similar challenges of habitat or way of life. In the case of the marsupial mole the challenge is how to live buried in the desert sand.

Two of a Kind

The marsupial mole (sometimes also called the southern marsupial mole) has been known about since the 19th century. However, individuals are rarely seen—which is not surprising given the animal's way of life. In 1920 a new sort of marsupial mole was discovered close to Eighty Mile Beach on the northwestern coast of Western Australia. This variety, called the northern marsupial mole, was a little smaller than the southern marsupial mole, and it had a differently shaped nose-shield and tail.

Whether the northern marsupial mole qualifies as a separate species is the subject of a debate that is unlikely to be resolved, since the animals are so hard to find. However, from time to time specimens of the southern marsupial mole are discovered. People finding the moles are usually puzzled enough to contact a museum or university, and dead or dying specimens have been collected at a rate of five to 15 animals every 10 years.

The real challenge is to find and study a living marsupial mole of the northern variety. Scientists

DATA PANEL

Marsupial mole (southern marsupial mole)

Notoryctes typhlops

Family: Notoryctidae

World population: Unknown and almost impossible to estimate

Distribution: Northwestern Australia

Habitat: Desert burrows

Size: Length head/body: 4–6 in (10–16 cm); tail: 1 in (2.4 cm). Weight: 1.2–2.5 oz (35–70 g)

Form: Flat-bodied animal with pale-golden fur; very short legs; spadelike front feet; no functional eyes, ear hole hidden in fur; nose has tough, horny shield, tail short and stubby. Female has a pouch opening to rear

Diet: Insect grubs, particularly larvae of beetles and moths

Breeding: Unknown

Related endangered species: Northern marsupial mole *(Notoryctes caurinus)* EN, although it may not qualify as a separate species. Its scientific classification is the subject of a debate

Status: IUCN EN; not listed by CITES

AUSTRALIA

have spent years searching the deserts, enlisting the support of local people living in remote Aboriginal communities. In 1998 two schoolboys found and captured a living specimen of the northern marsupial mole, which ended up at the Museum of Western Australia. It did not adapt to life in captivity and died after about eight weeks, having not eaten well in all that time.

Marsupial moles do occasionally come to the surface, usually after rain. When they emerge, their bodies leave distinctive furrows in the sand, with marks either side where they have used their legs to haul themselves along. Further proof that the moles are around can be found by taking core samples of firm sand and looking for the oval-shaped areas of looser material that show a mole has passed through. Scientists have tried burying sound-sensitive microphones in the sand to detect passing moles. The problem with all such techniques is that, while they show that there are moles around, they do not give any idea how many there are. Until researchers can get some idea about population size, it is very difficult to prove what position the species is in.

There is no shortage of goodwill toward the moles, since they do not appear to damage human activities such as farming. They have been killed out of curiosity or for their silky fur, but are not deliberately hunted. The marsupial moles' chief problem is likely to be changes in their habitat due to controlled burning of bush and grass to create grazing pastures. Predation by introduced species, such as cats, could be a problem too. A high proportion of fox droppings have been found to contain marsupial mole remains, thus proving that the marsupial mole's predators are better at finding them than people are.

The marsupial mole *has fine, sandy-colored silky fur and shovellike hands, which it uses to "swim" through sand. It can be found up to 5 feet (1.5 m) below the surface. It has no eyes or obvious ears, which would quickly clog with sand, and the female's pouch opens toward the rear, so it does not get full of sand.*

Koala

Phascolarctos cinereus

The koala has enjoyed considerable conservation success. However, although it is no longer threatened with extinction, managing the remaining populations is proving problematic for conservationists.

Koalas manage to survive on a diet that no other mammal will touch—eucalyptus leaves. Tough, dry, and with a very low nutritional value, the leaves also contain indigestible materials and compounds that are highly poisonous to most other animals. Koalas are able to exist on this poor diet by having efficient digestive systems that will not only break down the toxins but also extract every available calorie. They also conserve energy by spending up to 20 hours a day resting. Until the arrival of European settlers in Australia in the late 18th century the ability of the koala to eke out a living from a food that no other animal could eat meant that it was a highly successful animal, well adapted to its diet and environment.

Consequences of Colonization

European settlement brought a number of threats to Australia's native wildlife. It destroyed the natural habitat and caused a marked increase in forest fires. The koala was also hunted for its fur. By the early 20th century koalas were facing a very real threat of extinction. Disaster was narrowly averted when the koala was made a nationally protected species in 1927. The koala has now returned to much of its original range; but because its habitat is patchy, it will never be as common as it once was. Although the koala as a species is out of immediate danger, individuals and localized populations are still threatened. Many koalas are killed on the roads or attacked by dogs, and forest fires can wipe out whole colonies at a time.

Victims of Success

The biggest problem is the patchy, isolated nature of the remaining koala habitat. The species responds so well to conservation that protected populations often increase to the point where the animals begin to damage the trees that they rely on for survival. Yet surplus animals cannot easily disperse if their forest home is surrounded by urban development or vast areas of open pastureland, as is now the case in much of eastern Australia. In overcrowded

DATA PANEL

Koala

Phascolarctos cinereus

Family: Phascolarctidae

World population: About 40,000, but estimates vary widely and are controversial

Distribution: Eastern Australia

Habitat: Eucalyptus forests below 2,000 ft (600 m)

Size: Length head/body: 28–31 in (72–78 cm); animals from south of range larger than those in north. Weight: 11–24 lb (5–11 kg); males can be half as heavy again as females

Form: Stout, bearlike animal with thick, woolly, grayish-brown fur on back, fading to white on belly. Head large with rounded furry ears, beady black eyes, and large black nose. Legs short with 5 large claws on each foot.

Tail short and stumpy. Female has pouch that opens to the rear

Diet: Leaves of various species of eucalyptus

Breeding: Single young (occasionally twins) born in midsummer after gestation of 25–30 days; young spend 5–7 months in pouch, weaned at 6–12 months; mature at 2 years. Life span up to 20 years

Related endangered species: No close relatives, but the northern hairy-nosed wombat (*Lasiorhinus krefftii*) of northeastern Australia is listed as CR

Status: IUCN LRnt; not listed by CITES

AUSTRALIA

conditions the koala is especially vulnerable to a disease caused by the *Chlamydia psittaci* bacterium. Conservation programs therefore face the difficult task of establishing healthy koala populations without creating overpopulated, disease-ridden colonies in which surplus animals have to be culled.

The least damaging solution is to move the excess koalas to other areas of suitable habitat. However, after 200 years of logging, development, and clearance for agriculture there are very few large areas of eucalyptus forest available. Consequently, koalas are often moved to other isolated patches of woodland where they soon become overcrowded again. The only real solution is to create "corridors" of habitat linking the isolated patches so that koala populations can

Koalas, *like other Australian marsupials, are born very early and suckled by their mother—often in a pouch—for the first months of life. Koala young are weaned on to "pap," a special form of the mother's droppings that provides the baby with the gut bacteria it needs to digest eucalyptus leaves.*

spread themselves more evenly. Tracts of suitable land connecting isolated koala populations would benefit the species in other ways: When koala colonies are decimated by natural events such as forest fires or outbreaks of *Chlamydia*, koalas dispersing from other areas would be able to recolonize the affected sites.

Long-Beaked Echidna

Zaglossus bruijni

The long-beaked echidna is a reclusive animal that feeds mainly on the worms and small grubs it finds in the wet forest leaf litter. A slow breeder, it is hunted for food and suffers from habitat loss.

The long-beaked echidna is an egg-laying mammal that inhabits the thick, humid forests of New Guinea, an island north of Australia. It lives alone, sheltering in a burrow or other hideout during the day. Since it seems to be active largely at night and is rare, even in undisturbed habitats, it is difficult to study, and little is known of its habits. A 1998 report suggests that there may be three species of long-beaked echidna, but one is known from only a single specimen and may already be extinct.

Unlike its cousin the short-beaked echidna, which feeds extensively on ants and termites, the long-beaked echidna seems to specialize in eating worms. It seeks them out by poking its long, curved snout into rotting wood or under moss and leaves. The jaws do not open far, and they are weak and have no teeth, so the food must be swallowed without being chewed. Worms, beetle larvae, and grubs of all sorts are abundant in wet forest leaf litter, so there is normally sufficient food even for such a large creature.

Rare Animals

When the forests are cut down, the ground dries out, and the staple foods of the echidna's diet become less abundant. Felling trees also removes the availability of rotten wood, a vital source of invertebrate food. Large areas of forest have been cleared in New Guinea to make way for new villages, roads, mines, and farms. Still more has been felled for timber. The echidnas can now only survive in the remote areas where they are not troubled by such developments. They appear to have become extinct in the central highlands within the last 50 years, and they are no longer found in most of the northern areas of New Guinea.

Echidnas have been hunted by specially trained dogs and their meat is highly prized by native people as a rare delicacy to be eaten at traditional feasts. Echidnas cannot climb, run fast, or attack predators, so they are easily captured. It is said that echidnas live at an average density of 4 per square mile (1 or 2 per sq. km).

DATA PANEL

Long-beaked echidna

Zaglossus bruijni

Family: Tachyglossidae

World population: Unknown, probably low thousands

Distribution: New Guinea (Papua New Guinea and West Irian, a province of Indonesia)

Habitat: Various habitats from lowland tropical jungles to mountain forests and grasslands at more than 13,000 ft (4,000 m) above sea level

Size: Length: 18–30 in (45–77 cm); height at shoulder: about 10 in (25 cm). Weight: 11–22 lb (5–10 kg)

Form: A small animal covered in short, thick spines and dense, black hair. Long, tubular, downcurved snout. Feet have large claws; hind ones point sideways; walks slowly with rolling gait

Diet: Invertebrates, mainly earthworms

Breeding: Details unknown, but probably lays 1 egg per year in July; egg is incubated in temporary pouch on the mother's belly. Young fed on milk for several months before becoming independent. A long-beaked echidna has lived more than 30 years in captivity; life span in the wild unknown

Related endangered species: Short-beaked echidna *(Tachyglossus aculeatus multiaculeatus)* LRnt

Status: IUCN EN; CITES II

INDONESIA

New Guinea

PAPUA NEW GUINEA

AUSTRALIA

Multiplying this by the area of suitable habitat suggests that there may be over 300,000 animals in total, but such a figure is unlikely. In a sample of skulls from the remains of several thousand native animals killed for consumption in traditional feasts there was only one long-beaked echidna.

The long-beaked echidna breeds very slowly, producing only a single baby each year. The young are extremely vulnerable and almost defenseless for many months (apart from their spines). As a result of its slow breeding rate, the species is unable to sustain heavy losses. Echidnas are not at risk from large natural predators since there are none living on New Guinea. Consequently, their spines have evolved to offer the animal only limited protection. However, introduced dogs and increasing numbers of people present

The long-beaked echidna *is one of the few egg-laying mammals. In this young echidna (above) the black fur is not yet fully developed. The spines show up clearly in the photograph, taken at night with flash illumination.*

dangers that the animal cannot withstand. Long-beaked echidnas have full legal protection, but the law is not always enforced in remote areas.

Little is known about the breeding biology of echidnas; outside New Guinea specimens are kept in only one zoo in Sydney, Australia. Even the short-beaked echidna has rarely bred in captivity, so there seems to be little prospect of developing a "safety net" of captive-bred echidnas as an insurance against extinction. Maximum protection in the Lorenz National Park and other nature reserves in New Guinea is vital. **147**

Platypus

Ornithorhynchus anatinus

Platypuses are no longer hunted for their fur, but they face threats from pollution and the environmental consequences of modern development. The platypus has become a well-known conservation symbol for its freshwater habitat of southeastern Australia.

European settlers in Australia first saw and described the duck-billed platypus in 1797, but it was another hundred years before the animal's unique anatomy and reproductive habits were scientifically studied. In the past the platypus was hunted extensively for its fur, which, like that of other aquatic mammals, is extremely dense, so it keeps the animal warm even when wet. Thousands of platypuses were killed for their skins, while the heads and bills were sold as curios.

Hunting has all but exterminated the platypus population of South Australia: The last sighting of the animals on the lower Murray River, one of Australia's major rivers, was as long ago as 1960. The only platypuses living in the state these days are an introduced population on Kangaroo Island off South Australia and a few animals in captivity. Today wild platypuses still occasionally come across the border from New South Wales.

People are not the only predators to have taken a serious toll. In the days before European settlement the only predator of the platypus was the native Australian water rat. In recent times, however, introduced foxes, cats, rats, and dogs have all killed platypuses, especially young ones. Road deaths are also becoming a problem in urban areas.

The Costs of Development

The main problems facing platypuses today are those associated with modern development. Pollution and physical changes threaten the waters where they live. Many rivers have become unsuitable for platypuses through dramatically altered rates of flow as a result of the diversion of water for human use. Artificial structures such as weirs, drains, dams, and grilles built

AUSTRALIA

DATA PANEL

Platypus (duck-billed platypus)

Ornithorhynchus anatinus

Family: Ornithorhynchidae

World population: Unknown; low thousands

Distribution: Fresh waters of eastern Australia; throughout Tasmania and King Island in the Bass Strait; introduced population on Kangaroo Island off South Australia

Habitat: Freshwater rivers, lakes, and lagoons

Size: Length: 12–22 in (30–55 cm); males up to 20% bigger than females on mainland, but in Tasmania the sexes are similarly sized. Weight: 1–5.5 lb (0.5–2.5 kg)

Form: Unlike any other mammal; body is robust and slightly flattened, covered in dense, brown fur; legs short, feet large and webbed; tail flattened from above and paddlelike; head dominated by large, soft, rubbery beak, eyes small, ears hidden in fur; male has prominent sharp spurs on hind feet

Diet: Mostly freshwater crustaceans, worms, and insect larvae; some small fish and frogs

Breeding: One to 3 (usually 2) sticky-shelled eggs laid August–October after 2-week gestation; incubated by mother for further 2 weeks before hatching; young feed on milk from ducts on mother's belly; weaned at 4–5 months; mature at 2 years. Life span up to 15 years in the wild

Related endangered species: No close relatives

Status: Not listed by IUCN; not listed by CITES

The platypus's bill *is not really like that of a duck. Soft and leathery, it is well supplied with nerve endings. When hunting underwater, the platypus keeps its eyes closed and "feels" its way around with the bill, which can even sense electrical activity in the nerves of invertebrate prey.*

across rivers to trap debris can make it difficult for platypuses to travel far.

Pollution is a problem for all freshwater animals. The particular threat for the platypus is that the fine, dense fur that it relies on for warmth underwater can be fouled by waste chemicals, while detergents in the water may destroy the natural oils that keep it waterproof. An adult platypus eats a great deal—up to half its own body weight every night—so anything that affects its food soon has a carry-over effect on platypus numbers. For example, nutrient enrichment by fertilizers washed off farmland may seem like the opposite of poisoning, but ultimately it is just as damaging. In a process known as "eutrophication" sudden blooms of algae—caused by the extra nutrients—can quickly choke a river or lake, using up all the available oxygen so that other plants and invertebrates cannot survive. It is also the case that some kinds of blue-green algae are highly toxic and can kill even quite large animals.

Studies of the platypus in captivity are allowing a better understanding of the problems it faces in the wild. For example, recent studies in South Australia—aimed at improving the success of captive-breeding programs—highlighted the importance of maintaining the natural chemical balance of the platypus's remaining wild habitat. Before 1990 only one platypus had ever been produced in captivity. As a result of the captive research it is now clear that factors such as the relative acidity of the water play a crucial role in breeding success.

The platypus is a popular animal that attracts much public attention. As such, it is a fine example of a "flagship species." Conservation measures designed to help it also benefit the rest of the ecosystem in which it lives. What is good for the platypus turns out to be helpful for less publicized aquatic creatures too.

Brown Kiwi

Apteryx mantelli

The mainland populations of the unique brown kiwi—found only in New Zealand—have suffered huge declines in the 20th century, mainly due to plundering by introduced predators.

The female brown kiwi *lays large eggs: Each egg weighs as much as 20 percent of her body weight.*

With its shaggy, hairlike plumage, a plump, round body, a lack of visible tail or wings, and an ability to track down food in the dead of night, kiwis resemble nocturnal mammals rather than typical birds. Like many mammals, they also rest and shelter their young in burrows and mark their boundaries with strong-smelling droppings; the bristly modified feathers at the base of the bill serve as whiskers for feeling in the dark. Isolated for millions of years on New Zealand—where there are no native mammals except bats—the brown kiwi has occupied a niche that elsewhere would be filled by a mammal.

Kiwis are the smallest living ratites—a group of flightless birds that includes the ostrich, rheas, cassowaries, and the emu, none of which are nocturnal. Until recently ornithologists recognized three species of kiwi: the little spotted kiwi, the brown kiwi, and the great spotted kiwi. Genetic research has led to the brown kiwi being split into two distinct species, the brown kiwi and the tokoeka of a few areas in South Island. The Maori name kiwi comes from the shrill call of males, which punctuates the night, especially during the breeding season.

Long-Term Decline

Brown kiwis were once widespread throughout North Island and the northern part of South Island. Although they were hunted by the Maori—who had colonized New Zealand from the Pacific by the 12th century—this probably had little effect on overall numbers. It was not until the European settlers arrived in the mid-19th century that persecution of the birds began in earnest, as hunters tried to satisfy the demand for kiwi plumage by the clothing trade. A law banning the hunting, capture, or killing of kiwis was passed in 1908, but the pace of land clearance for agriculture and settlements destroyed much of the kiwi's forest habitat. The birds' fate was further sealed by the introduction of predatory mammals such as cats, dogs, and stoats. As a result of the combined threats, large-scale losses of brown kiwis occurred.

Researchers think that numbers of brown kiwis have fallen by at least 90 percent over the last 100 years and continue to decline at about 6 percent every year (in studied sites). This represents the halving of the population each decade. However, the species' overall decline is probably below 80 percent, thanks to the stability of the populations introduced to islands where predators are removed—and also to effective predator control in mainland sites.

The main threat facing the brown kiwi is still introduced predators, especially since it evolved with no native predators. At least 94 percent of kiwi chicks die before they reach breeding age (about 14 months for males and two years for females). Half of this mortality is due to predation. The other main cause of decline is the clearance of native forest, which threatens small, isolated populations. Many kiwis also

The brown kiwi ~~is nocturnal and has tiny, poorly~~
developed eyes that enable it to see only a few yards ahead.
Unusually for a bird, it detects its prey by smell.

used to die in traps set to catch predators or possums;
animals reached plague proportions in some areas.
Today this is avoided by raising traps above the ground
so that the kiwis do not stumble upon them.

Conservation

Conservationists have an accurate picture of kiwi
populations thanks to an intensive, nationally
coordinated program of monitoring. By culling
introduced predators and by removing
eggs and hand-rearing the young to
an age when they can fend off
attacks, key populations have been
helped. Continued protection is
needed to save the brown kiwi.

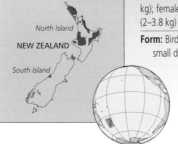

North Island
NEW ZEALAND
South Island

DATA PANEL

Brown kiwi

Apteryx mantelli

Family: Apterygidae

World population: About 35,000 birds

Distribution: North Island in Northland;
Coromandel Peninsula from Gisborne to
northern Ruahine Range, and Tongariro
to Taranaki. Introduced to Little Barrier,
Kawau, and Pounui Islands. Isolated
population on Okarito, South Island, may
be a separate species with Critical status

Habitat: Subtropical and temperate
forests; regenerating forest, shrubland,
pine plantations, and pastureland

Size: Length: 16 in (40 cm). Weight:
male 3–6.5 lb (1.4–3
kg); female 4.5–8 lb
(2–3.8 kg)

Form: Bird the size of a
small dog; small

head; long, slightly downcurved bill with
bristles at base; long neck (usually
drawn in); rotund body covered with
coarse, hairlike plumage that is dark
gray-brown with red-brown streaks;
rudimentary wing stubs in plumage;
strong legs; 4 toes on each foot

Diet: Invertebrates in soil and leaf litter,
especially earthworms, spiders, and
insects; also fruit, seeds, and leaves

Breeding: Female lays 1 or 2 very large
eggs in August–September in burrow or
natural cavity; egg(s) incubated by male
for 11–12 weeks; chick(s) independent
at 14–20 days; fully grown by 20
months

Related endangered species: Great
spotted kiwi *(Apteryx haastii)* VU; little
spotted kiwi *(A. owenii)* VU; tokoeka
(A. australis) VU

Status: IUCN EN; not listed by CITES

Galápagos Penguin

Spheniscus mendiculus

The only species of penguin to live on the Equator, the portly Galápagos penguin breeds on at least five of the Galápagos Islands. Because of its restricted range and very small population, a sharp decline in numbers is particularly disturbing.

Penguins are normally associated with cold habitats in and around Antarctica, although several species have ranges that include warmer climates. The Humboldt penguin, for instance, breeds in coastal Chile and Peru. However, the Galápagos penguin—a close relative of the Humboldt—is the only species that lives entirely within the tropics, on at least five islands of the Galápagos group. Life at such latitudes is challenging for the birds, since their insulating plumage, underlying fat, and specialized blood heat exchange—all adaptations for surviving in very cold water—make it difficult for them to cope with the tropical heat when on land. Temperatures in the Galápagos Islands can rise to more than 104°F (40°C).

Adaptations to Heat

In order to survive the heat, the Galápagos penguin has various anatomical and behavioral adaptations. It is one of the smallest penguin species, and the smaller an animal, the greater its surface area relative to its total size. Consequently, the Galápagos penguin has a large surface area from which to dissipate (lose) heat when on land. Heat loss is made easier by its having shorter feathers than any other species of penguin.

When ashore, the adults seek shade. They lose more heat by increasing the blood flow to their flippers, feet, and bare facial patches. The flippers are proportionately larger than those of cold-climate penguins, increasing the area where heat exchange can take place. The animals' blood supply can also bypass the heat-transfer system that helps maintain their body temperature in cold water.

Galápagos penguins often breed in rock crevices and caves, such as lava tubes (natural tunnels in lava flows) that shade the birds and their chicks from the sun.

Major Threats

The Galápagos penguin depends directly on the surrounding ocean for its survival.

DATA PANEL

Galápagos penguin

Spheniscus mendiculus

Family: Spheniscidae

World population: Fluctuates greatly; currently estimated at 1,200 individuals

Distribution: Galápagos Islands, Ecuador

Habitat: Breeds on low-lying areas of coastal, volcanic desert, rarely more than 55 yards (50 m) inland; feeds around upwellings of cool, nutrient-rich inshore waters

Size: Length: 19–21 in (48–53 cm); height: 14 in (35 cm). Weight: average 3.8–5.7 lb (1.7–2.6 kg)

Form: Small with black head; white stripes on face; black to brownish back and tail; chin and underparts white; variable pattern of black spots and irregular black bands on breast; flippers brown-black above, white below; male more boldly marked. Juveniles have grayish upperparts and lack distinctive face pattern

Diet: Schools of ocean fish, including sardines and mullet. Possibly crustaceans

Breeding: Breeds at any time, in small colonies or singly, when food supply is adequate; nests in lava tubes, rock crevices, or caves, at least partly shaded from the sun; 2 white eggs laid per breeding attempt; pair shares incubation that lasts 5–6 weeks; young leave nest at 8.5–9 weeks

Related endangered species: Nine other penguin species are threatened, including African penguin (*Spheniscus demersus*) VU; Humboldt penguin (*S. humboldti*) VU; erect-crested penguin (*Eudyptes sclateri*) EN; Snares penguin (*E. robustus*) VU

Status: IUCN EN; not listed by CITES

COSTA RICA
PANAMA
COLOMBIA
Galápagos
Islands
(Ecuador)
ECUADOR
PERU

The Cromwell Current, an upwelling of cool, nutrient-rich water, maintains the fish stocks that the penguins rely on for food. The current is susceptible to a periodic climatic event called the El Niño Southern Oscillation (ENSO). Records show that a population of 3,400 penguins declined by 77 percent between 1982 and 1983—an ENSO year that adversely affected the Cromwell Current, reducing fish stocks and causing thousands of birds to starve. It is likely that more females than males died, which would have slowed the recovery of the population. Another ENSO event in 1997 caused a further decline of 66 percent.

Galápagos penguins are known to be slow breeders, the birth rate averaging out at only 1.3 chicks per year. In ENSO years the entire population can fail to breed at all. The animals also have a restricted breeding range, with about 95 percent nesting on just two islands. Chicks and eggs are vulnerable to natural predators such as rice rats, snakes, and crabs. More serious threats are posed by introduced predators, including feral dogs, cats, and brown and black rats, which kill adults and chicks.

Galápagos penguins *feed on the rich fish stocks around the Galápagos Islands. The small, dapper bird has large flippers and feet that help it dissipate body heat.*

A tenfold increase in the permanent human population of the Galápagos in the last 40 years has led to disturbance of breeding sites and an expansion of coastal fisheries. Penguins are caught in nets and suffer from competition for fish stocks. Tourism adds to disruption; visitors come to look at the birds.

To ensure the continued survival of the Galápagos penguin, controls on fisheries, oil spills, human disturbance, and the introduction of mammalian predators are urgently required, as are scientific studies of the penguins to help increase their breeding success rate. Most importantly, we need to cut fossil fuel emissions to reduce global warming, which is likely to increase ENSO events.

Bermuda Petrel

Pterodroma cahow

The story of this graceful seabird is an extraordinary saga of rediscovery after hundreds of years of presumed extinction, followed by a steady increase in numbers due to the efforts of conservationists. The population is still dangerously small, however, and the bird continues to face several threats.

Bermuda is made up of about 150 small islands in the northwestern Atlantic Ocean, 750 miles (1,200 km) off the east coast of the United States. As well as serving as a useful stopover site in spring and fall for windblown migrants, it is home to one of the world's rarest seabirds, the Bermuda petrel.

Also known as the cahow in imitation of its eerie mating calls, the bird is one of the so-called gadfly petrels of the *Pterodroma* genus. They are graceful, long-winged birds, fast in flight, alternating bursts of rapid wingbeats with long glides. They rarely alight on the water, feeding on the wing by seizing small sea creatures such as squid from just below the water's surface with their sharp, hooked bills. In contrast, they are awkward on land, managing only a shuffling walk due to the position of their feet at the back of their bodies. To avoid the attentions of predators, the birds visit their colonies only under cover of darkness.

Lost and Found

Bermuda remained uninhabited until 1609, when an English expedition was shipwrecked there. At the time the islands teemed with seabirds, including vast numbers of Bermuda petrels. Soon, however, settlers arrived in force, bringing with them pigs, rats, and other animals that raided the petrels' nesting burrows. To make matters worse, the settlers themselves also caught and ate huge numbers of the birds, until by 1621 the species was thought to be extinct.

No specimens were recorded for more than 300 years, but then, miraculously, the bird turned up again. The first clue that it still existed came in 1906, when a dead petrel was found on Castle Island, one of the smallest in Bermuda. At first it was taken to be a previously unknown capped petrel from the

DATA PANEL

Bermuda petrel (cahow)

Pterodroma cahow

Family: Procellariidae

World population: About 180 birds

Distribution: Breeds on a few islets in Castle Harbor, Bermuda; outside the breeding season (mid-June–October) the birds live at sea, probably wandering across the Atlantic Ocean; has been recorded off North Carolina

Habitat: Breeds on rocky islets; spends nonbreeding season flying over open ocean

Size: Length: 15 in (38 cm); wingspan: 35 in (89 cm)

Form: Medium-sized, long-winged, short-tailed seabird with hooked black bill bearing nostrils in tubes on top; webbed feet set at hind end of body

Diet: Little known; probably mainly squid and crustaceans, plus some fish

Breeding: January to mid-June; colonies once nested in burrows in soil, but now use natural crevices in soft limestone and artificial burrows; single, large white egg is incubated for 7–8 weeks; young fledge in 13–14 weeks

Related endangered species: Thirty-five other petrel and shearwater species are threatened, and a further 2 are extinct. In the *Pterodroma* genus to which the Bermuda petrel belongs they include: Chatham Islands petrel (*Pterodroma axillaris*) CR; Galápagos petrel (*P. phaeopygia*) CR; Jamaica petrel (*P. caribbaea*) CR; black-capped petrel (*P. hasitata*) EN; Barau's petrel (*P. baraui*) EN; Trindade petrel (*P. arminjoniana*) VU; Atlantic petrel (*P. incerta*) VU; Murphy's petrel (*P. ultima*) NT

Status: IUCN EN; not listed by CITES

Caribbean region, but then in 1916 another individual turned up—and it seemed to fit 17th-century descriptions of the missing species. The clinching record came in 1931, when a bird that hit St. David's lighthouse was retrieved and identified as a Bermuda petrel. Another definite record was of an individual that struck a telephone pole in St. George, at the northeastern end of the main island.

The Bermuda petrel was considered extinct for more than 300 years and was only rediscovered in the early years of the 20th century.

The puzzle of where these birds came from remained, since none could be found nesting on any of the inhabited islands. In 1951 a search turned up 18 pairs of the petrels nesting on rocky islets in Castle Harbor, near St. George. The total area of these islets was only 2.4 acres (1 ha). Instead of nesting in burrows as they had done in the 17th century, the petrels were now using natural crevices created by water erosion of the soft limestone rock, since there was little soil on the islets.

Building Up the Numbers

After its rediscovery the tiny breeding population was carefully observed. Worryingly, numbers increased only slightly in the early years; by 1961 there were still only 20 pairs. Like all other members of the tubenose order, which includes albatrosses and shearwaters as well as petrels, Bermuda petrels are slow breeders: Roosting birds lay a single egg, and the young take five or more years to become sexually mature.

Subsequently, research into the reasons for the petrels' poor productivity revealed that one problem facing the birds came in the shape of another seabird, the white-tailed tropicbird, which competed for the rock crevices where the petrels bred, killing the young in the nest after they hatched. Conservationists built artificial burrows for the petrels, but these too were attacked. Eventually, researchers solved the problem by fitting stone or wooden baffles over the burrow entrances that allowed the petrels to pass in but kept the bulkier tropicbirds out. This has had some success: The population is increasing, and breeding success is up to 25 percent from 5 percent in the 1950s.

A lingering threat comes from DDT and other pollutants, which become concentrated in the petrels' bodies and may be responsible for the growing number of eggs that fail to hatch. The bright lights of a nearby airport and NASA tracking station also cause problems by disrupting the petrels' nighttime aerial courtship rituals. More worrying still is the risk of rising sea levels as a result of global warming; after 25 years without major problems half a dozen serious floods affected petrel burrows in the 1990s. Conservationists have replanted other potential breeding islands with native flora; at some future time a new colony may be established on one of them, Nonsuch Island.

Andean Flamingo

Phoenicoparrus andinus

The rarest of the world's five species of flamingos, the Andean flamingo lives in a few remote high mountain lakes of the Andes Mountains. Its survival is threatened by the continuing exploitation and deterioration of its habitat.

The Andean flamingo belongs to one of the oldest of all bird families, which originated over 50 million years ago. Today they are found on the puna—a high, cold, dry plateau in the Andes Mountains, usually at heights of between 7,500 and 14,750 feet (2,300 and 4,500 m). They live in lakes, where they wade in water 10 times as salty as the sea.

Although the lakes appear to be inhospitable, they are productive habitats, containing huge concentrations of diatoms, or microscopic single-cell algae (plants that have no true stems, roots, and leaves) on which the flamingos feed. The bizarre-looking bills of Andean flamingos are specially adapted for feeding in shallow water. The birds dunk their heads in the water, holding the bill upside down. The bill contains rows of comblike structures with which the birds sieve out the tiny food items by pumping water through the bill with a pistonlike action of the large tongue.

Multiple Threats

Only one species of flamingo, the greater flamingo, is not considered threatened. The other four, even with a combined population of several million birds, are considered at risk from hunting, because of a long breeding cycle, and because there are fewer than 30 major breeding sites in the world. The situation for the Andean flamingo is particularly serious: It has the smallest population, which has recently shown a serious decline—equal to 24 percent in the 15 years since the mid-1980s. Breeding success is consistently low; and since the adults are long-lived (up to 50 years), numbers are unlikely to recover for many years.

The species nests at only 10 or so major colonies; and despite their remoteness, the breeding sites are coming under increasing pressure. Away from the protected colonies the flamingos are still regularly hunted (on a small scale) for their meat, feathers, and fat, which is used in traditional medicine and considered to be a cure for tuberculosis in some parts of the Andes. Most of the birds killed are juveniles.

A more serious threat is posed by the removal of eggs by local people, especially if they are sold in quantity rather than being used for personal consumption. The problem was especially acute during the 1950s to the early 1980s, when many eggs were taken from nests each year.

Both an increase in mining activities near breeding colonies and the towns that service the mining developments pose major threats to the flamingo's habitat. Along with the problem of water pollution, increased disturbance at the colonies from human activity can cause breeding failure. The diversion of streams for mining operations and other uses or changes in weather also result in fluctuating water levels. Such factors can cause droughts and consequently a lack of food or destruction of nests by flooding.

Surveys of the high-altitude salt and alkaline lakes of the Andes have revealed the species' status and population trends and located new colonies. A priority in the future is to maintain habitat, halt deterioration, and prevent hunting and egg-collecting by protecting more breeding sites. Four sites currently receive official protection to some degree.

The Andean flamingo *is endangered for many reasons, but low breeding success is a critical factor.*

DATA PANEL

Andean flamingo

Phoenicoparrus andinus

Family: Phoenicopteridae

World population: Fewer than 34,000 birds

Distribution: The high Andean plateaus of Peru, Argentina, Bolivia, and Chile

Habitat: High mountain alkaline and salt lakes

Size: Length: 39–42 in (99–110 cm)

Form: Large waterbird with long neck and long legs. Downward-bent bill, pale yellow at the base, black on the downcurved portion. Plumage pale pink with bright upperparts and deep wine-red tinge to head, neck, upper breast, and wing coverts (small feathers covering the base of the flight feathers). Primary flight feathers of wingtips form a large black triangular patch when the wings are closed. Young birds are gray with heavily streaked upperparts

Diet: Diatoms (microscopic single-cell algae)

Breeding: Breeds in large social colonies of birds (including other species). Female lays 1 white egg in shallow pit atop a nest of mud. Incubation period about 4 weeks; chicks have pale-gray down and are at first fed on a milklike secretion from the adults' upper digestive tract; they fledge at 10–12 weeks; acquire adult plumage at 3 years

Related endangered species: Chilean flamingo (*Phoenicopterus chilensis*) LRnt; lesser flamingo (*P. minor*) LRnt; puna flamingo (*Phoenicoparrus jamesi*) LRnt

Status: IUCN VU; CITES II

Northern Bald Ibis

Geronticus eremita

With its red face and long, downcurved, red bill framed by a scruffy ruff of black feathers, the northern bald ibis has an odd charm of its own. It is one of the world's rarest birds, with a very small range and population.

The northern bald ibis was once widespread and abundant, but it is now extremely localized. Its representation in hieroglyphics dating back 5,000 years shows that it was revered as a holy bird in ancient Egypt. It bred in many places in North Africa and the Near and Middle East and until the 17th century in the mountains of Germany, Austria, Switzerland, and the former Yugoslavia. At the beginning of the 20th century the bird was rediscovered in North Africa and the Middle East to Western science. It looked very like the bird in a 16th-century Swiss drawing, but experts did not believe such an exotic species could ever have lived in Europe until a semifossilized specimen that was definitely a northern bald ibis was found there.

Decline and Persecution

The reasons for the species' decline are not known for certain. From the Middle Ages onward it was hunted for food, which may have contributed to its eventual extinction in Europe. Other factors probably included the conversion of the mountain meadows where it fed into farmland and possibly a cooling of the climate.

Following its scientific discovery, the northern bald ibis faced increased persecution as museum collectors raced to secure specimens of this rare, semimythical bird. Aided by local hunters, they wiped out whole colonies, including, by the 1930s, most of the remaining Algerian colonies and all those in Syria. The bird also faced increasing threats from the conversion of its habitat to farmland, the rising use of pesticides, and frequent droughts. By the mid-20th century the world breeding population had declined to one colony in Turkey, one in Algeria, and a few in Morocco.

Turkey

The Turkish bald ibis colony at the town of Birecik on the Euphrates River survived only because local people believed that the bird was a symbol of fertility and that it served as a guide to pilgrims to

---

DATA PANEL

Northern bald ibis

Geronticus eremita

Family: Threskiornithidae

World population: About 220 birds

Distribution: In Morocco breeds only at Sous-Massa National Park and nearby Tamri; captive-bred, released colony breeds at Birecik in Turkey

Habitat: Arid to semiarid, sparsely vegetated steppes on plains and rocky plateaus; cultivated fields and pastures. Wild birds breed on cliff ledges by sea

Size: Length: 27.5–31.5 in (70–80 cm); wingspan: 4.1–4.4 ft (1.3–1.4 m); male usually larger. Weight unknown

Form: Large, dark, storklike bird; iridescent black plumage shows bronze-green, copper, blue, purple, and violet gloss in sunlight; naked red face and crown; long, narrow feathers project from nape to form wispy ruff; long, red downcurved bill and relatively short reddish legs; broad wings show 3–4 separated primary feathers at tips in flight

Diet: Mainly grasshoppers, locusts, beetles, and small lizards; also woodlice, spiders, snails, scorpions, small fish, frogs, and tadpoles; occasionally nestling birds and small mammals; berries, young shoots, and other plant matter

Breeding: Breeds in colonies of 3–40 pairs; nest is loose platform of branches lined with grass, straw, and other material, including paper; female lays 2–4 brown-spotted, bluish-white eggs; incubation period lasts 3–4 weeks. Chicks fledge in 6–7 weeks

Related endangered species: Southern bald ibis (*Geronticus calvus*) VU; dwarf olive ibis (*Bostrychia bocagei*) CR; white-shouldered ibis (*Pseudibis davisoni*) CR; giant ibis (*P. gigantea*) CR; crested ibis (*Nipponia nippon*) EN

Status: IUCN CR; CITES I

MOROCCO
Tamri
Sous-Massa
National Park
ALGERIA

Mecca. They held an annual festival to celebrate its return each February from winter quarters in Sudan and southern Arabia. However, when Birecik grew, the newcomers did not share the local people's reverence for the ibis, and the festival was not held after 1958. As the town expanded, the bird's nesting grounds were absorbed. From an estimated 3,000 pairs in 1890 the population was reduced to 530 pairs by 1953 and 23 pairs by 1973.

The chief causes of this catastrophic decline were the use of pesticides in the surrounding habitat and the increasing human disturbance at the colonies. In 1977 a colony of captive-bred birds was created by conservationists 1.3 miles (2 km) north of Birecik, with the aim of encouraging the wild birds breeding in the town to relocate to this site. However, most of the released birds failed to integrate with the wild population, which meant that they did not migrate (the young have to learn to migrate from their parents) and so perished during the winter.

Lack of food, problems capturing wild birds, the late release of juveniles, plus the failure of the Turkish government to ban the use of pesticides resulted in a steeper decline in the population. By spring 1989 only three wild birds returned from their winter quarters, and two later died in accidents. With one bird left, the species was effectively extinct in the wild at Birecik.

Morocco

The ibis has fared better at its two surviving sites in Morocco, but has still faced severe problems, especially hunting, pesticide poisoning, and habitat loss as a result of dam building. In 1991 the Sous-Massa National Park was established specifically to protect the breeding and feeding areas of the ibis. In 1994 the Moroccan breeding population was estimated to be 300. In May 1996, 40 birds died mysteriously, possibly from botulism or unknown toxins. By 1998 numbers had declined to about 200 birds, but there has been a slight increase since then.

The northern bald ibis *uses its long, downcurved bill to extract prey. It probes into crevices, among tufts of vegetation, in sand, soft soil, and under stones.*

Labrador Duck

Camptorhynchus labradorius

The distinctive and attractive Labrador duck was never common and became extinct in the late 19th century. The reason for its disappearance remains a mystery.

The male Labrador duck was one of the most attractive among a colorful group of birds. It had a white head, black body, and large white wing patches. As with other species of ducks, the female was a drab brown, probably indicating that she alone was responsible for incubating their eggs. Such sexual "dimorphism" (two distinct forms) is seen in most species of duck. Dull colors are an advantage to the female, concealing her and her precious brood from the eyes of predators. The male, meanwhile, is free to exploit his fine appearance to attract other mates or to display in competition with other males.

Mysterious Birds

However, this is all guesswork based on what we know of duck species in general; we know almost nothing about the Labrador duck itself. Today it seems amazing that such a large and distinctive bird living in a well-populated part of North America should remain such a mystery. After all, it has been extinct for barely a century.

Little information is available about Labrador ducks. Records show that they used to turn up in the meat and fish markets in New York, New Jersey, and Maryland, having been shot along nearby coasts in the winter. The famous American naturalist and bird painter J. J. Audubon claimed to have seen them as far south as Chesapeake Bay, Virginia. They were also known to be winter visitors in the Bay of Fundy, between Nova Scotia and New Brunswick, and along the coast of Long Island.

The Labrador ducks' breeding areas seem to have been farther north, probably along the Gulf of St. Lawrence and coastal Labrador, and would have been frozen for many months of the year. The ducks apparently retreated south to sandy bays, sheltered inlets, harbors, and estuaries. Here the sea would not freeze, and they would be able to find food.

Despite the fact that Labrador ducks were seen regularly in markets, they were not a popular food, and it would appear that nobody made special efforts to hunt many of them. The ducks were said to be wary and difficult to shoot anyway. This is in direct contrast to many extinct and endangered bird species that were highly sought after and hunted down ruthlessly.

Death by Natural Causes

Instead, the Labrador duck seems never to have been a successful or

---

DATA PANEL

Labrador duck

Camptorhynchus labradorius

Family: Anatidae

World population: 0 (Extinct)

Distribution: Unknown; probably bred along the Gulf of St. Lawrence and coastal Labrador, Canada, and wintered from Nova Scotia to Chesapeake Bay, Virginia

Habitat: Unknown; wintered along seacoasts

Size: Length head/body: 12–15 in (30–40 cm); tail: 2 in (5 cm)

Form: Male strikingly black and white; female brown

Diet: Unknown; probably a specialized diet, perhaps soft plant material or invertebrates such as mollusks

Breeding: Unknown

Related endangered species: Chubut steamerduck *(Tachyeres leucocephalus)* LRnt

Status: IUCN EX; not listed by CITES

CANADA

probable former range

UNITES STATES

abundant species and appears to have died out from natural causes. Perhaps there was some catastrophic event in its breeding areas, which may have been marshes or on small islands offshore. Or maybe its extinction was due to specialization.

The Labrador duck was peculiar in having an unusually large number of special plates or grooves inside its beak and soft corners to the end of the bill. Such features usually indicate a particular feeding method, one that probably relied heavily on specific foods. Perhaps the special beak was used to deal with mollusks or to sieve tiny insect larvae or shrimp from mud or water. Such a lifestyle would be risky, relying on an abundance of food and little competition for it.

A rare species will always be in danger of extinction simply because its population is small to begin with. Breeding, feeding, or habitat problems will have an immediate effect on numbers. We will never know for sure what happened to the Labrador duck, but it is not thought that the small numbers shot by hunters could in themselves have caused its extinction.

The Labrador duck *was always rare, and its habits and lifestyle are still a mystery. The male had striking black-and-white plumage, while the female was mainly brown.*

Perhaps the birds or their eggs and young were taken from their few breeding grounds by people or by an invasion of predators, reducing numbers to such low levels that hunting then finished them off completely. Populations seem to have declined gradually. The duck disappeared from the markets between 1850 and 1870. The last recorded specimen was probably the one shot in the fall of 1875 on Long Island, New York. (This is now in the Smithsonian Institution.) A less likely final record is for 1878, when one was said to have been shot near Elmira, New York. Another had been shot in 1871 on Mana Island, New Brunswick. Today there are about 50 known specimens in museums, five of them in a single glass case in the American Museum of Natural History in New York. It is one of five or six species of American birds that have become extinct in the last 200 years.

White-Headed Duck

Oxyura leucocephala

Long-term population declines for the white-headed duck have recently intensified as a result of habitat loss at a key wintering site. Threats of competition from the introduced North American ruddy duck have also been a problem.

The white-headed duck probably had a global population of over 100,000 in the early 20th century; in the 1930s an estimated 50,000 wintered on the Caspian Sea. However, by 1991 the population was estimated at a mere 19,000 ducks. This reduction in numbers was matched by a large decline in breeding range. Over the last 100 years the white-headed duck has become extinct as a breeding bird in Albania, Azerbaijan, Corsica, Hungary, Italy, Israel, Morocco, and the former Yugoslavia. Despite the historical declines, however, there was some optimism in 1991, since the population was thought to be relatively stable.

Since 1991 that optimism has faded. Numbers appear to have plummeted over the last decade to fewer than 10,000 birds. The decline has been most severe at what was the most important wintering site, Burdur Gölü in Turkey. In 1991 about 10,900 birds wintered there, but in 1996 only 1,270 were recorded. Obviously, some of the birds have simply scattered to other wetland sites, and wintering numbers have increased elsewhere in the eastern Mediterranean region. They include the doubling of the population at Lake Vistonis, Greece, with other large increases in Bulgaria and Romania. However, the counts do not compensate for the very large declines at Burdur Gölü.

Reasons for the Decline

The large historical declines are mostly the result of extensive drainage of wetlands, particularly in the former Soviet Union and Spain. Over 50 percent of breeding habitat was destroyed during the 20th century, and the remaining sites are especially vulnerable to eutrophication (overenrichment by nutrients, particularly nitrates and phosphates) and pollution. The range of threats includes industrial, domestic, and agricultural pollution, sedimentation, and water extraction, as seen at Burdur Gölü and the Sultan marshes in central southern Turkey. At Lake Vistonis drowning in fishing nets is a severe threat. Dead birds have also been found in nets at sites in Spain and Turkey.

DATA PANEL

White-headed duck

Oxyura leucocephala

Family: Anatidae

World population: Fewer than 10,000 birds

Distribution: Algeria, Spain, and Tunisia; most birds breed in Russia and Kazakhstan, smaller populations in Afghanistan, Iran, Mongolia, Turkey, and Uzbekistan. Eastern populations occur and winter in the eastern Mediterranean, Middle East, Central Asia, and the Indian subcontinent

Habitat: Breeds on small, shallow, freshwater or brackish lakes with dense vegetation at fringes. Winter lakes are larger and deeper with little emergent vegetation. In Spain and Tunisia, artificial lagoons and reservoirs

Size: Length: 17–19 in (43–48 cm); wingspan: 24.5–27.5 in (62–70 cm). Weight: male 25–32 oz (720–900 g); female 19–28 oz (550–800 g)

Form: Chestnut-brown diving duck; long tail, often cocked vertically. Male has white head, black cap, and blue bill, swollen at base. Female has pale face with dark cap, and cheek stripe; blackish, less swollen bill

Diet: In Spain benthic (bottom-dwelling) chironomid larvae and pupae; wintering birds in Greece feed primarily on polychaete worms

Breeding: Polygamous (has more than 1 mate); nests in dense reedbeds, often on top of old coot nests. Timing is variable, with 4–9 eggs laid April and early July. Incubation takes 3–3.5 weeks, fledging 8–9 weeks

Related endangered species: Twenty-one others, including pink-headed duck (*Rhodonessa caryophyllacea*) CR

Status: IUCN EN; CITES II

White-headed duck populations have suffered through widespread habitat loss and cross-breeding with the ruddy duck.

Ruddy Duck Danger

While a major problem for the white-headed duck is habitat loss, western European populations are also threatened by hybridization and competition with the North American ruddy duck. The ruddy duck was introduced to Britain in the 1950s and is now spreading across western and into central Europe. It has been seen in 20 countries, and breeding has been recorded in six. This introduced species cross-breeds readily with the white-headed duck, and hybrids are fully fertile; second-generation birds have also been collected in Spain. The real concern is that the ruddy duck will spread eastward into the core of the white-headed duck's range. If it spreads into Algeria, Turkey, or Russia, the size of the wetlands—which are infrequently monitored—will make control impossible.

Conservation Measures

Measures are being taken to control the ruddy duck in France, Portugal, Spain, and the Netherlands. In Britain a regional control trial is assessing whether a wider, longer-term strategy is necessary and practicable. The Spanish control program is one element of a highly effective conservation strategy that was started in 1979. Since then a reduction in illegal hunting, the regeneration of natural vegetation, the release of captive-bred birds into the wild, and from 1989 shooting of ruddy ducks and hybrids has led to a dramatic population recovery.

The challenge is to replicate the success of the Spanish program for more easterly populations. The effective protection of wetlands in Russia and Kazahkstan is a high priority. Without such protection it is almost certain that the white-headed duck will continue its dramatic decline.

Nene

Branta sandvicensis

Unique to the Hawaiian Islands, the nene was driven to the verge of extinction by the destruction of its wild habitats and the introduction of predators. By 1950 there were only about 30 left on Hawaii, but captive breeding has helped, and the nene may soon be thriving again in the wild.

The volcanic Hawaiian Islands were once home to a unique variety of birdlife, including at least 11 species of waterfowl found nowhere else in the world. Perfectly adapted for life on the islands, where the only native predators were birds of prey, several of the geese and ducks were flightless. When the Polynesians arrived about 1,600 years ago, they were sitting targets, and most are now extinct. Only three of the 11 now survive, including the one big goose that was able to fly: the nene.

Also known as the Hawaiian goose, the nene is named for its high, nasal, two-note "né-né" call. Although it can fly, it has quite short wings—too short for a long migration. Fossil evidence shows that it once occurred throughout the Hawaiian chain. To make up for its short wings, it has unusually long legs, with big, strong feet. Since there is little wetland on the islands, it has little webbing between its toes, which are padded

to help it scramble over the rocky lava flows that spill down the flanks of the island volcanoes.

Drinking water is hard to find on the islands, so the essentially vegetarian nene seeks out moisture-rich plants for food. In season it plucks berries from the bushes between the lava flows, making the most of its long legs to reach up into the foliage.

Hunted Out

The Polynesian settlers brought their pigs, dogs, and—accidentally—the Polynesian rat. They all played havoc with the ground-nesting nene. People also burned off the lowland scrub to create pasture, destroying vital cover for the breeding geese. Yet the nene survived, and there were at least 25,000 of them at the end of the 18th century, when Europeans reached the islands. The new settlers introduced more killers: black rats, cats, and in 1883 the small Indian mongoose. They also had guns; between them human hunters and predators eliminated the nene from the lowlands.

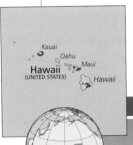

DATA PANEL

Nene (Hawaiian goose)

Branta sandvicensis

Family: Anatidae

World population: About 960–1,000

Distribution: Originally throughout Hawaiian archipelago, but reduced to a few wild birds on Hawaii by 1950; following reintroductions, it now lives wild on Hawaii, Maui, and Kauai

Habitat: Grassy shrublands and sparsely vegetated, semiarid basalt lava flows on volcanic slopes; lowland pasture on Kauai

Size: Length: 25–27 in (63–69 cm). Weight: 2.9–6.6 lb (1.3–3 kg)

Form: Small, erect goose with short wings, long legs, and strong feet with reduced webbing. Black bill, face, and crown; golden-buff neck with unique dark furrows; upperparts and breast sepia brown with pattern of dark gray and white; white belly

Diet: Moist vegetation such as grass, leaves and berries, and seeds

Breeding: Birds pair for life and breed in November–January; 3–5 white eggs laid in a nest scrape and incubated by female for about 4 weeks while male stands guard; young fledge in about 10–12 weeks

Related endangered species: In Hawaiian Islands, Laysan duck (*Anas laysanensis*) CR; Hawaiian duck (*A. wyvilliana*) EN. Other threatened geese include the lesser white-fronted goose (*Anser erythropus*) VU and the red-breasted goose (*Branta ruficollis*) VU

Status: IUCN VU; CITES I

By 1907, when hunting was banned, the nene was probably found only on Hawaii itself. It had retreated into the volcanic uplands where mongoose and cats were scarce, yet while the near-barren slopes provided enough food for bare survival, the extra nutrients needed for producing eggs and feeding young were often lacking. In poor seasons many adult geese failed to breed, and the young birds that did hatch often died from malnutrition. By 1949 there were perhaps only 30 left.

Rescue

The recovery of the nene is almost entirely due to captive breeding. In 1950 three birds were acquired by what is now the Wildfowl and Wetlands Trust at Slimbridge, England, and they became the foundation of a captive-bred flock of 2,000 or so. Meanwhile, the birds were also being bred in captivity on Hawaii. In 1960 a reintroduction program started, and since then over 2,300 geese have been released into protected areas on Hawaii and the neighboring island of Maui.

On Hawaii and Maui the reintroduced nene live in the uplands, where they still suffer from bad weather and malnutrition. On Hawaii the nene population of about 400 has to be boosted by new introductions and given extra food. On Maui the population of about 280 is stable or growing.

Since 1985 some 137 nene have been introduced to the more distant island of Kauai. There the population has more than doubled to over 260. There is no mongoose predation, allowing the nene to live in the coastal lowlands, where they enjoy a better diet.

Conservation bodies aim to establish large, predator-free reserves in lowland areas. The elimination of poaching and reduction of roadkills are also planned. If coupled with translocations of stock between islands to minimize inbreeding, the nene may be on track for a full recovery.

The nene is a relative of the Canada goose. It evolved on the Hawaiian Islands into a species with shortened wings and half-webbed feet.

Philippine Eagle

Pithecophaga jefferyi

One of the rarest of the world's birds of prey, the Philippine eagle is in a precarious situation. Its small and rapidly declining population is threatened by forest destruction and fragmentation.

The Philippine eagle is a flagship species for wildlife conservation on four of the Philippine group of islands. Predictions of its imminent extinction have been made since the 1960s, but the species hangs on in the face of immense odds. Conservationists believe that most of the population is equally distributed between the large islands of Luzon and Mindanao (an estimated 105 pairs), while the smaller islands of Samar and Leyte house only an estimated eight pairs between them. However, these figures are based mostly on forest-cover data, and more precise information on numbers is not available.

The Philippine eagle is a huge and powerful predator. It waits on a perch high in the rain forest canopy, looking and listening for the slightest movement or sound that betrays prey beneath. Its relatively short, rounded wings and long tail equip it for weaving deftly among the trees. It often begins a hunt at the top of a hillside and works its way down; it starts the process again when it reaches the bottom.

The Philippine eagle was once known as the monkey-eating eagle. Although it eats various species of monkey, it more often feeds on two cat-sized mammals: the flying lemur and the palm civet. It is likely that the eagle is also an opportunistic hunter, taking different prey according to its availability and abundance. Each pair hunts in a large territory of about 23 to 38 square miles (60 to 100 sq. km). As in other eagle species, the pairs mate for life.

Lost Forest

As with so many other species, the main threat facing the Philippine eagle is the relentless destruction of its habitat. Every year some of the remaining primary forest on the islands is felled for timber: The great

DATA PANEL

Philippine eagle (monkey-eating eagle)

Pithecophaga jefferyi

Family: Accipitridae

World population: 350–650 birds; possibly only 226 mature adults

Distribution: Philippine islands of Luzon, Leyte, Mindanao, and Samar

Habitat: Primary dipterocarp (hardwood) rain forest on steep slopes; sometimes lives among secondary growth and gallery forest along riverbanks and floodplains. Occurs from the lowlands to 5,900 ft (1,800 m)

Size: Length: 34–40 in (86–102 cm); wingspan: about 6.5 ft (2 m). Weight: 10.3–17.6 lb (4.7–8 kg)

Form: Huge eagle with large, arched, powerfully hooked blue bill. Dark area around eyes (which have pale blue-gray irises) contrasts with buff crown and nape; long, spiky, black-streaked feathers form scruffy crest; cheeks, throat, underparts, and underwings white; upperparts and upperwings dark brown; legs and feet yellow

Diet: Tree-dwelling mammals such as flying lemurs, palm civets, monkeys, and flying squirrels; also tree-dwelling birds, including hornbills, owls, and hawks; bats, monitor lizards, and snakes

Breeding: Female lays 1 white egg in huge stick nest high in canopy of tall tree, usually on an epiphytic fern (one that grows on another plant). Both sexes incubate for about 9 weeks; eaglet fledges after about 5 months; remains dependent on parents for another year or more

Related endangered species: New Guinea harpy eagle (*Harpyopsis novaeguineae*) VU; harpy eagle (*Harpia harpyja*) LRnt

Status: IUCN CR; CITES I

PHILIPPINES

Luzon

Samar
Panay
Palawan
Negros
Mindanao

MALAYSIA
BRUNEI
Borneo

dipterocarp (tall hardwood) trees growing there are a major source of tropical timber for the rest of the world. When the loggers leave, settlers who practice "slash-and-burn" cultivation frequently move in. Slash-and-burn agriculture produces poor-quality, weed-infested grassland with bamboo or other scrub in place of a rich forest and is of little value to the eagles.

With the increasing numbers of people moving into the forests, it is probable that only 3,560 square miles (9,220 sq. km) of forest remain. Even national parks are severely affected; in Mount Apo National Park, for instance, over 50 percent of the original forest has disappeared.

Other threats facing the Philippine eagle include hunting by local people for food or trophies and, until recently, the capture of young for sale to zoos and the cage-bird trade. Plans for mining operations have also caused concern. There is evidence that the eagles accumulate pesticides from their prey in their body, a factor that is likely to affect their breeding success—a serious problem in a species that produces only one young every two years, at most.

Last Hope

Over the past 30 to 40 years various conservation initiatives have been launched to assure the future of the Philippine eagle. Plans include protective legislation, surveys, captive breeding, public awareness programs, and a sustainable agriculture project designed to improve conditions for both eagles and local people. However, relatively little is still known of the bird's ecology, and the work has been hampered at intervals by natural disasters and serious political unrest, as well as by the difficult nature of the remote habitats the eagle favors.

The Philippine eagle *perches high up in the rain forest canopy, watching for prey. Plans for its conservation include a campaign to foster national pride in the bird. If that is successful, the eagle may yet avoid extinction in the wild.*

Spanish Imperial Eagle

Aquila adalberti

One of the world's rarest birds of prey, the Spanish imperial eagle was thought to be in recovery in the early 1980s, but recently numbers have declined again. Like many other birds of prey, it has come into increasing conflict with the demands of people and is now seriously threatened.

At the beginning of the 20th century the Spanish imperial eagle was still relatively common and widespread. It could be found over most of Spain in areas of dry, uncultivated habitat. It also bred in Portugal and Morocco.

Today the species has disappeared from much of its range as a result of the loss and fragmentation of its forest habitat. By the 1960s the Spanish imperial eagle was almost extinct, with only 30 pairs recorded. Conservationists tried a new rescue technique. First,

they located nests with three or four eaglets. The last chicks to hatch often die as a result of the so-called Cain and Abel conflict. The "conflict" describes the tendency of the stronger nestlings to kill their younger siblings—as Cain killed his brother Abel in the biblical story. Sometimes the weaker siblings starve, since they are not strong enough to compete for the food brought by their parents.

Rescued eaglets were then put into nests with only a single chick. The number of surviving fledglings increased by up to 43 percent. From the early 1980s the species started to recover, and an average of five new breeding pairs appeared each year until 1994. Unfortunately, the population has since declined from 148 pairs in 1994 to 131 pairs in 1998. More significantly, even in major strongholds breeding success has plummeted.

Threats to Survival

Spanish imperial eagles need large areas of open forest with scattered trees or clumps of woodland for nesting and rough grassland or open ground for hunting. The birds avoid areas that have been irrigated for crops and site their nests well away from settlements, roads, and other developments. Wild places are increasingly difficult to find as more people move into undeveloped areas. The eagles are sensitive to disturbance, which can affect their breeding success.

Another major factor affecting the eagle's success is the availability

DATA PANEL

Spanish imperial eagle (Adalbert's eagle)

Aquila adalberti

Family: Accipitridae

World population: About 260 birds

Distribution: Breeds in central and southwestern Spain, in the Sierras of Guadarrama and Gredos, the plains of the Tajo and Tiétar Rivers, the central hills of Extremadura, Montes de Toledo, the Alcudia Valley, Sierra Morena, and the Guadalquivir marshes; also Salamanca and Málaga

Habitat: Open, wooded areas away from irrigated and cultivated farmland; high mountain slopes; hills and plains; sand dunes and alluvial plains

Size: Length: 29.5–33 in (75–84 cm); wingspan: 6–8 ft (1.8–2.4 m). Weight: 5.5–7.7 lb (2.5–3.5 kg)

Form: Huge bird of prey with dark plumage. Brown-black coloration with white "shoulders," pale-golden nape,

and pale-gray base to upper tail. Juveniles have rust-colored plumage that fades to pale buff; dark flight feathers; white fringes to wing coverts (feathers covering the flight feathers)

Diet: Mainly mammals, especially rabbits; also pigeons, waterbirds, gamebirds, and members of the crow family; occasionally snakes and lizards. Also dead cows and other grazing mammals

Breeding: Large stick nest built in tree; female usually lays 2–4 brown-blotched whitish eggs that are incubated for about 6 weeks; young fledge in about 10 weeks

Related endangered species: Imperial eagle *(Aquila heliaca)* VU; greater spotted eagle *(A. clanga)* VU

Status: IUCN EN; CITES I

of rabbits. Rabbits usually form more than half of the eagle's total prey—in some places as much as 70 percent. However, the viral disease myxomatosis, deliberately introduced to control rabbit populations in 1957, was very effective. In a few areas eagles switched to hunting alternative prey. It is likely that many pairs were forced to stop breeding due to the shortage of rabbits. Another viral disease— hemorrhagic pneumonia—has added to the drop in rabbit numbers: in some areas by 80 percent.

Deliberate and accidental poisoning of the eagles is another cause of the bird's decline, especially in hunting preserves where game animals are commercially exploited. Carcasses baited with powerful poisons are now a significant cause of death. Such traps kill other species, too, including domestic dogs. Between 1989 and 1999 at least 57 Spanish imperial eagles died from poisoning—probably more than by any other means.

The eagles are also vulnerable to electrocution by power cables. Inexperienced juveniles are most at risk, especially when their plumage is wet. There are more deaths when power lines are sited away from roads and in areas where there are large numbers of rabbits.

Conservation Plans

Although 60 percent of the breeding population lives in 20 protected areas, the species still needs urgent help. A coordinated conservation plan is being implemented. Priorities include annual censuses of the breeding population, protecting nesting areas, increasing the rabbit population, working toward the elimination of poisoning, and surveying and modifying power lines to prevent electrocution.

The Spanish imperial eagle *is a huge bird of prey with a wingspan of between 6 and 8 feet (1.8 and 2.4 m).*

Red Kite

Milvus milvus

After an apparently relentless decline stretching over three or four centuries, the red kite is staging a comeback in the northwest of its range, thanks largely to the efforts of conservationists.

Big, beautiful, and almost balletic in its mastery of the sky, the red kite is one of the world's most spectacular raptors. Instantly identifiable by its rich, chestnut plumage and forked tail, it flies with a buoyant, airy grace that seems to defy gravity. It flourishes particularly in open, half-wild country with scattered woodlands, where it can locate food from the air and find plenty of trees for roosting.

At one time the kite was a common sight over much of Europe, even in major cities, for although it is a hunter, its real talent lies in scavenging easy meals from carcasses and refuse dumps. Back in the 16th century there were rich pickings to be had from every back alley, and the practice of allowing farm animals to roam over unfenced land ensured a steady supply of carrion. Yet by the end of the Middle Ages it was on the brink of a long, slow decline in numbers.

It disappeared from the cities first. Improved hygiene eliminated edible garbage from the streets. Like many other raptors, the kite was declared vermin, but its leisurely flight style made it an easier target than most. As guns became widespread during the 18th and 19th centuries, the red kite was gradually shot out of the skies. Others were trapped or poisoned; since they feed from carcasses, they can fall victim to poisoned bait laid out for other animals.

At the same time, agriculture was becoming more scientific, and farmers were abandoning the old ways in favor of more intensive systems. In the lowlands the supply of carrion began to dry up; and when chemical pesticides came into common use, live prey began to disappear too. Gradually, the kites retreated to the mountains and moors, where they could still find food and secure nesting sites.

In many places they are still declining. In eastern Europe the intensification of agriculture following land privatization has reduced their habitat. Yet the most endangered population is the distinctive, smaller race that once flourished on the Cape Verde Islands, off West Africa. Its numbers began to dwindle in the 1960s, partly because of the virtual destruction of the natural ecosystem on many of the islands and partly because the red kites were interbreeding with similar black kites. By the year 2000 the population had crashed to just four birds. Barring a virtual miracle, the Cape Verde red kite will be extinct within five years.

Welsh Revival

In sharp contrast, conservation efforts in northwestern Europe have led to a kite revival. In Britain, for example, a tiny relict population of red kites managed to survive in the mountains of central Wales, where they were able to exploit a steady supply of rabbit and sheep carcasses. Yet in 1903, when conservation

began, they were on the edge of extinction, with only 12 birds left. Since then intensive research, better protection, supplementary feeding, and the cooperation of local farmers have gradually enabled the Welsh kites to bounce back. By 2000 there were some 800 individuals, with 259 breeding pairs. Meanwhile, kites from southern Sweden and northern Spain have been introduced into hill country in England and Scotland, with similar success.

The Welsh experience shows that the red kite is a survivor; given the right conditions, it can breed its way back from near-oblivion. Other countries in northwestern Europe are reporting similar increases, which partly offset the losses in other parts of its range. Yet ultimately its future may depend on the survival of another endangered species: the organic farmer, whose pesticide-free fields nurture the wild plants and insects that form the basis of the ecosystem on which the bird depends.

The red kite *includes carrion in its diet and is susceptible to both deliberate and accidental poisoning of carcasses.*

DATA PANEL

Red kite

Milvus milvus

Family: Accipitridae

World population: 19,000–32,000 breeding pairs

Distribution: From western Russia west to Wales, Spain, and the Cape Verde Islands; from southern Sweden south to Sicily and northwestern Morocco

Habitat: Mixed country, often hilly, with woodland for nesting and meadows, lakes, and rivers

Size: Length: 24–26 in (60–66 cm); wingspan: 5.7–6.4 ft (1.8–2 m). Weight: 1.8–2.9 lb (0.8–1.3 kg); females larger than males

Form: Sleek, graceful bird of prey with long wings, long, deeply forked tail, and feathered legs. Gray-white head; red-brown upperparts with black wingtips; rich chestnut underparts and tail; large, pale patches on undersides of outer wings. Bright yellow eyes, black-tipped yellow bill, yellow feet, black talons

Diet: Birds, small mammals, fish, large insects, earthworms, carrion, and scraps

Breeding: In March–May 2–4 eggs are laid in a nest of sticks and mud, often incorporating scraps of paper, plastic, or cloth, high in a tall tree or, rarely, on a cliff. The nest is often built on top of an abandoned buzzard's or crow's nest, and the same site is often reused every year for decades. The female incubates the eggs for 31–32 days, and the chicks fledge after 48–60 days

Related endangered species: Many birds of prey in the family Accipitridae, including the Cuban kite (*Chondrohierax wilsonii*) CR and the white-collared kite (*Leptodon forbesi*) CR

Status: Not listed by IUCN; CITES II

California Condor

Gymnogyps californianus

The California condor has already been extinct in the wild once, and only the reintroduction and management of captive-bred birds is preventing its disappearance for a second time.

There is evidence that the massive California condor once lived across a wide range in the United States. Since 1937, however, it has been confined to California in the nation's southwestern corner. This decline in range was matched throughout the 20th century by a continuing fall in numbers, driven by human activity and in particular by the widespread availability of firearms. Many birds were shot and killed; others suffered indirectly by ingesting lead from the carcasses of animals that had been shot and abandoned, leading to death by lead poisoning. By 1987 the California condor's situation had become so critical that the last six wild individuals were captured for inclusion in a captive-breeding program. The magnificent creature had formally become extinct in the wild.

At that time there were already 16 birds in captivity, so the total population stood at only 22 birds. Since then a large-scale, integrated breeding and reintroduction program has been in operation. It has had notable success; the total population has increased almost sevenfold to 147 birds. Of them 97 are still in captivity, split between three breeding facilities managed respectively by the Peregrine Fund at the World Center for Birds of Prey, by the Los Angeles Zoo, and by the San Diego Wild Animal Park. The remaining 50 birds have been reintroduced back to the wild at five separate sites. There are now 28 birds in California, at Lion Canyon, in Los Padres Natural Forest, and at Castle Crags on the western border of San Luis Obispo County. The other 22 are in northern Arizona, at Vermillion Cliffs and at Hurricane Cliffs 60 miles (100 km) to the west.

Problems in the Wild

Unfortunately, the recovery program is all that is stopping the species from becoming extinct in the wild for a second time, since the released birds still depend on the ongoing work of the program for their continued survival. None of the birds has yet reached reproductive maturity, and in addition they all currently rely on food provided by the program. Nor have they found it easy to readapt

---

DATA PANEL

California condor

Gymnogyps californianus

Family: Cathartidae

World population: At the end of 1998 the total population was 147, including 50 in the wild

Distribution: Birds have been reintroduced in 5 areas, 3 in California and 2 in northern Arizona

Habitat: Rocky, open-country scrubland terrain, coniferous forests, and oak savanna

Size: Length: 46–54 in (117–134 cm); wingspan: 9 ft (2.7 m). Weight: 17.6–31 lb (8–14 kg)

Form: Huge, unmistakable raptor (bird of prey). Mostly black with white wing-linings and silvery panel on upper secondaries. The head is naked and orange-red. Immatures have black heads and dark mottling on the underwing. When soaring, the wings are held horizontally, with the outermost wing feathers curled up

Diet: Scavenges the carcasses of large mammals, although the reintroduced birds currently rely on food provided by the recovery program

Breeding: Nest sites are located in cavities in cliffs, on rocky outcrops, or in large trees. Clearly adapted for very low reproductive output

Related endangered species: Andean condor *(Vultur gryphus)* LRnt

Status: IUCN CR; CITES I and II

to conditions in the wild. The first birds to be released suffered from behavioral difficulties and tended to collide with powerlines. This had not previously been a problem with the species and such accidents may have been caused by the captive-bred birds getting used to man-made structures. Following the deaths of a number of newly released individuals, a program of "aversion training" was introduced that has involved conditioning the birds to avoid powerlines and all contact with humans. The first of the conditioned birds was released in 1995, and so far the training appears to have been successful.

Other grounds for optimism include the fact that at some of the release sites the birds are increasingly finding food of their own. In addition, at certain times of the year they are now ranging up to 250 miles (400 km) away from the sites. In the meantime the provision of clean carcasses does have the added benefit of avoiding any possibility of lead poisoning.

Ambitious Targets

The current conservation action plan for the species has set several ambitious targets. A long-term goal is to establish two self-sustaining populations of at least 150 individuals each, including 15 breeding pairs. For this goal to be realized, all aspects of

California condors
came close to extinction in the late 1980s, when the total population of the species was reduced to just 22 birds.

the current program must be continued. One key factor is the maintenance of the birds' habitat. Another is the implementation of information and education programs, which will raise awareness of the California condor's plight. Without such efforts persecution may begin again as the birds become increasingly widespread.

Mauritius Kestrel

Falco punctatus

Reduced to a population of just four wild birds by 1974, the Mauritius kestrel has clawed its way back from the edge of extinction to become a spectacular success story.

The island of Mauritius in the Indian Ocean will always be notorious as the former home of the dodo: the universal symbol of extinction. Until recently the Mauritius kestrel seemed bound to suffer the same fate since its numbers had reached a point from which recovery seemed impossible.

The Mauritius kestrel hunts like a short-winged sparrowhawk. Its relatively short wings give it the maneuverability to pursue prey beneath the canopy of dense evergreen forest that once covered much of the island. It usually hunts from a perch, moving swiftly and swerving through the branches to snatch prey (songbirds, dragonflies, or lizards) from the air or the trees. Among its favorite targets are the iridescent green geckos found only on Mauritius; the kestrel is expert at locating them as they bask, immobile in the sun. Occasionally, it hovers to pinpoint prey in low vegetation, but its wings are not really adapted to the task. It is a bird of the forests. As the forests were felled to provide farmland for a growing population, the kestrel gradually disappeared.

Relentless Decline

Mauritius kestrels have never been abundant. Each breeding pair occupies a large territory, and the entire island is no bigger than a large city. At most there were probably only 1,000 birds. By the 1970s rampant deforestation had eliminated most native forest cover, leaving only a few pockets of habitat in rocky gorges on the southwest of the island. The kestrels were also shot by farmers—who believed they stole poultry—and poisoned by pesticides. Their tree nesting sites

were vulnerable to the egg-thieving nonnative macaque monkeys, as well as introduced cats, rats, and mongoose. It was a deadly combination, and by 1974 there were just four birds.

That season one pair nested in a tree in the usual way, but their nest was raided by monkeys. For some reason the other pair chose to nest in a hole in a sheer cliff. The choice of this unusual nesting site saved the species because the cliff face was monkey-proof. Three chicks fledged, and for the first time in years the Mauritius kestrel population increased. The young birds adopted the

Mauritius kestrels are currently being studied to determine their genetic variation so that their genetic diversity can be maintained.

cliff-nesting habit when they matured, and by 1976 they had boosted the population to 15 birds.

Revival

Early attempts to breed Mauritius kestrels in captivity ended in failure. The first success came in 1984, and since then many birds have been bred in captivity both in Mauritius and at the World Center for Birds of Prey in Boise, Idaho. By 1993 there were 200 birds.

The object was always to reintroduce the birds to the wild. Released captive-bred birds initially had trouble establishing territories in areas where there were wild kestrels; only about 50 percent of birds released in prime habitat survived their first year.

It was assumed that Mauritius kestrels would not thrive in other types of terrain, but the captive-bred birds have proved adaptable.

Released into areas of degraded secondary forest, their survival rate after a year is about 80 percent. By the end of the 1999 to 2000 breeding season there were three subpopulations, including between 145 and 200 breeding pairs. At first the birds were sustained by supplementary feeding, nest-guarding, predator control, and other conservation measures. But since 1994 there have been no more reintroductions, and apart from careful monitoring, the kestrels have virtually been left to their own devices.

The Mauritius kestrel will never be quite safe: Its total population is so small that it will always be vulnerable to natural disasters such as tropical storms and infectious diseases. However, its story shows what can be done, given the will and a little luck.

175

Whooping Crane

Grus americana

Intensive conservation efforts have pulled the whooping crane back from the brink of extinction. There is now hope that this rescue initiative is turning into a conservation success story.

In the mid-19th century the population of whooping cranes numbered between 1,300 and 1,400 birds. By 1938 heavy hunting pressure, widespread habitat conversion, and general disturbance by people had reduced the population to just 14 adults. Such a large reduction in numbers was inevitably accompanied by a huge contraction in range, and many populations became extinct.

There is now only one self-sustaining wild population, breeding in the wet prairies of Wood Buffalo National Park in central Canada. This population of 183 birds includes 50 breeding pairs and has been increasing slowly at about 5 percent per year since 1966. The major hope for the species' continuing survival rests with the wild Canadian flock.

Reintroduced Birds

A reintroduced population that includes six territorial pairs exists in Florida, but numbers are maintained by the annual introduction of more birds from captivity. However, there are hopes that the Florida population will become self-sustaining, which is not the case for the reintroduced birds in Idaho. This was an experimental flock, cross-fostered by sandhill cranes, but the birds have not reproduced.

Current Problems

Hunting and large-scale habitat loss are no longer key threats to the populations. Currently the largest known cause of death or injury to fledglings is collision with powerlines. Since overall numbers are still low, predation by golden eagles is also believed to be highly significant, especially on migration routes.

Drought is thought to be a cause of the deterioration of some breeding habitats, but availability of habitat on breeding grounds is not considered to be a limiting factor for the near future. There are more important threats, such as those affecting the major wintering site, Aransas National Wildlife Refuge in Texas. There, the risk of oil and chemical pollution is always present, along with problems related to boat traffic, wave erosion, and dredging.

DATA PANEL

Whooping crane

Grus americana

Family: Gruidae

World population: About 380 birds in the wild and captivity

Distribution: Wild population breeds in Wood Buffalo National Park, on the border of Northwest Territories and Alberta, Canada. Winters at Aransas National Wildlife Refuge, Texas. Flocks have been reintroduced to Florida and Idaho, with former nonmigratory and latter wintering south to New Mexico

Habitat: Breeds in prairie wetlands and winters in coastal brackish wetlands

Size: Length: 4.4 ft (1.3 m); wingspan: 7–8 ft (2–2.4 m). Weight: 16.5 lb (7.5 kg)

Form: Huge bird with large, horn-colored bill. Adults show black forehead, lores (area between eyes and base of bill), and "moustache," tipped red. Red crown and facial skin around bill. Black primary feathers visible in flight. Immatures whitish, with scattered brown feathers over wings and paler red-brown head and neck

Diet: In Canada snails, larval insects, leeches, frogs, minnows, small rodents, and berries; sometimes scavenges on dead ducks, marsh birds, or muskrats. During migration aquatic animals, plants roots, and waste grain in stubble fields. In Texas shellfish, snakes, acorns, small fish, and wild fruit

Breeding: Two eggs laid between late April and mid-May and incubated for about 1 month; usually only 1 fledges

Related endangered species: Include blue crane (*Grus paradisea*) VU; black-necked crane (*G. nigricollis*) VU; Siberian crane (*G. leucogeranus*) CR; wattled crane (*G. carunculatus*) VU

Status: IUCN EN; CITES I

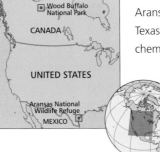

Wood Buffalo National Park

CANADA

UNITED STATES

Aransas National Wildlife Refuge

MEXICO

Conservation Targets

Only an intensive conservation effort has prevented the whooping crane from disappearing into extinction. Its objectives have been to maintain one self-sustaining population and to increase the captive population for further releases of birds into the wild.

The 124 captive birds are held at four main locations in Maryland, Texas, and Wisconsin in the United States, and at Calgary in Canada. In the special facilities whooping crane chicks are kept in isolation from humans. They are fed through a hole in the wall by an adult whooping crane glove puppet. Simulation of this kind is designed to make the birds' eventual introduction to the wild as successful as possible. Since the choice of migration routes, nesting locations, and wintering sites is learned rather than instinctive, the captive-breeding programs also focus on teaching birds to migrate by following light aircraft or vehicles on the ground.

The species is the subject of a transnational recovery plan, which has a number of ambitious but necessary targets. Current efforts are designed to increase the size of the existing wild population and to establish two further self-sustaining reintroduced populations. An important part of the conservation plan is to ensure that the self-sustaining populations in the wild grow to at least 1,000 birds.

The whooping crane *is a huge white crane that is threatened by the high incidence of collisions with powerlines among fledglings. A recent experiment aimed at making the lines more visible has reduced collisions by 40 to 60 percent.*

Takahe

Porphyrio hochstetteri

Once believed extinct, the flightless takahe of New Zealand was rediscovered in 1948 in the cold, wet, and remote mountains of Fiordland on South Island. Since then its numbers have fluctuated fairly constantly between 100 and 160, but a recent steady increase offers hope for the future.

Isolated in the South Pacific, between the coral seas of Polynesia and the windswept pack ice of Antarctica, New Zealand has been cut off from the rest of the world for 80 million years. Inaccessible to the mammals that spread over other regions of the world during this time, it became the home of an extraordinary variety of birds adapted for every conceivable lifestyle. Since the birds had no need to escape from enemies such as cats, foxes, or humans, many of them lacked any fear of predators and the power of flight.

One of the most spectacular of these flightless islanders is the takahe, a giant bird that once ranged all over the North and South Islands, originally occurring throughout the islands' forests and grasslands. Its troubles began with the arrival of

Polynesian colonists about 1,000 years ago. These colonists—the Maori—found the takahe easy meat and probably wiped out local populations by hunting them. This probably drove the birds into suboptimal grassland habitats, where there was little hunting.

The Maori also brought the first of many mammal invaders: pigs, rats, and dogs. Some 800 years later European settlers arrived and began introducing a whole menagerie of cats, foxes, stoats, possums, rabbits, deer, cattle, and sheep to the islands. While predators such as the stoat attacked the takahe, the grazers destroyed its food supply. By degrees the takahe disappeared, and by the 1930s the species was believed to be extinct.

New Zealand map showing Tiritiri Matangi Island, North Island, Islands of Kāpiti, Mana, and Maud, South Island, Murchison and Stuart Mountains

DATA PANEL

Takahe (notornis)

Porphyrio hochstetteri

Family: Rallidae

World population: About 150–220 birds

Distribution: Occurs naturally on South Island, New Zealand, but has been introduced to 4 predator-free islands off New Zealand

Habitat: Mountain tussock grassland in summer; beech forest and scrub in winter

Size: Length: 25 in (63 cm). Weight: male 4.8–8.8 lb (2.2–4 kg); female 4–7.7 lb (1.8–3.5 kg)

Form: A bulky, flightless bird with a large red bill and frontal shield, reduced wings, and a short tail. Head and neck iridescent blue; peacock-blue shoulders; green and blue back and wings; red legs. Juveniles duller

Diet: Mainly juices from the tender bases of snow tussock grasses; grass seeds and fern rhizomes in winter; also some insects and small lizards

Breeding: Pairs mate for life and usually breed October–December. A nest is built on the ground; 2 brown-blotched, pale-buff eggs are incubated for 4–4.5 weeks by both parents. Chicks depend on parents for 4 months

Related endangered species: One of 33 threatened species in the family Rallidae, including Invisible rail (*Habroptila wallacii*) VU; Guam rail (*Gallirallus owstoni*) EW; Makira moorhen (*Gallinula sylvestris*) CR; Samoan moorhen (*G. pacifica*) CR; and horned coot (*Fulica cornuta*) NT

Status: IUCN EN; not listed by CITES

Rediscovery

In fact, the takahe had retreated to the remote Murchison Mountains in the Fiordland of South Island. When it was rediscovered in 1948, there were between 250 and 300 birds left, surviving in a region of heavy snows and high rainfall. It is a hard life, and it has been made harder by introduced red deer that overgraze and eliminate the most nutritious grasses, leaving little for the takahe to eat. The takahe also suffers predation by stoats, and as a result it has a low breeding success rate. Since 1980 the wild population has fluctuated at levels of 100 to 160 birds, and without intensive conservation actions its chances of survival would have been slim.

Conservation

Red deer have been controlled in the Murchison Mountains since the 1960s, but despite this the takahe population failed to recover. In an effort to boost its numbers, a captive-breeding unit was established in the 1980s and captive-bred birds were released into the wild. From 1984 to 1991 small populations were also established on four predator-free islands and intensively managed to maximize their breeding success. Even so, these islands' populations have reached a total of only about 60 adults.

There is a plan to establish a second mainland population. The ultimate goal is to reach a total, self-sustaining population of over 500 birds; if the recovery program achieves this, the takahe will be off the Endangered list, but will be classified as Vulnerable.

The takahe *is the largest and one of the most colorful members of the rail family.*

Kakapo

Strigops habroptilus

Conservationists saved this extraordinary parrot by translocating the few remaining birds to predator-free islands, but the population is still extremely small and inherently at risk.

The kakapo is the heaviest parrot, one of the few nocturnal species in its family, and the only one that is completely flightless. It lives mainly on the ground, where its massive legs and feet enable it to travel far and quite fast. It uses its wings to balance when running at speed and climbing up leaning trunks and branches, and to break its fall as it parachutes from branches or down steep slopes. It is incapable of gliding, let alone powered flight.

Like so much about this exceptional parrot, its social life (or lack of it) and reproductive behavior are remarkable. In contrast to other parrots, which are among the most gregarious and sociable of birds, the kakapo is solitary except during courtship, and then the interactions between males are highly aggressive; researchers who kept kakapos together found they would attack and even kill one another.

The kakapo is the only parrot species with a "lek" breeding system, in which several rival males assemble at a shared "arena" on summer nights to attract females to mate with them. This arena consists of a complex system of well-defined paths, linking a number of bowl-shaped depressions in the ground. Both paths and bowls are made by the males, and each male has a bowl of his own. He fits inside it and inflates the air sac within his chest until he swells up like a big green balloon, then releases the air to produce the loud, booming calls that act as a magnet for the waiting females. The bowl amplifies the strange sound, which is audible to humans from up to 3 miles (5 km) away.

Each male has to spend many nights booming— up to 1,000 times an hour—to secure a mate. He also carefully cleans his tracks and bowl, and defends them

fiercely against rival males. After mating, a female is on her own. Having laid her eggs, she must incubate them for a month and may care for the young for a further nine months. All this activity requires a great deal of energy from both sexes. It is hardly surprising, then, that kakapos do not breed every year, but only irregularly at intervals of three to five years, triggered by the periodic abundance (known as "masting") of seeds and fruit of certain key plant species, such as the native rimu tree.

To the Brink of Extinction

Evidence from preserved bones shows that for some time after the first Maori settlers arrived in New Zealand about 1,000 years ago, the kakapo was found throughout most of the country. However, with the Maori colonization of the land the kakapo's range started contracting. The birds suffered as the settlers altered habitats, and especially as they introduced dogs and Pacific rats, which hunted down the birds— as did the Maori themselves. The Maori ate them and also valued their feathers for making cloaks.

Evolving on a group of oceanic islands that had no native mammalian predators (New Zealand lacks any native mammals apart from three species of bat), the kakapo had no need to evolve defenses against them and so was especially vulnerable. Kakapo mothers had to search for food at night, leaving their eggs and chicks unattended and so even more vulnerable.

After Europeans colonized New Zealand from the early 19th century, they introduced other carnivorous mammals such as stoats, cats, dogs, black and brown rats, and Australian brush-tailed possums. These animals caused even more devastation among kakapo populations. By 1976 only 18 birds were known to exist in the remote mountain country of Fiordland, in the southwest corner of South Island, and all of them were males. By 1989 the Fiordland birds—the last mainland population—were gone. However, in 1977 the dramatic discovery was made of about 150 kakapos living on Stewart Island, the largest of New Zealand's offshore islands. Over half the birds were being killed each year by feral cats. Between 1980 and 1992 the 61 kakapos on Stewart Island were moved to predator-free offshore islands.

Today kakapos are tagged with miniature radio transmitters, and every nest is constantly monitored using infrared video cameras. Kakapo eggs and nestlings are kept warm with heating pads when the females leave to forage at night. Providing extra food has increased the frequency and the success of breeding attempts, and researchers are currently investigating whether rimu trees can be induced to fruit using plant hormones.

Thanks to the work of conservationists and to a run of three successful breeding seasons, the kakapo population is at last increasing. There are currently 62 kakapos, comprising 36 males and 26 females, of which 50 are capable of breeding, six are subadults, and six are juveniles. Even so, there is a long way to go before the kakapo is secure.

*The kakapo is a giant, flightless parrot that resembles an owl in its facial disks (*Strigops *means "owl face").*

DATA PANEL

Kakapo (owl parrot)

Strigops habroptilus

Family: Psittacidae

World population: 62 birds

Distribution: Translocated birds on 4 New Zealand offshore islands: Maud, Inner Chetwode, Codfish, and Pearl

Habitat: Mainly forest edges and forests in younger stages of growth

Size: Length: 23–25 in (58–64 cm); wingspan: 33–36 in (84–91 cm)

Form: Large, stout-bodied parrot with hairlike facial disk, short, broad bill with cere (bare skin at base containing nostrils) prominent and swollen; short, broad wings; scruffy, downcurved tail; massive, fleshy legs and feet with powerful claws; plumage moss-green on upperparts and greenish-yellow on underparts; mottled and barred with brown and yellowish; male has wider head and much bigger bill and is about 25% heavier than female

Diet: Leaves, stems, roots, fruit, nectar, and seeds of trees, shrubs, etc.

Breeding: Breeds every 2–5 years, coinciding with bumper crops of food plants; nests inside rotting fallen tree trunks, in hollow tree stumps, or under clumps of vegetation; 1–3 white eggs incubated by the female for 30 days; fledging period 10–12 weeks; may not attain sexual maturity until 6–9 years old

Related endangered species: There are no other members of the subgroup Strigopini, but 2 other threatened New Zealand parrots, the kaka *(Nestor meridionalis)* VU and kea *(N. notabilis)* VU, may be related; some experts think that the kakapo may be related to the night parrot *(Pezoporus occidentalis)* CR and the ground parrot *(Pezoporus wallicus)* of Australia

Status: IUCN CR; CITES I

North Island

NEW ZEALAND
Islands of Maud and Inner Chetwode

South Island

Codfish Island
Pearl Island

Hyacinth Macaw

Anodorhynchus hyacinthinus

The world's largest parrot, the hyacinth macaw is a spectacular vivid blue South American bird. It has suffered a massive decline in numbers over the last 40 years due mainly to illegal trapping for private collectors.

Once relatively numerous across much of its range in Brazil, the hyacinth macaw is now rare in most of its former strongholds. The largest population occurs in the Brazilian part of the Pantanal region—a huge, grassy plain about the size of Iowa that straddles the southwestern Brazilian states of Mato Grosso and Mato Grosso do Sul, extending southeast into Bolivia and Paraguay. Dotted with palms and other trees and shrubs, the habitat is flooded during the rainy season, peaking in about February to become the biggest freshwater wetland in the world. Even here numbers of the great blue parrots have declined alarmingly in recent times.

The two other, smaller, populations are in the Gerais region of central Brazil and in Amazonia.

In contrast to most of the more familiar macaws of the genus *Ara*, such as the blue-and-yellow and scarlet macaws, which eat a wide range of plants, hyacinth macaws depend on a few species of palm trees for their staple diet of palm nuts.

The massive black bill of the hyacinth macaw is an adaptation to its specialized diet. Accounting for about one-fifth of the entire weight of the bird and worked by powerful muscles, it is immensely strong and forms an impressive and efficient tool for crushing the large, hard nuts of palm trees.

As well as taking them straight from the trees, the birds also feed on the palm nuts where they have fallen on the ground. On ranchlands where cattle are raised they can take advantage of concentrations of palm nuts that remain undigested in cowpats. The cattle digest the soft, fleshy mesocarp surrounding each nut, thereby saving the birds the effort.

Although birds in northeastern Brazil nest on remote cliff crevices, most hyacinth macaws need suitable nesting trees if they are to breed. In the Pantanal only a few of the trees grow big enough to have developed large hollows in which the birds can conceal their nests from predators. However, such big trees and big birds are so prominent that local people cannot fail to be aware of the nest sites. Sometimes, trappers return year after year to steal chicks, while other long-established nesting trees are felled or burned by landowners clearing the land for cattle; both scenarios spell disaster for the hyacinth macaws.

Habitat in the Gerais region is being rapidly converted to mechanized agriculture, cattle ranches, and exotic tree plantations.

Illegal Trade

During the period between 1970 and 1980 huge numbers of young hyacinth macaws were taken from their nests and sold to dealers or middlemen, who then sold them on to private collectors in the United States, Europe, Japan, and other countries. Some illegal trade still exists. An equal but persistent demand for captive macaws within Brazil, and the taking of birds for feather headdresses or food adds to the problem, despite Brazilian legislation protecting the species. Estimates suggest that up to 10,000 hyacinth macaws may have been taken from the wild in the 1980s alone.

In 1987 the situation regarding international trade was judged to be so serious that the hyacinth macaw was moved from Appendix II to Appendix I of CITES, but for a while this had the unfortunate effect of

DATA PANEL

Hyacinth macaw (hyacinthine macaw, blue macaw, black macaw)

Anodorhynchus hyacinthinus

Family: Psittacidae

World population: About 2,500–10,000 individuals in Brazil; perhaps fewer than 100 in Bolivia; small numbers in Paraguay

Distribution: Three main areas of interior Brazil: on the southern side of the Amazon in the northeast; the Gerais region of central Brazil; the seasonally flooded Pantanal region of the Upper Río Paraguay basin, just extending into eastern Bolivia and northern Paraguay

Habitat: Lightly wooded areas, especially where clumps of trees are mixed with open grassland or swamps

Size: Length: 35–39 in (90–100 cm)

Form: Bird of great size with huge, hooked black bill; long, narrow wings; long tail; cobalt-blue plumage, purple on wings and tail, blackish on underwings and undertail

Diet: Mainly nuts of various palm trees; fruit, including figs; occasionally water snails; liquid from unripe palm fruits

Breeding: Usually in dry season; 2 (rarely 1 or 3) eggs laid; incubation 3–4 weeks, fledging about 3.5 months

Related endangered species: Lear's macaw (*Anodorhynchus leari*) CR; glaucous macaw (*A. glaucus*) CR; Spix's macaw (*Cyanopsitta spixii*) CR; blue-throated macaw (*Ara glaucogularis*) CR; military macaw (*A. militaris*) VU; red-fronted macaw (*A. rubrogenys*) EN

Status: IUCN EN; CITES I

stimulating even greater demand by unscrupulous dealers and collectors willing to pay $8,000 or more for each bird.

Recent efforts to save the hyacinth macaw have included studies of its ecology, an investigation into trade in the bird, and the establishment of nest boxes. Most encouragingly, many ranch owners in the Pantanal and Gerais regions no longer allow trapping on their properties.

The hyacinth macaw *is a slow breeder, taking about five months from egg-laying to fledging (the time when the young start to fly). The birds rarely succeed in rearing more than one of the usual two chicks.*

Pink Pigeon

Columba (Streptopelia) mayeri

Thanks to the dedicated work of conservationists, the pink pigeon has been saved from extinction, and numbers have dramatically increased over the last decade. But without continued intensive management, including a captive-breeding program, the species would be likely to become extinct.

A close relative of the abundant and widespread wood pigeon of Europe and parts of Asia, the pink pigeon is one of the most attractive members of the large family of pigeons and doves. This group has suffered more than most from extinction, with almost a third of the 309 surviving species classified as Threatened or Lower Risk, near threatened. Over 80 percent of them are island species, as were all but one of the 13 species of pigeons and doves that have recently become extinct.

The pink pigeon is found only on the island of Mauritius and the neighboring Ile aux Aigrettes. Discoveries of bones of the birds indicate that it was once widespread in forests throughout the whole of Mauritius. Now it is confined to the southwestern part of the island. The precarious position the species is in today is entirely due to a variety of human factors.

Multiple Threats

Along with many other unique animals and plants, the pink pigeon has suffered from the massive destruction of the native forests of Mauritius by colonists from the late 18th century onward. Uncontrolled hunting also played its part in reducing the species to a perilously low and fragmented population.

In addition, the pink pigeon—and other unique Mauritian wildlife—has been affected by predation by the legion of animals deliberately introduced or accidentally brought to the island by sailors and settlers. They include the crab-eating macaque, originally from Southeast Asia, which preys on adult pigeons, also taking eggs and young from their nests. The small Indian mongoose, which was introduced to control black rats, also preys on young pigeons. However, black rats that take the pigeon's eggs and young have survived and prospered; feral cats are also predators of pigeons.

Other threats affecting the birds include disease and shortages of suitable food in late winter. The remaining small and fragmented populations and their forest habitat are increasingly at the mercy of tropical cyclones that hit the island from time to time. Winds blowing at up to 155 miles per hour (250 km/h) or more not only damage the forest by stripping trees of the shoots and fruit on which the pigeons feed but also blow down the bird's nests.

By 1990, as a result of all these factors, the total world population of this once common species was reduced to just 10 individuals, all of which nested in a single grove of introduced Japanese red cedar trees.

Rescue Plans

The pink pigeon has been the focus of a major international rescue program for many years. It has involved sponsorship by BirdLife International (a global partnership of conservation organizations), the World Wide Fund for Nature, and the New York Zoological Society. There is also a long-term program of research and rescue involving the Mauritian government working together with several zoos—the Durrell Wildlife Conservation Trust, Vogelpark Walsrode in Germany, and the New York and Alberquerque zoos.

Attempts at captive breeding at the zoos began in the mid-1970s. Careful reintroduction into the wild has recently helped achieve a dramatic increase in the pigeon's numbers. Other elements in the program

DATA PANEL

Pink pigeon (Mauritius pink pigeon, chestnut-tailed pigeon)

Columba (Streptopelia) mayeri

Family: Columbidae

World population: 360–380 birds

Distribution: Restricted to 4 sites in southwestern Mauritius and introduced to Ile aux Aigrettes, off eastern coast

Habitat: Subtropical evergreen forests, including remnant native trees and introduced species; most pairs nest in introduced Japanese red cedars

Size: Length:14–14.8 in (36–40 cm). Weight: male 8.5–14.5 oz (240–410 g); female 7.5–13 oz (213–369 g)

Form: Slightly larger than feral pigeon, with smaller head, larger body, and broad, rounded wings; plumage pink-white; duskier on upper back, belly, flanks, and undertail; rest of upperparts and wings dark chocolate-brown; primary flight feathers darker; lower back and rump blue-gray; uppertail coverts and tail red-orange or chestnut; eyes surrounded by red ring of bare skin with white or pale-yellow iris; bill red at base with a yellow or creamy tip; red feet

Diet: Wide variety of fruit and berries as well as leaves and flowers

Breeding: Nest is platform of twigs; 2 white eggs incubated for 13–18 days; young fledge in about 20 days

Related endangered species: Sixty-one species of pigeons are threatened, including 17 other species in the genus *Columba*: silvery wood pigeon (*C. argentina*) CR; yellow-legged pigeon (*C. pallidiceps*) EN; white-tailed laurel pigeon (*C. junoniae*) EN; maroon pigeon (*C. thomensis*) VU; and Sri Lanka wood pigeon (*C. torringtoni*) VU

Status: IUCN EN; CITES III

include restoring habitat, controlling introduced predators and guarding nests to prevent predation, rescuing eggs and young from failing nests, providing the birds with extra food, and controlling disease.

The rescue program came barely in time to save the pink pigeon. The intensive management has seen a dramatic increase in the numbers of the pigeons. A few more years of decline and the species would probably have suffered the same fate as its closest relative, the long-extinct Réunion pigeon.

The pink pigeon has undergone a remarkable improvement in status. Once classified by the IUCN as Critically Endangered, it was downgraded to Endangered in 2000, a status that was confirmed in 2004.

185

Dodo

Raphus cucullatus

The dodo was first discovered on a remote island in the Indian Ocean in about 1507. Few people ever saw it alive, but it has since become world famous as a symbol of extinction.

The dodo is a kind of giant ground pigeon that somehow reached the island of Mauritius long ago and developed into a unique, flightless bird. The island had no native mammals and no human inhabitants, so flight was unnecessary to escape enemies. The birds could nest on the ground and roam around without risk.

Portuguese navigators discovered the dodo on Mauritius in about 1507. It was described as being unintelligent (the name possibly comes from the Portuguese *doudo*, meaning "stupid") and easy to catch and kill. The sailors would stock up with fresh meat in the form of dodos before continuing their travels. A later Dutch expedition fed their entire crew on four dodos with some to spare, but noted that the dead birds needed to be boiled for a long time before they were tender enough to eat.

Island Colonization

Subsequent visits by French and British ships led to colonization of the island. The settlers cleared the forests to make way for sugarcane. They imported pigs, monkeys, cats, and dogs; with them also came rats. The introduced animals were highly effective scavengers and predators. Although the adult dodos were large enough to defend themselves, their eggs—laid on the ground—could be swiftly gobbled up by the first pig or monkey that spotted them. The fruit trees that provided a vital part of the bird's diet vanished, and within about 155 years of its discovery the dodo was extinct.

Dead as a Dodo

No dodos were found during a visit to Mauritius in 1682. The dodo has since become an international symbol for extinction and a reminder of the pressures facing wildlife in the modern world. The expression "dead as a dodo" has even entered our language to describe something that is dead or defunct.

Our impression of what a dodo looks like may be based on drawings of the bird done long ago. The pictures make the bird look very plump. In fact, analysis of the dodo's skeletal structure suggests that it was actually a slimmer bird, more like a modern wild

DATA PANEL

Dodo

Raphus cucullatus

Family: Raphidae

World population: 0 (Extinct)

Distribution: Mauritius, Indian Ocean

Habitat: Lowland forests

Size: Length: about 30 in (75 cm). Weight: up to 50 lb (23 kg)

Form: Gray, turkey-sized bird, often depicted as plump. Large, fleshy feet; tuft of tail feathers; thick, long bill measuring 9 in (20 cm) with hooked tip

Diet: Large fruit gathered from forest floor, perhaps supplemented by invertebrates, including snails and worms

Breeding: Said to lay single white egg

Related endangered species: Probably Rodrigues solitaire (*Pezophaps solitaria*) EX

Status: IUCN EX; not listed by CITES

turkey. It is possible, however, that the plumpness shown in the pictures was real. It was thought that the dodos ate large quantities of fruit in season and stored the fat in their bodies. On occasion they were said to have reached a weight of 50 pounds (23 kg).

Dodo Remains

Unusually for a forest bird, a number of bones exist for study. Some dodos appear to have fallen into rock crevices or were trapped in small caves in the volcanic lava of Mauritius, leaving their bones for scientists to discover centuries later. However, most of the bones in the world's museums come from a swamp where the modern international airport now lies. Many dodos seem to have drowned here, and collectors used to employ local people to wade around in the mud feeling for dodo bones with their bare feet.

There are no dodo skins in existence, just the head and foot of a specimen that had been kept alive in Europe. The body parts were stuffed after the bird died, but were attacked and partly defaced by insects.

The remains were rescued and are now on display in the University Museum in Oxford, England. Some museums exhibit life-sized models of the dodo, created using goose and chicken feathers.

There were stories of another species of dodo— the white dodo—living on the island of Réunion. The island is situated about 120 miles (200 km) west of Mauritius. Being flightless, it is difficult to imagine that the Mauritian dodo could have colonized Réunion. In fact, the evidence for the existence of white dodos relies on old eyewitness accounts, which may well be inaccurate. Either the sailors were mistaken about which island they saw the dodo on, or they confused the bird with a flightless ibis that lived on Réunion and is now also extinct.

The dodo *was extinct by 1682. It was probably not as plump as it was depicted in illustrations.*

Spotted Owl

Strix occidentalis

Largely restricted to the ancient conifer and oak forests that once extended all along the Pacific coast of North America, the spotted owl is being driven from its ancestral habitats by logging operations that target the biggest, oldest, and most valuable trees.

Found in four distinct populations from southwestern Canada to Mexico, the spotted owl is primarily a bird of mature, moist, temperate forests. Throughout its range it is a night hunter that uses its acute hearing and night-adapted eyesight to pinpoint small mammals and birds in the darkness as it perches above the forest floor. Swooping down on silent wings, it seizes its victim in its feathered talons and returns to the perch to sever its spinal cord with its bill. Then it swallows the prey whole, headfirst.

The forests of great redwoods, pines, hemlocks, cedars, and oaks provide the spotted owl with a wealth of prey and plenty of quiet roosting sites where it can spend the day undisturbed.

They also offer ideal nesting holes in big, mature trees, although the owl will sometimes use a rock cavity or even an abandoned squirrel nest. Many spotted owls stay on their nesting territories throughout the year, defending them against trespassing rivals with loud whoops and shrieks that echo through the forest. It is an eerie, evocative, and increasingly rare sound.

Logged Out

As is the case elsewhere, ancient forests of western North America are being destroyed for their timber. Secondary forest is no replacement for the rich, multilayered patchwork of trees, shrubs, and undergrowth that develops naturally over the centuries. It does not have the same diversity of wildlife—which for the spotted owl means prey—and the young trees lack holes and snags where birds can

DATA PANEL

Spotted owl

Strix occidentalis

Family: Strigidae

World population: About 15,000 birds in 4 races

Distribution: Western North America: northern race *S. o. caurina* from southern British Columbia to northern California; California race *S. o. occidentalis* through central and southern California; Mexican race *S. o. lucida* scattered from southern Utah to central Mexico; the fourth, from the State of Mexico in southern central Mexico, recently described and named *juanaphillipsae*

Habitat: Mainly moist, temperate old-growth conifer or oak forest, but Mexican race also occurs in warmer, drier, secondary pine-oak forest and rocky canyons

Size: Length: 16–19 in (41–48 cm). Weight: 1.1–1.7 lb (520–760 g)

Form: Medium-sized, upright, round-headed owl with well-defined facial disk, black eyes, and fully feathered feet. Upperparts rich red-brown, with white spots on head and neck; mottled buff on back and wings; underparts barred whitish and rust-brown. Mexican race paler. Juvenile pale brown with dark barring

Diet: Mainly small mammals; also roosting birds (including small owls) and insects

Breeding: Birds pair for life, nesting March–June. Usually 2 eggs, laid on bare floor of tree cavity or crevice and incubated by female for 30 days. Downy chicks brooded by female for 2 weeks while male brings food, then both parents forage; fledged young leave nest at 35 days

Related endangered species: Twenty-three other owls in the family Strigidae, including Blakiston's eagle owl (*Ketupa blakistoni*) EN; São Tomé scops-owl (*Otus hartlaubi*) VU; Sokoke scops-owl (*O. ireneae*) EN; rufous fishing-owl (*Scotopelia ussheri*) EN; and long-whiskered owlet (*Xenoglaux loweryi*) EN

Status: IUCN NT; CITES II

nest and perch. Spotted owls avoid plantations that are fewer than 100 years old, and a forest has to be at least 200 years old for it to become suitable breeding habitat.

The old trees are the biggest and most valuable. Consequently, tracts of prime old-growth forest have been clear-felled, leaving nothing but stumps. Where big trees are more scattered, they are often selectively felled to leave younger, smaller trees. Both strategies are catastrophic for the owl, especially the northern race. It is estimated that in the northwestern United States the degree of spotted owl habitat loss ranges from 54 percent to over 99 percent.

Logging and the spread of farmland and towns, reservoir development, and mining have led to a steep decline in the population of spotted owls. There are some 8,500 of the northern race surviving in the huge swath of coastal forest from Canada to northern California. The California race is in trouble too, with about 3,000 left. The more adaptable Mexican race numbers up to 1,500 in the American part of its range, with perhaps 2,000 in Mexico itself; the southern owls seem to be holding their own, partly because they are less tied to old-growth forest, but also because they are not suffering such heavy habitat losses.

The spotted owl is classified as Lower Risk, near threatened rather than Endangered, but its decline is accelerating, and it has become the subject of six management plans in Canada and the United States. It has also been the focus of a heated debate between conservationists, timber companies, and politicians over the future of the forests.

The spotted owl, *like many other nocturnal owl species, has a facial disk that helps reflect sound to the ears, helping the birds locate prey.*

Bee Hummingbird

Mellisuga helenae

Bee hummingbirds are found only on the island of Cuba, and the males of the species are famous for being the world's smallest living bird. Although they were once relatively common and widespread, they are now becoming increasingly rare and localized.

As its name suggests, the bee hummingbird can easily be mistaken for a large bee as it hovers to sip nectar from the blossom of a hibiscus plant or an aloe. About half of its diminutive length is taken up by its long, slender bill and short tail. Among the smallest of all vertebrate animals, it weighs about 75,000 times less than the world's largest bird, the male ostrich, and is about the same size as an ostrich eye. Bee hummingbirds are dwarfed by many of the butterflies found in their tropical forest home.

Like other hummingbirds, the bee hummingbird feeds in flight. It is a superb flyer and has wings with bones that are fused except at the shoulder joint. This wing design enables it to rotate its wings. Such prowess in the air allows it to hover in one spot, remaining almost motionless in front of a flower to feed. It can also fly sideways, straight up and down, and even backward.

When hovering, a bee hummingbird beats its wings 70 times per second. This uses up large amounts of energy—and such a tiny animal can store very little. Consequently, it must have a constant source of energy-rich food that it can convert quickly into fuel to power its proportionately large wing muscles and maintain its high metabolism. It finds this food in the form of nectar, which it sips from tubular flowers by inserting its long, slender bill and lapping up the sugary liquid with its long, grooved tongue. The bee hummingbird needs to feed every few minutes. It can only survive short periods without food, and it does so by becoming torpid, reducing its metabolic rate by 80 to 90 percent and thereby saving up to 60 percent of its energy requirements. The male bee hummingbird is fiercely territorial, driving off any intruder of the same or different species that attempts to feed from his patch of nectar-rich flowers.

Spectacular Displays

A male attracts a mate in three ways. First, he expands his gorget—a bib of feathers—and lateral plumes, which take on a glittering, jewellike appearance in sunlight and are iridescent—the colors change depending on the viewing

DATA PANEL

Bee hummingbird

Mellisuga helenae

Family: Trochilidae

World population: Over 10,000 birds (estimated)

Distribution: Cuba; formerly occurred on the Isla de la Juventud (Isle of Youth) to the southwest of Cuba

Habitat: Mainly coastal forests and forest margins, with thick tangles of lianas and abundant epiphytes (plants that grow on other plants); also interior forests, wooded mountain valleys, swamps, and gardens

Size: Length: 2–2.3 in (5–6 cm); male slightly smaller than female. Weight: 0.05–0.07 oz (1.6–1.9 g)

Form: Tiny bird with long, straight, black bill. Male's head, throat, lateral plumes, and gorget (bib of feathers) glitter fiery red in sunlight; rest of upperparts bluish; rest of underparts

off-white. Female and immatures have green upperparts and whitish underparts

Diet: Adults eat nectar from a wide range of flowers; also small insects

Breeding: Season from March to June. Female weaves nest from dried plant fibers, camouflaged on the outside with lichens, usually partly hidden by leaves and lined with soft plant wool; 2 white eggs incubated for 21–22 days. Young fledge at 13–14 days, leaving nest at about 18 days

Related endangered species: No close relatives, but 9 hummingbird species classed as Critical, 9 as Endangered, and 9 as Vulnerable

Status: IUCN NT; CITES II

UNITED STATES

BAHAMAS

CUBA

Cayman Islands (U.K.)

JAMAICA

angle. Second, he zooms around in an aerial display. Third, he beats his wings to make a humming noise.

Pairs of birds mate in flight, after which the female builds a tiny, deep, cup-shaped nest in a forked twig or on a branch of a tree. Into it she lays two pea-sized eggs. She must keep the young supplied with a nourishing diet of nectar and partly digested insects.

Threatened Habitat

The bee hummingbird was once found throughout Cuba and the Isla de la Juventud (Isle of Youth) to the southwest of Cuba. Today it may survive only in a few sites in La Habana, Sierra de Anafe, Guanahacabibes Peninsula, Zapata Swamp, Moa, Mayarí, and the coast of Guantánamo. The bird seems to be heavily dependent on mature forest.

Much of Cuba's native vegetation has been converted for growing crops or for cattle pasture, and only 15 to 20 percent of the land remains in its natural state. Large areas of rain forest have been destroyed to make way for plantations of cacao, coffee, and tobacco, while dry forest is threatened by logging, charcoal production, and slash-and-burn cultivation. In the Zapata Swamp, burning, drainage, and agricultural expansion take their toll.

Although there are some 200 conservation areas in Cuba, making up about 12 percent of the total land area, some are probably too small to support their wildlife, and few afford sufficient protection from logging and other threats. Conservation efforts must be improved to save the bee hummingbird.

The bee hummingbird *beats its wings 70 times per second when feeding.*

Regent Honeyeater

Xanthomyza phrygia

The strikingly patterned regent honeyeater has suffered serious declines in range and numbers as a result of the destruction and fragmentation of its forest habitat, and probably also because it has lost out in competition with more adaptable rivals.

The honeyeater family is one of the major groups of Australian birds. Almost 40 percent of the 170 species in the world occur in Australia; the family evolved there and in New Guinea. At least one species occurs in every different land habitat in Australia, and 10 or more species may occur in a single area: Honeyeaters may account for over half of all the birds in a locality.

Brush Tongues

The most distinctive adaptation of the regent honeyeater is its brush-tipped tongue. When the bird pushes its beak into a flower and extends its tongue beyond the beak's tip, the tongue laps up nectar or other sugary fluids the way a paint-brush collects paint. Most honeyeaters can lap up all the nectar from a flower in less than a second. This adaptation is a major factor in the group's success.

Nevertheless, some species of honeyeater are not thriving. One of the most threatened is the regent honeyeater. This attractive and characterful bird feeds on nectar mainly from the flowers of trees—red ironbark, yellow gum and other eucalypts, and yellow box. The bird also eats manna (a sugary sap produced on tree bark in response to injury, especially by insects) and lerps (or honeydew), as well as fruit. All the foods are rich in energy but low in nutrients, so the birds have to spend a lot of time feeding; they live a partly nomadic life, moving around to find the best feeding

DATA PANEL

Regent honeyeater
Xanthomyza phrygia

Family: Meliphagidae

World population: About 1,500 birds

Distribution: Southeastern Australia; mainly at a few sites in northeastern Victoria, along the western slopes of the Great Dividing Range and central coast of New South Wales, with only small numbers elsewhere; now extinct in South Australia

Habitat: Dry, open forests and woodlands, especially those dominated by yellow box, red ironbark, and yellow gum trees; also riverside forests of river she-oaks in New South Wales

Size: Length: 8–9.5 in (20–24 cm)

Form: Slim-bodied, thrush-sized bird with downcurved, sharp-tipped bill; long tail. Male has black head, neck, upper back, and upper breast; patch of bare, pink or yellow skin around each eye; rest of upperparts black with pale-yellow scaly pattern; wings black with broad white fringes to some coverts; 3 broad yellow panels in each folded wing; lower breast, upper belly, and flanks creamy with black chevrons, rest of underparts white; tail black above with yellow edges and tip, bright yellow below. Female smaller and duller. Juvenile browner with yellow bill

Diet: Nectar from various flowers; also insects, manna (sugary sap produced by trees in response to injury), lerps (or honeydew—sugary secretions of aphids and plant-eating insects), and fruit, including mistletoe berries

Breeding: Mainly August–January (may not nest some years); nest of bark and grass strips lined with plant down and hair, built in tree 6.5–33 ft (2–10 m) tall, in an upright fork or among mistletoe; 2–3 salmon-buff eggs with red-brown spots; incubation about 15 days; fledging period about 14 days

Related endangered species: Crow honeyeater (*Gymnomyza aubryana*) EN; black-eared miner (*Manorina melanotis*) EN; stitchbird (*Notiomystis cincta*) VU; dusky friarbird (*Philemon fuscicapillus*) VU; long-bearded melidectes (*Melidectes princeps*) VU; painted honeyeater (*Grantiella picta*) NT; white-chinned myzomela (*Myzomela albigula*) DD; Chatham Island bellbird (*Anthornis melanocephala*) EX

Status: IUCN EN; not listed by CITES

sites. When breeding, they need more protein, and they include insects in their diet in order to satisfy this requirement. They take them from the trunks, branches, or foliage of trees, but sometimes catch them in flight.

Honeyeaters are quarrelsome birds, often chasing away rivals of their own and other species from flowering trees and other plants. It has been discovered that regent honeyeaters mimic the calls of larger species of honeyeater, such as friarbirds, wattlebirds, and the spiny-cheeked honeyeater, in an attempt to prevent these more dominant relatives from driving them away from sources of nectar.

Fragmented Forests

Despite the skilled mimicry, fragmentation of the regent honeyeater's habitat seems to be favoring more aggressive species, such as the noisy miner, which may be replacing the regent honeyeater in parts of its range. The habitat loss may be affecting the less adaptable regent honeyeater to such an extent that it is unable to gather in sufficient numbers at breeding sites to share the effort of driving rivals away from good nectar sources. Today only about a quarter of its habitat remains, the rest having been cleared for agriculture, timber, and other developments. What remains is often of inferior quality, with larger trees removed and an increasing number of unhealthy trees.

In many places the regent honeyeater appears only sporadically. When breeding, the birds are concentrated at relatively few sites, but numbers fluctuate greatly between sites and from one year to the next. In places where they have been scarce or absent for years they may suddenly return in large numbers. Years when few or no birds breed at a site may be a result of their failure to nest or because they have moved elsewhere to breed. Little is known about the birds' movements outside the breeding season.

The regent honeyeater, *an attractive, brightly plumaged bird, lives, feeds and breeds in dry, open forests.*

Conservationists carry out annual surveys of the species' range and abundance. A captive colony has now been established. Logging and grazing have been restricted at some major sites, and many of the trees favored by the honeyeaters have been planted to replace those destroyed or in poor health.

Plans to build on this work include studying the movements and population dynamics of the species, measuring the degree of isolation between different breeding populations, assessing the effect of noisy miners, and surveying and monitoring the birds' habitat to ensure that it is not degraded.

193

Blue Bird of Paradise

Paradisaea rudolphi

One of the most beautiful species in a family containing many spectacular-looking birds, the blue bird of paradise is also one of the most threatened—mainly by the loss of its habitat, but also by hunting for the stunning blue display plumes of the male.

As with many other birds of paradise, male blue birds of paradise are among the most stunning-looking birds in the world. An adult male is adorned with brilliant blue and violet filmy plumes that cascade from tufts of deep-crimson flank plumes on either side of his belly. In addition, two exceptionally long central tail feathers extend like narrow black ribbons and end in bright-blue spatula shapes. Over millions of years competition between rival males to appeal to females has led to the evolution of increasingly spectacular plumage and dramatic courtship displays.

Having prepared a special display site by stripping leaves from the surrounding branches, the male hangs upside down by his feet from a branch and gently sways back and forth. At the same time, he expands his iridescent display plumes to shimmer in the sunlight that penetrates the forest canopy. His scarlet-bordered black belly patch pulsates as he moves. After a few minutes he narrows his eyes to emphasize the white patches above and below them. All the while he utters an extraordinary buzzing, crackling, and whirring song, which sounds like radio static.

The gorgeous plumes and amazing display are the badge of adult males. The plumage of immature males resembles that of females, but with longer, narrower central tail feathers that grow with age. As the males mature, they also acquire more blue and violet feathers that will equip them to perform the displays.

Patchy Distribution

The blue bird of paradise is found only on the island of New Guinea. It is restricted to forests in the eastern Central Ranges in Papua New Guinea on the eastern half of the island. It is not known why the species' range does not extend into Papua, the Indonesian province on the western half of the island.

Within its limited range the blue bird of paradise is common in some areas, but rare or patchy in many places and absent from others—especially on the northern slopes of the southeastern mountains. The male blue bird of paradise spends much of his life defending his territories and attracting

DATA PANEL

Blue bird of paradise	Female lacks ornamental plumes and has chestnut underparts, but otherwise resembles male
Paradisaea rudolphi	
Family: Paradisaeidae	
World population: Estimated at 2,500–10,000 birds	**Diet:** Mainly fruit, including figs, wild peppers, and wild bananas; also insects, including crickets, and spiders
Distribution: Papua New Guinea, in mountains of eastern Central Ranges	
Habitat: Mainly montane primary oak forest, forest edge, and older secondary growth at lower levels 4,600–5,900 ft (1,400–1,800 m)	**Breeding:** Nest bowl built in tree or bush; usually 1 pale-pink egg with lavender-gray and brown markings; incubated by female for about 18 days; young cared for by female alone
Size: Length: male 26 in (67 cm), including elongated tail feathers; female 12 in (30 cm). Weight: 4–7 oz (124–189 g)	**Related endangered species:** Three other birds of paradise: MacGregor's bird of paradise (*Macgregoria pulchra*) VU; black sicklebill (*Epimachus fastuosus*) VU; Wahne's parotia (*Parotia wahnesi*) VU
Form: Pigeon-sized bird with dark plumage, white eye-ring, and stout, blue-white bill; male has glossy black plumage with blue feathers on wings, lower back, and tail; long, gauzelike plumes; 2 central feathers in tail form long ribbons with spatula-shaped tips.	**Status:** IUCN VU; CITES II

New Guinea
PAPUA NEW GUINEA
INDONESIA

AUSTRALIA

mates. Males are usually found only in primary forest, but some have been seen in fragmented areas of primary forest or in secondary forest. Female-plumaged birds (immature males or females) are often seen at the edge of the forest, and in areas of denser, older secondary growth.

Typically, there is also an altitude difference in the distribution of male and female blue birds of paradise; mature males occupy the central portion of the habitat, between 4,600 and 5,900 feet (1,400 and 1,800 m), and the female-plumaged birds tend to live in the upper and lower edges of the forest, up to 6,600 feet (2,000 m) and down to 3,600 feet (1,100 m).

Adult males are essentially solitary birds, but female-plumaged birds are sometimes encountered in small groups feeding at fruit-bearing trees. They may also feed with other species of bird of paradise. Although they find some fruit high in the forest canopy, most feeding occurs at lower levels, and individuals have been recorded foraging to within 3.3 to 6.6 feet (1 to 2 m) of the ground. While the bulk of their diet is the fruit of many different trees and shrubs, they also eat insects, including cockroaches, grasshoppers, and spiders.

Forest Clearance and Hunting

In the 1950s researchers looked at the distribution of the blue bird of paradise and recorded that it had gone from huge areas of forest that had been cleared for subsistence agriculture. Habitat loss still poses a major threat to the species today. Unfortunately, its range lies entirely within the zone most favored in Papua New Guinea for new settlements, agriculture, and logging.

Hunting is another threat. The species has been hunted by the islanders for hundreds of years for its spectacular plumes, which are used in headdresses and other ritual ornamentation. Where males are regularly hunted, they may abandon an area. The losses from hunting may be compounded by unfavorable competition with the Raggiana bird of paradise, which is better able to adapt to disturbed habitat.

Information about numbers and the rates of decline of the blue bird of paradise is lacking, but records suggest that its total population is relatively small and fragmented into small subpopulations. More data may result in reclassification of the species up to Endangered or down to Lower Risk, near threatened.

Conservation Priorities

Conservationists have identified several targets for protecting the blue bird of paradise, including pinpointing the species' exact distribution and determining its western, northern, and eastern boundaries. Studies into the effects of habitat change and hunting are also planned. Other priorities include the enforcement of existing protective legislation and the implementation of various public education programs.

The male blue bird of paradise *is hunted for its feathers, which are used in headdresses. The bird's appeal should help publicize conservation initiatives.*

195

Raso Lark

Alauda razae

With one of the smallest ranges of any bird in the world, the Raso lark—a close relative of the skylark—is critically threatened by adverse changes on the tiny Atlantic island to which it is restricted. Its total population is currently in the low hundreds or fewer.

The Raso lark is found only on the islet of Raso (or Razo) in the Cape Verde group, 310 miles (500 km) off the west coast of Africa. Volcanic in origin, Raso is low-lying and lacks natural water supplies. It experiences only slight and erratic rainfall that does nothing to relieve the dry conditions. Although the larger islands in the group have human populations, Raso is uninhabited.

Raso is also small—less than 3 square miles (7 sq. km) in area—and suitable breeding habitat for the lark occupies less than half of the islet's total area. Most of the birds feed and breed on a flat expanse of decomposing volcanic lava and soft rocks deposited from hot, lime-rich springs that support a sparse growth of herbaceous plants and low scrub. Although individuals have sometimes been recorded elsewhere

on the island, the Raso lark has never been recorded anywhere beyond its shores.

Raso larks feed on insects and seeds. Analysis of the stomach contents of two birds collected in the late 1960s showed them to contain ants, beetles, seeds, and other vegetable matter, as well as grit, probably swallowed to aid digestion. Since then the larks have been observed using their bills—which are heavier and longer than those of skylarks—to pry pebbles out of the soil, presumably to expose items of food.

An interesting feature of the species is the difference—of almost 21 percent—in the length of the bill in males and females. The gap has probably evolved in response to the island's relatively meager food resources—plants and animals that depend for their existence primarily

DATA PANEL

Raso lark (Razo lark)

Alauda razae

Family: Alaudidae

World population: Fluctuates between 40 and 250 birds

Distribution: Found only on the tiny island of Raso, in the Cape Verde Island group in the Atlantic off the west coast of Africa

Habitat: Mostly volcanic plains with patches of sparse vegetation, where it feeds and breeds; sometimes ventures farther afield to feed

Size: Length: 5 in (13 cm); wingspan: 8.5–10 in (22–26 cm)

Form: Similar to Eurasian skylark, but less than 75% of its size, with wings that are 30–40% shorter and more rounded; bigger bill, shorter tail,

and proportionately longer legs; short, erectile crest. Plumage dull grayish, with buff and blackish streaks above; blackish tail has white outer feathers; legs brownish pink

Diet: Seeds and insects

Breeding: Governed by scarce, irregular rainfall; builds fragile nest of grass in small hollows under creeping vegetation or a boulder; eggs whitish, with fine grayish to brownish spots; clutch of 3 recorded. Incubation and fledging periods unknown

Related endangered species: Seven other species of larks are threatened, including Rudd's lark (*Heteromirafra ruddi*) CR, Ash's lark (*Mirafra ashi*) EN, and Botha's lark (*Spizocorys fringillaris*) EN

Status: IUCN CR; not listed by CITES

Santo Antão
São Vicente
Raso ▣   Sal
São Nicolau
Boa Vista
CAPE VERDE
Maio
Brava   Fogo   São Tiago

on the nutrients provided by the guano (droppings) from seabird colonies. The bill difference enables both sexes to feed on different food items, reducing competition for the limited food supply.

Past records refer to the species as being easy to approach and showing no fear of humans, although more recent observations have suggested that the birds are now somewhat warier.

Fluctuating Population

Censuses carried out by visiting ornithologists reveal that the Raso lark population has fluctuated over the years. Between the mid-1960s and the early 1980s estimates suggested that there were only between 20 and 50 pairs. However, a survey in early 1985 showed that there were at least 150 birds on the islet, and by 1992 the figure had risen to about 250. When a count was made in 1998, though, the researchers found a total of only 92 birds, restricted to the south and west of the islet, suggesting that the population had contracted in range and also fallen back to the alarmingly low levels found in the 1960s.

Recent droughts are almost certainly responsible for the decline. However, they indicate something other than natural climatic variability. There is evidence of long-term reversion of the land to desert in the Cape Verde Islands, probably as a result of emissions of greenhouse gases. In addition, since the lark nests on the ground, its already small population is in danger of being wiped out by rats, cats, and dogs accidentally carried to the islet by fishermen. A dog was seen on Raso in 1994, and evidence that cats were present was found during the 1998 survey. Signs of nest predation have also been found—the culprit was possibly a brown-necked raven.

Although Raso was declared a nature reserve and given legal protection in 1990, there has been no actual enforcement of protection. To ensure the survival of the Raso lark, it will be essential to check if cats or other predators have become established on the island and, if so, to eradicate them as quickly as possible. Another urgent task for conservationists is to continue to carry out regular surveys, so that they can be alerted to the first signs of further declines.

The Raso lark *is found on a single uninhabited island where, until recently, it has been protected by its isolation.*

Gouldian Finch

Erythrura gouldiae

Once abundant and widespread over much of northern Australia, the beautiful and colorful Gouldian finch is greatly reduced in numbers and breeding sites, due mainly to habitat changes.

Records suggest that in the early 20th century the Gouldian finch was a common and familiar member of its family with an extensive range. During the 20th century, however, the species suffered a dramatic decline both in numbers and distribution. During the 1960s a survey at Pine Creek, Cape York, Australia, caught about 1,000 individuals in one week. A second survey in the same area in 1996 found only half a dozen birds in three months.

It is not surprising that such a stunning-looking bird was popular with cage-bird enthusiasts. Large numbers were caught—legally and illegally—for the Australian and international trade in captive birds until the early 1980s. The numbers of birds legally caught each year by licensed bird trappers were recorded until the end of 1986, when the trapping of Gouldian finches was banned. The statistics showed that between 1972 and 1981 there was an 87 percent decline in numbers caught in Western Australia. At the end of this period—five years before the trapping ban—no Gouldian finches were caught commercially. Large-scale trapping is likely to have depleted populations, but landscape changes are thought to be much more significant.

Gouldian finches are primarily birds of open tropical woodland with a grassy understory, where they are highly selective both in their diet and choice of breeding sites. They feed exclusively on grass seeds; the grass species varies seasonally and geographically. The birds travel over large distances to find supplies to build up their reserves before breeding.

Environmental Change

Gouldian finches are the only members of their family to nest almost exclusively in tree hollows rather than building their own nests. Highly sociable, they breed in loose colonies, preferring clumps of smooth-barked eucalyptus trees, although the species of eucalyptus varies from area to area. At present none of the known breeding sites has long-term protection as a nature reserve.

The Gouldian finch's dependence on a specialized diet makes it sensitive to changes in land management, especially the burning of grasses by farmers. Low-intensity fires

DATA PANEL

Gouldian finch (painted finch, rainbow finch, purple-breasted finch, Lady Gould's finch)

Erythrura gouldiae

Family: Estrildidae

World population: Fewer than 2,500 adults may remain in the wild at the start of the breeding season

Distribution: Northern Australia

Habitat: Dry savanna grassland; fringes of mangroves and thickets; rarely far from water. Woods and scrubland with spinifex grasses in wet season; avoids human habitation

Size: Length: 5–5.5 in (12.5–14 cm). Weight: 0.4–0.5 oz (12–15 g)

Form: Multicolored plumage in adults. Male has green upperparts with circular or oval patch on purple breast; yellow belly and flanks; black tail with long, pointed central feathers. Female duller, with shorter central tail feathers. Juveniles have gray heads and lack bright colors and long tail feathers

Diet: Ripe and part-ripe grass seeds, mainly sorghum in dry season; seeds of other grasses in the wet season

Breeding: Female usually lays 4–8 white eggs directly into tree hollow or termite mound in January–April (rainy season). Incubation 12–13 days; fledging about 21 days

Related endangered species: Green-faced parrotfinch (*Erythrura viridifacies*) VU; Shelley's crimson-wing (*Cryptospiza shelleyi*) VU; Anambra waxbill (*Estrilda poliopareia*) VU; green avadavat (*Amandava formosa*) VU

Status: IUCN EN; not listed by CITES

AUSTRALIA

Gouldian finches *come in many color varieties. About 75 percent of birds have black faces and 25 percent have crimson heads; there is also a rare yellow-headed form.*

during the dry season can help the birds find food: Fallen seed is more accessible to the birds after any covering of dead stems and leaves has been burned off. At the end of the dry season, however, intense fires burn off tree leaves, destroying suitable shelter. Fierce fires during the wet season can destroy sorghum grassland, including any emerging seedlings. Food shortages after such fires are often made worse by the fact that cattle graze the affected areas, preventing grasses from seeding. Grazing and the uniform fire regime destroy the mosaic of habitats on which the finches depend. The regular burning destroys clumps of breeding trees, and the birds are known to avoid badly burned tree hollows.

Mite Attack

A symptom of these landscape changes is the high level of infection with a parasitic mite that affects the finch's respiratory system. When birds in captivity are infected, they wheeze and become listless, fail to breed, and die if they are not treated with antibiotics. Although the effects of the mite had not been reported in wild birds, researchers checking for its presence found it occurred in 62 percent of the birds examined. Even though the parasites were not the cause of the massive declines, they may be preventing the species from recovering its numbers.

Recovery Plan

A recovery plan for the Gouldian finch was announced in 1998. Its chief emphasis is an in-depth study of the ecology and habitat needs of the species. The main objective is to stabilize numbers. Initially the numbers and occurrence of the Gouldian finch must be determined. With a small, scarce bird with a huge range this is no easy task, although counts at waterholes have gained useful results so far.

Blunt-Nosed Leopard Lizard

Gambelia silus

The decline of this attractive lizard dates back to the California Gold Rush of 1849, when parts of its habitat were turned over to agriculture to feed the influx of miners.

The habitat of the blunt-nosed leopard lizard is now restricted to a number of scattered areas in the San Joaquin Valley in California. The lizards use the deserted burrows of small mammals for shade, shelter, and hibernation in winter. Although they are diurnal (active during the day), leopard lizards tend to shelter during the hottest part of the day. They are often active at air temperatures of up to 104°F (40°C), when the soil temperature is about 122°F (50°C). From September onward the lizards take to their burrows to spend the colder months in a dormant state. Leopard lizards have predators, which is part of the natural balance; but when the lizards are forced into smaller areas by human disturbance, and their vegetation cover is destroyed, they become more exposed and vulnerable to these predators.

The Human Threat

As the human population increased in the San Joaquin Valley, so did agriculture and urban development. This inevitably encroached on the habitat of the blunt-nosed leopard lizard. Further damage occurred as industries developed around the extraction of oil and minerals. By 1985 barely 10 percent of the original wild land on the San Joaquin Valley floor had been left undeveloped.

The road building and landfill dumping that accompanied development in the valley were also destructive to the lizard's habitat, and the damage to the delicate balance of the desert ecosystem largely ignored. Lizards and their habitats were destroyed under construction machinery; roads and irrigation ditches fragmented the lizard's territory. Pesticides sprayed on crops also had a detrimental effect on much of the wildlife. Leopard lizards are insectivorous—a large part of their diet includes insects—so their food supply can be drastically reduced, or contaminated, by the drift from crop spraying. Where the land has been adapted for pastoral farming, grazing animals eat the natural vegetation and trample rodent burrows and lizard egg

---

DATA PANEL

Blunt-nosed leopard lizard

Gambelia silus

Family: Iguanidae

World population: Unknown

Distribution: San Joaquin Valley, California

Habitat: Arid areas, often alkaline, saline or sandy soils with sparse vegetation, rarely above 2,500 ft (800 m)

Size: Length: up to 13 in (33 cm)

Form: Slender lizard with long, "whippy" tail, blunt nose, and spotted throat; variable pattern of dark spots and light bars on yellow, fawn, gray, or dark- brown background; body color lightens with increased temperatures, so spots become indistinct; mated females and juveniles develop orange spots; males have red coloration in the breeding season

Diet: Mainly insects, other lizards, and small mammals

Breeding: One clutch of 2–6 eggs laid per year

Related endangered species: None

Status: IUCN EN; not listed by CITES

Oregon Idaho Wyoming
Nevada Utah Colorado
UNITED STATES
California
Arizona New Mexico
MEXICO

sites. They also break the soil surface, which can cause soil erosion. The removal of natural vegetation through grazing allows nonnative plants to invade, eliminating the open spaces preferred by the lizard.

The threats to the blunt-nosed leopard lizard from continuing habitat destruction were highlighted as far back as 1954, but the species was not listed as endangered by the United States Department of the Interior until 13 years later. It was given state listing in 1971.

Recovery Plans

The first recovery plan for the species was not prepared until 1980 (revised in 1985). Since then numerous studies have been carried out, including aerial surveys, to determine the amount of suitable territory still existing. Some areas have been purchased as reserves, but lack of funding has prevented this in many areas.

Conservation is a complex business needing comprehensive studies of numerous aspects: ecology, population, feeding habits, breeding, and genetic variability. Although much information has now been gathered, the scattered nature of the remaining lizard sites complicates matters because of environmental

The blunt-nosed leopard lizard *is active by day and prefers hot, dry, and sparsely vegetated areas. It can run on its hindlegs to escape predators, which include snakes, birds, and mammals.*

variation. It may be a long time before all the necessary knowledge is accumulated.

The blunt-nosed leopard lizard has proved itself to be adaptable, often colonizing sites that have been disturbed then abandoned. However, unless the decline of its habitat and its continued isolation in ever-shrinking areas are halted, the species may never recover. Its survival depends on further land acquisition and the construction of "corridors" to allow groups to move between fragmented sites, so preventing the genetic problems that develop in small populations. Its habitat must be protected, improved, and managed in such a way that the land is only used in a manner compatible with the lizard's existence. This is a tall order given the conflicting interests over land use. Recovery of this species will take a very long time; it remains to be seen if it will be successful.

201

Pygmy Blue-Tongued Skink

Tiliqua adelaidensis

The pygmy blue-tongued skink—once a common lizard—was presumed to be extinct, since there had been no sightings after 1959. In 1992, however, one was found inside the body of a dead snake. Surveys carried out in the surrounding region—the grasslands of South Australia's Mount Lofty Ranges—revealed a dozen small sites containing pygmy blue-tongued skinks.

Although less than half the size of the larger blue-tongued skinks familiar to many reptile keepers, the pygmy blue-tongued skink is otherwise similar in appearance. Its common name comes from the blue tongue displayed by most lizards of the genus *Tiliqua*. However, while the pygmy skink's mouth lining is pinkish-blue, its tongue is actually pink. The dramatic color combination provides a startling effect that deters attackers.

The lizard is found in the Mount Lofty Ranges north of Adelaide in South Australia. Unfortunately, the animal's preferred habitat is also highly suitable for farming. The climate is ideal, and the native grassland can be easily plowed. Pasture improvement—a process of replacing native plant species with agricultural species such as hay grasses and crops like alfalfa and clover—has further altered the plant diversity in favor of nonnative species.

Habitat Destruction

At the time when the lizards are most active—during the warm months—the soil is too hard for them to dig their own burrows. As a result, they often live in empty spider burrows dug by the spiders during the winter and early spring, when the soil is moist and soft. Plowing of the land is likely to be particularly destructive to the skink's survival, depriving them of shelter and leaving them exposed to snakes, birds, and other predators.

Before Europeans settled in South Australia, much of the area was native grassland supporting other reptile species, as well as birds and plants. Now only about 2 percent of the original grassland is left. All pygmy blue-tongued sites are found in the few unplowed areas. The undisturbed patches also support rare orchids and other plants, butterflies, and an endangered bird: the plains wanderer. Conserving the remaining grasslands will benefit the pygmy blue-tongues as well as the other rare fauna and flora.

Conservation Projects

The discovery of an extinct species was exciting, and various government bodies, museums, zoos, and universities cooperated in the search for new habitat sites. A recovery plan was devised; its first task was to study skinks in the wild and in captivity.

DATA PANEL

Pygmy blue-tongued skink

Tiliqua adelaidensis

Family: Scincidae (subfamily Lygosominae)

World population: About 5,500

Distribution: North Mount Lofty Ranges, southern South Australia

Habitat: Grassland with tussocks and open areas; open woodland

Size: Length: 7 in (18 cm); males often slightly smaller than females

Form: Heavy body with relatively short limbs; scales small and smooth. Male has larger head than female. Color varies from gray-brown to orange-brown with darker flecks along back

Diet: Insects and some plant material

Breeding: Gives birth to 1–4 live young per year

Related endangered species: No close relatives, but more than 40 other skink species are listed by IUCN

Status: IUCN EN; not listed by CITES

A group of pygmy blue-tongued skinks was taken to Adelaide Zoo to be studied. Specimens were also displayed to increase public awareness of the lizard's plight. After seven years in captivity the colony had not bred. It was decided to set up another group in private, free from disturbance by the public. Little was known about the animal's behavior and requirements, but captive breeding for possible release into the wild was an important part of the recovery plan.

Pygmy blue-tongues are listed under the Endangered Species Protection Act and the South Australia National Parks and Wildlife Act. An important task has been to persuade landowners to protect known skink habitat sites on their land. There are also several laws that could be enforced to prevent habitat destruction. Law enforcement is perhaps the most important task, since the habitat is fragile and small in area. Recently owners of land enclosing three habitat sites signed a 10-year agreement to run their properties as wildlife sanctuaries. Other landowners are eager to sign up, but legal problems over grazing rights have caused some delay. Two previously unknown sites have also been discovered, although they are at some distance from the existing sites.

By early 2000 the situation for the pygmy blue-tongued skink had improved. An area of native grassland—unpopulated by the species but close to its other habitats—was made into a conservation park in the hope that it will be suitable for translocations. The

The pygmy blue-tongued skink *has a heavy body with relatively short limbs and a fairly short tail, and its scales are small and smooth. Despite its name, the skink's tongue is, in fact, mainly pink.*

park could be the first secure home for the animals.

The total number of blue-tongues is difficult to estimate because of their patchy distribution, but it may be about 5,500. However, the figure is still too low to justify changing the lizard's Endangered status to Vulnerable. Although relatively few populations are unprotected now, the lizard will keep its status until larger populations exist in secure habitats.

One project to increase numbers involves the provision of artificial burrows. They are made from wooden tubes that are the same length and diameter as the favored spider hole, but less easily destroyed. Advising landowners on habitat management, such as weed clearance, grazing, and the use of pesticides, is also an important part of the program. Community involvement is a high priority, and a local school has been involved in studies as part of the plan. Despite such efforts, the outlook for the pygmy blue-tongued skink is by no means certain, since funds for wildlife conservation are limited.

Komodo Dragon

Varanus komodoensis

Known locally as buaja daret *("land crocodiles"), these giant lizards were named after the mythical dragon because of their size and fierce predatory nature.*

It seems inconceivable that the enormous Komodo dragon could remain unknown (at least to western scientists) until the early 20th century. Referred to locally as the *ora* or *buaja daret* ("land crocodile"), early reported sightings were probably dismissed as superstition or simply as crocodiles. In 1912 a Dutch pilot, having swum ashore to the island of Komodo after crashing in the sea, reported seeing them; further investigation verified their existence. The first scientific description was by Major P. A. Ouwens, director of the botanical gardens in Buitenzorg, Java, in 1912. Soon afterward a government order closed the area in which they were found and limited the number of specimens allowed to go to zoos.

The Komodo dragon is found only on Komodo and the neighboring islands of Rinca, Padar, and western Flores. Some of the populations are probably transient—

they are powerful swimmers and go from island to island in search of food. The total area of their natural habitat is roughly 390 square miles (1,000 sq. km), and it is generally hot, with an average daytime temperature of 80°F (27°C) or higher. Usually conditions are very dry, too, apart from a short monsoon season, when the Komodo dragons use pools caused by rain for wallowing. During hot weather and overnight they take to burrows.

Komodo dragons are top predators in their range. Adults will tackle anything, including deer, pigs, and goats. Occasionally even humans are said to feature in the diet. They are armed with a strong tail as well as powerful limbs and claws. Their teeth are serrated like those of sharks and can easily rip a carcass. They also produce bacteria that cause blood poisoning and death. Prey that is not killed immediately often dies later. Komodo dragons can scent the carrion up to

Borneo
Sulawesi
INDONESIA
Java
Sumbawa Flores
Sumba Timor

DATA PANEL

Komodo dragon

Varanus komodoensis

Family: Varanidae

World population: 3,000–5,000 in the wild

Distribution: Indonesia; islands of Komodo, Rinca, Padar, and western Flores

Habitat: Lowland islands, arid forest, and savanna

Size: Length: males over 8 ft (2.4 m); females 7 ft (2.1 m). Weight: males 200 lb (90 kg); females 150 lb (67 kg)

Form: Lizard with large, bulky body and powerful tail, strong limbs, and claws. Rough scales give a

beaded appearance. External ear openings are visible on each side of the head. Sharp teeth for ripping carcasses. Coloration is brown, black, reddish brown, or gray

Diet: Hatchlings and juveniles eat insects, reptiles, eggs, small rodents, and birds. Adults eat deer, pigs, goats, possibly water buffalo, and reputedly, humans

Breeding: Up to 30 eggs, buried. Incubation period about 8 months

Related endangered species: Gray's monitor lizard *(Varanus olivaceus)* VU

Status: IUCN VU; CITES I

5 miles (8 km) away and come to gather at the site of the death.

The Indonesian government regards Komodo dragons as a national asset, and they are protected. Hunting is strictly forbidden; trade in Komodos (or their parts) is banned under CITES. Tourists on Komodo are carefully controlled to prevent disturbance. The islands of Padar and Rinca are nature reserves where no tourists are allowed. However, Komodo dragons have been smuggled. In 1998 a Malaysian was arrested in Mexico City after investigation by the United States Fish and Wildlife Service, and Komodo dragons were seized.

Protecting the Species

The main threat to Komodo dragons comes from habitat destruction and the poaching of their prey by inhabitants on Komodo Island. Padar and Rinca are uninhabited, so this is not a problem; however, there, as on Komodo, natural fires destroy the plants and animals on which the dragons depend. Recent reports claim that many specimens on Komodo are emaciated from lack of food.

The first captive-breeding attempt was carried out in the National Zoo, Washington, in 1992, when 13 out of a clutch of 26 eggs hatched; this was followed by two successful hatchings at Cincinnati Zoo in 1993. Currently around 300 specimens are held in zoos worldwide; 186 of the specimens are juveniles bred in captivity. This is encouraging, but many zoos are unable to set up breeding groups due to lack of space. Zoo populations are seen as a "reservoir" from which specimens could be reintroduced into the wild. No further introductions will be made, however, until the genetic makeup of wild and captive-bred specimens has been studied, since variations between the two have been observed.

The Komodo dragon is a giant lizard about 8 feet (2.4 m) long. The largest recorded example, which was displayed in Saint Louis in the 1930s, measured 10.2 feet (3 m) and weighed over 350 pounds (160 kg).

Hawksbill Turtle

Eretmochelys imbricata

For centuries the hawksbill's attractive shell has been the main source of tortoiseshell. Despite international legislation, illegal trade in this commodity continues, and the hawksbill is one of the most seriously threatened sea turtles in the world.

Sea turtles such as the hawksbill have always been exploited by humans for food, oil, and skins. On a local scale a balance can be maintained, but the pressure of human activities over the last 50 years has resulted in all sea turtle species becoming endangered. Although all species are listed on CITES Appendix I, some of the 150 signatory countries flout the ruling. The hawksbill is classed by the IUCN as Critical, making it one of the most severely endangered sea turtles in the world.

For many years the hawksbill's attractively colored shell has been the main source of tortoiseshell, used for glasses frames, combs, ornaments, and jewelry. The scutes (hornlike shields) of the hawksbill shell are exceptionally thick, making them ideal for carving. Japan has been the largest user, importing an average of 30 tons (305 kg) of shell per year between 1970 and 1994. More than half of this was from the Caribbean—particularly Cuba—and Latin America. In the 1980s Japan's stockpile of hawksbill shell represented the death of over 170,000 turtles.

Although a member of CITES, Japan did not ban shell imports until 1993. Proposals by Cuba to allow the exportation of hawksbill shell to Japan by transferring the species from CITES Appendix I to Appendix II were defeated in 1997 and 2000. However, turtle meat and eggs are still consumed and sold in many countries. Illegal shipments of shell are often intercepted, and tourist souvenirs, including whole turtles, stuffed and lacquered, are openly traded in many countries. Bringing any part of a sea turtle back from vacation is illegal, and seizures, sometimes followed by fines, are common.

Hawksbills have been recorded on the coasts of at least 96 different countries, and nesting takes place only on sandy beaches. Suitable sites exist in the Caribbean (particularly Puerto Rico), Central and South America, and Florida. In at least two of their former haunts the species is now thought to be extinct. Often four or more clutches—of up to 140 eggs each—are laid, usually overnight. This process takes up to three hours, during which time the females and their eggs are vulnerable to predators, including people. An interval of two or three years occurs between each breeding. Hawksbills take at least 30 years to mature to breeding age, a factor that badly affects the replenishment of the population.

Human Interference

Although classed as endangered since 1970, the hawksbill's situation has not improved. Estimates of the worldwide population are impossible to arrive at, but observers who monitor breeding females in various countries are convinced that numbers are falling. Even without human interference sea turtles' eggs and hatchlings face severe predation from wild pigs, monitor lizards, crabs, dogs, and seabirds.

Humans multiply the threats. The sandy beaches needed for turtle nesting are encroached on by building, mainly for tourist facilities. Beach leveling and mechanical raking can destroy nests, while offroad vehicles compact the sand, crushing eggs and producing tire tracks that prevent hatchlings reaching the sea. People simply walking on nesting sites, especially at night, deter nesting female turtles and compact the sand. In addition, artificial lighting along

DATA PANEL

Hawksbill turtle

Eretmochelys imbricata

Family: Cheloniidae

World population: Unknown

Distribution: Atlantic, Pacific, and Indian Oceans

Habitat: Shallow tropical and subtropical seas; coral reefs; mangrove bays; estuaries

Size: Length: female 24–37 in (62–94 cm); male up to 39 in (99 cm)

Form: Oval shell with serrated (toothed) edge; dark pattern on amber background

Diet: Sponges and mollusks; algae

Breeding: Up to 140 eggs per clutch; 4–5 clutches per season

Related endangered species: All other sea turtles

Status: IUCN CR; CITES I

The hawksbill, *like other sea turtles, is toothless and slow-moving, with a protective shell and paddlelike limbs.*

beaches has increased, and hatchlings that would naturally head toward the light on the horizon at sea instead make for the shore lights and die from either dehydration or predation. Other threats come from fishing nets and lines. Some countries insist on turtle-excluder devices on the nets, but they are not always used. Turtles are often killed or mutilated by boat propellers. Pollution by sewage, pesticides, and other chemicals causes further problems. The hawksbill is gravely endangered by the destruction of coral reefs from silting and excavation for building purposes. Illegal capture of the turtles is also widespread.

207

Yellow-Blotched Sawback Map Turtle

Graptemys flavimaculata

Map turtles are sometimes called "sawbacks" because of the toothlike projections down the center of their shell. The yellow-blotched sawback increasingly faces threats of pollution in its river habitat.

Of the 12 or so species of map turtle, seven are in decline. The yellow-blotched sawback has the smallest range, living mainly along the Pascagoula River and the Leaf and Chickasawhay Rivers in Mississippi. Exports of map turtles to Britain, Europe, Japan, and Taiwan rose from 325 in 1985 to 84,546 in 1995. It is not known whether the yellow-blotched was among this number, but it has been taken in the past by private and commercial collectors. Many turtles sold in the trade are said to have been farmed, but it is claimed that adults are taken from the wild to replenish breeding stocks.

When the yellow-blotched sawbacks were placed on the IUCN Endangered Species List as Threatened in 1991, many aspects of their behavior and biology were unknown. However, recent studies are providing more information. In the wild females tend to live on mollusks, while males prefer aquatic plants, insects, and larvae. Females become mature when they are about 5 inches (13 cm) long, males when they are about 2.5 inches (6.5 cm) long. In zoo collections females have produced small clutches of between one and five eggs, sometimes laying two or three clutches in a year. The low breeding rate is a problem for a declining species.

Toxic Rivers

Yellow-blotched sawbacks are adapted to living in clean, slow- to moderate-flowing rivers where they use the sandy river banks and sandbars for nesting. They like to bask, making use of rocks or fallen logs for the activity. Most turtle species will only bask in warm, sunny weather, but the yellow-blotched sawbacks will bask even when temperatures are low or when it is raining; This behavior leaves them vulnerable to being killed by thoughtless people who use them as target practice.

However, today, as in the past, the greatest threat is from habitat alteration and destruction. As human settlement spread, trees along the rivers were felled for timber and the land cleared for building. Turtle nesting and basking sites were lost as sandbars and beaches were excavated to improve navigation. Turtle food was swept away during these activities, and some areas of the river became unsuitable for the

DATA PANEL

Yellow-blotched sawback map turtle

Graptemys flavimaculata

Family: Emydidae

World population: Unknown

Distribution: The Pascagoula River system in Mississippi

Habitat: Rivers with slow to medium currents and sandy banks for nesting

Size: Males 2.7–4 in (7–11 cm); females 6–7 in (15–17 cm)

Form: Green-brown shell with yellow blotches; yellow and black stripes on head and limbs; yellowish mark behind each eye; ridge of toothlike projections along back

Diet: Plants and insects

Breeding: Between 1 and 5 eggs per clutch; 2–3 clutches per year

Related endangered species: Barbour's map turtle *(Graptemys barbouri)* LRnt; Cagle's map turtle *(G. caglei)* VU; Escambia map turtle *(G. ernsti)* LRnt; Pascagoula map turtle *(G. gibbonsi)* LRnt; ringed map turtle *(G. oculifera)* EN; Texas map turtle *(G. versa)* LRnt

Status: IUCN EN; not listed by CITES

turtles because of their greater depth and increased water flow. Industries sprang up along the rivers and began to dump waste products into the water. They killed off food sources, in turn killing off the turtles.

Storm water drains, as well as the construction of dams, levees (embankments to protect against flooding), and flood walls have so altered the riversides that determining the original natural habitat of the yellow-blotched turtle is virtually impossible. In many areas increased recreational use of the rivers and adjacent banks is also obstructing efforts to improve the habitat. Camper vans and offroad vehicles also cause problems for nesting turtles. Some reserves have been established—notably the Pascagoula River Wildlife Management Area, which covers 37,000 acres (15,000 ha) of state-protected land in Mississippi. However, pollution threats from upstream still put the turtles at risk.

The yellow-blotched sawback map turtle *basks on riverbanks, rocks, and logs, a habit that makes it vulnerable to unscrupulous hunters.*

Protective Measures

The turtle's future lies in habitat protection and improvement, especially the reduction of effluent. The species is now protected at both state and federal levels. In some areas of turtle habitat roads are gated and entry prohibited, but signs are ignored by collectors and others. Protection against collecting and deliberate killing requires persuasion and education.

Captive breeding in zoos and private collections has been successful and could help maintain numbers, as long as this goes hand-in-hand with a conservation program for the turtle's river habitat.

209

Egyptian Tortoise

Testudo kleinmanni

The Egyptian tortoise is the smallest tortoise species in the Northern Hemisphere and one of the smallest in the world. In 1982 it was classified as Vulnerable; today it is officially Critical.

The Egyptian tortoise has a relatively small range: mainly the narrow coastal strip along the North African coast from Libya, through Egypt into Israel, extending at the most some 56 miles (90 km) inland. It was discovered in Israel in 1963. The largest population there lives between Beersheba and the Egyptian border; others inhabit scattered areas of the Negev Desert. A field survey in 1994, financed by the Turtle Recovery Program, concluded that it had all but disappeared from its former territory in Egypt, although a few unsurveyed, remote areas may still hold small populations. Its CITES rating was immediately moved from Appendix II to Appendix I, which prohibits trade, but enforcement of the law and CITES regulations is lax in North Africa.

Diminishing Numbers

Uncontrolled collecting has been accompanied by severe habitat destruction. In the recent past house building and tourist development have expanded rapidly along the coast over much of the tortoise's former habitat. Large areas have been reclaimed for agriculture, and programs of road building, irrigation, and sand extraction have been implemented. Many suitable tortoise areas have disappeared forever.

Further degradation of the habitat had been caused by the goats and sheep belonging to the wandering Bedouin herdsmen; the animals eat the same plants as the tortoise. Traditionally the Bedouin moved them around on foot when the sparse grazing was exhausted. However, the animals can now be moved using trucks and are taken to remote areas that might have remained untouched.

All species of small tortoise fetch high prices in Britain, Europe, and the United States. Illegal consignments, sometimes including Egyptian tortoises, are occasionally seized. Commercial collection in Egypt has ended due to the lack of tortoises, but they still come in from Libya. The Libyan authorities occasionally crack down at the border, but at one time they were demanding a tax on tortoises taken across. Israel recently banned the export of all its wildlife, but its tortoise populations are under pressure as a result of building development and agricultural expansion.

Tortoise Care

Steps are being taken in Egypt to save the species. In 1997 Tortoise Care was set up after 200 tortoises were seized by

DATA PANEL

Egyptian tortoise

Testudo kleinmanni

Family: Testudinidae

World population: Unknown

Distribution: North Africa

Habitat: Arid, sandy areas with sparse vegetation

Size: Length: males up to 3.8 in (9.5 cm); females up to 5 in (12.7 cm)

Form: Head, legs, and soft parts light yellow; most specimens bear 2 V-shaped dark marks on the plastron (lower shell)

Diet: Grasses and annual plants

Breeding: Typically 1 egg (occasionally 2) laid at monthly intervals until 4 or 5 have been laid

Related endangered species: Greek tortoise *(Testudo graeca)* VU; Hermann's tortoise *(T. hermanni)* LRnt; western Hermann's tortoise *(T. h. hermanni)* EN; Horsfield's tortoise *(T. horsfieldii)* VU

Status: IUCN CR; CITES I

GREECE
TURKEY
SYRIA
CYPRUS
LIBYA
EGYPT
SAUDI ARABIA

The Egyptian tortoise *is distinguished from other tortoises mainly by its small size, which has made it popular with collectors.*

Egyptian police. They were given medical treatment, and shelters were built—some tortoises even produced eggs, which were successfully hatched. The project has grown, thanks to local and outside assistance from bodies including the Cairo American College, the Tortoise Trust (an American-British organization), the Danish government, the Netherlands government, and the Zoological Society of London.

Captive breeding is under way in Egypt (160 eggs hatched successfully in 1999), and supervised releases using radio-tracking equipment have taken place. The Tortoise Trust and some British zoos are also breeding Egyptian tortoises.

A tortoise sanctuary has been established in a nature reserve at Zaranik on the north Sinai coast, with the help of the Egyptian Environmental Affairs Agency. The sanctuary also includes a visitor center where local Bedouins are employed as guards, and craft items based on the theme of tortoises are sold. Zaranik was formerly part of the Egyptian tortoises' natural range; although it is listed as an internationally important wetland and is also the Egyptian coast's largest green turtle nesting site, the area is still under pressure from proposed development.

Many Egyptian tortoise specimens are owned by collectors in Europe and the United States, and their young are sometimes offered for sale, particularly in the United States. The legality of such sales varies from one country to another.

The Tortoise Care organization in Egypt is pressing the government to give greater protection to the Egyptian tortoise and its habitats. Its members are also planning to set up more reserves in which the diminutive tortoise may live and breed in safety.

211

Galápagos Giant Tortoise

Geochelone nigra

Before permanent settlers arrived on the Galápagos Islands in the 1830s, there were huge numbers of giant tortoises. Since then habitat destruction and immigrant predators have taken their toll.

Lying off the coast of Ecuador and almost on the equator, the Galápagos Islands achieved lasting fame after the English naturalist Charles Darwin published his theory of evolution in *The Origin of Species* (1859). The book was written after his visit to the islands in 1835. The area was already well known to whalers and other seamen who, between 1789 and 1860, took tortoises to keep on their ships as sources of fresh meat. The tortoises, with water stored in their bladders, would survive on the ships for several months until they were needed. Whaling declined after 1860, when petroleum started to be used instead of whale oil for lighting. Apart from humans, the tortoises had no predators except some birds, which took hatchlings.

Galápagos tortoises are the largest in the world. One male specimen measured 4.3 feet (1.3 m) and weighed about 425 pounds (200 kg). There is considerable variation in the shape of the shell, depending on which island they inhabit, a phenomenon that was noted by Darwin and helped form his theories. Some tortoises have domed shells; others have "saddleback" shells that allow the head to be raised higher. The length of the neck and size of the head also vary; they were considered to be a single species, but scientific study showed that there were 15 different "races" from the various islands, and each one has a third name to distinguish it from others. Three races are now extinct, and some of the others are very rare.

When settlers came to the islands in the 1830s, they brought pigs, goats, dogs, cattle, and burros (donkeys), some of which escaped and began to breed, causing a further decline in tortoise numbers. Pigs and dogs eat eggs and hatchlings; the other animals destroy the vegetation and trample tortoise nests. Rats and fire ants, both introduced species, also eat large numbers of hatchlings.

DATA PANEL

Galápagos giant tortoise

Geochelone nigra

Family: Testudinidae

World population: About 10,000

Distribution: Galápagos Islands, Pacific Ocean

Habitat: Volcanic islands; hot and dry with rocky outcrops; some forested areas with grassy patches

Size: Length: up to 4 ft (1.2 m). Weight: up to 500 lb (227 kg)

Form: Huge tortoise with gray-brown shell and hard-scaled legs; some have domed shells; others are saddleback (resembling a saddle in shape)

Diet: Almost any green vegetation

Breeding: About 7–20 eggs buried in soil

Related endangered species: All subspecies of *Geochelone nigra* are on the IUCN Red List, including the Abingdon Island tortoise *(Geochelone nigra abingdoni)* EW; Duncan Island tortoise *(G. n. ephippium)* EW; Charles Island tortoise *(G. n. galapagoensis)* EX; Hood Island tortoise *(G. n. hoodersis)* CR. The Brazilian giant tortoise *(G. denticulata)* is VU

Status: IUCN VU; CITES I

In 1928 a New York Zoological Society expedition collected 180 tortoises and allocated them to zoos as far away as Australia. Some of them have bred to second generation, and one from San Diego zoo was returned to the islands for a captive-breeding program. Following pressure from scientists, the Charles Darwin Foundation was formed in 1959, followed in 1964 by the Charles Darwin Research Station. The islands became a national park, and laws were passed to prevent the removal of any animals.

Long-Term Plans

It is estimated that some islands may need 100 years to recover their vegetation and tortoise populations.

The recovery program instituted by the research station has included collecting eggs from the wild and incubating them artificially, and removing introduced animals. The first young were released in 1970.

Collecting eggs in the wild for incubation has progressed to breeding some tortoises at the research station. The first hatchlings were released in 1975, and in 1991 the first wild-bred hatchling was found on the island. The highlight of the program was the release, early in 2000, of the thousandth tortoise on Espanola.

The tortoise population of the islands has almost doubled in recent years, and laws have been passed to restrict settlement and protect the coastal waters. Quarantine laws forbid the introduction of nonnative plants and animals.

One problem was that some of the races had been reduced to very low numbers, and their lack of genetic diversity was a cause for concern. Even today it is possible that more tortoises may be found on islands where populations are low. This would seem to be the only hope for a tortoise nicknamed Lonesome George, the sole survivor of a race from Pinta Island. He was discovered in 1971 and moved to the station with two females of another race, but as yet no eggs have been produced, and no Pinta female can be found.

Galápagos giant tortoises *are now rare or extinct on many of the islands because of habitat destruction and the introduction of animals that prey on the young or compete with adults for food.*

Jamaican Boa

Epicrates subflavus

Native only to Jamaica, the Jamaican boa—known locally as "yellowsnake"—has suffered from habitat destruction, predation, and deliberate killing. It is now difficult to find in many parts of its former haunts, but sizable captive populations exist in the United States and Europe.

The genus *Epicrates,* to which the Jamaican boa belongs, contains 10 species, one of which lives in South America. The other nine are distributed throughout the West Indies. They are all nonvenomous, using constriction to kill their prey. Although they are harmless, they are, like many snakes, often killed out of fear.

The present distribution of the Jamaican boa is patchy as a result of habitat fragmentation and destruction over the years. During the period of European settlement in Jamaica, which began with the Spanish in the 15th century, land was increasingly cleared for agriculture. Farmers brought in pigs, goats, cats, and dogs, and they attracted rats. Mongoose were introduced to control rats, and they started

preying on the native fauna, particularly young snakes.

Agriculture is the main source of income in Jamaica, but there is also bauxite mining and tourism, both of which encroach on the boa's natural habitat. There are still some fairly remote, forested areas where the boa thrives, but more roads are being built into the forest, giving easier access to subsistence farmers, woodcutters, charcoal burners, and hunters. Charcoal burning is particularly destructive to the boa's habitat—large amounts of timber are needed to produce a relatively small amount of charcoal.

The Jamaican boa is not in immediate danger of extinction in its main areas, but small, localized populations are at risk. Exactly how many Jamaican boas remain outside captivity is hard to estimate; the boa is difficult to spot in the wild, preferring quiet

DATA PANEL

Jamaican boa

Epicrates subflavus

Family: Boidae

World population: Unknown

Distribution: Jamaica

Habitat: Mainly forests on honeycomb limestone, although it can be found in moist, tropical forest areas. Safest population in the Blue Mountains in Portland, eastern Jamaica, and the Cockpit Country in Trelawny, northern Jamaica. It is adaptable and has been found in coconut and banana plantations, often near houses

Size: Length: 6–8 ft (1.8–2.4 m)

Form: Long, slender snake with a broad head; anterior part of body yellowish tan or orange to reddish brown, variable black spots become irregular dark bands in the middle of the body; posterior part of body dark blue to black with irregular markings; short dark stripe behind each eye; males smaller and slimmer than females, with prominent pelvic spurs either side of the cloaca (cavity into which alimentary canal, genital, and urinary ducts open)

Diet: Mainly mammals such as rodents and bats, but also birds; young feed mainly on lizards; heat-sensitive pits located on each lip are used to detect warm-blooded prey

Breeding: Livebearer (gives birth to living young). The 5–40 young have pale orange bodies with dark orange to brown crossbands; adult coloration develops at about 18 months

Related endangered species: Cuban tree boa (*Epicrates angulifer*) LRnt; Puerto Rican boa (*E. inornatus*) LRnt; Round Island keel-scaled boa (*Casarea dussumieri*) EN; Asiatic rock python (*Python molurus*) LR

Status: IUCN VU; CITES I

caves or holes in limestone, and is nocturnal (active at night). Continued fragmentation of the habitat will endanger them further. One population, on Goat Island off Jamaica, has been completely destroyed by mongoose. This island once supported the endangered Jamaican iguana, which is now restricted to a small area in Hellshire on the southern coast. Part of Hellshire has been proposed for national park status. Goat Island may be restored as a habitat, but it would have to be cleared of mongoose first.

Breeding in Captivity

The problems of breeding Jamaican boas in captivity have largely been solved—a number of zoos and private keepers in the United States and Europe hold substantial numbers. The species is known to live for over 20 years in captivity and to produce sizable litters under these conditions. This should provide a good supply of young boas for reintroduction to the wild. Hope Zoo in Kingston, Jamaica, would be an ideal breeding facility, and other zoos, particularly Fort Worth Zoo in Texas, are assisting the staff in Kingston with advice.

Although IUCN listed and designated on CITES Appendix I, the boa's protection in Jamaica has left much to be desired. It was recommended for total protection over 30 years ago, but this was not fully implemented. There is a need to educate and persuade the public to protect this harmless snake. As the population and tourist industry grow, pressure on the land—and the boa's habitat—will increase.

An iridescent sheen *covers the boa's body, particularly when the skin has been newly shed.*

Woma Python

Aspidites ramsayi

According to Aboriginal folklore the woma python once roamed Australia in human form, creating the famous Ayers Rock and other mountains in Western Australia during a time known as "dreamtime" in the long-distant past.

The main woma territory is a large area in central Australia that takes in parts of Queensland, Northern Territory, South Australia, and New South Wales. Two populations of woma occur in Western Australia: one in the southwest, the other on the northwestern coast.

Little was known about the species until recently. Its habitat—mainly arid desert and scrubland—was sparsely populated, and the snake was considered rare until herpetologists (those who study reptiles and amphibians) began to observe it and found it to be more common than previously thought. In 1982 the first womas were bred in captivity. Since then it has become a popular species with hobbyists. It is good natured, not too large to accommodate, and reasonably easy to breed in captivity.

Coloration and size vary in woma pythons from different areas. The background color may be drab brown, yellowish, reddish brown, or olive, with darker brown crossbands of varying widths. The head can be light yellow or golden, and is usually unmarked, but in some individuals the juvenile head markings are retained. The snout is pointed, with the upper lip slightly overlapping the lower one. The protruding lip is possibly an adaptation for digging; the woma and its relative, the black-headed python, dig in loose soil using a scooping motion of the head. Unlike other pythons, woma and black-headed pythons do not have heat-detecting pits along the lips to sense warm-blooded prey. Much of their prey is ectothermic (cold-blooded) lizards and, occasionally, snakes.

Studying pythons in the wild in Australia has not been easy because of the vast areas involved, the difficult terrain, and the mainly nocturnal nature of the snakes.

DATA PANEL

Woma python (Ramsay's python)

Aspidites ramsayi

Family: Boidae

World population: Unknown

Distribution: Central Australia: arid regions of Queensland, Northern Territories, South Australia, and Western Australia

Habitat: Arid and semiarid areas, including sand dunes, rocky regions, grasslands, woodlands, and scrub

Size: Length: adults usually 5 ft (1.5 m); occasionally up to 8 ft (2.5 m)

Form: Cylindrical body with short tail and vestiges of hind limbs; eyes with vertically elliptical pupils. Coloration brown, yellowish, reddish brown, or olive with darker brown bands; juveniles more intensively colored. Pointed snout

Diet: Mammals and reptiles (mainly lizards, occasionally snakes)

Breeding: One clutch of 6–19 eggs laid; female incubates eggs

Related endangered species: None

Status: IUCN EN; not listed by CITES

Habitat Loss

Human activity is destroying the outer parts of the woma's range. There is no estimate for total numbers of woma pythons in the wild, but they are known to have declined in certain areas; the last specimen reported in New South Wales was in 1890.

In Queensland land clearance for agriculture and grazing is threatening much suitable habitat; the most severely threatened is the southwestern population of Western Australia. The last confirmed record of woma pythons in the area was in 1987, when a specimen was supplied to the Western Australia Museum.

A large part of woma habitat in Western Australia has been turned over to agriculture, and an area known as the wheatbelt has been increasing for many years. Urban expansion, road construction, and related activities such as crop spraying are all threats. Snakes are also victims of road kills because of their habit of basking on road surfaces. In addition, feral and domestic cats are known to kill snakes, although the extent of predation has not been assessed: An assessment would have to be made if captive-bred young were to be released.

In Captivity

Specimens owned by hobbyists tend to come from the central part of the woma's range. No southwestern womas are held in captivity, although illegally held specimens may exist.

The species as a whole is recognized as being in danger and is listed under government conservation legislation. Even so, snakes are not popular; about 80 percent of Australia's snakes are venomous, and many people are ready to kill snakes of any species, classing them all as deadly.

Herpetologists are trying to investigate the population numbers, particularly of the southwestern form (if it still exists). Conservation bodies and herpetological societies are also trying to increase public awareness and encourage reports of sightings. The Western Australia Amateur Herpetological Society has offered to set up a captive-breeding program at its own cost if any southwestern womas are found and provided that government permission is granted.

The woma, *like other pythons, is nonvenomous; all pythons kill their prey by constriction.*

Milos Viper

Macrovipera schweizeri

The Milos viper has been endangered for 14 years, but practically nothing has been done to protect it or its habitat. However, the causes of its decline are well known, and proposals for conservation measures have been made.

The Milos viper occurs only on the islands of Milos, Kimolos, Polyaigos, and Siphnos in the western Cyclades, Greece. Milos, the largest island with an area of 100 square miles (160 sq. km), has the biggest viper population, but suitable habitat has been deteriorating for more than 15 years. The viper's preferred habitat is rocky hillsides with small trees and bushes interspersed with open areas. Much of Kimolos is used for agriculture; it is arid and has little suitable habitat. Polyaigos contains some good areas of habitat since it is not disturbed by people. Siphnos is also used for agriculture. Its viper population has not yet been fully surveyed.

Adult Milos vipers feed mainly on birds, and their young feed on lizards; both avoid areas of dense vegetation, as do their prey. The islands are staging posts for many migratory birds in spring and fall, and some stay there to breed. The vipers are frequent visitors to the watercourses where the birds gather to drink. Although mainly a terrestrial species, the viper is often seen in bushes sheltering from the sun and waiting to ambush birds. Its activity patterns are dictated by the weather. In hot weather it is active mainly at night; in cooler weather it is active during the day. Winter is spent in hibernation, but on mild days the vipers come out to bask.

One unusual feature of the Milos viper is that it lays eggs; other European vipers are livebearers (give birth to live young). Female vipers lay eggs only every other year; breeding may not take place at all if the spring has been cold and they have not fed well. In captivity clutches of up to 10 eggs have been recorded. Eggs and young are eaten by predators such as rats and feral (wild) cats or destroyed by human activity. The cats also kill adult vipers.

Balancing Act

Milos has a population of fewer than 5,000 people concentrated mostly in the eastern corner of the island. The vipers live on the sparsely populated, more mountainous west. Other islands have fewer people. The current viper population on Milos is estimated at 2,500; Polyaigos and Kimolos each have between 600 and 900. This may sound a lot, but unless they can maintain a balance between births and deaths, they will become extinct. Habitat destruction has been ongoing on Milos for several years. Quarrying for minerals and cement production has laid waste much of the suitable viper

DATA PANEL

Milos viper (Cyclades blunt-nosed viper)

Macrovipera schweizeri

Family: Viperidae

World population: About 4,300

Distribution: Western Cyclades islands, Greece

Habitat: Mostly rocky areas with open spaces between bushes

Size: Length: 30 in (75 cm)

Form: Heavy-bodied snake; 2 hollow fangs on short maxilla (upper jaw); red-brown blotches on lighter background

Diet: Birds and lizards

Breeding: Between 8 and 10 eggs laid every other year

Related endangered species: Several species of viper in Europe and Asia, including Latifi's viper *(Vipera latifi)* VU of Iran and mountain viper *(V. albizona)* EN of Turkey

Status: IUCN CR; not listed by CITES

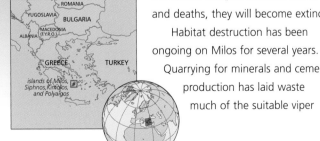

The Milos viper's venom is quite strong, but few people are bitten, and no fatalities have been recorded.

habitat in the west. The mineral industry on Milos is vital to the national economy, and expansion of the business is planned. Traffic supports the industry, and road kills are becoming more common, particularly at night in summer. Wildlife was not moved before the quarrying began, and spoiled areas have not been restored. Natural restoration takes several years, even if the new growth is not grazed; overgrazing by sheep and goats is an additional problem in some areas.

Until recently Milos has not been badly affected by tourism, but now tourist numbers have increased, and a second airport is planned. House building and land clearance for agriculture are also changing the viper's habitat. Tourism may prove a mixed blessing, possibly slowing down industrial expansion, but it might also destroy more habitat and increase disturbance. Vipers found near tourist areas might be deliberately eradicated so that they do not deter visitors. Recent surveys have found that vipers have been deliberately killed. Until 1977 trappers could claim 10 drachmas (then about 15 U.S. cents) from the authorities for each viper caught, but in 1981 a presidential decree

on wildlife protection outlawed the collection or killing of all wildlife. A cause of decline had been collection by hobbyists and by people intending to sell the vipers. Substantial numbers were taken in the 1980s, but collecting has been reduced in recent years.

In 1985 creation of a biogenetic reserve was recommended after a report by the Societas Europaea Herpetologica (SEH). Another report by the SEH in 1986 proposed greater control of quarrying, the employment of game wardens, and education programs to inform the public and so protect the species. A survey between 1993 and 1997 examined the viper's ecology, population, and threats to its habitat. Recommendations were made, but no action taken. Since then the need for conservation has been pressed at annual meetings, but to no effect. The government seems reluctant to aid the conservation of endangered species. Most of the areas considered for conservation are of archaeological importance and do not contain any viper habitats. However, habitat protection is vital for the future of the Milos viper.

Chinese Alligator

Alligator sinensis

The Chinese alligator is one of the smaller crocodilians (large, predatory reptiles of the order Crocodilia), and possibly the rarest. Its range has been restricted by expanding human populations in China, and it is now endangered, although farmed specimens are restoring numbers overall.

Like all crocodilians, the Chinese alligator is an efficient predator that is well adapted to its lifestyle. It is reclusive, feeding mainly at night and spending six to seven months hibernating in burrows. The burrow system is complex, often having ventilation holes up to the surface. The alligators' habits, together with their efficient camouflage, mean that they can often go undetected even when they are near human habitation.

Once widespread, the species is now mainly restricted to 13 small protected areas within Anhui Chinese Alligator National Nature Reserve, an area of 167 square miles (433 sq. km). The alligators'

association with the dragons of Chinese mythology offers no protection. Their habitat is in an area of dense human population that has been heavily cultivated, principally by draining swamps and clearing vegetation. Pressure to expand cultivation is growing as the population increases.

The Chinese alligator is not a man-eater, but is feared by local people and considered an expensive nuisance because of its burrowing, which destroys irrigation dams. Although the alligator's diet is mainly snails and mussels—the broad teeth are adapted to crushing mollusk shells—they will take fish and ducks, which brings them into conflict with humans.

The alligator is a protected species, but that does not stop it from being killed and sold for meat and medicinal use. The meat and skins are not as sought-after as those of some other species; the skin is difficult to tan due to the large osteoderms (bony plates) under the scales. Its lower value means that it is not worth hunting the alligators on a commercial basis. However, occasional kills remove a pest and earn a little money.

Surviving Populations

When the species was added to the IUCN listing in 1965, the estimated wild population was 50 specimens. Today the estimate is about 1,000, roughly 500 of which are in the Anhui Reserve. A few live in other reserves and possibly in scattered isolated areas along the Yangtze River's tributaries. There are more alligators in captivity than in the wild.

DATA PANEL

Chinese alligator

Alligator sinensis

Family: Alligatoridae

World population: About 1,000 wild adults

Distribution: Lower Yangtze River in China

Habitat: Slow-moving freshwater rivers and streams; lakes, ponds, and swamps

Size: Length: up to 6 ft (2 m). Weight: up to 85 lb (40 kg)

Form: Similar to the American alligator, but smaller and with a more tapered head. Snout is slightly upturned near the nostrils. Color is dark brown to black. Young carry bright-yellow crossbands that fade with age

Diet: Snails, mussels, fish, and ducks

Breeding: Clutch of 10–40 eggs per year laid under mounds of decaying vegetation. Average clutch size in captivity is 15 eggs. Females may occasionally miss breeding one year. Incubation about 70 days

Related endangered species: Black caiman (*Melanosuchus niger*) LRcd

Status: IUCN CR; CITES I (farmed specimens in China are classed as CITES II)

NORTH KOREA

SOUTH KOREA

CHINA

Captive-breeding programs have been successful; starting in the early 1960s with 200 wild alligators and 780 wild eggs, numbers increased to just over 4,000 by 1991. Breeding centers have been set up in China, and Chinese alligators have been bred at several American and European zoos. Currently the number of alligators in establishments in China is about 5,000; outside China about 230 exist in zoos and one or two private collections. Space is limited in zoos, however. The young will live together quite well up to the age of three or four years; but as they grow, fights and cannibalism can become a problem. At the moment breeding from second-generation animals is not carried out for these reasons.

Future Prospects

It may seem odd that although the wild alligators are listed in CITES Appendix I, the farmed specimens are

The Chinese alligator's *survival in the wild depends on a change in people's attitudes and greater protection of the animal's habitat.*

in Appendix II, which means that they can enter trade. The original idea was to produce them for meat and for the European pet market, although it is doubtful if the demand in Europe would be great enough to make breeding worthwhile. However, the industry provides much-needed jobs for many people.

The Chinese alligator has been proven to thrive in captivity. Females are mature at between four and five years, which makes them ideal for captive breeding. Its longevity and reasonable clutch size mean that wild areas could be repopulated if the habitat was not being constantly threatened.

American Crocodile

Crocodylus acutus

The American crocodile has a much wider distribution than the American alligator. Although in the United States it is restricted to southern Florida, it is found in 16 other countries. Like the alligator, it has been hunted to supply the lucrative trade in leather made from crocodile skin.

In the United States crocodiles live in the tidal marshes in the Everglades along Florida Bay and in the Florida Keys. The American crocodile is also found in western Mexico through Central America down to northeastern Peru and into Venezuela. It occurs on some Caribbean islands, mainly Cuba (which has the largest wild population) and also Jamaica, Haiti, and the Dominican Republic. In all these countries crocodile populations have declined.

Crocodiles are fairly adaptable; they are excellent swimmers, they can travel considerable distances overland, and they can live in fresh or salt water. However, urban development—for example in Dade and Monroe counties, Florida— has reduced their habitat. One population has taken refuge in brackish water cooling channels at Turkey Point nuclear power station in Florida.

Like alligators, crocodiles do not usually attack humans unless they or their nests are disturbed. In Florida the crocodiles and their nests are strictly protected; killing, feeding, or disturbing them in any way is illegal.

Crocodiles are good burrowers, excavating deep holes for shelter and nesting. In the absence of suitable soil they will cover the eggs with a mound of loose vegetation. Eggs and youngsters are vulnerable to predators. Racoons in the United States dig up their nests, as do teiid lizards in Central America. Flooding can also destroy nests before the eggs hatch.

Souvenir Hunt

The American crocodile is threatened both by urban development and by other forms of habitat destruction. In Ecuador, for example, mangroves have been cleared for shrimp aquaculture. Crocodiles are also sometimes killed out of fear or because they are seen as a threat to

DATA PANEL

American crocodile

Crocodylus acutus

Family: Crocodylidae

World population: Unknown

Distribution: Southern Florida, Central America, Peru, and Venezuela

Habitat: Fresh and salt water; swamps, rivers, lakes, reservoirs, and mangrove swamps

Size: Length: male 16–19 ft (5–6 m); female up to 16 ft (5 m). Reports of specimens 22 ft (7 m) long in Central America. Weight: 700–800 lb (318–363 kg)

Form: Large lizardlike reptiles with longer and narrower snouts than alligators and a body that is not as well armored. The fourth tooth on each side of the lower jaw is visible when the mouth is closed. Coloration is green-gray or gray-tan with dusky markings. Adults have a prominent swelling in front of each eye

Diet: Fish, crabs, turtles, birds, and small mammals; can attack livestock

Breeding: Clutches of 20–60 eggs are laid in excavated holes or buried in mounds of loose vegetation. Incubation takes about 3 months

Related endangered species: Orinoco crocodile (*Crocodylus intermedius*) CR; Philippines crocodile (*C. mindorensis*) CR; marsh or mugger crocodile (*C. palustris*) VU; Cuban crocodile (*C. rhombifer*) EN; Siamese crocodile (*C. siamensis*) CR

Status: IUCN VU; CITES I

UNITED STATES

BAHAMAS
MEXICO
CUBA
NICARAGUA
VENEZUELA
COLOMBIA
ECUADOR
BRAZIL
PERU

livestock. Illegal hunting for the trade in skins or for making tourist souvenirs is common. Other threats include accidental capture in fishing nets, tropical storms, and overfishing; fish form a large part of their diet.

Conservation

The Crocodile Specialist Group (CSG) consists of experts and other interested parties who advise the Species Survival Commission of the IUCN on crocodilian conservation. Operating from the Florida Museum of Natural History, the group monitors crocodile populations and draws up conservation programs; by 1971 the CSG had set up a conservation program for all 23 crocodilian species throughout the world. Monitoring the crocodiles is a mammoth task. The most detailed study has been that of the Florida population, but in several countries very little up-to-date information is available, and there is a need for more fieldwork. The CSG is funded by voluntary donations, so funds are not always sufficient to do what is needed.

The American crocodile *feeds in the water (often floating at the surface to lie in wait for prey) and comes onto land to bask in the sun and to lay eggs.*

The American crocodile was listed as Endangered in 1979, and a recovery plan was initiated by the United States Fish and Wildlife Service in 1984 to cover aspects such as habitat protection and captive-breeding programs. Captive breeding for the skin trade and restocking exists in six countries, but recent reduced demand for skins may remove the financial incentive for this to continue. Few zoos have captive-breeding programs, although one notable success was the hatching of 10 young crocodiles in 1996 at Cleveland Metroparks Zoo. In Venezuela protection and releases of captive-bred stock are aiding recovery.

Florida's crocodile population is slowly increasing, but in several countries (such as El Salvador and Haiti) they are still declining. There is an urgent need for restocking of the wild populations.

Gharial

Gavialis gangeticus

One of the largest crocodilian species, the gharial (or gavial) came close to extinction in the 1970s. Traditionally, gharials were not threatened by humans since they were regarded as sacred. Today they have disappeared from much of their original range. Conservation programs have increased numbers, but the gharial's future is still uncertain.

An unusual crocodilian, the gharial's common name comes from the Indian word "ghara," a pot, and refers to the bulbous growth on the male's snout. The growth is thought to act as a resonator when the male calls, or it may be used for recognition of males by females.

The gharial's distinctive narrow, tooth-lined snout, which seems at odds with the heavy body, is an adaptation to a diet of fish. The snout can be quickly slashed sideways, and the razor-sharp, slightly angled teeth are able to gain a firm grip on the slippery fish. Large specimens sometimes seize larger prey such as mammals, but youngsters feed on aquatic invertebrates and small creatures such as frogs.

Gharials spend much of their time in water, crawling onto land to bask or nest. Once out of water, their legs cannot raise the body off the ground, but they are capable of rapid movement by slithering on the belly. Unlike most crocodilians, gharials do not transport hatchlings from the nest to water, possibly because of their jaw structure, but the mothers do guard their young once they have hatched and reached water.

Population Decline

The gharial was once found in the major rivers and their tributaries in the northern parts of the Indian subcontinent, namely the Brahmaputra (India, Bhutan, Bangladesh); the Indus (Pakistan); the Ganges (Nepal and India); the Mahandi (India); and the Narayoni River and

DATA PANEL

Gharial (gavial)

Gavialis gangeticus

Family: Gavialidae

World population: Fewer than 2,500

Distribution: Northern Indian subcontinent

Habitat: Largely aquatic; calmer areas of deep rivers with sandbanks for nesting

Size: Length: male 19–22 ft (6–7 m); female about 16 ft (5 m)

Form: Typical crocodilian shape. Elongated, narrow snout with many interlocking, sharp teeth. Males have a bulbous growth on the end of the snout.

Adult color: uniform olive gray, sometimes with brownish blotches or bands, especially on the tail. Juveniles have dark spots and crossbands on a yellow-brown background

Diet: Fish; sometimes small mammals

Breeding: Clutch of 30–50 eggs buried in loose sand; eggs take 12–13 weeks to hatch

Related endangered species: None

Status: IUCN EN; CITES I

its tributaries (Nepal), with smaller populations in the Kaladan and Irrawaddy Rivers in Myanmar (Burma). Today the remaining populations are in India and Nepal, with perhaps a few specimens in isolated areas.

The gharial's decline has been due to human activity. Settlements set up along the rivers have destroyed or disturbed breeding areas. Fishermen regard the gharials as direct competitors and destroyers of fishing nets. Furthermore, gharials are reputed to be man-eaters. While they do not attack people, they are thought to scavenge on human remains in the river (traditionally corpses are placed in the Ganges during funeral ceremonies). In some areas people hunt gharials for meat, and the eggs and body parts are also used in traditional medicine.

Chances of Survival

The gharial has benefited from a recovery plan set up in India in the 1970s to prevent poaching losses. Nine protected areas were established along the Ganges and its tributaries, and six captive-breeding and ranching centers were started, where eggs were taken from the wild to be hatched and raised in captivity. Several thousand young gharials have been released into the wild, which has steadied the decline in some areas. At smaller sites, however, numbers have not increased since youngsters do not always remain in the release area. In Nepal captive breeding and releases have produced only a small improvement in gharial numbers.

The gharial is still rare in India and Nepal and remains at risk from habitat degradation, fishing, and hunting. There is a shortage of suitable release sites in the protected areas, and the high cost of captive breeding and protection is also a problem. Ideally, youngsters should not be released until they are about five years old. However, the cost of feeding and caring for them means that some have been prematurely released, which reduces their chances of survival in the wild.

The gharial *is distinguished by its long, slender snout and sharp-toothed jaws.*

Japanese Giant Salamander

Andrias japonicus

Restricted to just two mountainous areas, the Japanese giant salamander's mountain stream habitat is under threat from damming and deforestation. Collection has also depleted numbers. Fortunately, the salamander is now fully protected by international trade restrictions.

The Japanese giant salamander and its close relative the Chinese giant salamander from China and Taiwan are the largest salamanders in the world. An inhabitant of mountain streams with clear, cool water, the Japanese giant salamander is similar in anatomy and habits to the hellbender of North America, and the two Asian species are sometimes known as Oriental hellbenders.

The Japanese giant salamander has a heavily built, slightly compressed body and a flat head, with small eyes and nostrils at the tip of its snout. Its skin is rough and warty, with many wrinkles and folds, giving the impression that its body is too small for its skin. Two prominent folds run along the whole length of its body. The tail, which makes up about a quarter of its total length, is flattened from side to side and has a fin along the upper side. The limbs are small and also slightly flattened. In color the salamander is reddish or grayish brown with a darker mottled pattern, and it is paler on the underside. Males and females are similar in size and appearance, except that the male develops a swollen cloaca (cavity into which the alimentary canal, genital, and urinary ducts open) during the breeding season.

The Japanese giant salamander is a retiring animal by day, hiding under rocks or in a burrow. It emerges at night in search of food, which includes fish, worms, and crustaceans such as crayfish. It has an unusual arrangement of jawbones and muscles, which enables it to suck its prey into its mouth. It requires the clean, well-oxygenated water that is found only in fast-flowing streams and so is confined to altitudes between 980 and 3,300 feet (300 and 1,000 m). The Chinese giant salamander is found in a similar habitat, but also occurs in mountain lakes.

Breathing through the Skin

The giant salamanders show a form of pedomorphosis, retaining many aspects of the larval form into adult life. Unlike some pedomorphic salamanders, however, giant salamanders lose their external gills when they are about 18 months old and about 4.5 inches (12 cm) in length. Thereafter they rely on their skin to absorb oxygen from the water. The skin of giant salamanders contains a higher density of blood capillaries than most

DATA PANEL

Japanese giant salamander

Andrias japonicus

Family: Cryptobranchidae

World population: Unknown

Distribution: Southern Japan; islands of Honshu and Kyushu

Habitat: Rocky mountain streams with clear, fast-flowing, and well-oxygenated water

Size: Length: 8–56 in (20–140 cm)

Form: Large salamander; long, flattened body; rough, warty skin with many wrinkles and folds. Laterally compressed tail with dorsal (back) fin. Broad, flat head; small eyes. Reddish or grayish brown on upper body; paler below

Diet: Fish, worms, and crustaceans

Breeding: Fall (August–September)

Related endangered species: Chinese giant salamander (*Andrias davidianus*) CR

Status: IUCN NT; CITES I

salamanders, and the many wrinkles and folds in the skin increase the surface area over which oxygen is absorbed. When resting, the salamanders sway slowly from side to side; this serves to gently stir up the water, ensuring that well-oxygenated water is always close to their skin.

Paternal Care

Breeding begins in the fall (August to September). The male Japanese giant salamander plays a more active role than is true for most salamanders. He digs a pit in the gravel on a stream bed, defending his territory aggressively against rival males. At the same time, he displays to attract a female into the pit. The female lays 400 to 600 eggs in strings that are between 7 and 60 feet (2 and 18 m) in length, and the male sheds sperm onto them. Mating attracts the attention of other, usually smaller males, who enter the nest and also shed sperm on the eggs. After mating, the female leaves the male, who guards the eggs until they hatch, after about two months. The newly hatched larvae disperse from the nest and reach maturity at about three years of age. Giant salamanders are very long-lived; one animal, in Amsterdam Zoo, lived to be 52 years old.

Protected Species

The large size of the Japanese giant salamander, together with its specific habitat requirements, means that it was never an abundant creature. As a result, it has been particularly badly affected by deforestation and the damming of rivers, activities that destroy the clear, well-oxygenated streams it prefers.

Japanese giant salamanders have also been collected in the past and sent to many museums, aquaria, and zoos throughout the world. However, this kind of trade is now tightly controlled, the species having been given full protection under the CITES treaty.

The Japanese giant salamander *loses its external gills at about 18 months, when it is about 4.5 inches (12 cm) in length.*

227

Great Crested Newt

Triturus cristatus

Although the great crested newt is widely distributed across Europe, the species has declined over much of its range. Changes in land use and agricultural practices over the last 50 years have destroyed much of its pond and woodland habitat.

The great crested newt of northwestern Europe—along with other European newts of the genus *Triturus*—gets its name from the large, deeply notched crest that runs along the back of the breeding male. The European newts are unique among tailed amphibians: During the breeding season the males develop elaborate decorations that serve to attract and stimulate females during courtship.

Although great crested newts spend much of their lives on land, breeding takes place in water. Adults migrate to ponds in early spring. Females start the breeding season already full of large, yolk-filled eggs. It takes the males several weeks to fully develop their deep tail and crest, features that play an important part in the mating process. Males that emerge from their winter hibernation with larger fat reserves develop larger crests, and it is likely that they are more attractive to females.

Mating usually occurs at dusk. The male takes up a position in front of the female and displays to her with rhythmic beats of his tail. If the female responds by moving toward him, the male deposits a package of sperm, called a spermatophore, on the floor of the pond. The female then moves over it and picks it up with her open cloaca (cavity into which the genital ducts open).

Two or three days after mating the female begins to lay her eggs, a process that takes many weeks. Great crested newts usually produce between 150 and 200 eggs, each of which is laid individually and carefully wrapped in the leaf of a water plant. After two to three weeks the eggs hatch into tiny larvae, which, once they have used up their reserves of yolk,

start to feed on tiny aquatic animals, such as water fleas. Larval development takes two to three months, and the young emerge from their pond as miniature adults in late summer and fall. Females mate several times during the breeding season, interrupting egg-laying to replenish their supplies of sperm.

Risk Factors

Together with its close relative, the marbled newt, the great crested newt has a remarkable abnormality of its chromosomes. As a result, 50 percent of its young die as early embryos. This is one reason, perhaps, why crested newts have declined more rapidly than other European newt species.

Predation is not a significant problem for great crested newts. When handled, glands in their skin produce a bitter, milky secretion that humans and potential predators, such as water birds and hedgehogs, find highly distasteful. In addition, the bright orange and black pattern on the belly appears to warn off predators.

However, crested newts are at risk from habitat alteration and destruction. The main problem has been changes in land use since World War II. Woodlands have been cleared, hedges destroyed, and land drained to make way for crops and livestock. Ponds, which were a common feature of the European landscape, have been filled in. In some parts of Britain, for example, 90 percent of farm ponds have disappeared in the last 50 years.

Another threat to crested and other newt species comes from fish that eat newt larvae. The eggs and larvae of crested newts are also sensitive to a variety of pollutants, such as herbicides and pesticides.

In the southern parts of its range the crested newt is found in a number of forms that differ from the northern form in having longer bodies, shorter legs, and a different shape of crest on the male. Such forms are now recognized as three distinct species: the Italian crested newt, the Danube newt, and the southern crested newt. All are threatened by habitat loss and protected, to varying degrees, by national and European laws.

At the southwestern edge of its distribution, however, the crested newt is expanding its range. In some parts of France it appears to be adapting to new patterns of land use and is even spreading into ponds previously used only by marbled newts.

DATA PANEL

Great crested newt (warty newt)

Triturus cristatus

Family: Salamandridae

World population: Unknown

Distribution: Northwestern Europe

Habitat: Woodland, scrub, and hedgerows close to ponds, lakes, or ditches

Size: Length: male 3.9–5.5 in (10–14 cm); female 3.9–6.3 in (10–16 cm)

Form: Dark gray or brown newt with large black spots on upperside; bright orange underside with black spots. In breeding season male (only) has large, dorsal crest and deep tail with white stripe

Diet: Small invertebrates

Breeding: Mates in spring and early summer. Between 70 and 600 (usually 150–200) eggs laid; larvae hatch after 2-week gestation; young develop over 2–3 months. Life span up to 16 years

Related endangered species: Danube newt *(Triturus dobrogicus)* NT

Status: IUCN LC; CITES not listed

In the breeding season *the male great crested newt develops a distinctive crest and tail, which he displays during courtship. The tail has a conspicuous white stripe that shows up clearly in the dim light of dusk—when mating occurs.*

Olm

Proteus anguinus

A bizarre, permanently aquatic salamander that lives almost entirely underground, the olm is vulnerable to a variety of factors that threaten its restricted and specialized habitat.

The olm is a strange and obscure amphibian. It is highly adapted to a habitat of underground streams, pools, and lakes, and shows a classic example of pedomorphism. This is an evolutionary change that results in the retention of juvenile characteristics in the adult form. The species does not exist as a terrestrial, lung-breathing salamander. During the course of its normal pattern of development the olm has become "frozen" in the larval stage, retaining the large, feathery external gills and laterally compressed tail, which it beats to propel itself through the water.

Adapted for Life in the Dark

The olm's underground streams and pools occur in the "karst" landscape that is associated with limestone.

Living in permanent darkness, it has only tiny rudimentary eyes that are covered by skin. Its larvae, on the other hand, have quite well-developed eyes, but they degenerate during life. The adults lack dark pigment in their skin, but vary in color, being white, pink, gray, or yellowy; younger individuals often have darker blotches on the skin.

Unable to see, the olm must rely on other senses to find its food and for social communication. It has an excellent sense of smell, and its skin contains large numbers of tiny lateral line organs that are sensitive to water-borne vibrations. It uses its sense of smell and sensitivity to vibrations to detect the moving invertebrates on which it feeds. These senses are also important during aggressive interactions between males and during courtship and mating.

As recently as 1994 a distinct form of the olm has been discovered. Given the status of a subspecies, *Proteus anguinus parkelj* is black, has well-developed eyes, and is found only in the Bela Krajuna region of southeastern Slovenia. Individuals have been observed emerging from caves at night and swimming around in open pools and streams.

Breeding

Living underground, the olm is not exposed to the seasonal variations in temperature and rainfall that are experienced by amphibians living on the surface. Water temperature in its cave habitat is more or less constant all year round. As a result, the olm has no obvious breeding season but may breed at any time of year. When breeding, the slightly smaller

DATA PANEL

Olm (blind cave salamander)

Proteus anguinus

Family: Proteidae

World population: Unknown

Distribution: Southeastern Europe: the Adriatic coast from northern Italy to Montenegro (former Yugoslavia)

Habitat: Caves and underground lakes and streams in limestone mountains

Size: Length: 8–11 in (20–28 cm)

Form: Large, flat head with rounded snout; white, pale-gray, pink, or creamy-yellow elongated body; darker blotches in younger animals; large pink, feathery external gills. Small rudimentary limbs

Diet: Small aquatic invertebrates, mainly crustaceans

Breeding: Any time of year. Eggs fertilized internally. Twelve to 70 eggs laid under a stone and guarded by female until hatched; alternatively, just 1–2 eggs develop inside body of female, who gives birth to well-developed larvae. Young mature at 7 years. Life span up to 58 years

Related endangered species: None

Status: IUCN VU; not listed by CITES

males become aggressive toward one another, defending their territory. If a female enters a male's territory, he performs a tail-fanning display—similar to that of European newts—in which he beats the tip of his tail rapidly against his flank. This creates a water current that he directs toward the female, who receives both vibratory stimuli and odor cues. If she is sexually responsive, she will approach the male. He then turns away, stopping to deposit a packet of sperm (called a spermatophore) on the ground. The female follows him and passes over the spermatophore. As she does so, her cloaca (cavity in the pelvic region into which the genital ducts open) passes over the spermatophore, and the sperm is drawn up into her body.

The female then creates a simple nest in the debris on the cave floor and lays a clutch of eggs. She guards them against predators until they hatch. Alternatively, between one and two eggs develop inside the body of the female, who gives birth to well-developed larvae.

The olm *lacks any dark pigment. Instead, individuals show a variety of pale colors, from pink to creamy yellow.*

Habitat at Risk

The olm's specialized habitat requirements—places where there are underground caves containing water—mean that even under ideal conditions it will always be a rare species.

Although it is reasonably safe from many of the changes that have adversely affected surface-living amphibians, such as habitat destruction, it is not wholly unaffected by events on the surface. Much of the water that fills the underground caves flows in from the surface, where it can become contaminated by a range of pollutants, such as agricultural runoff or industrial waste. It is believed that pollution is a major factor in the reduction of the olm population.

The olm is a fascinating animal, both to scientists and to amateur enthusiasts. In the past olms were collected as pig food. Today it is collection by enthusiasts that is having a more serious effect on natural populations.

Mallorcan Midwife Toad

Alytes muletensis

The Mallorcan midwife toad has an unusual reproductive strategy. Confined to a restricted habitat, it is now being sustained by a captive-breeding and release program.

The tiny Mallorcan midwife toad was known as a fossil long before it was discovered alive; it was found alive and named as recently as 1977. Now confined to about 10 isolated localities in the Sierra de Tramuntana, a mountainous region in western Mallorca, it once lived throughout the island. Its natural habitat is now fully protected, and a captive-breeding program is producing a steady supply of young animals that are released annually into suitable new sites.

Smaller than the three species of midwife toads that live on the European mainland, the Mallorcan midwife toad became isolated about 7 million years ago, when a rise in sea level separated Mallorca from Spain. Living in streams, pools, and wells throughout the island, its survival came under threat in Roman times, when nonnative animals were introduced to the island. The viperine snake is a predator of midwife toads, while the Spanish green frog is a competitor, its tadpoles feeding on the same kind of food. Both species thrive at low altitudes, but have not been able to colonize Mallorca's impressive mountainous regions. As a result, the Mallorcan midwife toad is confined to a few remote limestone ravines.

Call of the Wild

Following winter rains, which briefly turn their habitat into a raging torrent, Mallorcan midwife toads begin to call. The call is a soft, simple "peep" and, unusually, is produced by both sexes. It enables individuals to find each other in deep, rocky fissures. Mating, which takes place on land, is complex and protracted, and involves an elaborate series of leg movements by which a string of ten to 20 large, yolk-filled eggs becomes tightly wrapped around the male's hindlegs. The male then carries them around for several weeks until they are ready to hatch.

The brooding period lasts for three to 10 weeks and averages four weeks; it is longer in cold weather and can be costly for males. While carrying eggs, males are not able to pursue prey actively and so tend to lose weight. In addition, the egg string sometimes becomes so tightly wrapped around a leg that its blood supply is cut off and the leg is lost.

When the eggs are fully developed, the male briefly enters a pool and deposits them; soon afterward they hatch into tadpoles. Tadpole development and growth can take more than a year, and the tadpoles grow to a considerable size. Indeed, growth in the tadpole stage represents a greater proportion of total lifetime growth than in any other frog.

DATA PANEL

Mallorcan midwife toad (ferreret)

Alytes muletensis

Family: Discoglossidae

World population: Unknown

Distribution: Mallorca

Habitat: Around pools in deep ravines at high altitude

Size: Length: 1.2–1.8 in (3–4 cm)

Form: Pale yellow or ocher with numerous dark-brown, black, or dark-green spots

Diet: Small invertebrates

Breeding: Spring and summer (March–July). Male carries eggs wrapped around hindlegs for several weeks; tadpole development lasts about 1 year

Related endangered species: Betic midwife toad *(Alytes dickhilleni)* VU

Status: IUCN VU; not listed by CITES

SPAIN

Majorca · Minorca

Ibiza · Balearic Islands

Formentera

ALGERIA

Having passed a string of eggs to a male, the female, liberated from parental duties, develops a new batch of eggs; by the time they are mature, after about three weeks, there are males available who have gotten rid of their first batch of eggs. The breeding season lasts several months, and during it a female can lay up to three or four batches of eggs. Because females can generally produce eggs faster than males can brood them (an effect that is especially marked in cool weather), females commonly have to fight one another to mate with a willing male.

On the Brink of Extinction

When zoologists discovered the Mallorcan midwife toad alive, they realized that it was not only extremely rare, but also in danger of extinction. Its restricted habitat was a major cause for concern. It was immediately protected, and in 1985 a captive-breeding program was established involving a number of zoos and universities across Europe. The Mallorcan midwife toad thrives and breeds readily in captivity, and by

1989 large numbers of tadpoles and young adults were being shipped back to Mallorca to be released into the wild. Releases were made at localities with a suitable habitat where there were no wild toads. The species is now established at 12 new sites, in addition to the 13 natural ones. The range over which the species occurs has been doubled, and it is estimated that about 25 percent of the total population was bred in captivity. In 2004 its status was reduced from Critically Endangered to Vulnerable.

The Mallorcan midwife toad illustrates the potential of captive-breeding programs in the conservation of endangered animals. It is a particularly suitable technique for amphibians because they have a high reproductive potential that is only rarely realized under natural conditions. Amphibians typically produce a large number of eggs. However, most die, either as eggs or tadpoles, through a variety of natural causes in the wild. In captivity eggs and tadpoles can be protected from such hazards so that the reproductive potential of a species can be exploited.

The Mallorcan midwife toad *now provides a focal point for an environmental education program that involves other threatened species in Mallorca.*

Golden Toad

Bufo periglenes

The golden toad has become a symbol of declining amphibian populations. Although living in a protected habitat, the species disappeared along with several other frog and toad species, and in 2004 was listed as extinct. The cause of this dramatic decline is unknown.

Most toads belonging to the genus *Bufo* are dull in color. Males and females are generally similar in appearance, with the females slightly larger than the males. The golden toad is highly unusual in that the coloration of the male is strikingly different from that of the female. While the female is greenish-yellow and black, decorated with yellow-edged red spots, the male is bright orange or red. The biological significance of the color difference is unknown.

Golden toads live in "elfin" cloud forest, so called because the trees' growth is stunted by powerful winds. When the forest is shrouded in dense cloud, it creates a damp climate that favors the growth of epiphytic plants and creepers (plants that grow on other plants, but are not parasitic). The toads have been seen only in the breeding season from March to June following the rain and lasting only a few days or weeks. The rain fills small pools—many form around the roots of trees—that are essential for the breeding

biology of the species. Large numbers of golden toads gather at the shallow pools, with males typically outnumbering females.

Tadpole Survival

Most toads lay very large numbers of small eggs (several thousand in many species) that hatch into tiny tadpoles. The eggs of the golden toad, however, are large, with a sizeable part consisting of yolk, and the average clutch size is only about 300. It is thought that this pattern evolved because the breeding pools used by the golden toad could become very crowded and did not support a sufficient growth of algae to provide food for large numbers of tadpoles. Golden toad tadpoles need the nutrients provided by the yolk if they are to grow quickly and metamorphose (transform into an adult) before their breeding ponds dry out.

DATA PANEL

Golden toad (sapo dorado)

Bufo periglenes

Family: Bufonidae

World population: Probably 0

Habitat: Montane (mountainous) cloud forest

Distribution: Monteverde Cloud Forest Preserve, Cordillera de Tilaran, Costa Rica

Size: Length: male 1.5–2 in (4.1–4.8 cm); female 1.8–2.3 in (4.7–5.4 cm)

Form: Male bright red or orange; female mottled black, red, and yellow

Diet: Insects and other invertebrates

Breeding: Clutch size of about 300 eggs laid March–June; hatch into tadpoles

Related endangered species: Amatola toad (*Bufo amatolicus*) EN; boreal toad (*B. boreas*) NT; Yosemite toad (*B. canorus*) EN; black toad (*B. exsul*) VU; Houston toad (*B. houstonensis*) EN; Amargosa toad (*B. nelsoni*) EN

Status: IUCN EX; CITES I

The golden toad

appears to have been a victim of climate change. It has probably gone extinct because its habitat became too dry for breeding.

Most toads lay their eggs in large, permanent ponds that are rich in algae and other nutrients.

Mysterious Decline

The golden toad was first described in 1964, having been observed during the breeding season. In 1987 1,500 animals were counted, but in both 1988 and 1989 only one individual was recorded at Monteverde in Costa Rica. Since then not a single golden toad has been seen. Over the same period about 20 percent of the frog and toad species found at Monteverde declined dramatically in numbers. During this time 25 species disappeared; only five have reappeared since. The species that were affected were those most dependent on standing water for breeding.

The cause of the dramatic population decline is not understood.

Monteverde is a nature reserve and is not subject to habitat destruction of any kind, nor are any herbicides, pesticides, or other chemicals used in the locality.

A detailed analysis of the climate at Monteverde suggests that climate change may be responsible for the demise of the golden toad and other frog and toad species. Since the 1970s the number of days each year when the forest is shrouded in cloud has diminished, affecting the local fauna. Bird and reptile species that once occurred at lower, drier altitudes have moved into higher altitudes. It seems that the golden toads died out when their habitat became too dry for successful breeding.

Western Toad

Bufo boreas

Once common throughout the western United States and Canada, the western toad has vanished from many parts of its range over the last 30 years. Although its decline is well documented, the causes of its depleted numbers are not known.

The huge geographical range of the western toad, stretching from the Baja California region of Mexico in the south to Alaska in the north; from sea level to altitudes of over 11,800 feet (3,600 m), suggests that it is a very adaptable species. It is found in a wide variety of habitats, including desert streams, grassland, woodland, and mountain meadows—its main requirement is only some kind of temporary or permanent water body nearby where it can breed. The western toad's remarkable ability to live in such a diversity of habitats has not, however, prevented it from declining and, in some areas, probably becoming extinct.

Gray or green in color with dark blotches, the western toad has a distinctive white or cream stripe running down the middle of its back. Its skin is warty, the warts mostly positioned within the dark blotches, some of which may be a rusty red color. Compared to many toads, it has rather small hind legs, and it typically runs over the ground, rather than hops. The male is, on average, slightly smaller than the female and somewhat less warty.

Two subspecies are recognized. The boreal toad occupies the northern part of the range, whereas the California toad is found farther south in California, western Nevada, and Baja California in Mexico.

Explosive Breeding

The western toad spends much of its life underground, either digging into soft soil or using the burrows of other animals, such as ground squirrels. It is described as an "explosive breeder," meaning that it has a very short and frenetic breeding season. Early in the spring—which can be any time from late January to July, depending on latitude, altitude, and local climatic conditions—large numbers of toads suddenly emerge from their winter hiding places and move toward ponds, lakes, and streams. Males do not call to attract females, but simply move around a breeding pond looking for females. At lower altitudes western toads are generally active only during the night, but at higher altitudes where it is cold at night, they are active by day. In the water the more numerous males grapple over females. Once a pair is firmly clasped

DATA PANEL

Western toad (boreal toad)

Bufo boreas

Family: Bufonidae

World population: Unknown

Distribution: Western U.S. and Canada

Habitat: Varied: includes desert streams and springs, grassland, woodland, and mountain meadows; in or near ponds, lakes, reservoirs, rivers, and streams

Size: Length: 2.5–5 in (6.2–12.5 cm)

Form: Brown, gray, or greenish with large, dark blotches; often also some rusty-red blotches; white or cream stripe down the middle of the back; warty skin

Diet: Small invertebrates

Breeding: Spring and summer (January–July, depending on latitude, altitude, and local conditions); explosive breeder; female produces thousands of eggs in long strings

Related endangered species: Amargosa toad *(Bufo nelsoni)* EN; Amatola toad *(B. amatolicus)* VU; black toad *(B. exsul)* VU; Houston toad *(B. houstonensis)* EN; Yosemite toad *(B. canorus)* EN

Status: IUCN NT; not listed by CITES

Alaska (U.S.)

CANADA

UNITED STATES

together, the male on the female's back, they make their way to a spawn site, where the female lays two long strings of eggs. Spawning is usually communal, with all the females in a population laying their eggs in one spot. The most likely benefit of such behavior is that the temperature inside a mass of spawn is slightly higher than that of the surrounding water, encouraging more rapid development of the eggs.

Population Decline

A survey carried out in Colorado in 1982 revealed that 11 populations of western toads known to exist in 1971 had vanished. In 1988 surveys in the central Rocky Mountains found western toads in only 10 of the 59 historically recorded sites. In Yosemite National Park in 1992 they were present in only one of many sites where they had been recorded in 1924. The species is now virtually extinct in Utah, and in Wyoming it has declined in the Yellowstone and Grand Teton National Parks.

Over much of its range the western toad has probably been adversely affected by deforestation, which has destroyed and fragmented its habitat. The period over which it has declined has also been a time when several serious droughts have occurred, preventing breeding in some years. Such factors do not explain the decline of the species in protected areas where its habitat has not been destroyed.

At some sites up to 95 percent of eggs have failed to hatch, a rate of mortality that is associated with an infection by the freshwater fungus, *Saprolegnia ferax*. The tendency of the species to breed communally exacerbates the effect of fungal infection. Experimental studies have shown that mortality among the eggs of western toads, as for other species, is increased by exposure to the elevated levels of ultraviolet radiation (especially UV-B) that now frequently occur in areas such as Oregon as a result of thinning of the ozone layer. Disease has also been suggested as a cause of the toad declines. Another

possibility is that one or more environmental factors, such as increased UV-B or pollution, has weakened their immune systems so that they have lost their resistance to once-harmless diseases.

The western toad *is an adaptable species inhabiting a huge range throughout the western United States. It is found in a variety of habitats, from mountain meadows to deserts.*

Golden Mantella

Mantella aurantiaca

The golden mantella frog is only found in one small forest on the island of Madagascar. It is threatened by the destruction of its habitat and by the international pet trade in frogs.

The golden mantella is one of a small group of frog species found only in Madagascar. It is brightly colored, poisonous, and active by day. It shares such characteristics with the poison-dart (dendrobatid) frogs of Central and South America. In evolutionary terms, however, the golden mantellas and poison-dart frogs are not related. The golden mantella thus represents an example of "convergent evolution" by which organisms come to closely resemble one another not as a result of common evolutionary ancestry, but through the action of natural selection (the survival of individuals best adjusted to their environment). The exact relationships of the mantellas are not clear. Some authorities put them in the large family Ranidae; others in a small family of their own: the Mantellidae.

Like the poison-dart frogs, the mantellas acquire poisonous compounds, called alkaloids, from their insect prey. They incorporate the toxic substances into secretions made in numerous poison glands in their skin. Predators that attack toxic, brightly colored prey quickly learn to associate the striking color pattern with an unpleasant experience and thereafter avoid that particular kind of prey.

Terrestrial Mating

Unlike many frogs, mantellas do not mate in standing water. However, they need damp conditions to breed and consequently mate in the rainy season. Males call to females, producing a sound like a cricket's chirp that consists of a series of notes, with three "clicks" in each. When a receptive female approaches, the male clasps her in a brief amplexus (mating embrace), during which the eggs are laid in hollows in the damp

soil. There are suggestions that fertilization is internal, but mating has not been properly observed. The eggs are whitish in color, and there are between 20 and 75 in a clutch. They hatch after about 14 days; the tadpoles push their way up to the soil surface and then wriggle over the damp ground to a nearby pool. There they complete their development, emerging as tiny frogs about two months later. In contrast to the vivid adult coloration, newly metamorphosed golden mantellas are green and black.

A Race against Time

The golden mantella lives only in one small forest area between Beforona and Maramanga in western Madagascar. The forests of Madagascar have been largely destroyed. Trees have been felled over large areas to be exported as timber and to create land for agriculture. All kinds of animals that are unique to the island are threatened by such activity, and biologists are currently exploring the remaining forest fragments to catalog the endemic (native) fauna before it disappears. As a result of the intense exploration, a growing number of newly described Madagascan species, including mantellas, are emerging. A few years ago only three mantellas had been described, but the most recent analysis lists 12 species, all of which are listed by IUCN at some level of threat.

Mantellas are also threatened by international trade, being popular as pets in Europe, the United States, and elsewhere. Since they are small and mainly terrestrial, the frogs are relatively easy to keep in captivity. In addition, they can be induced to breed, a factor that may be crucial for their conservation. All species are listed under CITES.

DATA PANEL

Golden mantella

Mantella aurantiaca

Family: Ranidae/Mantellidae

World population: Unknown

Distribution: Eastern Madagascar

Habitat: Deep leaf litter in wet tropical forests

Size: Length: 0.8–1.3 in (2–3 cm)

Form: Adults bright yellow, orange, or red; newly metamorphosed frogs green and black; black eyes

Diet: Small invertebrates

Breeding: Clutch of 20–75 whitish eggs laid in dark cavities on land; eggs hatch after about 14 days; tadpoles wriggle to small pools and emerge as tiny frogs about 2 months later

Related endangered species: 11 other mantellas listed by IUCN as threatened

Status: IUCN CR; CITES II

Adult golden mantellas *are both vividly colored and poisonous, a combination known as aposematic or warning coloration.* **239**

Tomato Frog

Dyscophus antongilii

The red or orange-colored tomato frog of Madagascar has been threatened by habitat destruction, pollution, and overcollection for the pet trade. It is now protected and responding well to captive-breeding programs.

The tomato frog gets its name from the rounded shape of the female and her red coloration, which makes her resemble a ripe tomato. Not all tomato frogs are red; some are orange, others dark brown, and males are generally less vividly colored than females. The frog has a flat head, a rounded body, and white underside; females are considerably larger than males. Their striking coloration, combined with the fact that they thrive in captivity, have made them popular animals in the international pet trade.

Found only in Madagascar, the tomato frog has a small range. It occurs in two main areas on the coastal plain in the northeast of the island. Its preferred habitat is soft soil, where standing water for it to breed in accumulates during the rainy season. A secretive, nocturnal animal, it hides during the day, emerging at night to hunt ground-dwelling invertebrates. The frog's round shape and lack of adhesive disks on its fingers and toes mean that it is unable to climb. Nor is it particularly well adapted for swimming, having only partial webbing between its toes and none between its fingers. During the dry season it burrows deep into sandy soil, using horny protuberances on its hind feet.

Sticky Defense

In many amphibians bright coloration is associated with skin toxins that make them unpalatable or poisonous to potential predators. The tomato frog's bright color serves to warn predators that it is not good to eat. When attacked or handled, it secretes copious amounts of sticky mucus from its skin; any animal trying to eat it is likely to find its jaws glued together. A number of amphibians have this kind of defense, but the tomato frog produces mucus with stronger sticking power than that of any other frog. It is also mildly toxic, often causing an allergic reaction in humans.

Breeding after Rain

With the first indication of rain male tomato frogs emerge from underground and head for ditches, ponds, and pools as they fill with water. It is thought that the sound of rain falling on the ground is a sufficient stimulus to bring males out of hiding. Males call to attract females

---

DATA PANEL

Tomato frog

Dyscophus antongilii

Family: Microhylidae

World population: Unknown

Distribution: Eastern coastal plains of Madagascar

Habitat: Lowland habitats with soft soil; some agricultural areas

Size: Length: male 2.5 in (6.5 cm); female 3.3–4.8 in (8–12 cm)

Form: Flat head, plump body, partial webbing between toes. Female bright red, occasionally orange or dark brown on the back; belly white. Male has duller, yellow-orange coloration

Diet: Small invertebrates

Breeding: 1,000–1,500 black-and-white eggs laid on water surface; tadpoles hatch within 36 hours; metamorphosis complete at 6.5 weeks; fully mature at 12 months. Life span 10 years

Related endangered species: Neither of the 2 other known species of *Dyscophus* is threatened

Status: IUCN NT; CITES I

TANZANIA
COMOROS
MALAWI
MADAGASCAR
MOZAMBIQUE

from the edge of the water, inflating a single vocal patch under the chin. Females lay between 1,000 and 1,500 eggs that float on the surface of the water. Filter-feeding tadpoles hatch from the eggs within two days and take a further six weeks to metamorphose into juvenile froglets. The young frogs are about 0.4 inches (1 cm) long by this stage and black or brown with a tan stripe down the back. They develop the characteristic adult colors at about three months and are fully mature by one year.

Threats and Conservation

The tomato frog has a restricted range in Madagascar, and much of its natural habitat has been destroyed to make way for building and agricultural land. This has not been as disastrous for the tomato frog as for other species, since they thrive alongside human activities and habitations. Large breeding populations form in man-made drainage ditches, rice fields, and flooded meadows, but these habitats are susceptible to pollution from pesticides, herbicides, and detergents.

The main threat to the tomato frog comes from the worldwide trade in amphibians. Large numbers used to be exported from Madagascar to Europe and the United States. Although it is nocturnal, the frog's distinctive nighttime call made it possible for poachers to identify and capture it in the dark.

The trade in tomato frogs for pets has now been stopped. The species is fully protected under CITES and breeding successfully in captivity, although lack of genetic diversity is a problem. To help increase diversity, attempts will be made to crossbreed frogs from European and American collections. The aim is also to build up captive populations in Madagascar for export to foreign breeding programs. The pet-trade market could then be met by captive-bred, rather than wild-caught frogs, and captive-bred animals could be used to reestablish populations in the wild.

The female tomato frog's *vivid red color has made it a target of poachers in its native Madagascar. CITES legislation has now outlawed this practice.*

Coelacanth

Latimeria chalumnae

Until the late 1930s it was thought that the coelacanth had been extinct for 70 million years. Closely related to the ancestors of land vertebrates and so-called living fossils, the coelacanths alive today are primitive deep-sea bony fish. The name refers to the fish's hollow fin spines (the Greek koilos means "hollow" and akantha means "spine").

In 1938 a fishing boat was trawling at a depth of about 240 feet (70 m) off the coast of South Africa near Port Elizabeth when the crew spotted an unusual fish in the catch; none of them had ever seen one like it before. On returning to port, they informed Marjorie Courtenay-Latimer, curator of the local natural history museum. She could not identify it.

Marjorie Courtenay-Latimer measured, examined, and photographed the fish and then had it stuffed. She also wrote to James Leonard Brierly Smith, an ichthyologist (fish specialist) in Grahamstown in South Africa, enclosing a sketch.

The fish measured about 5 feet (1.5 m) in length and was mauvish-blue with iridescent silver markings. Its odd-looking fins were perhaps its most unusual feature. The caudal (tail) fin had an extra portion sticking out at the end, like an additional fin lobe. There were also two dorsal (back) fins, instead of one. The paired fins were even more strange in that they had "stems" that looked like limbs, with fin rays fanning out at the edges.

Fossil Record

The rest, as they say, is history. The fish was a coelacanth, a primitive marine bony fish of the genus *Latimeria*. Fish of the genus *Coelacanthus* had been found as fossils in rocks from the end of the Permian period—225 million years ago—and at the end of the Jurassic period 136 million years ago. The coelacanths were believed to have become extinct about 70 million years ago, so the find was a rare creature, a "living fossil." As such, it provoked much public interest. The modern coelacanth was larger than most fossil fish and had a powerful body.

Reports of other catches of coelacanths have been recorded in more recent years. However, none of the catches has occurred in South Africa until the latest finds in Sodurana Bay. Until the late 1990s the 200 or so finds all came from the waters around Comoros, a small group of islands between southeastern Africa and Madagascar in the Indian Ocean. However, in September 1997 Mark

DATA PANEL

Coelacanth

Latimeria chalumnae

Family: Latimeriidae

World population: Unknown, but estimated at 200–500

Distribution: Comoro Islands, Indian Ocean (between Madagascar and southeastern Africa)

Habitat: Cold waters in deep ocean at 240 ft (70 m)

Size: Length: up to 5.9 ft (1.8 m). Weight: 210 lb (95 kg)

Form: Primitive fish with limblike pectoral fins. Bluish base color with light pinkish-white patches

Diet: Fish

Breeding: Livebearer (gives birth to living young). Up to 20 large eggs, each measuring 3.5 in (9 cm) in diameter and weighing 10.6–12.4 oz (300–350 g) are released from ovaries into oviduct. Developing embryos reach a length of at least 12 in (30 cm) before birth. Life span at least 11 years

Related endangered species: Sulawesi coelacanth (*Latimeria menadoensis*) not listed by IUCN

Status: IUCN CR; CITES I

Erdman, a scientist visiting the Indonesian island of Sulawesi, saw an unusual-looking fish being taken into the local market; he immediately identified it as a coelacanth. In 1998 a further specimen was found near Sulawesi, questioning the long-held belief that coelacanths inhabited a limited range in the Indian Ocean—Sulawesi is separated from the Comoro Islands by more than 6,000 miles (10,000 km). The Sulawesi coelacanths seem to be identical in every way except coloration—they are brown with golden-colored flecks. Analysis of genetic structures, however, indicated that the fish is, in fact, a separate species.

Keeping the Past Alive

Although it is not possible to gauge how abundant coelacanths are (scientists estimate that only between 200 and 500 remain in the western part of their range), there is no doubt that they are very rare.

In recognition of its rarity CITES has listed the coelacanth under Appendix I, thus making trade in the fish illegal. Another protective measure involves the safe release of any specimens accidentally caught by fishermen. The coelacanth favors cold waters at depths of about 240 feet (70 m). A "deep release kit" (first suggested by Raymond Walner, a visitor to one of the coelacanth websites) allows specimens to be lowered rapidly in a sack to a depth where the water is sufficiently cold and where the fish can release itself safely. So far the method has proved to be the most effective way of returning coelacanths to the wild.

Coelacanths found today have changed little from their ancestors, although they are larger than most "fossil fish." They have powerful bodies and limblike fins, which they use to move themselves around on the sea bottom when they are looking for prey.

Great White Shark

Carcharodon carcharias

The great white shark is a hunter par excellence. It frequents a wide range of habitats, and within its domain its success is matched only by that other major predator, the orca, or killer whale.

The great white shark is magnificently designed. Torpedo-shaped and armed with multiple rows of replaceable saw-edged triangular teeth, it also has a battery of receptors that almost defy human comprehension. It can sense its prey from distances of over 1 mile (1.6 km); low-frequency sound waves can be picked up from this distance by the shark's ears, while low-frequency vibrations in the water are detected by its hypersensitive lateral line system (a system of sensory organs that detect even the slightest pressure changes and vibrations).

In addition to its long-distance senses the shark has an acute ability to detect weak electrical fields, such as those emitted by fish and other prey. The tiny pulses of electricity are picked up by the ends of ducts (ampullae of Lorenzini) located on the shark's snout. Such is the sensitivity of the ampullae that some sharks can locate prey such as flatfish even if it is buried in the sand.

Sharks can also sense blood—the unmistakable "signal" sent out by injured prey—at extremely weak dilutions. In experiments to find out more about the shark's capacity to detect weak solutions, lemon sharks were shown to sense tuna remnants or "juice" at an incredibly weak dilution of one part juice to 25 million parts of water.

The shark's ability to detect movement in dim light is aided by a membranous reflecting layer of cells located under the retina in the eye. It acts as a mirror, reflecting rays back through the retina, reactivating the light-sensitive cells in the process, and thus optimizing the eye's ability to detect movement in even minimal levels of illumination. This exceptional

DATA PANEL

Great white shark

Carcharodon carcharias

Family: Lamnidae

World population: About 10,000

Distribution: Worldwide, but predominantly in warm-temperate and subtropical waters; may also be found in warmer areas. Only infrequently encountered in cold northern regions

Habitat: Wide range of habitats from surf line to offshore (rarely in mid-ocean). Found between the surface and depths of 820 ft (250 m) or more

Size: Unconfirmed reports refer to specimens in excess of 23 ft (7 m). Confirmed data, however, indicates a maximum size of 18–20 ft (5.5–6 m)

Form: Torpedo-shaped fish with saw-edged triangular teeth. System of sensory organs for detecting prey; light-sensitive membrane below retina for tracking movement in dim light

Diet: Mainly bony fish but also cartilaginous fish (including other sharks); marine mammals, including cetaceans (whales and dolphins) and pinnipeds (seals and sea lions)

Breeding: Gives birth to 5–10 live young (probably more) after a gestation period that could last as long as 1 year

Related endangered species: Whale shark (*Rhincodon typus*) VU

Status: IUCN VU; CITES III

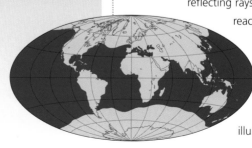

sensory system, combined with the other attributes possessed by sharks, has ensured their survival for over 200 million years.

Pressure from Humans

Exploitation by humans has taken its toll over the years. Direct killing for the entertainment of professional anglers or to obtain shark products for the souvenir trade has caused significant decline. Passive killing, with great white sharks being caught in nets set out for other target species, has also exerted pressure on populations, as have shark nets installed to protect bathers along shark-threatened coastlines.

The combined effects of these and other threats have led to a significant decline in great white shark numbers. The actual extent of this decline and the total number of great whites that remain in the wild are difficult to quantify. There are several reasons for this, including the diversity of nomadic and homing habits exhibited by the species. Some specimens, for

The great white shark *is an aggressive sea predator with a finely tuned sensory system. However, hunting and accidental killings by humans have taken their toll on population numbers.*

instance, tend to frequent relatively localized "territories," while others are known to roam over large distances. Another complicating factor is that, worldwide, the species is relatively scarce.

As a result, although a figure of 10,000 has been cited as a global total, it can only be approximate. Concerned by the decline, several countries have implemented protection programs. Measures range from banning all great white shark products to prohibiting activities such as fishing or underwater viewing by tourists. Further action is being urged by conservation bodies who fear that the current IUCN listing as Vulnerable may be incorrect and that the great white shark may already be Endangered.

Common Sturgeon

Acipenser sturio

It is difficult to imagine that some European rivers can hide giant fish measuring up to 20 feet (6 m) long that are capable of producing many millions of eggs in a single spawning. Such a fish is the common sturgeon. In spite of its prolific breeding habits, the species is at risk.

The common sturgeon usually grows to a length of 3.3 to 6.6 feet (1 to 2 m), but can be longer. At least one report indicates that the species can attain a length of 20 feet (6 m) and a weight of about 1,300 pounds (600 kg). Despite this report, probably the largest specimen actually on record was 11.3 feet (3.4 m) long and 705 pounds (320 kg). The female has the potential to deliver close to 2.5 million eggs in a single spawning episode.

As with some 40 or so other sturgeon species, the common sturgeon is under severe threat. It was once found in large numbers along the coast of Europe, from the North Sea to the Mediterranean and Black Seas. Today it is scarce throughout its range.

Sturgeons are famous primarily for their eggs, known universally as caviar. However, many species have also been fished for their flesh. All species are long-lived, with ages beyond 50 years being common.

Double Life

The common sturgeon is anadromous, which means that it spends its life at sea but migrates into freshwater habitats during the spawning season. One notable exception to the rule is the common sturgeon population that lives in Lake Ladoga in Russia. Another is the sterlet, which lives permanently in fresh water.

Spawning migrations upriver occur in early or mid-spring, with actual breeding taking place during early summer. Spawning is usually in pools that are several feet deep and have a flow of water. Alternatively, it may occur along river banks covered by spring floods. The eggs—up to 2.5 million for a largish female—are scattered over a gravelly bottom and abandoned.

By now the condition of the adults has deteriorated, since they do not feed during their migrations: Many, in fact, will not make it back to sea to resume feeding. In better days such losses would not have been a problem, owing to the large number of adults in the population, not to mention the high numbers of offspring. Today every adult that dies adds to the scarcity of the species as it struggles to survive in the modern world.

DATA PANEL

Common sturgeon (Baltic sturgeon)

Acipenser sturio

Family: Acipenseridae

World population: Unknown, but close to extinction in parts of its range

Distribution: Atlantic Ocean from Norway south to North Africa and into the western Mediterranean; Baltic, and Black Seas

Habitat: Relatively shallow, mainly coastal seas, usually over sandy or muddy bottoms; some specimens move to deeper waters

Size: Length: on average 3.3–6.6 ft (1–2 m). Weight: a 10-ft (3-m) specimen may weigh about 440 lb (200 kg)

Form: Elongated body with distinct snout and characteristic caudal (tail) fin in which upper lobe is larger than lower one. Five rows of large, stout scales down body. Underslung mouth has distinctive barbels (whiskers)

Diet: Adults feed on bottom-dwelling marine invertebrates, but will also take small fish; juveniles feed mostly on bottom-dwelling freshwater invertebrates

Breeding: Migrates up to 620 miles (1,000 km) upriver in early to mid-spring; spawning occurs over gravel or pebbles, usually in flowing water pools. Each female is usually accompanied by more than 1 male. Hatching takes about 7 days, and juveniles may stay in their river of birth for up to 4 years

Related endangered species: Over 40 populations of the 25 species are under varying degrees of threat, including the ship sturgeon (*Acipenser nudiventris*) EN

Status: IUCN CR; CITES I

Young common sturgeon stay fairly close to the spawning grounds at first, but gradually move downriver as they grow. Some reports suggest that by the fall of the same year they move out to sea; others state that this may be delayed for one to four years. Whatever the case, males mature at between seven and nine years (some estimates indicate later maturation between nine and 13 years), while females may take eight to 14 years (some estimate it to be between 11 and 18 years) to mature and return to their waters of birth to breed for the first time.

Overfishing and Habitat Destruction

Overfishing is usually cited as the main reason for the sharp decline in numbers. Undoubtedly, fishing has had a severe effect on natural populations, not just of the common sturgeon, but of many of its relatives. Some of the eastern populations and species in particular are still the focus of illegal trade in caviar. In some cases arguments have been put forward to ban fishing altogether. However, others argue that to do so would drive the market underground and into the hands of organized illegal groups, thus probably accentuating rather than solving the problem.

The common sturgeon's best hope for the future appears to lie in coordinated captive-breeding programs to rear stocks for commercial exploitation of the roe (caviar). Such farms are likely to produce more fish than may eventually be needed for harvesting purposes, thus acting as a potential

source of fish for restocking former habitats. A beneficial spinoff from such programs is that they also reduce pressure on existing wild stocks.

However successful such breeding projects may be, the survival of the species in the wild needs to be urgently addressed. One problem is the pollution of watercourses. While it presents a daunting challenge, there are other potentially more difficult pressures facing the common sturgeon, including the building of dams, water channeling, and allied habitat-altering developments that plague the waterways.

The common sturgeon *has a number of distinctive features, including an elongated snout and barbels (whiskers) below its underslung mouth.*

Danube Salmon

Hucho hucho

Unlike its oceangoing cousins, the Danube salmon lives, breeds, and dies in the inland waters of the Danube River, where it is exposed to habitat destruction and environmental pollution.

Salmon are majestic fish, and the Danube species is the largest of all. While the Danube salmon lives in rivers, many species live at sea. On reaching maturity, sea-dwelling salmon undertake a migration of epic proportions to the river in which they were spawned. Compelled by instinct, each fish battles against unbelievable odds—sometimes including rapids or even falls—to reach the mouth of its home river to spawn. The female digs pits in the gravel in which to lay her eggs, which take about five weeks to hatch.

Although the life cycle of sea-dwelling salmon is physically challenging, its migratory habits have helped safeguard its success as a species. Juveniles that manage to negotiate the journey from their spawning grounds to the sea stand a better chance of reaching maturity than those that stay in the rivers of their birth. Unlike the Danube salmon, sea salmon avoid exposure to the pollution or irreversible habitat alteration that can occur in rivers as a result of environmental disasters.

International Pressures

The Danube River flows through 12 countries inhabited by a total of more than 70 million people. Enforcement of environmental controls is therefore complicated. Some problems are historical, relating to industrial sites that were built before environmental

DATA PANEL

Danube salmon (European salmon, Danube trout, European river trout)

Hucho hucho

Family: Salmonidae

World population: Unknown; estimates are low

Distribution: Rivers of Danube basin; introduced elsewhere in Europe, U.S., Canada, and Morocco

Habitat: Deep, well-oxygenated regions of fast-flowing water; also found in backwaters at temperatures of 43–64°F (6–18°C)

Size: Up to 6.5 ft (2 m). Weight: over 220 lb (100 kg)

Form: Similar to salmon *(Salmo salar)*, but slimmer; large head and jaws. Greenish back, silvery sides with diffused pink sheen, white along belly. Numerous small star-shaped black spots on back, gradually decreasing in number down body

Diet: Adults feed on other fish, amphibians, reptiles, waterfowl, and even small mammals. Juveniles feed predominantly on invertebrates

Breeding: Spawning March–May after migration to shallow, gravelly areas with fast-flowing, oxygen-rich water. Female excavates nest with tail and (with help of male) covers fertilized eggs. Hatching period 5 weeks

Related endangered species: Satsukimasa salmon *(Oncorhynchus ishikawai)* EN; carpione del Garda *(Salmo carpio)* VU; Ohrid trout *(S. letnica)* VU; ala Balik *(S. platycephalus)* CR; Adriatic salmon *(Salmothymus obtusirostris)* EN; beloribitsa *(Stenodus leucichthys leucichthys)* EN

Status: IUCN EN; not listed by CITES

The Danube salmon *(also known as the European salmon, Danube trout, and European river trout) is the largest of all the salmons, and faces an uncertain future.*

legislation had to be taken into account. Others are political, where one country is not bound by the environmental laws of another. Both situations apply to the Danube, along which there are approximately 1,700 industries, many producing wastes that are known to be toxic. Aquatic organisms cannot survive the levels of toxicity and must find new areas or perish. Escape is not always possible, and the result is often the destruction of many thousands of creatures and their habitats.

Pollution Crises

In 2000 a dam leaked cyanide from a Romanian gold mine into the Tiza River, a tributary of the Danube, killing all forms of aquatic life for 250 miles (400 km) downstream. In Hungary alone about 85 tons of dead fish were removed. Some environmentalists claimed that the whole ecological system of the river had been wiped out by the spillage.

By early February 2000 cyanide was detected at the confluence of the Tiza with the Danube, and it was feared that the poisoning might cause the extinction of the Danube salmon. The outcome has been less devastating, but the situation illustrates the precarious future faced by the Danube salmon.

Such pollution crises are serious enough to threaten the existence of any Danube species. In the case of the Danube salmon there are other significant threats, including overfishing, water extraction for a wide range of industrial and other uses, and river alteration (primarily channeling and damming).

The Danube salmon is being pressurized from many quarters, to the extent that its long-term survival looks uncertain. Repeated attempts to introduce hatchery-bred stocks into a number of watercourses have been largely unsuccessful. However, in 1968 stocks were introduced from Czechoslovakia into Spanish waters, well outside the species' natural range. Over the years the stocks have become established. Restocking might not be the answer to the Danube salmon's problems, but it could be an essential lifeline.

249

Lake Victoria Haplochromine Cichlids

Haplochromis **spp.**

Restricted by nature to a certain habitat, many animal and plant species will evolve into several types, to fill every possible niche with little or no overlap. Such "species flocks" are able to survive side by side without much competition. This is the situation in the Great Rift lakes of Africa.

Africa's three major lakes, or "inland seas"— Lakes Malawi, Tanganyika, and Victoria— contain a bewildering array of fish species so diverse and colorful that they are often compared with coral reef fish. Each lake has its own endemic species (species found nowhere else). Lake Malawi is famous for *Aulonocara*, *Melanochromis*, and *Pseudotropheus* species, while Lake Tanganyika has *Lamprologus*, *Neolamprologus*, and *Julidochromis* species. Lake Victoria is renowned for haplochromine cichlids.

Lake Victoria

Lake Victoria is a massive body of fresh water. In surface dimensions it is the third largest lake in the world after Lake Superior and the Caspian Sea. It is, however, relatively shallow; its maximum depth is only 260 feet (80 m). Owing to its highly irregular coast profile, its shoreline is about 2,200 miles (3,500 km) long. Despite its colossal size, it is surrounded by land and is virtually cut off from major external influences. As a result, it has developed its own special characteristics, including hard and alkaline water.

Victoria Cichlids

Within this special environment habitats vary across the thousands of bays and inlets along the lake coastline, where a large number of fish species can be found. Estimates vary, but over 200—and probably closer to 400—endemic species of cichlids have evolved. More than half belong to the genus *Haplochromis*. Owing to the relative "youth" of Lake Victoria, the evolution of so many different cichlid species in such a short time has been referred to as an example of "explosive radiation," or "evolutionary avalanche."

Catastrophic Developments

A series of developments has affected these haplochromine populations. For example, pressures were created by a fast-expanding human population around the lake, and greater demand for arable land has resulted in forested areas

---

DATA PANEL

Lake Victoria haplochromine cichlids

Haplochromis **spp.**

Family: Cichlidae

World population: Some 200 species are known to have become extinct since mid-1950s; population levels of remaining species are estimated to have decreased from about 80% of total biomass of the lake to about 1%

Distribution: Lake Victoria, East Africa

Habitat: Wide range of habitats mostly close to the lake bottom and in relatively shallow water

Size: Length: about 4 in (10 cm)

Form: Most species have laterally compressed bodies, large eyes and mouths, and well-formed fins. Dorsal (back) fin has spinous front half and soft-rayed back half. Males of most species exhibit egglike spots (egg dummies) on anal (belly) fin

Diet: Diverse, but specific to each species. Phytoplankton and zooplankton encrusting algae, insects, mollusks, crustaceans, eggs, larvae, or even scales of other fish

Breeding: Female lays small number of eggs (sometimes only 5, depending on size and species). Males stimulated to release sperm by females pecking at egg dummies. Eggs and sperm brooded orally by females; female guards young, taking them back into mouth if danger threatens

Related endangered species: All species of haplochromine in Lake Victoria

Status: Not individually listed by IUCN because too many, but *Haplochromis obliquidens*, for example, is EN; not listed by CITES

Lake Albert   Lake Kyoga
CONGO (D.R.O.)   UGANDA
Lake Edward   KENYA
Lake Kivu   Lake Victoria
RWANDA
BURUNDI
TANZANIA
Lake Tanganyika

The emerald-backed cichlid *(above) may be prey to the voracious Nile perch (below right) that was introduced to Lake Victoria in the 1950s.*

being cleared. This has led to increased runoff into the lake—both physical (silt) and chemical (fertilizers)—and to changes in the vegetation of near-shore areas.

In addition, an increasing demand for protein arose. Traditionally gotten from fishing practiced at a sustainable level, the situation became critical when populations of some of the best food fish species dramatically collapsed. By the 1950s at least one species was commercially extinct. In order to provide people with a regular supply of cheap animal protein, two food fish species were introduced into the lake: *Tilapia* and the Nile perch.

For nearly 30 years there appeared to be no major change in the lake's endemic fauna. However, in 1980 a survey revealed a sudden drop in haplochromine cichlids. From originally forming about 80 percent by weight of catches, they had dropped to 1 percent, with 80 percent represented by the Nile perch.

The Nile perch fishing industry has become hugely important to the local economy. However, a large Nile perch consumes vast quantities of smaller fish. They are therefore blamed for the large-scale decimation leading to the extinction of about 50 percent of the lake's haplochromines. As a result, the Nile perch has turned to other foods, including its own young.

Ray of Hope

For the cichlids the future is still uncertain. Several national and international projects are, however, addressing factors concerning their continued survival. One such development is a wide-ranging captive-breeding program. Some 40 species have already been bred; and while rates of success vary, this is encouraging news. Additionally, aquaculture is being encouraged among the fishermen of the lake in the hope of reducing pressure on remaining cichlid stocks.

The Lake Victoria situation is complex. Yet with appropriate encouragement and dedication further losses may be prevented in the years to come.

251

Dragon Fish

Scleropages formosus

A fishing eagle hunting over the forests of central Sumatra spotted a large fish in the foaming waters of a stream below. It swooped from the skies, dived into the water, and mated with the armor-plated fish. Thus the dragon fish was born.

So went the legend of the dragon fish. As is often the case, the story is a somewhat fanciful but not unreasonable explanation of the facts. The remarkable union between a fish and a bird seemed plausible given the large yolks to which baby dragon fish are attached during the first weeks of their development when they incubate inside their father's mouth. Dragon fish eggs have a spherical yolk that can measure up to 0.7 inches (1.8 cm) in diameter, making them larger than those of many bird species.

It is likely that the legend of the dragon fish was also reinforced by observations. People may have seen predatory birds attempting to prey on dragon fish, although the fish's thick, immensely strong scales probably protected it from such aerial attacks. If a fishing eagle or other bird of prey were to dive onto a dragon fish, causing a great deal of splashing and foaming in the process, the chances are that it would leave empty-handed (or empty-taloned). It is easy to see how a failed attack (or more likely many failed attacks observed over time) could have been interpreted as mating rather than hunting.

A Fish of Many Forms

Dragon fish are found in eastern Asia, including Malaysia, the Philippines, Vietnam, and Indonesia. Doubt exists about the Myanmar (Burma) populations, and the species may now be extinct in Thailand. The fish are known variously as the Asian arowana, Asian bonytongue, Malayan bonytongue, and emperor fish. In their native waters three names are regularly used: *cherek kelesa*, *ikan arowana* (in Malaysia), and *Lóng Yú* (in Chinese-speaking countries).

The dragon fish occurs in three color forms in the wild (with regional modifications):

CHINA
MYANMAR LAOS
THAILAND VIETNAM
PHILIPP
MALAYSIA
INDONESIA

DATA PANEL

Dragon fish

Scleropages formosus

Family: Osteoglossidae

World population: Unknown

Distribution: Cambodia, Malaysia, Philippines, Vietnam, Indonesia (Kalimantan and Sumatra). Possibly Myanmar (Burma); may now be extinct in Thailand

Habitat: Still or slow-flowing waters that may be turbid (muddy) or heavily vegetated

Size: Length: up to 35 in (90 cm); usually much smaller

Form: Torpedo-shaped body with pointed head, large eyes, and large mouth with barbels (whiskers). Thick, strong scales. Three color forms: green/silver, gold, and red

Diet: A wide range of invertebrates and small vertebrates may be eaten. They are usually taken from the surface or upper part of the water column, but may occasionally also be plucked off branches above water

Breeding: About 30 eggs (but as many as 90 or more) are laid and are incubated orally by the male for 5–6 weeks; main breeding season July–December. Mature at 3–4 years

Related endangered species: Spotted or southern saratoga (*Scleropages leichardti*) LRnt; pirarucu (*Arapaima gigas*) DD

Status: IUCN EN; CITES I

The dragon fish, *particularly the red color form, is highly regarded throughout east Asia, where captive-breeding programs have ensured its survival.*

green/silver, gold, and red. The last of these is deemed the most valuable. Captive-bred varieties include crosses between the different color forms as well as color-selected types, such as the rainbow dragon. Occasionally, albinos have been reported.

Breeding can occur throughout the year, but is at its peak between July and December. Actual mating is preceded by a long period of courtship and bonding that can last two or three months. The females (which have a single ovary) will lay about 30 eggs—although over 90 have been reported—which, once fertilized, are picked up by the male in its mouth. From that point onward the female plays no further part in the process. The male, however, will incubate the eggs in its mouth for between five and six weeks, by which time the young fish (fry) can attain a length of nearly 3.5 inches (9 cm).

Fears for the Fish of Good Fortune

The dragon fish is held in high esteem in Asia, where it is believed to bring health, wealth, and luck to its owners. It is kept in aquaria throughout the region and is also much sought after by east Asian communities all over the world. Specialized Western aquarists are also interested in the species, but the large size that adult specimens can attain places the dragon fish outside the reach of most enthusiasts.

Fears for the continued survival of the dragon fish in the wild—probably as a result of overcollection—led to the species being listed under Appendix I of CITES in 1975. At one time the dragon fish was classified as Insufficiently Known by the IUCN, but its status has since been changed to Endangered.

Whether the concern over the fish's survival is fully justified or not remains open to debate. Populations have become established from captive-bred specimens in a government plan in Singapore. Monitored captive-breeding programs in other forms and other east Asian countries have also resulted in the establishment of registered farms that are licensed to export the species under a CITES Appendix I provision.

Devil's Hole Pupfish

Cyprinodon diabolis

The Devil's Hole pupfish gets its name from the freshwater limestone cave pool in which it lives. Its entire life cycle is spent largely within the boundaries of a shelf near the surface of the pool. If conditions on the shelf are less than ideal, the pupfish is in immediate danger.

The Devil's Hole pupfish has been known since 1891. However, for 40 years it was assumed to be a variant of another well-known species, the desert pupfish. In 1930 its distinctive nature was fully realized, and it was named as a separate species.

The "devil" that the pupfish bears in its common name is not a reflection of its form or habits, but rather of its natural habitat: Devil's Hole cave pool in Nye County, Nevada. The narrow but deep dimensions of the pool make diving difficult for those allowed to use it (researchers and others involved in scientific work on the pool and its inhabitants). Devil's Hole is 55 feet (17 m) long, 10 feet (3 m) wide, and over 300 feet (90 m) deep. The pupfish has been found at depths of up to 80 feet (25 m). However, much of its everyday life is based around a shallow ledge or shelf measuring 18 by 10 feet (5.5 by 3 m). The Devil's Hole pupfish congregate here to spawn and to feed on the tiny aquatic invertebrates that live and feed on an algal "mat."

Life on the Shelf

The Devil's Hole pupfish lives in precarious conditions, and the Devil's Hole shelf plays a pivotal role in the survival of the species. As with other species, water level is critical; even a minor drop spells real danger for the pupfish. If the shelf were deeper within Devil's Hole, then water level fluctuations would present less of a problem. As it is, a decrease in water level of only 39 inches (100 cm) exposes the shallowest area of the shelf and destroys much of the algal growth. As a result, the invertebrate population is reduced, and the

DATA PANEL

Devil's Hole pupfish

Cyprinodon diabolis

Family: Cyprinodontidae

World population: About 650

Distribution: Devil's Hole, Ash Meadows National Wildlife Refuge, Nye County, Nevada

Habitat: Largely confined to shallow water over an algae-covered shelf; specimens also found in deeper water down to 80 ft (25 m). Water temperature about 86°F (30°C)

Size: Length: males 1 in (2.5 cm); females smaller

Form: Relatively large head; dorsal fin set well back on body; lacks pelvic (hip) fins. Males in breeding condition have bluish tinge to body and black edges to the yellowish-golden fins. At other times the body is brown with silvery sides and numerous black specks

Diet: Small, aquatic invertebrate fauna of shelf's algal mat

Breeding: Eggs laid among algae on the shallow spawning shelf from spring into summer

Related endangered species: Other Cyprinodonts, including Cachorrito lodero (*Cyprinodon beltrani*) EN; Leon Springs

pupfish (*C. bovinus*) CR; Comanche Springs pupfish (*C. elegans*) EN; Perrito de carbonera (*C. fontinalis*) EN; Cachorrito cangrejero (*C. labiosus*) EN; large-scale pupfish (*C. macrolepis*) EN; Cachorrito gigante (*C. maya*) EN; Cachorrito de mezquital (*C. meeki*) CR; Cachorrito cabezon (*C. pachycephalus*) CR; Pecos pupfish (*C. pecoensis*) CR; Owen's pupfish (*C. radiosus*) EN; Cachorrito boxeador (*C. simus*) EN; Cachorrito de dorsal larga (*C. verecundus*) CR; and Cachorrito de charco azul (*C. veronicae*) CR

Status: IUCN VU; not listed by CITES

The Devil's Hole pupfish

is believed to be the vertebrate species with the smallest natural habitat in the world. Despite the problems of its range, its future appears to be in good hands.

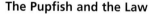

fish are deprived of a significant part of their food supply. A further reduction in water level, leading to exposure of the whole ledge, would cause the destruction of spawning sites. The result would be possible extinction if levels remained low for any length of time.

The Pupfish and the Law

In 1952 Devil's Hole was incorporated into the Death Valley National Monument, offering the cave pool official protection. It took 15 more years for the pupfish to be recognized as an endangered species. However, its newfound legal status, which should have been enough to ensure its continued survival, did not produce the desired results. In what is sometimes reported as a serious error, some of the land in the vicinity of Devil's Hole (now known as the Ash Meadows National Wildlife Refuge) passed into private ownership. Within a short time wells had been sunk in the area, with the result that water levels in the subterranean aquifers (water-bearing layers of permeable rock, sand, or gravel) supplying Devil's Hole began to suffer.

By 1969, 60 percent of the Devil's Hole shelf was exposed by the drop in water level, posing a serious threat to the fish. Urgent action was taken. Specimens were transferred to several fishless desert springs, aquarium breeding projects were set up, and a fiberglass ledge with overhead lights was installed at a suitable depth within Devil's Hole itself. The last measure proved considerably more successful than the other salvage attempts. After several years of further campaigning, and a series of court hearings, the

Devil's Hole pupfish obtained its legal lifeline in 1976. The ruling set out to limit the amount of water that could be pumped from the area. The pupfish has experienced further threats since, but has managed to survive with the help of scientists and conservationists.

Conservation Measures

To check natural population levels, researchers carry out a count at least twice a year, diving 80 feet (25 m) to the shelf known as Anvil Rock. They record every fish encountered during the gradual ascent to the surface. In addition, an above-water count of fish on the shallower ledge is carried out. Depending on the time of year, counts vary from under 200 specimens to over 500. The highest numbers are recorded following the spawning season in the summer; they drop off during the winter when the algal mat dies back, largely due to lack of sunlight. A species "safety net" can be found in three specially built ponds or "refugia." Each contains subpopulations of pupfish; two of the ponds have about 200 fish, while in the third, breeding has only just begun.

As long as conditions in Devil's Hole remain within certain limits, it would seem that naturally fluctuating population levels may not adversely affect the continued survival of the species.

Silver Shark

Balantiocheilos melanopterus

Despite its name and a passing visual similarity to true sharks, the silver shark could not really be more different from its namesakes. It is not ferocious, it lacks true teeth, and it feeds on tiny insects and plants, rather than fish, squid, and other marine animals.

The silver shark is a popular aquarium fish. Ever since it was first imported into Europe in 1955, it has been in great demand worldwide, in particular the very attractively colored juveniles.

Shark Appeal

The label "shark" made the fish appealing to millions of aquarium keepers around the world, even though the freshwater aquarium fish are not related to their predatory, marine namesakes. Although there are many other, smaller, more colorful aquarium species, the demand for silver sharks is high.

The silver shark is a cyprinid (a member of the family Cyprinidae). The family includes other "sharks"—the red-tailed black shark, the rainbow or ruby shark, and the black shark; all have a profile with only superficial resemblance to a true shark.

One of the reasons for the popularity of the silver shark and other freshwater aquarium "sharks" is the relative ease with which they can be kept. They do not have exacting dietary or water chemistry demands, and assuming that appropriately roomy accommodation can be provided, it is perfectly possible to keep such fish in peak condition until they die of old age (after several years). Modern aquarium technology and husbandry techniques mean that even fully mature specimens of silver shark, or even the larger black shark, can be kept.

Wild Populations Under Pressure

At one time the silver shark was so abundant throughout its range in Southeast Asia that it was regarded as a Category I species for home aquaria.

DATA PANEL

Silver shark (bala shark, tricolor shark)

Balantiocheilos melanopterus

Family: Cyprinidae

World population: Virtually extinct in some parts of the range but abundant in others

Distribution: Kalimantan (Borneo), Sumatra (Indonesia), Thailand, and peninsular Malaysia

Habitat: Flowing, oxygen-rich waters

Size: Up to 14 in (35 cm)

Form: Elongated fish with a passing resemblance to true sharks. Body almost entirely covered in silvery, highly reflective, scales. Pectoral (chest) fins uncolored, but others are golden yellow and black

Diet: Wide range of aquatic insects and other invertebrates; delicate submerged vegetation

Breeding: In the wild mass spawnings occur following migration to breeding grounds. Eggs are scattered among vegetation or over the substratum and abandoned by the spawners

Related endangered species: None

Status: IUCN EN; not listed by CITES

The term applies to species that are in demand and are collected or bred in large quantities for aquarists.

The fish stocks appeared to be inexhaustible; but, as in so many instances, they eventually proved not to be. Demand continued, and local populations became overfished, so the search expanded into unexploited areas, including spawning grounds. Harvests removed not only juveniles from a population, but also a percentage of the breeding adults that would normally replenish the numbers. Existing stocks were therefore placed under unsustainable pressure.

Further pressures came from deforestation, with the accompanying habitat alteration, deterioration in water quality, and siltation. Eventually, the silver shark became scarce in parts of its range within Kalimantan and Sumatra, and was virtually wiped out in others. Thailand populations, however, remained almost untouched, so the species as a whole was not depleted to a point beyond recovery. Today, however, the Thai populations are also believed to be declining.

In recent years the main cause of decline has not been collection from the wild; demand by aquarists for the silver shark is now met from captive-bred stocks. Wild populations still face an uncertain future, however, as a result of various factors, including habitat alteration, water deterioration caused by the use of chemicals, and the small-mesh nets used in fishing. The problems are being addressed, but it will be some time before the solutions can be assessed.

Silver sharks are members of the Cyprinidae family, which includes the food fish carp, roach, and tench; they are typically toothless fish with rounded, smooth-edged scales. The silver shark's scales are shiny and highly reflective.

Northern Bluefin Tuna

Thunnus thynnus

Tuna are the long-distance specialists of the fish world, covering several thousand miles a year on their migrations. They are also among the fastest-swimming fish in the world. Some populations are now endangered as a result of the world demand for tuna meat.

Tuna are fish built for speed. Every aspect of their body form is suited to maximum performance in the water. Their body is fusiform (pointed at both ends) with a stiff, sickle-shaped caudal (tail) fin perfect for producing maximum thrust. The bluefin tuna also has several features designed to reduce water resistance. Its scales are tiny and lie tightly against the skin, so minimizing friction. Its large eyes are well-bedded within their sockets, so the outer layer lies flush with the skin surface. The two dorsal (back) fins and the single anal (belly) fin fit into grooves when they are folded, while the series of finlets between the fins and the tail allow water to flow between them. The pectoral (chest) and pelvic (hip) fins are small and have a stiff front edge, which prevents them from collapsing when they are extended at high speeds.

A striking feature of the tuna's body is the deep-red color of the muscle tissue. This characteristic is found in the family Scombridaea that includes other high-speed species such as mackerel, bonitos, and their relatives. Red muscle has a rich blood supply that is typical of a species constantly on the move. The blood supplies the high levels of oxygen that the fish need and gives them plenty of stamina.

However, tuna would be unable to maintain their constant day-and-night swimming at speed were it not for a further adaptation. Unlike the majority of fish whose internal body temperature matches that of their environment, a tuna's countercurrent blood circulation allows it to maintain a high internal body temperature whatever the water temperature.

All-Consuming Demand

Bluefin tuna have been fished for about 100 years. Originally only sport fishermen and a few small-scale

DATA PANEL

Northern bluefin tuna (Atlantic bluefin tuna)

Thunnus thynnus

Family: Scombridae

World population: Disputed: about 40,000 in the western Atlantic (no equivalent data available for the eastern Atlantic)

Distribution: Atlantic. On eastern side from Norway to Mediterranean Sea, along western African coast to Cape Blanc. On western side from Newfoundland south to Brazil. Seen in central and northwestern Pacific

Habitat: Open oceanic waters

Size: Length: 15 ft (4.6 m). Weight: up to 1,320 lb (600 kg)

Form: Fusiform (spindle-shaped), streamlined body. Coloration deep blue above, with purple or green iridescence (colors that shimmer as observer changes position); silvery sides and belly

Diet: Fish (including herring, mackerel, and whiting); also squid

Breeding: Spawning occurs in the Gulf of Mexico, the western Atlantic, and in the

Mediterranean Sea in the east. Western stocks spawn from mid-April to mid-June; their eastern counterparts breed from June–August. Female can release about 30 million eggs

Related endangered species: Albacore tuna (*Thunnus alalunga*) DD; bigeye tuna (*T. obesus*) VU; southern bluefin tuna (*T. maccoyii*) CR; Monterrey Spanish mackerel (*Scomberomorus concolor*) EN

Status: IUCN DD (western population CR; eastern population EN); not listed by CITES

enterprises supplying fish for human consumption fished the species. But starting in the 1930s—and continuing for the next 30 to 40 years—sport fishing soared in popularity.

Then in the 1970s a new commercial dimension was added to the sports angling industry, arising out of the fast-expanding demand for fresh (deep-frozen) tuna meat in Japan. The market for raw tuna provided by sushi and sashimi enthusiasts led to 40 percent of the global tuna catch being sent to the Japanese market. A major factor leading to the rapid expansion was the improvement in air freight and transport that began in the 1970s and made possible transglobal overnight deliveries of fresh-caught tuna.

Allied to major changes that had occurred within the commercial fishery—which had also led to ever-greater catches—the fishing of large tuna by sport anglers for profit as well as sport led to dramatically declining yields in the space of a few years. Total Atlantic harvests of bluefin tuna plummeted from a peak of 38,600 tons (35,000 tonnes) in 1964 to less than half—18,500 tons (16,800 tonnes)—by 1972. By the early 1980s catches in the western Atlantic had dropped even further to about 6,600 tons (6,000 tonnes). A report by the International Commission for

Northern bluefin tuna *are superbly adapted to their environment in shape and structure. The deep blue color on the back and pale-colored belly also makes them hard for predators to see from above or below.*

the Conservation of Atlantic Tunas (ICCAT) has estimated that by the early 1990s the population of adult bluefins in the western Atlantic had dropped to just 13 percent of its 1975 level.

Population Conundrum

It is clear that fishing controls need to be introduced to protect the northern bluefin tuna. However, differences of opinion, disputed scientific data, a lack of faith in ICCAT's ability to enforce quotas, demands for higher-than-stated quotas for the western Atlantic mean that there is no consensus on population levels. The picture is made even more complex by the migration of some stocks across the oceans.

Meanwhile, tagging programs, aerial surveys, captive breeding, and genetic analysis are some of the methods being used to establish the status of the bluefin tuna on both sides of the Atlantic. This should pave the way for enforcing realistic fishing controls.

Broad Sea Fan

Eunicella verrucosa

The sea fan is a type of coral made up of many simple polyps joined together to form a colony in a fanlike pattern. In common with a number of other marine invertebrates, sea fans are beautiful and often form major attractions in "submarine gardens." A slow-growing animal, it is now under threat from overcollection.

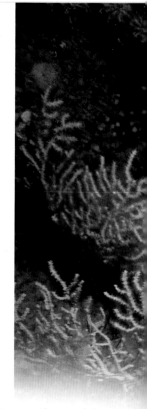

Sea fans are found in most of the world's seas and oceans. They may grow from shallow water down to the edge of the continental shelves and beyond; they are even found at depths of about 13,000 feet (4,000 m) in some parts of the world. The broad sea fan occurs in the northeastern Atlantic and in the Mediterranean Sea. Sea fans are attractive to souvenir hunters, and thoughtless collecting by divers has recently reduced their populations around European coasts.

Sea fans are colonial, that is, they are made up of many individual polyps, or zooids—cylindrical forms joined together to form a colony. Such a lifestyle is not unusual in the phylum Cnidaria to which they belong. In the broad sea fan the polyps are arranged in two rows along the top and bottom of the branches.

Each polyp is a miniature animal in its own right and has its own mouth that also serves as its anus. The mouth is surrounded by eight minute branching tentacles that are armed with stinging cells. The tentacle form is a feature of the order Gorgonacea (horny corals) and is ideal for sieving the passing water currents to trap microscopic plankton. Once collected, the prey is manipulated into the gastric cavity via the mouth. The gastric cavity extends into a number of tubes that increase the surface area for absorption and digestion of food products. Many species of sea fan are virtually two dimensional, and they grow so that the colony faces the prevailing currents at right angles, thus maximizing their ability to catch prey. Growth is slow, so some sea fans are very old.

The colony is supported by an internal horny skeleton made up of a substance called gorgonin. The tissue from which the polyps are made is further supported and protected by crystals of calcium carbonate that are embedded within it.

DATA PANEL

Broad sea fan

Eunicella verrucosa

Family: Anthozoa

World population: Unknown

Distribution: Mediterranean Sea; northeastern Atlantic; off coasts of France, Ireland, U.K., Mauritania, Morocco, Portugal, and Spain

Habitat: Rocks and hard surfaces from 49 ft (15 m) downward to about 984 ft (300 m)

Size: Colony grows to 11.8 in (30 cm) in height

Form: Plantlike pink or white colony made up of polyps—cylindrical sessile (attached) forms; branches in 1 plane only. Individual polyps arranged in double rows

Diet: Minute drifting plankton

Breeding: Details not well known; planula (free-swimming larva) results from fertilization of eggs; attaches itself to a new substrate; develops into a new colony, which produces new zooids

Related endangered species: Probably many, including red coral (*Corallium rubrum*)

Status: IUCN VU; not listed by CITES

Sperms and eggs develop inside the polyps, and fertilization results in the development of a planula (free-swimming larva), which escapes from the "parent" via its mouth and swims into the sea. The planula has a simple structure and is covered with microscopic beating filaments (cilia) that drive it through the water. However, the planula can detect a suitable substratum—usually rock—on which to settle and develop into a new colony, producing at first a founder polyp. The polyp grows and produces more individual polyps and the necessary skeleton so that a colony structure is developed once again.

Vulnerability

The emerging interest in marine conservation has led to an increased awareness of the effects of overcollection and human disturbance on some marine animals and plants. Although it has not been significantly at risk in the past, threats to the broad

Sea fans *come in a variety of colors, from deep red, yellow, and orange to pink and white. The polyps spread out their tentacles, forming a net with which they catch plankton.*

sea fan have risen recently with the increase in popularity of scuba diving. The broad sea fan and its Mediterranean relative, red coral (*Corallium rubrum*), are both slow growing, so they are potentially more vulnerable. Unlike the broad sea fan, *Corallium* has been collected for centuries, certainly since classical times. A rich red color, it was considered semiprecious and made into jewelry by the Greeks and Romans; it was also thought to be able to ward off illnesses. *Corallium* is now scarce in the Mediterranean and is found only at great depths. Collection of the animal seems as yet to be poorly regulated.

261

Giant Gippsland Earthworm

Megascolides australis

One of the largest earthworms in the world, the giant gippsland earthworm was discovered in 1878. Its large size and secretive habits have made it vulnerable to changes in land use resulting from the development of agricultural land from natural forest.

The giant Gippsland earthworm belongs to the Phylum Annelida, the segmented worms, which includes earthworms, ragworms, and leeches. Named after the area of Australia that is its home, it is found only in Gippsland, a fertile region of southeastern Victoria that extends along the coast from Melbourne to the New South Wales border.

The giant Gippsland earthworm lives in permanent and elaborate burrows, spending all its life underground. There it feeds on the roots of plants and on other organic matter in the soil. Most earthworm species deposit their waste material as obvious casts on the surface, but this species leaves its cast material below ground.

esult of its exclusively underground life the giant Gippsland earthworm is difficult to study. Consequently, many aspects of its biology are unknown. We do know that its body is divided up into between 300 to 500 visible segments. The head and front third of the body are a dark purple color, while the remainder, behind the "saddle," is a pinkish-gray.

Giant Gippsland earthworms are not easily kept in captivity, and because of their large size and fragility they are easily damaged or killed by scientists and farmers alike.

Patchy Distribution

The distribution of the giant Gippsland earthworm was previously much wider than it is today. When European settlers arrived in the 18th century, they transformed large areas of native forest into pasture for the dairy industry. The disturbances associated with this proved very damaging to the worms.

Today giant Gippsland earthworms tend to be restricted to steep hillsides and valleys where the soils cannot be plowed. Any activities that affect the moisture content and drainage of the soil can also be bad news for the worms. Building roads and dams,

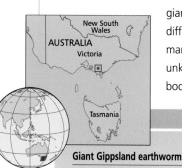

New South Wales

AUSTRALIA
Victoria

Tasmania

DATA PANEL

Giant Gippsland earthworm

Megascolides australis

Family: Megascolecidae

World population: Unknown

Distribution: Restricted to about 40 square miles (100 sq. km) of land in Gippsland, Victoria, Australia

Habitat: Burrows in organically rich soils

Size: Length: 31 in (80 cm); diameter 0.8 in (2 cm)

Form: Typical segmented worm; a definite head and 300–500 segments each with chaetae (bristles); well-developed respiratory and vascular system

Diet: Plant tissue and organic matter in soil

Breeding: Worms are hermaphrodite, but 2 individuals are required for fertilization to occur. Mating takes place in spring and early summer. Individuals lay a single amber-colored egg capsule containing 1 embryo, which takes about 12 months to hatch. The earthworms are presumed to reach adulthood about 4.5 years after hatching. Adults may be long-lived

Related endangered species: Washington giant earthworm *(Driloleirus americanus)* VU; Oregon giant earthworm *(D. macelfreshi)* VU

Status: IUCN VU; not listed by CITES

**The giant
Gippsland earthworm,**
*like other earthworms, is
beneficial to the fertility of soil.
However, more needs to be known
about this elusive and fragile creature
so that it can be protected.*

trenching, and laying cables are all damaging activities. Natural seasonal fluctuations of moisture content govern the normal movement of the worms within the soil.

Recent surveys of southern and western Gippsland have shown that the giant earthworm is restricted to about 40 square miles (100 sq. km) of land in an area bounded approximately by Loch, Korumburra, and Warragul. Much of this land is unsuitable, and the giant earthworm's distribution is very patchy. The population density of the adult worms within the acceptable areas is usually low, about two individuals per 35 cubic feet (two per cubic meter). The worms are mostly found in blue-gray clay soils on flats by the banks of streams or along ditches and watercourses where the slopes face a southwesterly direction.

Like all earthworms, the giant Gippsland worms have beneficial effects on the quality of the soil in which they live, contributing to an increase in its organic content and assisting aeration and increasing fertility. The giant Gippsland earthworm has become part of the folklore of southern Gippsland, and many landowners speak with pride about its presence on their properties.

Conservation

Conserving the giant Gippsland earthworm is difficult. Retaining natural vegetation alongside streams as well as on steep slopes and in valleys and keeping out livestock by fencing the remaining earthworm habitats are both thought to be helpful measures. However, such strategies rely heavily on the cooperation of private landowners and farmers who may need help in identifying the parts of their properties that accommodate the giant earthworms. One issue that has recently made this more difficult is the splitting up of larger properties into smaller ones used for small-scale farming.

California Bay Pea Crab

Parapinnixa affinis

Pea crabs are tiny crabs, almost always less than half an inch (1 cm) wide. As adults they live associated with other marine animals such as bivalve mollusks (clams) and tubeworms.

The California Bay pea crab inhabits the tubes and burrows of polychaete worms (marine annelid worms of the class Polychaeta that bear bristles and have paired appendages). Other species of pea crab, such as *Pinnotheres pisum*, are found in mussel and cockle shells in European coastal waters, while females of *Pinnotheres ostreum*, also known as the oyster crab, are found in oysters of the Atlantic coastal waters of North America and are abundant in oysters of Chesapeake Bay. (The males are usually free-swimming.)

Pea crabs live in other animal hosts but do not derive nourishment from their hosts' tissues; animals with this arrangement are not parasites but are known as commensal indwellers. The pea crabs appear to do no serious physical harm or damage to their hosts, although they do not seem to do any particular good either.

Unlike other crabs, which are protected by a hard exoskeleton made from calcium carbonate, pea crabs have a soft body. They rely on their hosts to provide them with shelter and protection.

The pea crabs intercept some of the food sieved from the water by the gills of the host animal. They feed on small prey items such as planktonic animals and carrion scraps that find their way near to or into the host's tube or shell.

Pea crabs sometimes live in pairs, although the male may move around between hosts. The female will carry the fertilized eggs under her abdomen until they hatch. At this point a planktonic larva swims away from the tube or burrow and goes through several stages, feeding on other planktonic organisms until it is sufficiently developed to settle on the seabed and seek out a new invertebrate host.

A study of the morphology (form and structure) of animals can tell us a lot about their lifestyles and adaptations to their favorite habitats. The strange shape of the California Bay pea crab, being much wider than it is long, is a perfect adaptation to life in a tube; It can move up and down its home by walking sideways, particularly aided by the well-developed next

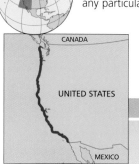

CANADA

UNITED STATES

MEXICO

DATA PANEL

California Bay pea crab

Parapinnixa affinis

Family: Pinnotheridae

World population: Unknown

Distribution: Western seaboard of U.S., especially coast of California

Habitat: The tubes and burrows of marine polychaete worms, including *Terebella californica* and *Amphitrite* species

Size: Minute crabs, reaching about 0.1 in (2.5 mm) long and 0.2 in (5 mm) wide

Form: Minute, wide crabs with very well-developed 4th pair of walking legs quite out of proportion to the rest of their body

Diet: Small marine animals and carrion

Breeding: Male fertilizes eggs that are carried on female's abdomen. Here they are guarded, oxygenated, and protected until they hatch into free-swimming planktonic larvae. They

pass through several stages, feeding on plankton before they metamorphose, settle on the seabed, and seek out a new suitable host worm

Related endangered species: None

Status: IUCN EN; not listed by CITES

The California Bay pea crab *(left) is less than 0.20 in (5 mm) wide— about a quarter of the size of the tiny California fiddler crab (below), which is distinguished by its large claw (in the male), used to signal to mates. The fiddler crab lives in burrows in sandy mud in bays and estuaries from Southern California to Baja California. Its future is also uncertain as a result of encroachment on its habitat by human construction.*

to last pair of walking legs. Pea crabs of the species *Pinnotheres pisum* have much more rounded bodies, reflecting the fact that they do not live in such confined spaces.

The relative softness of the California Bay pea crab's shell contributes to its overall flexibility and helps when it moves around in confined spaces. In some pea crab species there is a marked difference in the shape of the claws in the males and females, which probably assists the male in holding the female during mating.

Vulnerability

The viability of pea crabs depends on the availability of hosts as well as the presence of other essentials such as food and reproductive mates. Many of the worm species that the California Bay pea crab relies on are subjected to population fluctuations. These events in turn affect the population of the pea crabs that live with them.

Records of animals as small as pea crabs are often lacking, so it is difficult to establish a broad view of their distribution and abundance. The California Bay pea crab is listed as Endangered by the IUCN, and the extent of threats to the animal will be resolved only as a result of more scientific research.

265

Edible Sea-Urchin

Echinus esculentus

Sadly, the beautifully colored edible sea-urchin has become a familiar sight in beach souvenir shops. The animal is collected extensively because its test (shell-like internal skeleton) makes popular decorative objects and souvenirs.

Sea-urchins are spiny-skinned invertebrates that are in the same phylum—Echinodermata—as sea lilies, starfish, brittle stars, and sea cucumbers. Like other echinoderms, they have no head and no true brain, and their bodies have a skeleton of chalky plates. There are about 800 species of sea-urchin.

Sea-urchins are important grazers in marine communities. By eating young and developing algae (plants without true stems, roots, and leaves), they play a major role in controlling vegetation growth in the sea. They also feed on encrusting animals such as barnacles and sea mats. A lack of sea-urchins in a given area can result in rapid algal growth, and in some sensitive habitats such as coral reefs this can have serious effects on other organisms; the plants quickly outcompete the slower-growing corals for light and space.

The edible sea-urchin is a temperate species, living on hard substrates and among larger algae in coastal waters around northwestern Europe. Compared with other species of sea-urchin, it is quite large and has a pale, rosy-pink test. The test is the shell-like internal skeleton that is so close to the outside of the animal that it appears to be a shell. However, it is covered by thin living tissue. The skeleton of sea-urchins, as in other echinoderms, is made up of crystals of calcium carbonate perforated by spaces. (As a result, it is easily occupied by minerals after the animal's death, so it fossilizes well.)

The sea-urchin's test bears whitish-pink needle-shaped spines with purple tips. They are used for defense against predators and as an aid to the animal's movement. Between the spines are the pedicellariae—minute pincerlike organs carried on stalks—that are used for grooming.

As well as spines sea-urchins also have many long, branched tentacles, called tube-feet, with suckers on the end, which are arranged in rows up and down the animals. They are hollow and can be filled with water from inside the animal and extended by hydraulic pressure. They are used for movement and balance, and in some species help act as a sort of camouflage.

Like other sea-urchins, the edible sea-urchin has a mouth on the underside of the test with a complex arrangement of five jaws with teeth that are extruded (thrust out) to scrape

DATA PANEL

Edible sea-urchin

Echinus esculentus

Family: Echinidae

World population: Unknown

Distribution: Northeastern Atlantic

Habitat: Rocks and seaweeds from the low tide mark down to 164 ft (50 m)

Size: Up to 6.7 in (17 cm) diameter; often smaller

Form: Globular body with calcareous test bearing movable spines and extendible tube-feet ending in suckers

Diet: Encrusting animals such as barnacles; large algae

Breeding: Seasonal spawning; fertilization occurs in the open water; free-swimming larva feeds on minute drifting plants until it metamorphoses to form a juvenile urchin

Related endangered species: Probably several, including the rock borer *Paracentrotus lividus* (no common name) not listed by IUCN. The species has been seriously overfished for its edible roe in parts of France and Ireland

Status: IUCN LRnt; not listed by CITES

algae and other encrusting plant and animal life from the rocks. When removed from the test but still joined together, the jaws resemble a Greek lantern; Aristotle referred to them as lantern teeth, and today the jaw arrangement is called an Aristotle's lantern.

Hunted Out

The edible sea-urchin was for centuries fished for its roe (eggs); the food was considered a delicacy in Tudor times (between 1485 and 1603). Unlike the smaller Mediterranean species *Paracentrotus lividus*, which has a more delicate roe, the relatively coarse roe of the edible sea-urchin is no longer considered desirable to eat.

The edible sea-urchin, *which used to be fished for its edible roe (eggs), is now collected for its beautiful test.*

The species is easily seen and collected under water. When the test is cleaned out by removing the intestine and reproductive organs, it makes an attractive ornament. In recent decades divers have collected edible sea-urchins from southwestern Britain in such large numbers that scientists now believe that a population crash may be imminent. However, further information is needed about the state of the natural populations of edible sea-urchin around northwestern Europe and the sea-urchin's life span so that measures can be taken to protect them.

267

Velvet Worms

Peripatus spp.

Some scientists have regarded the velvet worms as "missing links" in the evolutionary chain of the animal kingdom. Their habitat—in the litter of the forest floor in moist areas—makes them vulnerable to human activities such as logging and forest clearance.

Velvet worms are terrestrial invertebrates that are placed in their own phylum: Onychophora (meaning claw-bearers). As a result of their widely scattered distribution and nocturnal habits, velvet worms are poorly known; few scientists have had the opportunity to observe live examples. The best known genus in the phylum is *Peripatus*, of which there are about 20 species. Velvet worms look like large caterpillars. They are covered in dry, velvety skin, and they have about 20 pairs of short legs.

Missing Links

Scientists have considered velvet worms as "missing links," lying somewhere in the evolutionary progression between annelids (earthworms and their allies) and arthropods (crustaceans, insects, and spiders). For example, velvet worms have antennae and clawlike mandibles (mouth parts) like arthropods, but their eyes are similar in structure to those of annelids, and they have a thin, flexible body wall (like annelids) rather than an exoskeleton. They move by contracting sheets of muscle (and with little assistance from their soft, unjointed legs), like worms.

Fossil evidence suggests that velvet worms existed 500 million years ago. There are about 70 species of Onychophora in widely separated parts of the world, indicating that the Onychophora are an animal group that evolved before the ancient land masses separated. However, whether velvet worms are forerunners of today's centipedes and millipedes (arthropods) is debatable. Recent research suggests that velvet worms may indeed be closer to modern-day arthropods than annelids and that they should

perhaps be classified as such. In due course the exact classification of velvet worms will be worked out on the basis of molecular investigations.

Slime Attack

The body of the velvet worm is divided into between 14 and 44 segments (depending on the species). Each segment has a pair of short legs with curved claws on the feet. Since they have no skeleton, the worms can squeeze through small holes. They hunt at night, feeding on small insects and cutting up prey with their strong jaws.

On either side of the intestine are glands that produce a sticky slime, which is squirted from a pair of papillae or fingerlike projections on both sides of the mouth. On contact with air the slime solidifies into sticky threads. Small animals readily become entangled in the threads, although the mechanism is thought to be more for defense than to subdue prey.

Moisture Dependent

Velvet worms live in leaf litter on the forest floor, under stones or logs, or in the soil. Their skin has pits that are connected to thin breathing tubes (tracheae). Since there

are so many openings and because they cannot be closed, water vapor is constantly lost from the body. (Arthropods have fewer such openings, and theirs can be closed.) In the velvet worm's moist habitat, however, water loss is compensated for: The worms take up water through minute pouches situated near the base of their legs. They fill the pouches by pressing up against damp surfaces. Water is also replaced by drinking the body fluids of insect prey.

Velvet worms are vulnerable to many aspects of human activity. Clearing of the forests by logging, the development of farmland, and the construction of highways all seriously damage the moist forest habitat on which the worms depend. The velvet worms are also at a disadvantage: Unlike many other animals, they cannot move rapidly enough over short periods to redistribute themselves into new habitats.

One of the *Peripatus* species, Macroperipatus insularis *of Jamaica, giving birth.*

DATA PANEL

Velvet worm

***Peripatus* spp. (about 20 species)**

Family: Peripatidae

World population: Unknown

Distribution: West Indies, Central America, and northern regions of South America

Habitat: Southern temperate and tropical forests, among leaf litter and under bark

Size: Length: females up to 5.9 in (15 cm) long; males shorter

Form: Cylindrical body; conspicuous antennae on head; clawlike mandible; thin body wall; 14–43 pairs of short, soft unjointed legs

Diet: Plant material; also insects and other worms

Breeding: Sexes separate; male places capsule of sperm on skin of female. Her white blood cells digest skin under capsule, allowing sperm to enter blood stream; when sperm have found their way to the ovary, they migrate through the ovarian wall and fertilize eggs. Eggs develop and are nourished in uterus. Live young born after a gestation period of about 13 months

Related endangered species: About 70 species of velvet worm; 20 species of the genus *Peripatus*. All are probably vulnerable to destruction of moist forest habitats by logging and development

Status: IUCN EN; not listed by CITES

Southern Damselfly

Coenagrion mercuriale

Damselflies and their close relatives the dragonflies are familiar waterside insects that hunt their prey on the wing. The drainage of ponds and marshes for agriculture and urban development—as well as an increase in the use of pesticides—threatens to wipe out these beautiful insects.

The brilliantly colored southern damselfly frequents sluggish streams in lowland areas. In Britain it is restricted to a handful of counties such as Hampshire and Dorset in the south of the country. It is more widely distributed across northwestern Europe, from France and Germany southward to the Mediterranean. Southern damselflies are also known to exist in North Africa.

Damselflies and dragonflies are familiar pond and streamside insects. Both have long, slender bodies, keen eyesight, and two pairs of wings. However, it is not difficult to tell the two insects apart. Damselflies are generally smaller and slimmer than their close relatives. In dragonflies the front wings and hind wings are of different shapes, with the hind wings being generally broader. In damselflies the wings are the same shape and taper into a narrow stalk just before they join the body. The two types of insect also alight and rest differently. Dragonflies always rest with their wings outspread, while damselflies perch with their wings only partly spread or held vertically over the body.

The southern damselfly is a day-flying insect, and eyesight is important in all its activities. In many cases the eyes are so large that the head appears to consist of little else. However, damselfly eyes are not quite as dominant as those of the dragonfly and are set farther apart, making the front end of the animal look slightly hammer shaped. Since the head can swivel on the neck, the insects have almost 360-degree vision.

Correspondingly, the senses of smell and touch are less well developed. The jaws are well equipped for biting and strongly toothed, a fact reflected in the name of the order: Odonata, meaning "toothed." The damselfiles are harmless to humans, but feed on a variety of small insects such as mosquitoes and small flies, which they hunt down on the wing.

Reproduction

The reproductive lives of southern damselflies are closely connected with the water by which they live. The long, slender abdomen of the male is equipped with a pair of claspers situated near its rear tip. Just in front of the claspers are the openings of the male reproductive organs. When preparing to mate, the male transfers a drop of sperm from the

---

DATA PANEL

Southern damselfly

Coenagrion mercuriale

Family: Coenagrionidae

World population: Unknown

Distribution: Southern Britain; northwestern Europe from France and Germany southward to the Mediterranean; North Africa

Habitat: Slow-running streams and boggy ground

Size: Length: 0.9–1.2 in (2.4–2.7 cm); wingspan: 1–1.4 in (2.5–3.5 cm)

Form: Resembles small dragonfly; long, slim, brilliantly colored body; conspicuous eyes; 2 pairs of wings

Diet: Adults feed on small insects, including mosquitoes; nymphs (larvae) feed on small aquatic animals such as other insect larvae

Breeding: Males go in search of females in spring. After courtship and copulation eggs laid under water in water plants. Free-living larvae hatch and may feed for many weeks before emerging to molt as adult damselflies

Related endangered species: Several, including Frey's damselfly (*Coenagrion hylas freyi*) CR

Status: IUCN VU; not listed by CITES

opening by bending his abdomen forward and underneath to touch special receptacles near the front of the abdomen (just behind the last pair of walking legs). He then flies off to find a female to mate with and takes hold of her by the neck using his claspers. Mating is then achieved as the male perches holding the female while she bends her abdomen around under his body to touch her tip against his sperm-filled receptacles. She then takes some sperm into her reproductive tract. After mating, the pair may fly around in the "tandem" position, with the male towing the female; this may often be observed in the spring. The female damselfly then dips the tip of her abdomen in the water to touch a suitable water plant. She makes a small cut with her egg-laying appendage and deposits her eggs in the plant tissue.

The eggs hatch into an aquatic larvae known as nymphs. The larvae live in the water and breathe by means of gills carried on three tail projections at the tip of the abdomen. Like adults, the nymphs are carnivores and hunt for aquatic food, small worms, and the larvae of other insects. They have a specially adapted set of mouthparts called the mask. It is normally kept folded under the head, but can be extended with great speed, effectively spearing the victim on the terminal clawlike extensions.

The southern damselfly's *brilliant coloration is due to pigments and the optical properties of the outer layer of the body.*

Conflict over Conservation

Because of its rarity the southern damselfly has recently become the subject of government-sponsored conservation efforts in Britain. Plans are in progress to allow swiftly flowing trout streams and the well-drained land associated with them to deteriorate naturally into habitat that is more suitable for the endangered southern damselfly, namely slower-running waters with boggy ground and soft banks.

The proposals have given rise to conflict between the trout-fishing lobby and conservationists, but this has only served to highlight the needs of the southern damselfly. It is difficult to convince some people of the need to protect the damselfly, but slow progress is being made.

Hermit Beetle

Osmoderma eremita

Hermit beetles live all their lives in decaying oak and lime trees; successive generations may continue to live in the same tree for many years. Since the beetles do not disperse well, isolated populations build up in each tree; and if the trees fail to survive, the beetles may be lost. The threat of collecting is now further reducing the stability of scarab beetle populations.

Scarab beetles—members of the family Scarabaeidae—display many diverse forms and habits. The family includes dung beetles, the hermit beetle, and the Egyptian sacred scarab beetle. It is thought that the Ancient Egyptians believed that the earth was rotated by a giant scarab beetle in the sky, in the same way that the dung beetle rolls balls of dung. This, at least, is one theory as to why the Egyptians held scarab beetles in such high regard.

Scarab beetles have short legs with flattened middle joints, and a number of species are attractively colored in metallic hues. The head has short antennae and is often equipped with spines or other projections. It is known that the scarab exudes a slightly perfumed scent, but the purpose of it is not understood.

Relatives of scarab beetles include some of the largest beetle species recorded, including the goliath beetle, which is up to 5.8 inches (15 cm) long, and the distinctive tropical rhinoceros beetle, which is about 4 inches (10 cm) long. However, most scarab beetles reach an average length of only 0.6 to 1 inch (1.5 to 2.5 cm).

Rolling Balls

Many members of the family Scarabaeidae are specialized scavengers. Those that forage for dung (animal droppings) are known as dung beetles or "tumblebugs" after the way in which they roll dung balls along the ground and appear to tumble at the same time. (Some beetles just drag the dung pellets along the ground.)

Typical dung beetle behavior involves finding a dung pile, removing a portion of it from the main mass, and rolling this portion into a ball that they roll along the ground. The dung ball is normally much larger than the beetle itself. A beetle measuring about 1 inch (2.5 cm) in length may roll a ball as big as about 4 inches (10 cm) in diameter. It does this while moving backward: It uses its front legs to walk on the ground while its hind legs press on the ball. The task of moving the ball may be shared between individual beetles of the

DATA PANEL

Hermit beetle

Osmoderma eremita

Family: Scarabaeidae

World population: Unknown

Distribution: Western, central, and northern Europe

Habitat: Decaying trees: oaks and limes

Size: Length: 1.4 in (3.6 cm), excluding antennae

Form: Beetle with dark-colored body shaped like a narrow shield

Diet: Decaying timber in mature forest

Breeding: Eggs laid in timber develop into grubs (larvae), which metamorphose into adult beetles

Related endangered species:
Ciervo scarab beetle (*Aegialia concinna*) VU; Giuliani's dune scarab beetle (*Pseudocotalpa giulianii*) VU

Status: IUCN VU; not listed by CITES

The hermit beetle *has a body shaped like a shield. It lives in and around hollow, decaying oak and lime trees.*

same species, regardless of their sex. The dung ball is stored in a hole excavated for this purpose, and the beetles return to feed on it. The beetles also store dung in which the females can lay their eggs. The larvae feed inside it, keeping the outer crust intact before emerging as adults.

Dung beetles are found on all continents except Antarctica, and the number of species per continent is roughly in proportion to the number of large mammal species present.

Timber-Loving Beetles

Although related to the dung beetles, the hermit beetle is a timber-loving species that is associated with decaying trees (they particularly like hollow trees). Host trees are usually common oaks or small-leaved lime trees, which are widely distributed across western, central, and northern Europe.

Recent research using radio transmitters suggests that the beetle populations associated with each tree are more or less self-contained, and there is not much exchange of individuals from one tree to the next; for some reason the beetles do not seem to disperse very freely. Consequently, several generations may live continuously in the same tree. This makes them particularly vulnerable if the trees are cut down or the habitat altered in some way.

The hermit beetle larva, or grub, also lives in the decaying wood of the same tree. The grubs of many hermit beetles can generate sounds by rapidly rubbing one part of their bodies against another. The purpose of the sound production, known as stridulation, is unclear. After spending their larval lives feeding on

and developing in the rotting wood, the grubs metamorphose into adult beetles.

Endangered

Areas where oak and lime trees have existed for years are the most likely habitats for hermit beetles, but they are becoming more scarce. Many of the trees favored by hermits have a rich fauna of various other beetle species associated with them, several of which are also threatened.

The hermit beetle is now believed to be endangered across its European distribution. However, it appears to be secure in southern Sweden, where it is being extensively studied. A recent report indicates that the beetles are now being openly traded by collectors using the Internet and other communications vehicles. This represents a further threat to the stability of the the natural populations of hermit beetles.

Birdwing Butterfly

Ornithoptera alexandrae; O. richmondia

For many years the large, tropical birdwing butterflies have been eagerly sought by collectors, and some birdwings now change hands for substantial sums of money, either legally or illegally. Many are now threatened, and their conservation is hindered by a lack of knowledge of their habits.

Some birdwing butterflies are very large; the Queen Alexandra's birdwing from Papua New Guinea is, in fact, the largest butterfly in the world, with a wingspan of almost 11 inches (27.5 cm). The Richmond birdwing from Australia, on the other hand, is one of the smaller birdwings, with a wingspan of less than 6 inches (15 cm).

The butterflies' common name is a result of their size and shape; at one time they were said to be shot by hunters who mistook them for birds. As in other *Ornithoptera* species, the sexes differ in color as well as in size: Queen Alexandra males are powder blue, green, gold, and black, and Richmond males are shades of iridescent green and black. The females of both species are dark brown, spotted with white and cream. Female birdwings are generally larger than their male counterparts, although their coloration is less spectacular.

The butterflies have adapted to forest habitats where occasional flowers provide enough nectar to feed the adults. The males exploit certain tall trees as vantage points and as mating sites. Females move around between patches of rain forest in search of specific vines on which to lay their eggs.

Birdwing butterflies have long been favorites with collectors. When all the species were listed by CITES, making it illegal for them to be offered for sale, a lucrative trade in smuggled specimens developed, with single Queen Alexandra's birdwings fetching more than $500 on the black market. Protection from collecting has done little by itself, however, to improve the butterflies' prospects, since the numbers actually changing hands are now small.

Habitat Destruction

A much greater threat comes from the destruction of their habitats and the food plants they live on. Birdwing caterpillars feed selectively on certain species of tropical forest vine belonging to the genus *Aristolochia*. These vines occur only in rain forest and frequently have a rather patchy distribution, especially where they have suffered from human interference in the form of timber-felling or forest clearing for urban development or farming. Over the past

DATA PANEL

Birdwing butterfly: Queen Alexandra's birdwing; Richmond birdwing

Ornithoptera alexandrae; O. richmondia

Family: Papilionidae

World population: Unknown

Distribution: Queen Alexandra's birdwing: Papua New Guinea. Richmond birdwing: subtropical Queensland and New South Wales, Australia

Habitat: Open woodland and tropical rain forest

Size: Wingspan: Queen Alexandra's birdwing: up to 11 in (27.5 cm). Richmond birdwing: less than 6 in (15 cm)

Form: Large butterflies with 2 pairs of conspicuous wings, the leading pair much longer than the second

Diet: Caterpillars feed on forest vine of genus *Aristolochia*; adults on nectar

Breeding: Eggs laid singly on upper side of leaves of host plant; they hatch into caterpillars that feed on plant for about 4 weeks before developing into a chrysalis. Chrysalis hatches into adult butterfly after about 3 weeks

Related endangered species: Obi birdwing butterfly *(Ornithoptera aesacus)* VU; Rothschild's birdwing butterfly *(O. rothschildi)* VU

Status: Queen Alexandra's birdwing IUCN EN; CITES I. Richmond's birdwing not listed by IUCN. Birdwing butterflies *(Ornithoptera* spp.) CITES II

10 years some important species of the vines have become scarce except in a few national parks, which are not always large enough to guarantee their long-term survival.

The loss of the vines has in turn threatened some of the birdwing species with extinction. The Queen Alexandra's and Richmond birdwings face particularly severe problems. Both have relatively small distributions that are especially vulnerable to forest clearance and the disappearance of food plants and breeding grounds.

Queen Alexandra's birdwing larvae apparently feed exclusively on a particular species of the vine *Aristolochia dielsiana*. Although the vine is widely distributed in Papua New Guinea, it is only available in sufficient quantities to support the huge, ravenous Queen Alexandra's caterpillars in the province of Oro.

Only Oro has enough of the volcanic, phosphate-rich soils that the vines need if they are to flourish. Richmond birdwing larvae depend on another vine, *A. praevenosa*. Their only natural food plant is found in lowland rain forests. However, at higher altitudes—above 2,500 feet (800 m)—on the border ranges of Queensland and New South Wales the Richmond birdwing larvae may also feed on a variant subspecies of *A. deltantha*.

Only when research has figured out all such complexities will biologists fully understand the life cycle of the remarkable birdwing butterflies. Yet such knowledge is necessary if strategies are to be designed to protect them.

Brilliant colors *mark the Richmond birdwing (above) and the Queen Alexandra's birdwing (right), shown here emerging from its chrysalis.*

Red-Kneed Tarantula

Euathlus smithi

Although there are many species of tarantula, the different forms generally share similar characteristics. Their large, hairy bodies are often strikingly marked, and some species have become popular as pets. Collection of the red-kneed tarantula has put the wild population at risk.

The red-kneed tarantula is arguably the most popular of all pet tarantulas, and people have been collecting specimens since the 1970s. First discovered in 1888, the spider was soon recognized as having potential as a pet. It was also used to heighten tension in films such as *Raiders of the Lost Ark*. Such publicity encouraged collection, and tarantulas were sold in pet stores for many years.

The red-kneed tarantula is found mainly in Mexico and Central America. Its natural habitat is scrubland and desert that provide temperatures of 70–90°F (20–30°C) and humidity of about 60 percent. The spider is found near cacti and bushes, and among logs, rocks, and other debris. It digs burrows in the ground that it lines with spider silk.

For most of the time the spider is relatively docile. However, a threatened red-kneed tarantula will rear up and display the red bristles on its body. As a defensive measure it will flick off urticating (irritant) hairs in the direction of its predator. The hairs are microscopically barbed (having tiny hooks) and can be irritating to the skin and lungs, causing a form of urticaria (an allergic disorder). Serious damage can occur if any hairs become embedded in the eye. Although most people are not seriously affected by the spider's venom, some are allergic to it and can have a strong adverse reaction.

Intriguing Habits

The red-kneed tarantula has a typical spider form, including a pair of fangs (chelicerae) that it uses to stab prey and inject venom. Pedipalps—small appendages near the mouth—have a number of functions, including handling prey. The spiders have poor vision, but sensory structures on the end of the legs allow them to smell, taste, and feel.

The tarantula does not spin a web to catch its food; insects, small amphibians, and sometimes mice are actively hunted at night. The prey is subdued with venom and then flooded with digestive juices. Tarantulas are unable to digest food internally, so the digested "soup" of nutritionally valuable parts of the prey are sucked back by the spider.

Males are often eaten by their mates after mating. When mature, a male spider spins a tubular web in which he deposits sperm. He then draws the sperm up into a special receptacle in his pedipalps. When mating is about to start, the male makes courtship signals, which help ensure that the female does not mistake him for prey. He uses tibial spurs (sharp projections) to grip the female's fangs while placing sperm in the female's reproductive tract.

Black Market

Although red-kneed tarantulas are relatively easy to keep, they are not easy to breed in captivity. The females live for a long time, often up to 20 years in captivity, but their reproductive rate tends to be slow. As a result of their popularity with collectors and the tarantula's vulnerability to habitat change, the species has become seriously threatened. Populations could not sustain the demands of the pet trade, and the wild spiders are now difficult to find. Mexico has prohibited their capture and export, but a black market still exists: Smugglers have been caught trying to take them out of their native countries.

DATA PANEL

Red-kneed tarantula

Euathlus smithi

Family: Theraphosidae

World population: Unknown

Distribution: Central America and Mexico

Habitat: Scrubland and desert

Size: Length: up to 2.5 in (6.4 cm); leg span: up to 5 in (12.7 cm)

Form: Cephalothorax (arachnid with joined head and thorax); opisthosoma (abdomen) with 4 pairs of strikingly patterned legs; claws for gripping. Eight eyes on head allow all-round (but poor) vision. Males have thin body and long legs; mature males have tibial spurs (sharp projections) on pedipalps (appendages on cephalothorax) to grip female's fangs during mating

Diet: Insects; also small animals such as lizards and mice

Breeding: Female produces up to 700 young a year (often fewer). Eggs wrapped in silk and carried by mother. Spiderlings guarded for several weeks after hatching. Life span of males 7–8 years; females 20–25 years in captivity

Related endangered species: None

Status: IUCN LRnt; not listed by CITES

The red-kneed tarantula *is strikingly patterned and has been a favorite with collectors.*

Kauai Cave Wolf Spider

Adelocosa anops

The Kauai cave wolf spider is both rare and unusual. Found only in three caves on Kauai Island, Hawaii, the species is blind—unlike other wolf spiders that are known to hunt using their keen eyesight. Endangered from habitat degradation, it is also thought to be at risk from the pesticide residues seeping into its cave dwelling.

Wolf spiders get their name from their habits as hunters. They are swift runners; instead of snaring their victims in silken webs like most other spiders, they rely on speed to chase their prey and run it down, although they may use silk to set up ambushes or "trip wires." They stalk their prey, watching every movement. Once it is trapped, they bite the victim and inject poison through their fang-tipped chelicerae—the first pair of head appendages, which look like miniature elephant tusks when seen through a lens. The venom paralyzes the prey and also digests its tissues, reducing it to a liquid, which the spider can suck out and swallow through its small mouth; they feed particularly on insects such as beetles and ants. There are many species of wolf spider: over 100 in North America and about 50 in Europe. The best-known wolf spider is probably the Mediterranean tarantula. The wolf spider's enemies are wasps, birds, and people. The spiders occur on all continents apart from Antarctica and on many islands, too: Spiders are often among the leading colonizers of volcanic islands.

Wolf spiders are not large and rarely exceed 1 inch (2.5 cm) in length. Their bodies are covered in short hair or bristles, and in the main they are brown or drab in color. As well as the fangs, the head carries a pair of pedipalps (small leglike appendages located in front of the first pair of long walking legs) and (usually) eyes arranged in three rows.

Usually a favorite habitat is leaf litter on forest floors. The spiders excavate shallow burrows and line them with silk spun by the spinnerets on the abdomen. In some species the burrow has a projecting silk entrance tube. The Kauai cave wolf spider, however, is an exception among wolf spiders. It is restricted in its distribution, being found only at three underground locations on the island of Kauai. The caves in which it lives were formed by ancient volcanic lava flows.

Eyes Wide Shut

Although the eyes of most wolf spiders are fairly simple (they have four large and four small eyes), they generally have

DATA PANEL

Kauai cave wolf spider

Adelocosa anops

Family: Lycosidae

World population: Unknown. Surveys of the 3 remaining populations could only find 30 members of each at any one time

Distribution: Kauai Island, Hawaii

Habitat: Dark, moist areas of Kauai cave system, formed from a lava flow and covering about 4 square miles (10 sq. km). About 75% of former habitat has been lost to human activity

Size: Length: 0.5–0.7 in (1.3–1.9 cm); legs: 1 in (2.5 cm)

Form: Head lacks eyes. Reddish-brown carapace (hard, outer covering); pale abdomen and bright-orange legs. Back part of chelicera (pair of fang-tipped appendages on head) has 3 large teeth

Diet: Small, cave-dwelling crustaceans

Breeding: Female lays up to 30 eggs after mating with male. Spiderlings hatch and ride on their mother's back

Related endangered species: Glacier Bay wolf spider (*Pardosa diuturna*) VU; Lake Placid funnel wolf spider (*Sosippus placidus*) VU; rosemary wolf spider (*Lycosa ericeticola*) DD

Status: IUCN EN; not listed by CITES

Kauai
Oahu
Maui
Hawaii
(UNITED STATES)
Hawaii

Kauai cave wolf spiders *have no eyes (below). More common wolf spiders (right) rely on sight for hunting and courtship rituals. (The male spider on the right is presenting the female with a gift.)*

good eyesight. This is important, since many hunt in poor light conditions. The Kauai cave wolf spider, like many cave-dwelling species, is blind. More unusually, it is eyeless—many cave dwellers cannot see but have vestigial eyes. This makes the species unique. It almost certainly detects the presence of potential prey by touch and smell, and is able to stalk its prey by following their scent trails. Hunting has not been observed, but this species probably feeds primarily on the Kauai cave amphipod, a type of crustacean that is also Endangered. Other species of arthropod that enter the caves from time to time may serve as food for the Kauai cave wolf spider.

Eyesight is usually an important tool in courtship and mating behavior for wolf spiders. How the Kauai cave wolf spider copes is unknown. After mating, the female Kauai cave wolf spider lays eggs—up to 30 at a time. They are laid in a round or oval silk cocoon made by the mother. She fastens it to the tip of her abdomen and carries it everywhere with her until the spiderlings hatch. The young climb onto the mother's back and are carried by her until they are old enough to fend for themselves.

At Risk

As a result of its restricted distribution, the Kauai cave wolf spider is highly endangered. Habitat destruction has occurred through soil filling, quarrying, and other activities associated with development and agriculture. The seepage of pesticide residues into the caves is also thought to be a source of risk. In the delicately balanced environment such problems also affect the Kauai cave amphipod, the spider's main prey. The amphipod feeds on rotting tree roots that work their way into the cave system. If the roots dry out or do not enter the cave, both species are affected.

The Kauai cave wolf spider was added to the IUCN Red List in January 2000. Of the 15 spider species considered to be at risk, six are cave spiders: The tooth cave spider of Texas, for example, was listed as Endangered under the United States Endangered Species Act in 1988. It is the limitation of their habitat that makes wolf spiders especially threatened.

Glossary

Words in SMALL CAPITALS refer to other entries in the glossary.

Adaptation features of an animal that adjust it to its environment; may be produced by evolution—e.g., camouflage coloration

Adaptive radiation where a group of closely related animals (e.g., members of a FAMILY) have evolved differences from each other so that they can survive in different NICHES

Adhesive disks flattened disks on the tips of the fingers or toes of certain climbing AMPHIBIANS that enable them to cling to smooth, vertical surfaces

Adult a fully grown sexually mature animal; a bird in its final PLUMAGE

Algae primitive plants ranging from microscopic, single-celled forms to large forms, such as seaweeds, but lacking proper roots or leaves

Alpine living in mountainous areas, usually over 5,000 feet (1,500 m)

Ambient describing the conditions around an animal, e.g., the water temperature for a fish or the air temperature for a land animal

Amphibian any cold-blooded VERTEBRATE of the CLASS Amphibia, typically living on land but breathing in the water; e.g., frogs, toads, newts, salamanders

Amphibious able to live on both land and in water

Amphipod a type of CRUSTACEAN found on land and in both fresh and seawater

Anadromous fish that spend most of their life at sea but MIGRATE into fresh water for breeding, e.g., salmon

Annelid of the PHYLUM Annelida in which the body is made up of similar segments, e.g., earthworms, lugworms, leeches

Anterior the front part of an animal

Arachnid one of a group of ARTHROPODS of the CLASS Arachnida, characterized by simple eyes and four pairs of legs. Includes spiders and scorpions

Arboreal living in trees

Aristotle's lantern complex chewing apparatus of sea-urchins that includes five teeth

Arthropod the largest PHYLUM in the animal kingdom in terms of the number of SPECIES in it. Characterized by a hard, jointed EXOSKELETON and paired jointed legs. Includes INSECTS, spiders, crabs, etc.

Baleen horny substance commonly known as whalebone and growing as plates in the mouth of certain whales; used as a fringelike sieve for extracting plankton from seawater

Bill often called the beak: the jaws of a bird, consisting of two bony MANDIBLES, upper and lower, and their horny sheaths

Biodiversity the variety of SPECIES and the variation within them

Biome a major world landscape characterized by having similar plants and animals living in it, e.g., DESERT, jungle, forest

Biped any animal that walks on two legs. See QUADRUPED

Blowhole the nostril opening on the head of a whale through which it breathes

Breeding season the entire cycle of reproductive activity, from courtship, pair formation (and often establishment of territory) through nesting to independence of young

Bristle in birds a modified feather, with a bare or partly bare shaft, like a stiff hair; functions include protection, as with eyelashes of ostriches and hornbills, and touch sensors to help catch INSECTS, as with flycatchers

Brood the young hatching from a single CLUTCH of eggs

Browsing feeding on leaves of trees and shrubs

Cage bird A bird kept in captivity; in this set it usually refers to birds taken from the wild

Canine tooth a sharp stabbing tooth usually longer than the rest

Canopy continuous (closed) or broken (open) layer in forests produced by the intermingling of branches of trees

Carapace the upper part of a shell in a CHELONIAN

Carnivore meat-eating animal

Carrion rotting flesh of dead animals

Casque the raised portion on the head of certain REPTILES and birds

Catadromous fish that spend most of their life in fresh water but MIGRATE to the sea for SPAWNING, e.g., eels

Caudal fin the tail fin in fish

Cephalothorax a body region of CRUSTACEANS formed by the union of the head and THORAX. See PROSOMA

Chelicerae the first pair of appendages ("limbs") on the PROSOMA of spiders, scorpions, etc. Often equipped to inject venom

Chelonian any REPTILE of the ORDER Chelonia, including the tortoises and turtles, in which most of the body is enclosed in a bony capsule

Chrysalis the PUPA in moths and butterflies

Class a large TAXONOMIC group of related animals. MAMMALS, INSECTS, and REPTILES are all CLASSES of animals

Cloaca cavity in the pelvic region into which the alimentary canal, genital, and urinary ducts open

Cloud forest moist, high-altitude forest characterized by a dense UNDERSTORY and an abundance of ferns, mosses, and other plants growing on the trunks and branches of trees

Clutch a set of eggs laid by a female bird in a single breeding attempt

Cocoon the protective coat of many insect LARVAE before they develop into PUPAE or the silken covering secreted to protect the eggs

Colonial living together in a colony

Coniferous forest evergreen forests found in northern regions and mountainous areas, dominated by pines, spruce, and cedars

Costal riblike

Costal grooves grooves running around the body of some TERRESTRIAL salamanders; they conduct water from the ground to the upper parts of the body

Coverts small feathers covering the bases of a bird's main flight feathers on the wings and tail, providing a smooth, streamlined surface for flight

Crustacean member of a CLASS within the PHYLUM Arthropoda typified by five pairs of legs, two pairs of antennae, a joined head and THORAX, and calcerous deposits in the EXOSKELETON; e.g., crabs, shrimps, etc.

Deciduous forest dominated by trees that lose their leaves in winter (or in the dry season)

Deforestation the process of cutting down and removing trees for timber or to create open space for growing crops, grazing animals, etc.

Desert area of low rainfall typically with sparse scrub or grassland vegetation or lacking it altogether

Diatoms microscopic single-celled ALGAE

Dispersal the scattering of young animals going to live away from where they were born and brought up

Diurnal active during the day

DNA (deoxyribonucleic acid) the substance that makes up the main part of the chromosomes of all living things; contains the genetic code that is handed down from generation to generation

Domestication process of taming and breeding animals to provide help and useful products for humans

Dormancy a state in which—as a result of hormone action—growth is suspended and METABOLIC activity is reduced to a minimum

Dorsal relating to the back or spinal part of the body; usually the upper surface

Down soft, fluffy, insulating feathers with few or no shafts found after hatching on young birds and in ADULTS beneath the main feathers

Echolocation the process of perception based on reaction to the pattern of reflected sound waves (echos); occurs in bats

Ecology the study of plants and animals in relation to one another and to their surroundings

Ecosystem a whole system in which plants, animals, and their environment interact

Ectotherm animal that relies on external heat sources to raise body temperature; also known as "cold-blooded"

Edentate toothless; also any animals of the order Edentata, which includes anteaters, sloths, and armadillos

Endemic found only in one geographical area, nowhere else

Epitoke a form of marine ANNELID having particularly well developed swimming appendages

Estivation inactivity or greatly decreased activity during hot weather

Eutrophication an increase in the nutrient chemicals (nitrate, phosphate, etc.) in water, sometimes occurring naturally and sometimes caused by human activities, e.g., by the release of sewage or agricultural fertilizers

Exoskeleton a skeleton covering the outside of the body or situated in the skin, as found in some INVERTEBRATES

Explosive breeding in some AMPHIBIANS when breeding is completed over one or a very few days and nights

Extinction process of dying out at the end of which the very last individual dies, and the SPECIES is lost forever

Family a group of closely related SPECIES that often also look quite similar. Zoological FAMILY names always end in -idae. Also used to describe a social group within a SPECIES comprising parents and their offspring

Feral domestic animals that have gone wild and live independently of people

Flagship species A high-profile SPECIES, which (if present) is likely to be accompanied by many others that are typical of the habitat. (If a naval flagship is present, so is the rest of the fleet of warships and support vessels)

Fledging period the period between a young bird hatching and acquiring its first full set of feathers and being able to fly

Fledgling young bird that is capable of flight; in perching birds and some others it corresponds with the time of leaving the nest

Fluke either of the two lobes of the tail of a whale or related animal; also a type of flatworm, usually parasitic

Gamebird birds in the ORDER Galliformes (megapodes, cracids, grouse, partridges, quail, pheasants, and relatives); also used for any birds that may be legally hunted by humans

Gene the basic unit of heredity, enabling one generation to pass on characteristics to its offspring

Genus (genera, pl.) a group of closely related SPECIES

Gestation the period of pregnancy in MAMMALS, between fertilization of the egg and birth of the baby

Gill Respiratory organ that absorbs oxygen from the water. External gills occur in tadpoles. Internal gills occur in most fish

Harem a group of females living in the same territory and consorting with a single male

Hen any female bird

Herbivore an animal that eats plants (grazers and BROWSERS are herbivores)

Hermaphrodite an animal having both male and female reproductive organs

Herpetologist ZOOLOGIST who studies REPTILES and AMPHIBIANS

Hibernation becoming inactive in winter, with lowered body temperature to save energy. Hibernation takes place in a special nest or den called a hibernaculum

Homeotherm an animal that can maintain a high and constant body temperature by means of internal

processes; also called "warm-blooded"

Home range the area that an animal uses in the course of its normal activity

Hybrid offspring of two closely related SPECIES that can breed; it is sterile and so cannot produce offspring

Ichthyologist ZOOLOGIST specializing in the study of fish

Inbreeding breeding among closely related animals (e.g., cousins), leading to weakened genetic composition and reduced survival rates

Incubation the act of keeping the egg or eggs warm or the period from the laying of eggs to hatching

Indwellers ORGANISMS that live inside others, e.g., the California Bay pea crab, which lives in the tubes of some marine ANNELID worms, but do not act as PARASITES

Indigenous living naturally in a region; native (i.e.,not an introduced SPECIES)

Insect any air-breathing ARTHROPOD of the CLASS Insecta, having a body divided into head, THORAX, and abdomen, three pairs of legs, and sometimes two pairs of wings

Insectivore animal that feeds on INSECTS. Also used as a group name for hedgehogs, shrews, moles, etc.

Interbreeding breeding between animals of different SPECIES, varieties, etc. within a single FAMILY or strain; Interbreeding can cause dilution of the GENE pool

Interspecific between SPECIES

Intraspecific between individuals of the same SPECIES

Invertebrates animals that have no backbone (or other bones) inside their body, e.g., mollusks, INSECTS, jellyfish, crabs

Iridescent displaying glossy colors produced (e.g., in bird PLUMAGE) not as a result of pigments but by the splitting of sunlight into light of different wavelengths; rainbows are made in the same way

Joey a young kangaroo living in its mother's pouch

Juvenile a young animal that has not yet reached breeding age

Keel a ridge along the CARAPACE of certain turtles or a ridge on the scales of some REPTILES

Keratin tough, fibrous material that forms hair, feathers, nails, and

protective plates on the skin of VERTEBRATE animals

Keystone species a SPECIES on which many other SPECIES are wholly or partially dependent

Krill PLANKTONIC shrimps

Labyrinth specialized auxiliary (extra) breathing organ found in some fish

Larva an immature form of an animal that develops into an ADULT form through METAMORPHOSIS

Lateral line system a system of pores running along a fish's body. These pores lead to nerve endings that allow a fish to sense vibrations in the water and help it locate prey, detect PREDATORS, avoid obstacles, and so on. Also found in AMPHIBIANS

Lek communal display area where male birds of some SPECIES gather to attract and mate with females

Livebearer animal that gives birth to fully developed young (usually refers to REPTILES or fish)

Mammal any animal of the CLASS Mammalia—warm-blooded VERTEBRATE having mammary glands in the female that produce milk with which it nurses its young. The class includes bats, primates, rodents, and whales

Mandible upper or lower part of a bird's beak or BILL; also the jawbone in VERTEBRATES; in INSECTS and other ARTHROPODS mandibles are mouth parts mostly used for biting and chewing

Mantle cavity a space in the body of mollusks that contains the breathing organs

Marine living in the sea

Matriarch senior female member of a social group

Metabolic rate the rate at which chemical activities occur within animals, including the exchange of gasses in respiration and the liberation of energy from food

Metamorphosis the transformation of a LARVA into an ADULT

Migration movement from one place to another and back again; usually seasonal

Molt the process in which a bird sheds its feathers and replaces them with new ones; some MAMMALS, REPTILES, and ARTHROPODS regularly molt, shedding hair, skin, or outer layers

Monotreme egg-laying MAMMAL, e.g., platypus

Montane in a mountain environment

Natural selection the process

whereby individuals with the most appropriate ADAPTATIONS are more successful than other individuals and therefore survive to produce more offspring. Natural selection is the main process driving evolution in which animals and plants are challenged by natural effects (such as predation and bad weather), resulting in survival of the fittest

Nematocyst the stinging part of animals such as jellyfish, usually found on the tentacles

Nestling a young bird still in the nest and dependent on its parents

New World the Americas

Niche part of a habitat occupied by an ORGANISM, defined in terms of all aspects of its lifestyle

Nocturnal active at night

Nomadic animals that have no fixed home, but wander continuously

Noseleaf fleshy structures around the face of bats; helps focus ULTRASOUNDS used for ECHOLOCATION

Ocelli markings on an animal's body that resemble eyes. Also, the tiny, simple eyes of some INSECTS, spiders, CRUSTACEANS, mollusks, etc.

Old World non-American continents

Olfaction sense of smell

Operculum a cover consisting of bony plates that covers the GILLS of fish

Omnivore an animal that eats a wide range of both animal and vegetable food

Order a subdivision of a CLASS of animals, consisting of a series of animal FAMILIES

Organism any member of the animal or plant kingdom; a body that has life

Ornithologist ZOOLOGIST specializing in the study of birds

Osteoderms bony plates beneath the scales of some REPTILES, particularly crocodilians

Oviparous producing eggs that hatch outside the body of the mother (in fish, REPTILES, birds, and MONOTREMES)

Parasite an animal or plant that lives on or within the body of another (the host) from which it obtains nourishment. The host is often harmed by the association

Passerine any bird of the ORDER Passeriformes; includes SONGBIRDS

Pedipalps small, paired leglike appendages immediately in front of the first pair of walking legs of spiders

281

and other ARACHNIDS. Used by males for transferring sperm to the females

Pelagic living in the upper waters of the open sea or large lakes

Pheromone scent produced by animals to enable others to find and recognize them

Photosynthesis the production of food in green plants using sunlight as an energy source and water plus carbon dioxide as raw materials

Phylum zoological term for a major grouping of animal CLASSES. The whole animal kingdom is divided into about 30 PHYLA, of which the VERTEBRATES form part of just one

Placenta the structure that links an embryo to its mother during pregnancy, allowing exchange of chemicals between them

Plankton animals and plants drifting in open water; many are minute

Plastron the lower shell of CHELONIANS

Plumage the covering of feathers on a bird's body

Plume a long feather used for display, as in a bird of paradise

Polygamous where an individual has more than one mate in one BREEDING SEASON. Monogamous animals have only a single mate

Polygynous where a male mates with several females in one BREEDING SEASON

Polyp individual ORGANISM that lives as part of a COLONY—e.g., a coral—with a saclike body opening only by the mouth that is usually surrounded by a ring of tentacles

Population a distinct group of animals of the same SPECIES or all the animals of that SPECIES

Posterior the hind end or behind another structure

Predator an animal that kills live prey

Prehensile capable of grasping

Primary forest forest that has always been forest and has not been cut down and regrown at some time

Primates a group of MAMMALS that includes monkeys, apes, and ourselves

Prosoma the joined head and THORAX of a spider, scorpion, or horseshoe crab

Pupa an INSECT in the stage of METAMORPHOSIS between a caterpillar (LARVA) and an ADULT (imago)

Quadruped any animal that walks on four legs

Range the total geographical area over which a SPECIES is distributed

Raptor bird with hooked beak and strong feet with sharp claws (talons) for seizing, killing, and dealing with prey; also known as birds of prey. The term usually refers to daytime birds of prey (eagles, hawks, falcons, and relatives) but sometimes also includes NOCTURNAL owls

Regurgitate (of a bird) to vomit partly digested food either to feed NESTLINGS or to rid itself of bones, fur, or other indigestible parts, or (in some seabirds) to scare off PREDATORS

Reptile any member of the cold-blooded CLASS Reptilia, such as crocodiles, lizards, snakes, tortoises, turtles, and tuataras; characterized by an external covering of scales or horny plates. Most are egg-layers, but some give birth to fully developed young

Roost place that a bird or bat regularly uses for sleeping

Ruminant animals that eat vegetation and later bring it back from the stomach to chew again ("chewing the cud") to assist its digestion by microbes in the stomach

Savanna open grasslands with scattered trees and low rainfall, usually in warm areas

Scapulars the feathers of a bird above its shoulders

Scent chemicals produced by animals to leave smell messages for others to find and interpret

Scrub vegetation dominated by shrubs—woody plants usually with more than one stem

Scute horny plate covering live body tissue underneath

Secondary forest trees that have been planted or grown up on cleared ground

Sedge grasslike plant

Shorebird Plovers, sandpipers, and relatives (known as waders in Britain, Australia, and some other areas)

Slash-and-burn agriculture method of farming in which the unwanted vegetation is cleared by cutting down and burning

Social behavior interactions between individuals within the same SPECIES, e.g., courtship

Songbird member of major bird group of PASSERINES

Spawning the laying and fertilizing of eggs by fish and AMPHIBIANS and some mollusks

Speciation the origin of SPECIES; the diverging of two similar ORGANISMS

through reproduction down through the generations into different forms resulting in a new SPECIES

Species a group of animals that look similar and can breed with each other to produce fertile offspring

Steppe open grassland in parts of the world where the climate is too harsh for trees to grow

Subspecies a subpopulation of a single SPECIES whose members are similar to each other but differ from the typical form for that SPECIES; often called a race

Substrate a medium to which fixed animals are attached under water, such as rocks onto which barnacles and mussels are attached, or plants are anchored in, e.g., gravel, mud, or sand in which AQUATIC plants have their roots embedded

Substratum *see* SUBSTRATE

Swim bladder a gas or air-filled bladder in fish; by taking in or exhaling air, the fish can alter its buoyancy

Symbiosis a close relationship between members of two SPECIES from which both partners benefit

Taxonomy the branch of biology concerned with classifying ORGANISMS into groups according to similarities in their structure, origins, or behavior. The categories, in order of increasing broadness, are: SPECIES, GENUS, FAMILY, ORDER, CLASS, PHYLUM

Terrestrial living on land

Territory defended space

Test an external covering or "shell" of an INVERTEBRATE such as a sea-urchin; it is in fact an internal skeleton just below the skin

Thorax (**thoracic**, adj.) in an INSECT the middle region of the body between the head and the abdomen. It bears the wings and three pairs of walking legs

Torpor deep sleep accompanied by lowered body temperature and reduced METABOLIC RATE

Translocation transferring members of a SPECIES from one location to another

Tundra open grassy or shrub-covered lands of the far north

Underfur fine hairs forming a dense, woolly mass close to the skin and underneath the outer coat of stiff hairs in MAMMALS

Understory the layer of shrubs, herbs, and small trees found beneath the forest CANOPY

Ungulate one of a large group of hoofed animals such as pigs, deer, cattle, and horses; mostly HERBIVORES

Uterus womb in which embryos of MAMMALS develop

Ultrasounds sounds that are too high-pitched for humans to hear

UV-B radiation component of ultraviolet radiation from the sun that is harmful to living ORGANISMS because it breaks up DNA

Vane the bladelike main part of a typical bird feather extending from either side of its shaft (midrib)

Ventral of or relating to the front part or belly of an animal (*see* DORSAL)

Vertebrate animal with a backbone (e.g., fish, MAMMAL, REPTILE), usually with skeleton made of bones, but sometimes softer cartilage

Vestigial a characteristic with little or no use, but derived from one that was well developed in an ancestral form; e.g., the "parson's nose" (the fatty end portion of the tail when a fowl is cooked) is the compressed bones from the long tail of the reptilian ancestor of birds

Viviparous (of most MAMMALS and a few other VERTEBRATES) giving birth to active young rather than laying eggs

Waterfowl members of the bird FAMILY Anatidae, the swans, geese, and ducks; sometimes used to include other groups of wild AQUATIC birds

Wattle fleshy protuberance, usually near the base of a bird's BILL

Wingbar line of contrasting feathers on a bird's wing

Wing case one of the protective structures formed from the first pair of nonfunctional wings, which are used to protect the second pair of functional wings in INSECTS such as beetles

Wintering ground the area where a migrant spends time outside the BREEDING SEASON

Yolk part of the egg that contains nourishment for a growing embryo

Zooid individual animal in a colony; usually applied to corals or bryozoa (sea-mats)

Zoologist person who studies animals

Zoology the study of animals

Further Reading

Mammals

Macdonald, David, *The New Encyclopedia of Mammals*, Barnes & Noble, New York, U.S., 2001

Payne, Roger, *Among Whales*, Bantam Press, U.S., 1996

Reeves, R. R., and Leatherwood, S., *The Sierra Club Handbook of Whales and Dolphins of the World*, Sierra Club, U.S., 1983

Sherrow, Victoria, and Cohen, Sandee, *Endangered Mammals of North America*, Twenty-First Century Books, U.S., 1995

Whitaker, J. O., *Audubon Society Field Guide to North American Mammals*, Alfred A. Knopf, New York, U.S., 1996

Birds

Attenborough, David, *The Life of Birds*, BBC Books, London, U.K., 1998

BirdLife International, *Threatened Birds of the World*, Lynx Edicions, Barcelona, Spain and BirdLife International, Cambridge, U.K., 2000

del Hoyo, J., Elliott, A., and Sargatal, J., eds., *Handbook of Birds of the World* Vols 1 to 6, Lynx Edicions, Barcelona, Spain, 1992–2001

Scott, Shirley L., ed., *A Field Guide to the Birds of North America*, National Geographic, U.S., 1999

Stattersfield, A., Crosby, M., Long, A., and Wege, D., eds., *Endemic Bird Areas of the World: Priorities for Biodiversity Conservation*, BirdLife International, Cambridge, U.K., 1998

Thomas, Peggy, *Bird Alert: Science of Saving*, Twenty-First Century Books, U.S., 2000

Fish

Buttfield, Helen, *The Secret Lives of Fishes*, Abrams, U.S., 2000

Dawes, John, and Campbell, Andrew, eds., *The New Encyclopedia of Aquatic Life*, Facts On File, New York, U.S., 2004

Reptiles and Amphibians

Corbett, Keith, *Conservation of European Reptiles and Amphibians*, Christopher Helm, London, U.K., 1989

Corton, Misty, *Leopard and Other South African Tortoises*, Carapace Press, London, U.K., 2000

Hofrichter, Robert, *Amphibians: The World of Frogs, Toads, Salamanders, and Newts*, Firefly Books, Canada, 2000

Murphy, J. B., Adler, K., and Collins, J. T. (eds.), *Captive Management and Conservation of Reptiles and Amphibians*, Society for the Study of Amphibians and Reptiles, Ithaca, New York, 1994

Stafford, Peter, *Snakes*, Natural History Museum, London, U.K., 2000

Insects

Borror, Donald J., and White, Richard E., *A Field Guide to Insects: America, North of Mexico*, Houghton Mifflin, New York, U.S., 1970

Pyle, Robert Michael, *National Audubon Society Field Guide to North American Butterflies*, Alfred A. Knopf, New York, U.S., 1995

General

Adams, Douglas, and Carwardine, Mark, *Last Chance to See*, Random House, London, U.K., 1992

Allaby, Michael, *The Concise Oxford Dictionary of Ecology*, Oxford University Press, Oxford, U.K., 1998

Douglas, Dougal, and others, *Atlas of Life on Earth*, Barnes & Noble, New York, U.S., 2001

National Wildlife Federation, *Endangered Species: Wild and Rare*, McGraw-Hill, U.S., 1996

Websites

http://www1.nature.nps.gov/ U.S. National Park Service wildlife site

http://www.abcbirds.org/ American Bird Conservancy. Articles, information about bird conservation in the Americas

http://animaldiversity.ummz.umich.edu/ University of Michigan Museum of Zoology animal diversity web. Search for pictures and information about animals by class, family, and common name

http://www.audubon.org National Audubon Society. Sections on education, local societies, and bird identification

http://www.birdlife.net BirdLife International, an alliance of conservation organizations working in over 100 countries to save birds and their habitats

http://www.birds.cornell.edu/ Cornell University. Courses, news, nest-box cam

http://www.cites.org/ CITES and IUCN listings. Search for animals by order, family, genus, species, or common name. Location by country and explanation of reasons for listings

http://cmc-ocean.org Facts, figures, and quizzes about marine life

www.darwinfoundation.org/ Charles Darwin Research Center

http://elib.cs.berkeley.edu/aw/ AmphibiaWeb. Information about amphibians and their conservation

http://endangered.fws.gov Information about endangered animals and plants from the U.S. Fish and Wildlife Service, the organization in charge of 94 million acres of wildlife refuges

www.EndangeredSpecie.com Information, links, books, and publications about rare and endangered species. Also includes information about conservation efforts and organizations

www.ewt.org.za Endangered South African wildlife

http://forests.org/ Includes forest conservation answers to queries

www.iucn.org Details of species, IUCN listings, and IUCN publications. Link to online Red Lists of threatened species at: www.iucnredlist.org

www.nccnsw.org.au Site for threatened Australian species

http://www.open.ac.uk/daptf/ DAPTF–Declining Amphibian Population Task Force. Provides information and data about amphibian declines

http://www.panda.org World Wide Fund for Nature (WWF). Newsroom, press releases, government reports, campaigns. Themed photogallery

http://www.pbs.org/journeytoamazonia The Amazonian rain forest and its unrivaled biodiversity

http://www.seaturtlespacecoast.org/ Website of the Sea Turtle Preservation Society

http://www.surfbirds.com Articles, mystery photographs, news, book reviews, birding polls, and more

http://www.traffic.org/turtles Freshwater turtles

http://www.ucmp.berkeley.edu/echinodermata The echinoderm phylum—starfish, sea-urchins, etc.

http://wdcs.org/ Whale and Dolphin Conservation Society site. News, projects, and campaigns. Sightings database

http://www.wwt.org.uk/ Wildfowl and Wetlands Trust (U.K.) aims to preserve wetlands for rare waterbirds. Includes information on places to visit and threatened waterbird species

Index

Animals that are the subject of a main entry in the book are listed under their common names, alternative common names, and scientific names. Animals that appear in the data panels as related endangered species are also listed under their common and scientific names. Common names in **bold** (e.g., **alligator, Chinese**) indicate a main entry under that name. Bold page numbers (e.g., **40–41**) indicate the location of an illustrated main entry under common, alternative, and scientific names.

Italic page references (e.g., *57*) indicate illustrations of animals in other parts of the book.

References to animals that are listed by the IUCN as Extinct (EX), Extinct in the Wild (EW), or Critically Endangered (CR) are found under those headings.

spp. means species.

Picture credits

Abbreviations

AL Ardea London; BCC Bruce Coleman Collection; C Corbis; E Ecoscene; FLPA Frank Lane Picture Agency; IUNC International Union for the Conservation of Nature; NHPA Natural History Photographic Agency; PEP Planet Earth Pictures; PW Premaphotos Wildlife; OSF Oxford Scientific Films; PP Papilio Photographic; PX Photomax; SP Still Pictures; WP Windrush Photos

t = top; **b** = bottom; **l** = left; **r** = right

Jacket: tl Geostock/Photodisc; **bc** Digital Stock Corp; **c** Digital Stock Corp; **tr** Alan and Sandy Carey/Photodisc; **br** Photos.com
Back Cover: Photolink/Photodisc

Title Pages: Photolink/Photodisc; Alan and Sandy Carey/Photodisc

7t PP; **7b** Newman, Mark/FLPA; **8** De Roy, Tui/OSF; **8-9** Rosing, Norbert/OSF; **9** IUCN; **11** Mickelburgh, Edwin/AL; **12-13** Osolinski, Stan/OSF; **14** Cordano, Marty/OSF; **15**/Hartmann, Frants/FLPA; **16** Gohier, François/AL; **17** Atkinson, Kathie/OSF; **18** Earth Scenes/Littlehales, Bates/OSF; **19t** DeVries, P. J./OSF;**19b** Cavendish, Piers/AL; **20-21** Ruiz, Jose B./BCC; **21** Iijima, Masahiro/AL; **22** Currey, David/NHPA; **23t** Amman, Karl/BCC; **23b** Taylor, Ron & Valerie/AL; **24** Monteath, Colin/OSF; **25** Bettmann/C; **26** Amman, Karl/BCC; **27t** Hall, Howard/OSF; **27b** Foott, Jeff/BCC; **28b** Hamblin, Mark/OSF; **28-29** Cordano, Marty/OSF; **29** Packwood, Richard/OSF; **30** Woodfall, David/NHPA; **31** Lundberg, Bengt/BCC; **32t** Ferrero, Jean-Paul/AL; **32b** Mcdonald, Mary Ann/BCC; **33** Pacific Stock/BCC; **34** Ratier, Christophe/NHPA; **35l** Fink, Kenneth W./AL; **35r** Harvey, Martin/NHPA; **36-37** Sinha, Vivek R./OSF; **39** Shah, Anup/BCC; **40-41** Pooley, Hilary/OSF; **41** Cox, Daniel J./OSF; **42-43** Carey, Alan & Sandy/OSF; **44-45** Harvey, Martin/NHPA; **46** Gordon, Nick/OSF; **49** Rico & Ruiz/BCC; **51** Stone, Lynn M./BCC; **52** Callan, Michael/FLPA; **55** Cooper, Anthony/E; **57** Bauer, Erwin & Peggy/BCC; **59** Watts, Dave; **60-61** Andrewartha, T./FLPA; **63** Rügner, Martin/PEP;**65** Su, Keren/OSF; **67** Sidorovich, Vadim/BCC; **69** Danegger, Manfred/NHPA; **71** Franz, Dr. Robert/PEP; **72-73** Ziesler, Gunter/BCC; **75** Gohier, François/AL; **77** Ulrich, Tom/OSF; **79** Panda/Di Domenico, F./FLPA; **81** Florence, Andrea/AL; **83** Hall, Howard/OSF; **85** Roy, Tui de/OSF; **87** Cox, Daniel J./OSF; **91** Soury, Gerard/OSF; **93** Animals Animals/Dick, Michael/OSF; **95** Colbeck, Martyn/OSF; **97** Cox, Daniel J./OSF; **99** Osolinski, Stan/OSF; **101** Wothe, Konrad/OSF; **103 inset** Haring, David/OSF; **103** Carey, Alan & Sandy/OSF; **105** Hill, Mike/OSF; **106-07** Survival Anglia/Paton, William/OSF; **109** Beames, Ian/AL; **110-11** Downer, John/OSF; **113** Chillmaid, Martyn/OSF; **115** Ulrich, Tom/OSF; **117** Fink, Kenneth W./AL; **118-19** Bartov, Eyal/OSF; **120-21** Hill, Mike/OSF; **123** Oxford, Pete/BCC; **125** Survival Anglia/Knights, Chris/OSF; **127** Morris, P.; **129** Survival Anglia/Strobing, Michael/OSF; **131** Survival Anglia/Harris, John/OSF; **135** Stebbings, Dr. R. E.; **139** Atkinson, Kathie/OSF; **143** A.N.T./NHPA; **145** Watts, Dave; **147** Ferrero, Jean-Paul/AP; **149** Watts, Dave; **151** Jones, Mark/OSF; **153** Parer D. & Parer-Cook E./AL; **153 inset** Osolinski, Stan/OSF; **156-57** Littlewood, Steve/OSF; **159** Savoie, Phil/BCC; **163** Bracegirdle, John R./PEP; **165** Mills, Stephen/OSF; **167** Heuclin, Daniel/NHPA; **169** Grande, J. L. G./BCC; **170-71** Sierra, Jorge/OSF; **173** Animals Animals/Chappell, Dr. Mark A./OSF; **174-75** Garbutt, Nick/PEP; **177** Lucas, Ken/PEP; **178-79** Cancalosi, John/BCC; **181** Bush, Robin/OSF; **183** Osolinski, Stan/OSF; **185** Garbutt, Nick/PEP; **189** Cancalosi, John/BCC; **191** Tyrrell, Robert A./OSF; **196-97** Pop, Rene/WP; **199t** Tilford, Tony/OSF; **199b** Tilford, Tony/OSF; **201**Animals Animals/Gerlach, John/OSF; **203** Hutchison, Mark; **204-05** Kay, Paul/OSF; **207** Webster, Mark/OSF; **209** Dennis, David M./OSF; **211** Animals Animals/Leszczynski, Zig/OSF; **212-13** Jones, Mark/OSF; **215** Animals Animals/Leszczynski, Zig/OSF; **217** Fogden, Michael/OSF; **219** Gibson, R.; **221** Gordon, Nick/OSF; **223** Bennett, Bob/OSF; **224-25** Animals Animals/Leszczynski, Zig/OSF; **227** Orion Press/BCC; **229** Wilmshurst, Roger/FLPA; **231** Morris, P./AL; **233** Mattison, Chris/FLPA; **235** Linley, Mike/OSF; **237** Animals Animals/Leszczynski, Zig/OSF; **239** Brakefield, Tom/OSF; **241** Oxford, Pete/PEP; **243** Scoones, Peter/PEP; **245** Animals Animals/Roessler, Carl/OSF; **247** Reinhard, Hans/BCC; **249** Okapia/Hartl, Andreas/OSF; **251t** Gibbs, Max/PX; **251b** Gibbs, Max/PX; **253** Gibbs, Max/PX; **255** Switak, Karl/NHPA; **257** Gibbs, Max/PX; **259** Herrmann, Richard/OSF; **261** Manuel, R. L./OSF; **263** Keller, Ralph & Daphne/NHPA; **265** Burton, Jane/BCC; **267** Ehrenstrom, Fredrik/OSF; **268-69** Cooke, J. A. L./OSF; **271** Preston-Mafham, K. G./PW; **275** Frith, D. W. & C. B./BCC; **275 inset** Compost, Alain/BCC; **277** Williams, Rod/BCC; **279l** Mull, William P.; **279r** Pfletschinger, Hans/SP